LIBRARY OF NEW TESTAMENT STUDIES

393

formerly the Journal for the Study of the New Testament Supplement series

Editor
Mark Goodacre

TEXT TO PRAXIS

HERMENEUTICS AND HOMILETICS
IN DIALOGUE

ABRAHAM KURUVILLA

t&t clark

Published by T&T Clark International
A Continuum imprint
The Tower Building, 11 York Road, London SE1 7NX
80 Maiden Lane, Suite 704, New York, NY 10038

www.continuumbooks.com

British Library Cataloguing-in-Publication Data
A catalogue record for this book is available from the British Library

ISBN-10: HB: 0-567-53854-0
ISBN-13: HB: 978-0-567-53854-3

Typeset by CA Typesetting Ltd, www.sheffieldtypesetting.com
Printed on acid-free paper in Great Britain by the MPG Books Group

Timothy S. Warren

Teacher
Colleague
Neighbour
Friend
Brother in Christ

CONTENTS

ACKNOWLEDGEMENTS

I thank my God in all my remembrance of you, always offering prayer with joy in my
every prayer for you all, in view of your participation … (Phil. 1.3-5)

As the modified version of a doctoral thesis presented to the University of Aberdeen, this work owes much to the many who aided and abetted its production. Most things in life are never accomplished solo. A *Philosophiæ Doctor* is no exception.

Without the unflagging love and tenacious support of my family – the rest of the Kuruvillas: my father, my brother and his wife, and my two nephews – that undertaking could not have been attempted, far less completed.

I will ever be grateful for their gracious tolerance of my idiosyncrasies, and for the benevolence and tangible love extended to this bachelor by the Morgans, my adopted folks in Texas, upon whom I inflicted myself time and again during my peripatetic meanderings across the Atlantic.

Of his keen eye and sharp mind, I have been a beneficiary; I have oft been encouraged by his kind words and sustained by his steadfast support; my work has only profited from his unremitting call for excellence. To my *doktorvater*, Francis Watson, I owe thanks. I have learnt much from him.

We were a bunch of divinity postgrads lamenting our infelicitous lot as students at the University of Aberdeen. But those times will be sorely missed – those hard-but-fun years sharing lives marked by the all-sufficient grace of God. The Gibsons and the Modys – you made that journey enjoyable.

In Old Aberdeen there used to exist a kennel-full of unusual specimens who called themselves the 'Dawgs'; our weekly sessions of prayer, especially during my early days at the university, were a great source of strength and sustenance. To that motley litter, I, *Canis medicus*, am in debt.

One of the delights of dwelling in that fair city in Northeast Scotland was the privilege of attending High Church, Hilton. I was ministered unto by, and had the privilege of ministering to, those dear people of God. Many thanks to the Revd Dickson; Peter's pastoral care was truly a godsend.

Prayer warriors galore undertook to intercede for my latest endeavour to obtain an education, among whom I remember, with much appreciation for their *labores orationis*, Ann Ledwith, the Aitkens, Burrows, Buies, Cortezs, DiMuzios, Kumars, Lyons, Reeds, Tablers and Tullochs. Over the years, these saints of God, and others at Plano Bible Chapel, Plano, Texas, where I was ordained, have depicted Christ to me in manifold ways. To them, my brothers and sisters – *Thank you!*

Without the magnanimity of the members of the Warren Adult Bible Fellowship at Lake Pointe Church in Rockwall, Texas, and the graciousness of numerous others who helped share the load, this project would not have gotten off the ground. God bless you all for your generosity. I am also thankful to the Gunasekera extended family; they were uncommonly bountiful in their support of my mid-life academic adventures in Scotland.

I acknowledge a special debt of gratitude to Dallas Theological Seminary, particularly to my colleagues (erstwhile and current) in the Department of Pastoral Ministries, and the President and Academic Dean of this fine institution, for collegial interaction, solicitous concern and generous support. It continues to be a privilege to collaborate with this great team in fruitful ministry for God's glory.

Timothy Warren, a pioneer in the consideration of theology in the preaching endeavour, has long been a bastion of strength and support since my student days at Dallas Theological Seminary, critiquing my sermons, affording me preaching opportunities, supporting my teaching enterprises, serving on my ordination committee, writing recommendation letters to all and sundry, praying for me, advising me, raising support for me .... We have enjoyed Tex-Mex together, trudged wearily through snow together, laughed, taught and bemoaned life together, and even gotten lost together! To him, for investing in my life, I dedicate this work with immense gratitude.

Soli Deo gloria!

Abraham Kuruvilla
Pentecost, 2008
Dallas, Texas

ABBREVIATIONS

Ancient Texts

1 Apol.	Justin Martyr, *First Apology*
1 Clem.	Clement of Rome, *First Epistle of Clement*
'Abot R. Nat.	*'Abot de Rabbi Nathan*
Ag. Ap.	Josephus, *Against Apion*
Ant.	Plutarch, *Antonius*
Apol.	Tertullian, *Apology*
b. Meg.	Talmud, Babylonian tractate *Megillah*
b. Soṭah	Talmud, Babylonian tractate *Soṭah*
Brut.	Cicero, *Brutus*
Can.	Council of Laodicea, *Canons*
Comm. Jo.	Origen, *Commentarii in evangelium Joannis*
Creation	Philo, *On the Creation of the World*
De or.	Cicero, *De oratore*
Decr.	Athanasius, *De decretis*
Doctr. chr.	Augustine, *De doctrina christiana*
Eloc.	Demetrius, *De elocutione*
Embassy	Philo, *On the Embassy to Gaius*
Ep. ad Dardanum	Jerome, *Epistula ad Dardanum*
Ep. ad Hedybiam	Jerome, *Epistula ad Hedybiam*
Ep. ad Paula	Jerome, *Epistula ad Paula*
Ep. ad Theodorum	
medicum	Gregory the Great, *Epistula ad Theodorum medicum*
Ep. fest.	Athanasius, *Epistulæ festales*
Ep. mort. Ar.	Athanasius, *Epistula ad Serapionem de more Arii*
Euripides	Satyrus, *Life of Euripides*
Haer.	Ireneaus, *Adversus haereses*
Hist. eccl.	Eusebius, *Historia ecclesiastica*
History	Thucydides, *History of the Peloponnesian War*
Hom. Col.	Chrysostom, *Homiliæ in epistulam ad Colossenses*
Hom. Gen.	Chrysostom, *Homiliæ in Genesim*
Hypoth.	Philo, *Hypothetica*
Inst.	Quintilian, *Institutio oratoria*
J.W.	Josephus, *Jewish War*
LXX	Septuagint
m. Pesaḥ.	Talmud, Mishnah tractate *Pesaḥim*
Marc.	Tertullian, *Adversus Marcionem*
Moses	Philo, *On the Life of Moses*
Or. Brut.	Cicero, *Orator ad M. Brutum*
Pan.	Epiphanius, *Panarion*
Phaedr.	Plato, *Phaedrus*

Phil.	Polycarp, *Epistle to the Philippians*
Poet.	Aristotle, *Poetics*
Praescr.	Tertullian, *De praescriptione haereticorum*
Princ.	Origen, *De principiis*
Rhet. Alex.	Anaximenes, *Rhetorica ad Alexandrum*
Spec. Laws	Philo, *On the Special Laws*
Strom.	Clement of Alexandria, *Stromata*
Summa	Aquinas, *Summa theologica*
t. Sanh.	Talmud, Tosefta tractate *Sanhedrin*

Periodicals and Reference Works

ANF	*Ante-Nicene Fathers*
BA	*Biblical Archaeologist*
BAR	*Biblical Archaeology Review*
Bib	*Biblica*
BSac	*Bibliotheca Sacra*
BTB	*Biblical Theology Bulletin*
BZAW	*Beihefte zu Zeitschrift für die alttestamentliche Wissenschaft*
CBQ	*Catholic Biblical Quarterly*
CCC	*College Composition and Communication*
CI	*Critical Inquiry*
Coll. Eng.	*College English*
Ess. Crit.	*Essays in Criticism*
EvJ	*Evangelical Journal*
ExpTim	*Expository Times*
Fordham L. Rev.	*Fordham Law Review*
GTJ	*Grace Theological Journal*
HTR	*Harvard Theological Review*
IEJ	*Israel Exploration Journal*
IJST	*International Journal of Systematic Theology*
Int	*Interpretation*
Iowa Rev.	*Iowa Review*
J Aes Art Crit	*Journal of Aesthetics and Art Criticism*
JAAR	*Journal of the American Academy of Religion*
JBL	*Journal of Biblical Literature*
JETS	*Journal of the Evangelical Theological Society*
JR	*Journal of Religion*
JSOT	*Journal for the Study of the Old Testament*
JSSR	*Journal for the Scientific Study of Religion*
LCL	Loeb Classical Library
NLH	*New Literary History*
NPNF	*Nicene and Post-Nicene Fathers*
NTS	*New Testament Studies*
OTS	*Oudtestamentische Studiën*
P&R	*Philosophy & Rhetoric*
PG	*Patrologia Græca*
Phil. Christi	*Philosophia Christi*
Phil. Rev.	*The Philosophical Review*
Phil. Sci.	*Philosophy of Science*
PL	*Patrologia Latina*

Pol. Sci. Q.	*Political Science Quarterly*
PRSt	*Perspectives in Religious Studies*
QJS	*Quarterly Journal of Speech*
SBET	*Scottish Bulletin of Evangelical Theology*
SJT	*Scottish Journal of Theology*
Texas L. Rev.	*Texas Law Review*
ThTo	*Theology Today*
TrinJ	*Trinity Journal*
TS	*Theological Studies*
TSF Bull.	*Theological Students' Fellowship Bulletin*
TynBul	*Tyndale Bulletin*
US	United States Reports
USQR	*Union Seminary Quarterly Review*
VTSup	Vetus Testamentum Supplements
WBC	Word Biblical Commentary
WTJ	*Westminster Theological Journal*
ZNW	*Zeitschrift für die neutestamentliche Wissenschaft*
ZPE	*Zeitschrift für Papyrologie und Epigraphik*

INTRODUCTION: GOALS AND ASSUMPTIONS

It was Søren Kierkegaard who exclaimed, 'As for ways of reading, there are thirty thousand different ways.'[1] For those who would accurately expound biblical texts for application, this is far too many. Kierkegaard's is a poignant cry of incredulity that has echoed through the corridors of the centuries preceding that philosopher and continues to do so in the halls of those decades following him. It might not be too farfetched to surmise that the philosopher's frustration resonates every week in the study of the preacher who attempts to make a legitimate move from ancient biblical text to contemporary Christian audience. If scriptural interpretation in the preaching endeavour encompasses the entire process from text to praxis, then hermeneutics – the art and science of reading – is of vital interest to homileticians (and to teachers of preaching). The one to whom is assigned the role of mediating the encounter between Scripture and God's people will, no doubt, confess to the arduous nature of the task of moving from the 'then' to the 'now' with authority and relevance. This struggle to bridge the gap between inscribed content and real lives of real people – the geographical, linguistic, psychological and chronological gulf between two worlds – is an attempt 'to conquer a remoteness, a distance between the past cultural epoch to which the text belongs and the interpreter'.[2] How does the interpreter construct this bridge and conquer this breach?

It is an unfortunate verity that in this building project, homileticians, abandoned to their own devices, flounder in the chasm. Theorists of interpretation, oblivious to ecclesial settings, preaching texts and sermonic intentions, have remained insensate to the plight of homileticians and contributed precious little to the arena in which is transacted one of the most crucial operations of the Church, the proclamation of Scripture. David Buttrick expresses it incisively:

> [M]any books have been written on 'biblical preaching'; specifically on how preachers can move step by step from the Bible passage to a sermon. Many of these works …have been genuinely helpful.… They have also described a set of homiletical

---

1. Søren Kierkegaard, *For Self-Examination, Judge for Yourself!* (vol. 21 of *Kierkegaard's Writings*; ed. and trans. Howard V. Hong and Edna H. Hong; Princeton: Princeton University Press, 1990), p. 25.

2. Paul Ricoeur, 'Existence and Hermeneutics', in idem, *The Conflict of Interpretations* (trans. Kathleen McLaughlin; ed. Don Ihde; Evanston: Northwestern University Press, 1974; repr. 2004), p. 16; Fred B. Craddock, *As One without Authority* (Nashville: Abingdon, 1981), p. 117.

procedures from initial outlining down to a final speaking of the sermon. But in all such books there seems to be a gap. There's something left out in between. The crucial moment between exegesis and homiletical vision is not described. The shift between the study of a text and the conception of a sermon – perhaps it occurs in a flash of imagination – is never discussed. So alert readers are left with the odd impression that we move from the Bible to a contemporary sermon by some inexplicable magic![3]

It is the aim of this work to render that 'magic' less mysterious, and to remedy the bemoaned lacuna between text and praxis by a fruitful dialogue between hermeneutics and homiletics. Hermeneutics, considered here as critical reflection on interpretive practice, appears to be a natural ally of homiletics – the application of a literary corpus, the canonical Scriptures, by and to an interpretive community of believers. Such an alliance, privileging the duty and role of the preacher as a 'theologian-homiletician' mediating between the past of the inscription and the present of the congregation, will prove to be fruitful in delineating a valid movement from text to praxis. In labeling the preacher a theologian-homiletician, this work reveals its tenor: the one proclaiming the biblical text to the Church ought not to be merely a homiletician, but a theologian as well. It is the working out of this nomenclature, especially the 'theologian' half of the appellation, that is the essence of this work, uniting as it does in one portfolio the responsibility of negotiating the demands of both hermeneutics and homiletics.

Goals

Application is 'the life and soul of a sermon, whereby these sacred truths [of Scripture] are brought home to a Man's particular conscience and occasions, and the affections ingaged [*sic*] unto any truth or duty'.[4] It is the culmination of the exercise of preaching, whereby the biblical text is brought to bear upon the lives of the congregation in a manner that seeks to align the community of God to the will of God for the glory of God. What is historical and distant (the text) is, in preaching, made contemporary and near (praxis). The Bible affirms that 'whatever was written in earlier times was written for our instruction' (Rom. 15.4). Therefore, a fundamental issue for preachers of the Bible has always been the determination of application that is faithful to the textual intention and fitting for the listening audience. Particularly pertinent is how this transaction may be conducted with respect to the self-contained and well-

---

3.   David Buttrick, *A Captive Voice: The Liberation of Preaching* (Louisville: Westminster/ John Knox Press, 1994), p. 89.

4.   John Wilkins, *Ecclesiastes, or A discourse concerning the Gift of Preaching As it fals under the Rules of Art: Shewing The most proper Rules and Directions, for Method, Invention, Books, Expressions, whereby a Minister may be furnished with such abilities as may make him a Workman that needs not to be ashamed* (3rd edn; London: Samuel Gellibrand, 1651), p. 19.

defined quantum of the scriptural text that is regularly employed in liturgical contexts – the pericope. As the fundamental units of the canonical text handled in the formal gatherings of the people of God, pericopes are the basic textual elements of their weekly rendezvous with Scripture.[5] Deriving valid application from pericopes, then, is a cardinal task of the homiletician. This work seeks to discover the answer to the question: In a sermon intending to proclaim application from a pericope, how does one move validly from text to praxis, that is, with authority and relevance? Pursuing a resolution to the issue, the two fields of hermeneutics and homiletics are allowed to engage each other in productive dialogue. Homiletics must draw from the insights of early and modern hermeneutics, and hermeneutics must attend to the ecclesial context and unique demands of the homiletical endeavour. A theological liaison between the two fields is called for, respecting both the literary entity of the text and the liturgical event of its proclamation. This cooperative enterprise, as is envisaged and essayed here, will alone be efficacious in relieving the dolour of the preacher; it is only by the bipartisan agency of hermeneutics and homiletics that biblical pericopes may be validly exposited for application.

Eternity intersects time in the text of scripture, with the divine gaining an entrée into the course of history, thus endowing those writings with critical significance for the life of the Church. In the assemblies of God's people, the instruments of life transformation are these assimilable units of the biblical canon, pericopes. The weekly burden of the preacher is the transposition of the particular pericope of Scripture rooted in the historical context of its inscription, into valid application in the lives of hearers grounded in their own contemporary contexts. This interpretive transaction is actually discernible within the canon itself, for earlier material of the corpus was adapted and rendered in subsequent texts in forms capable of addressing new situations with relevance. The reshaping is visible even with the first body of divine commands given at Sinai; these were reinterpreted and reapplied in later circumstances, Deuteronomy being an expanded commentary on Exodus 20–24, enabling the latter 'to speak afresh in a new context'.[6] How may this transition from Scripture to relevant application be continued validly today, without diluting the authority of the textual source of the sermon?

---

5.   While acknowledging its more common connotation of a portion of the Gospels, this work employs 'pericope' to demarcate a segment of Scripture, irrespective of genre, that forms the textual basis for a sermon. Chapter 4 will discuss the utility and function of pericopes for the act of preaching.

6.   John Goldingay, *Models for Interpretation of Scripture* (Grand Rapids: Eerdmans, 1995), pp. 121–2. He calls this 'a process of reinterpretation, rethinking, reworking, and reappropriation'. This elaboration is also visible in the canon with the juxtaposition of the two Testaments and in the manner in which the New handles the Old. See Paul Ricoeur, 'Preface to Bultmann', in idem, *The Conflict of Interpretations* (trans. Peter McCormick; ed. Don Ihde; Evanston: Northwestern University Press, 1974; repr. 2004), p. 379.

The lot of the theologian-homiletician is not easy: each week, the preacher has to negotiate this formidable passage from ancient text to modern audience – 'a perilous road' – by which this intrepid soul seeks to expound with accuracy the sense and significance of a specific biblical passage for the faithful.[7] Unfortunately, 'at no point within the Bible is there ever spelled out a system or a technique by which one could move from the general imperatives of the law of God, such as found in the Decalogue, to the specific application within the concrete situation'.[8] Indeed, it is not only from the imperatives of law that the journey to application encounters hazards. The question of what constitutes valid application is pertinent to all genres of the biblical text from which the theologian-homiletician seeks to preach. Though the Bible does not offer an explicit *modus operandi* for traversing that gap between text and praxis, this work, nevertheless, will attempt to provide a theological bridge spanning those waters by employing with profit concepts derived from the embrace of hermeneutics and homiletics.

Texts, intrinsically linguistic as they are, yield themselves to consideration as Wittgensteinian language-games played according to conventional and institutional 'rules' (see Chapter 1).[9] The image of the language-game is utilized throughout this work as the metaphorical thread connecting its various parts, in order to enable an examination of the rules of those games of Scripture (Chapters 2 and 3). These rules facilitate a valid movement from Scripture to sermon, one that respects both the authority of the biblical text and the need for praxis relevant to the circumstances of auditors. It will be proposed herein that the bridge between text and praxis is the theology of the pericope, discovered by deployment of the rules of language-games: *pericopal theology* grounds the sermon in the authority of the text and launches it with relevance for the audience. This intermediary ensures the validity of the movement from ancient inscription to modern application (Chapter 4). Derived from and dependent upon a specific text of Scripture, pericopal theology is the product of hermeneutical exertions on the part of the preacher and, by enabling application of that text, it forms the basis for the subsequent homiletical enterprise. In pericopal theology, hermeneutics and homiletics converge to bear rich dividends for the preaching endeavour in the ecclesial context.

---

7.   James D. Smart, *The Strange Silence of the Bible in the Church: A Study in Hermeneutics* (London: SCM Press, 1970), pp. 33–4.

8.   Brevard S. Childs, *Biblical Theology in Crisis* (Philadelphia: Westminster, 1970), pp. 129–30.

9.   Ludwig Wittgenstein, *Philosophical Investigations* (2nd edn; trans. G.E.M. Anscombe; London: Basil Blackwell, 1958), ¶85. These rules are neither decrees absolute nor edicts that brook no infractions; they have more in common with signposts than with injunctions. In this work, the rules of biblical interpretation also are considered persuasive directions rather than peremptory diktats, those that have implicitly presided over readings of Scripture all through the history of the Church.

Assumptions

Seeking to provide the hermeneutical and homiletical bases for the move from text to praxis via theology, this work operates with certain assumptions – hermeneutical, pragmatic and theological.

Hermeneutical assumptions

Realism asserts that entities independent of the mind do exist. This work subscribes to a form of realism that assumes that some things can be objectively known despite the influence of cultural schemas and individual presuppositions. A stance of *hermeneutical realism* is adopted herein that holds that meaningful discourses exist prior to and independent of the process of interpretation, antecedent to their apprehension by hearers of spoken words or readers of written texts. Meanings are therefore discovered, not created.[10] At its core, such a discrimination between the discovery and creation of meaning involves the question of which interpretive code governs the reading of a given text. E.D. Hirsch narrows the options to two potential norms that may be adopted by the interpreter: either the reader's own ('autocratic'), or that of another ('allocratic'). In all hermeneutical transactions, *somebody's* norm or act of authorship has to be invoked, for there is 'no meaning without an author of meaning'. Under the first, authority resides with the empowered reader, based on his or her preferences: meaning is created. Under the second, the reader delegates authority to the historical act of another person or community: meaning is discovered. The reader is free to choose between these norms of interpretation; the choice of neither is inherently required or mandated by the text but, rather, is driven by the goal of the interpreter.[11]

The goal of the biblical interpreter, it will be assumed, is to discern the meaning of the text of Scripture as affirmed by its authors, both divine and

10. See E.D. Hirsch, Jr., 'The Politics of Theories of Interpretation', in *The Politics of Interpretation* (ed. W.J.T. Mitchell; Chicago: University of Chicago Press, 1983), pp. 321–33 (328); and Kevin J. Vanhoozer, *Is There a Meaning in This Text? The Bible, the Reader, and the Morality of Literary Knowledge* (Grand Rapids: Zondervan, 1998), p. 48. *Hermeneutical idealism*, in contrast, holds that it is interpretation of the text that generates meaningfulness; thus meaning is created, not discovered (Stephen Mailloux, 'Rhetorical Hermeneutics', *CI* 11 [1985], pp. 620–41 [622]).

11. Hirsch, 'Politics of Theories of Interpretation', pp. 326–7; idem, *The Aims of Interpretation* (Chicago: The University of Chicago Press, 1976), p. 85; and idem, 'Criticism and Countertheses: On Justifying Interpretive Norms', *J Aes Art Crit* 43 (1984), pp. 89–91 (90). Knapp and Michaels would dispute the presumption of any readerly choice: 'meaning of a text is simply identical to the author's intended meaning'; there cannot be any intentionless meaning. See Steven Knapp and Walter Benn Michaels, 'Against Theory', *CI* 8 (1982), pp. 723–42 (724, 727); likewise, P.D. Juhl, *Interpretation: An Essay in the Philosophy of Literary Criticism* (Princeton: Princeton University Press, 1980), pp. 12, 47.

human. Representing the conviction that the people of God have maintained over several millennia, Augustine declared that 'the person examining the divine utterances must of course do his best to arrive at the intention of the writer through whom the Holy Spirit produced that part of Scripture' (*Doctr. chr.* 3.27.38). Authorial intention, as the historical cause of a text and the antecedent of the act of writing, is the only necessary and sufficient explanation for the intelligibility thereof. Paul Ricoeur calls it a fallacy to presume that a text is an authorless entity: 'It is impossible to cancel out this main characteristic of discourse'.[12] An allocratic norm thus receives priority in this current enterprise, with the reader assuming an 'intentional stance', the strategy that construes texts as literary products of rational agents who express their intentions through their inscriptions. The authorial intention as affirmed in the text is the norm that forms the basis of all subsequent analyses of the written act of communication.[13] For scriptural interpretation, this stance permits the congregation to seek, discover, and abide by the will of God in the canonical text.

Chapter 1 will build upon these hermeneutical assumptions as it outlines the characteristics and functions of language-games, textuality and genres.

Such an understanding of hermeneutical realism is not to assert that the task of the theologian-homiletician is exhausted in the elucidation of the text's original sense. Indeed, the labour of the preacher continues further, to the elements beyond the semantics of the text, that is, pragmatics (see below). Pragmatic analysis is essential for the discovery of the future-directedness of the text and thus its application. In other words, this work calls for more than merely establishing the stability and determinate meaning of the text as it was 'then'. It also affirms that the discourse must be interpreted in such a manner that it may be applied 'now' – a hermeneutical-homiletical undertaking that is both conscientious in respecting the authority of the ancient text and creative in making relevant application to contemporary auditors.

---

12. Paul Ricoeur, *Interpretation Theory: Discourse and the Surplus of Meaning* (Fort Worth, TX: Texas Christian University Press, 1976), p. 30; also see Vanhoozer, *Is There a Meaning in This Text?*, p. 44.

13. To consider what the author 'affirms', rather than what the author 'intends', is to focus on the textual product of intending, rather than on the mental process thereof (Millard J. Erickson, *Evangelical Interpretation: Perspectives on Hermeneutical Issues* [Grand Rapids: Baker, 1993], p. 23). The cognitive intentionalist approach in psycholinguistics has demonstrated that comprehension of a discourse must necessarily take into account what the speaker/author intended in and with the utterance, that is, the communicative intention. Such intentionality pertains not only to transactions of discourse but also for virtually all actions of mankind, linguistic or otherwise. Note, for instance, the elaborate formulæ jurisprudence utilizes for labelling 'felonious intent', 'criminal intent', 'malice aforethought', 'guilty knowledge', etc. See Raymond W. Gibbs, Jr., *Intentions in the Experience of Meaning* (Cambridge: Cambridge University Press, 1999), pp. 16, 72–3.

Pragmatic assumptions

The determination of how exactly application relates to the meaning of the text, and whether there are directions for future application in texts authored in the past, hinges upon the notion that 'meaning' involves more than the semantics of the inscription (*sentence* meaning); it involves the pragmatics of the text as well (*discourse* meaning) – what speakers/authors do with what they say/ write, those aspects of meaning not secured by a semantic theory (see Chapter 1). This, of course, does not preclude an inquiry into textual semantics. Indeed, pragmatics incorporates and is built upon the latter; an understanding of the text involves, in the first place, grasping its semantic content.[14] Yet, as the field of pragmatics claims, the semantics of an utterance is not the whole story (or game): the goal is to apprehend what the author was doing with the text. No less energetic in the performance of their communicative actions, writers of biblical texts also were *doing* something with their literary products – persuading their audiences to think, feel and act in particular ways. Indeed, the placing of a writing implement upon writing material constituted a rhetorical act. The crucial interaction to be discerned by the interpreter is not so much that between author and text or between text and reader, but rather that between author and reader *by way of the text* employed as an instrument to accomplish specific aims and elicit specific responses.[15] Therefore, while comprehension of the semantic aspect of the text under consideration is the essential first step of its interpretation, this initial move should advance the reader further, to a discovery of 'the pragmatic penumbra' accompanying semantics. In biblical hermeneutics, the text of Scripture is more than an object of literary creativity; pragmatics asserts that the textual unit is also an instrument of action, the agent that effectively promotes an alignment of the lives of the faithful to the demands of their God.[16] This is a key thrust of this work: pragmatics enables the identification of the critical intermediary between text and praxis, the *world in front of the text*, the second-order referent of the text.[17]

14. Quentin Skinner calls it a truism that 'good critical practice depends above all on close and sensitive reading of the text itself' ('Motives, Intentions and the Interpretation of Texts', *NLH* 3 [1972], pp. 393–408 [395]).

15. Vernon K. Robbins, 'Writing as a Rhetorical Act in Plutarch and the Gospels', in *Persuasive Artistry: Studies in New Testament Rhetoric in Honor of George A. Kennedy* (ed. Duane F. Watson; Sheffield: JSOT, 1991), pp. 142–68 (168); Martin Nystrand, 'An Analysis of Errors in Written Communication', in *What Writers Know* (ed. Martin Nystrand; New York: Academic, 1982), pp. 57–74 (70).

16. Scripture is '*doing* something that decisively shapes the community's identity' (David H. Kelsey, *The Uses of Scripture in Recent Theology* [Philadelphia: Fortress, 1975], p. 208). Also see Stephen C. Levinson, *Presumptive Meanings: The Theory of Generalized Conversational Implicature* (Cambridge, MA: The MIT Press, 2000), p. 1.

17. Chapter 1 will attend to these concepts in detail; Chapter 4 will consolidate them for an account of their ecclesial significance.

For the most part, what the author was doing in and with the text is recoverable from the text itself. Such a transaction does not entail a subjective free-for-all interpretive endeavour that has no bounds. Ricoeur is careful to note that the surplus of meaning that constitutes the pragmatics and second-order references of symbols, metaphors and entire texts is a regulated polysemy, constrained by the 'clues' of textual signs; it is not constructed *ad libitum*. The text remains the sole means of access to both the semantics and pragmatics of the utterance.[18] In the same fashion, the location of truth for the community of God's people is the scriptural text. There is no non-textually mediated access to the truths of God and his relationship to his creation that is as authoritative as Scripture. The textual embodiment of this extratextual reality, in its irreducible textuality, offers an indirect access to that second-order referent; the text is the only reliable doorway to its pragmatic element, the world in front of the text.[19]

Chapters 2 and 3 will consider how this pragmatic component of the biblical text may be discerned by means of a reading governed by the rules of textual language-games.

Theological assumptions

With praxis as the end-point of the homiletical undertaking that commences in the text of Scripture, the fundamental theological assumptions involved in this work may be expressed in the biblical assertion: 'all Scripture is profitable' (2 Tim. 3.16). To assent to this affirmation is to recognize the importance of application in the life of God's people, for application is the outcome of the Church's encounter with Scripture, serving to reorient its faith and practice according to biblical prescriptions.

All *Scripture* is profitable. This work concerns itself with the Old and New Testaments comprising the canon in its final form as available to the community of believers. The biblical corpus displays the characteristic properties of a text, the various contours and particular nuances of primary literary genres and the

18. Ricoeur, *Interpretation Theory*, pp. 55–6. Also see idem, *Hermeneutics and the Human Sciences: Essays on Language, Action and Interpretation* (ed. and trans. John B. Thompson; Cambridge: Cambridge University Press, 1981), p. 175; and idem, 'Structure, Word, Event', in *The Conflict of Interpretations* (trans. Robert Sweeney; ed. Don Ihde; Evanston: Northwestern University Press, 1974; repr. 2004), pp. 79–96 (90).

19. Francis Watson, *Text, Church and World: Biblical Interpretation in Theological Perspective* (Grand Rapids: Eerdmans, 1994), pp. 2–3. Watson argues for an 'intratextual realism' that understands 'the biblical text as referring beyond itself to extratextual theological reality, while at the same time regarding that reality as accessible to us only in textual form, in principle and not only in practice' (224–5). None of this is to imply that readers can determine with absolute and infallible precision what the determinate semantic and pragmatic meaning of the text is. See idem, *Text and Truth: Redefining Biblical Theology* (Grand Rapids: Eerdmans, 1997), pp. 123–4; and Kevin J. Vanhoozer, *First Theology: God, Scripture and Hermeneutics* (Downers Grove: InterVarsity, 2002), p. 277 n. 4.

unique traits of its secondary genre (that of the canonical classic, superimposed upon and enfolding primary genres). The completed text of Scripture is construed as adequate for the derivation of application; it is sufficient to render the Christian 'fully qualified and equipped for every good work' (2 Tim. 3.17). It is as Scripture – and all that that theological nomenclature entails, including inspiration that renders it divine discourse – that the biblical text is the object of interpretation for application purposes; therefore, it remains the primary focus of this work.[20]

All Scripture *is profitable*. The application of Scripture in the lives of its readers (and in the lives of hearers of sermons based upon Scripture) is a fertile endeavour, the undertaking of those who, like the good soil, hear the word 'and hold it fast, and bear fruit with perseverance' (Lk. 8.15); the Bible enjoins the reader to be a doer of the word and not just a hearer (Jas 1.22-3). The employment of Scripture as the foundation of the existence, beliefs and activities of the Church, as well as the means of edification for individuals and community, assumes that biblical interpretation will culminate in application – life change for the glory of God. Divine discourse always demands a response.

All Scripture is profitable. All pericopes of Scripture are relevant for application. While there may be a hierarchy of relevance, no part of the Bible is completely irrelevant; all pericopes therein may gainfully be utilized in the move from text to praxis, for 'whatever was written in earlier times was written for our instruction' (Rom. 15.4). All of Scripture – all of its constituent genres (primary and secondary), its canonical books and the assemblage of pericopes that compose it – may be employed in moulding believers unto Christlikeness and orienting the community in a right relationship with God. The corollary of the text's profitability is its 'preachability': if profitable for application, then preachable in the community of God's people.

The working out of these theological assumptions in the generation of valid application will be detailed in Chapter 4.

One primary divine personage who ought to figure prominently in any consideration of theological hermeneutics and homiletics will, regretfully, receive no significant attention here. The role of the Holy Spirit in the interpretation of the biblical text, as well as in the sermonic proclamation thereof, is a whole field of inquiry and an extensive subject of reflection in itself. Also not scrutinized is a related topic – the role of the spiritual formation of the preacher, reader and hearer of Scripture in the integrated enterprise involving hermeneutics and homiletics. These lacunæ reflect limitations of space, rather than any attempt to belittle those critical arenas of thought, investigation and practice in the Church's ministry of the word. Such omissions are all the more acute because the religious text that Scripture is cannot simply be considered as equivalent to

---

20. Nicholas Wolterstorff, *Divine Discourse: Philosophical Reflections on the Claim that God Speaks* (Cambridge: Cambridge University Press, 1995), pp. 38–57.

other kinds of utterances. While there is convergence between biblical and other discourses in that their contents and referents are similarly discoverable, they do diverge in at least these important criteria: Scripture, construed as the word of God, is divine discourse – its unique authorship; the biblical text, canonically bounded, is the ground for all discourse on the divine name – its unique content; the canon adopts a particular moral, ethical and socio-political orientation – its unique stance; and the interpreter is assumed to belong to a community that acknowledges the biblical corpus as its Scripture – its unique readership.[21] The joint task of biblical hermeneutics and homiletics, then, is to unpack, for the purposes of application, the manifold implications of this 'God-talk', so that, thereby, Scripture may govern the life of God's people.[22]

It is intended that, as a result of these investigations, a theological paradigm for the application of Scripture in an ecclesial context may be rendered more substantive in theory and successful in practice. Chapter 1 will provide the general hermeneutical bases for this undertaking, considering language-games, textuality and the properties of genres. This chapter will introduce the important concept of the *world in front of the text*, as well as the notion of a surplus of meaning. The next two chapters will propound the Rules of Primary and Secondary Genres and how the reading of the biblical text is to be conducted under the aegis of those rules in order to discern that world in front of the text. Chapter 2 will deal with the primary language-game and propose rules for four prominent literary genres – narrative, prophecy, law and hymnody. Chapter 3 will postulate rules for the 'playing' of the secondary language-game, that of the canon. Finally, Chapter 4 will further develop the concept of the projected world, focusing upon pericopes in the homiletical undertaking. The world they portray – the theology of pericopes – endows them with the capacity to generate valid application, and to effect covenant renewal in the community of God as that projected world is 'inhabited' by readers and hearers.

This work, uniting hermeneutics and homiletics, will thereby have delineated the move from text to praxis, charting the navigation in such a way as to render the move from text to praxis, from Scripture to sermon, valid.

---

21. See Paul Ricoeur, 'Poetry and Possibility', in *A Ricoeur Reader: Reflection and Imagination* (ed. Mario J. Valdés; Hertfordshire: Harvester Wheatsheaf, 1991), pp. 448–62 (455); and idem, 'Naming God', *USQR* 34 (1979), pp. 215–27 (219).

22. Paul Ricoeur, 'Philosophy and Religious Language', *JR* 54 (1974), pp. 71–85 (83–4); and idem, 'Philosophical Hermeneutics and Theological Hermeneutics: Ideology, Utopia, and Faith', in *Protocol of the Seventeenth Colloquy, 4 November 1975* (ed. W. Wuellner; Berkeley: The Center for Hermeneutical Studies in Hellenistic and Modern Culture, 1976), pp. 1–28 (15–16).

1

LANGUAGE-GAMES, TEXTUALITY AND GENRES

The overall goal of this work, as has been detailed in the Introduction, is to determine how a sermon proposing application from a specific biblical pericope may move validly from text to praxis, that is, with authority and relevance. Such an investigation into the workings of these two linguistic phenomena, text and sermon, is necessarily bifocal: due attention must be paid to the hermeneutics of theological discourse as well as to the homiletical specificities that govern the reading and exposition of the biblical text in an ecclesial gathering. Hermeneutics and homiletics, therefore, form the dual thrust of this work: broadly, Chapters 1, 2 and 3 will focus upon the hermeneutical side of this duality; Chapter 4 will attend primarily to the homiletical half – sermonic proclamations based on pericopes of Scripture with application as their goal.

The linguistic nature of texts lends itself to the consideration of these discourses as instances of 'language-games', communicative actions of specific types, equivalent to genres. In other words, a genre is a language-game in relation to a written discourse, with a given text being an instantiation of a particular genre. As are all games, those of language, too, are governed by rules, implicit mandates by which particular texts are both created and comprehended.[1] This work will propose that in a homiletical endeavour geared towards application, the rules of language-games enable the hermeneut to move validly from text to praxis.

An adequate accounting of the first half of the hermeneutical–homiletical binary will require a judicious and balanced utilization of both general and special (theological) hermeneutics. To this end, Chapter 1 addresses general hermeneutics, laying out concepts that will be utilized in subsequent chapters for the dialogue with homiletics; Chapters 2 and 3 concentrate on specifically theological matters pertaining to interpretation of Scripture.

---

1. 'Rule' should not be construed as a legislated norm that is binding upon interpreters. The utilization of that term in this work is an aid to extending the analogy of games to hermeneutical undertakings. E.D. Hirsch rightly cautioned: 'No methods [or rules] of legal, biblical, or literary construction have ever been devised which are not in some instances either misleading or useless' (*Validity in Interpretation* [New Haven: Yale University Press, 1967], p. vii). 'Rule', in this work, should be understood with full cognizance of Hirsch's caveat.

Before attention is directed towards particular aspects of general hermeneutics in this chapter, the necessity for employing general hermeneutical concepts in biblical interpretation must be justified. This is undertaken at the outset of Chapter 1. Following this discussion, the game-plan for the rest of the chapter will involve an analysis of language-games. The establishment of what the textuality of such games entails, as against orality, will bring into relief the capacity of texts to play a unique kind of language-game, that of genre, with properties that enable the subsequent application of those texts by readers far removed in time and space from the writing event. Special attention will be paid to the hermeneutical consequences of the Bible being a canonical classic; this is a unique genre, a secondary language-game that is superimposed upon, and that encompasses, the primary literary genres of Scripture. A significant aspect of the work of genres, both primary and secondary, is the projection of the *world in front of the text*. This world with the transhistorical intention it bears (concepts adapted from Paul Ricoeur and E.D. Hirsch) enables texts of the classic category to exert their influence into the futurity of potential readers.

Chapter 1 will thus have laid the foundation for the theological undertakings of Chapters 2 and 3, where the rules of primary and secondary genres, respectively, will be analysed for the world projection they facilitate. Chapter 4 of this work will show how all of these hermeneutical elements may be employed in the homiletical endeavour to validate the move from text to praxis.

General and special hermeneutics

General hermeneutics lays claim to a universal domain of textuality, since the dimension of language, the basis of all experience, is the universal medium of being. Thus it might appear that theological or special hermeneutics is simply a regional application of the larger general enterprise of discovering meaning. However, the relationship between general and special hermeneutics is more complex than a simple hierarchy. Ricoeur describes it in terms of 'mutual inclusion'. Indeed, for him, there is even a reversal in the relationship between the two, whereby theological hermeneutics circumscribes and embraces general hermeneutics, transforming the latter into the former's own 'organon' (instrument or tool). The reasons for this 'inverse filiation' are the peculiar features of theological hermeneutics that challenge the universality, or the claim thereto, of general hermeneutics: the singular nature of its textual referent ('God-talk'), its ultimate author, the normative quality of such texts, and the spiritual and moral character of the transformative act of reading.[2] John Webster's urging to

---

2. Paul Ricoeur, 'Philosophical Hermeneutics and Theological Hermeneutics: Ideology, Utopia, and Faith', in *Protocol of the Seventeenth Colloquy, 4 November 1975* (ed. W. Wuellner; Berkeley: The Center for Hermeneutical Studies in Hellenistic and Modern Culture, 1976), pp. 1–28 (2–4); also see James Fodor, *Christian Hermeneutics: Paul Ricoeur and the Refiguring of*

see Christian reading of the Bible as 'a spiritual affair', and hence a matter for theological description, is appropriate. General hermeneutical categories must not eclipse the character of the Bible as the '*viva vox Dei* addressing the people of God and generating faith and obedience'. The uniqueness of this address is what makes theological hermeneutics one of a kind, not just a small plot in the larger terrain of general hermeneutics.[3]

In addition, general hermeneutics instructs the interpreter to take into account the textuality of the Bible and the consequences of 'distanciation' in the radical passage from speech to writing.[4] Theological hermeneutics supplements this instruction from the general field with a unique mode of textual reference – the splitting of referents into two 'layers' (first- and second-order), as a consequence of which the normativeness of the written word of God can potentially be translated into application in circumstances far removed from the event of its inscription. For Ricoeur, the explication of the second-order referent, the *world in front of the text*, is *the* task of hermeneutics. Religious texts re-describe life by opening up this potential world.[5] Another particularity of theological hermeneutics is that while general hermeneutics bids the interpreter consider individual texts as works or primary genres, special hermeneutics enfolds this scheme within the secondary genre of the canonical classic. Forming a 'playground' of its own, the canon creates a delimited space for interpretation, exerting its interpretive pressure upon the kind of theological meanings that emerge.[6] Religious language, which appears as a polyphony of primary literary genres, is harmonized by the unity secured in the canon. In short, theological

---

Theology (Oxford: Clarendon Press, 1995), p. 241. In the same vein is the claim of Kevin J. Vanhoozer that all hermeneutics is theological ('The Spirit of Understanding: Special Revelation and General Hermeneutics', in *Disciplining Hermeneutics: Interpretation in Christian Perspective* [ed. Roger Lundin; Grand Rapids: Eerdmans, 1997], pp. 131–65 [160]). George Steiner declares that 'any coherent understanding of what language is and how language performs, ... any coherent account of the capacity of human speech to communicate meaning and feeling is ... underwritten by the assumption of God's presence', requiring, in effect, that every book be read as the Bible is (*Real Presences* [Chicago: The University of Chicago Press, 1989], p. 3).

3. John Webster, *Word and Church: Essays in Christian Dogmatics* (Edinburgh: T. & T. Clark, 2001), pp. 47, 58.

4. The concepts discussed in this paragraph – distanciation, second-order references, world in front of the text and secondary genre – will be considered in detail later in this chapter.

5. Ricoeur, 'Philosophical Hermeneutics and Theological Hermeneutics', p. 12. He claims that when poetic texts function in similar fashion, it is simply because such texts are read as are theological texts; this is to assert that special hermeneutics conditions general hermeneutics.

6. Despite the obsolescence of his reason for promoting special hermeneutics (the hybrid 'Hebraizing' nature of NT language), Friedrich Schleiermacher's basic demand is valid: specific differences between categories of texts call for discrete theoretical approaches to their peculiar problems. The Bible, as a unique canonical entity of divine discourse, thus merits a special hermeneutic ('Hermeneutics and Criticism', in *Hermeneutics and Criticism and Other Writings* [ed. Andrew Bowie; Cambridge: Cambridge University Press, 1998], pp. 1–224 [19–20]).

hermeneutics is in a dialectical relationship with general hermeneutics – interdependent and mutually inclusive.

In contrast, Hans W. Frei's concept of the perspicuity of the text enables him to analyse the text solely on its own terms. Its meaning and its truth is in its language and only in its language: 'The linguistic, textual world is in this case not only the *necessary* basis for our orientation within the real world… it is also *sufficient* for that purpose.'[7] As an intrinsic part of God's creation that was declared 'good', language, for Frei, is not a barrier to understanding; neither obscure nor incomprehensible, the linguistic medium permits the ascertainment of truth without hindrance. Texts are autonomous and self-referential in this reading.[8] In contrast, Ricoeur sees religious texts as related to poetic language and, though he agrees with Frei that meaning is found in the details of the text, he argues that that object of hermeneutics is the world in front of the text – a concern that arises from his seeing the biblical text as being about 'something'. Thus, another mutually constitutive level of meaning appears to be added on to that of textual sense. This is the crux of the discord between the hermeneutics of Ricoeur and Frei: the relation between the sense of the biblical text and its second-order referent, the projected world in which the reader is invited to participate. As will be seen, to produce an adequate account of text–world relations, especially with a view to application, Ricoeur's concepts appear more felicitous, holding as they do in dynamic balance (in mutual *inclusion*) general and theological hermeneutics, and proffering for habitation a potential world.[9] Frei's static and somewhat mutually *exclusive* opposition of the global and regional forms of hermeneutics, conditioned partly by his universalizing of text and textuality, tends to diminish the explanatory and descriptive power of interpretive endeavours, and thus the potential for future application of the text as well, as it precludes any reference to the world in front of the text.

Rather than a rigid hierarchical disposition of general and special hermeneutics, a mutually inclusive and interweaving relationship between the two is therefore more likely to bear fruit in a hermeneutical undertaking. Their complementarity makes it essential that an interpreter moving from biblical text to praxis employ the resources of both categories to advantage. Such an

---

7.   Hans W. Frei, 'The "Literal Reading" of the Biblical Narrative in the Christian Tradition: Does It Stretch or Will It Break?' in *The Bible and the Narrative Tradition* (ed. Frank McConnell; New York: Oxford University Press, 1986), pp. 36–77 (66–7).

8.   See Fodor, *Christian Hermeneutics*, p. 267. Webster, like Frei, also sees God as being self-communicative: his self-bestowal in his word is an effective operation that will not be impeded (*Word and Church*, pp. 75–6). Though neither is in favour of a 'high-level' use of general hermeneutics in a foundational and global manner for subsequent theological work, both Webster and Frei do allow for the use of general hermeneutical principles in a 'low-level' and *ad hoc* fashion (Webster, *Word and Church*, p. 57; Frei, ' "Literal Reading" of the Biblical Narrative in the Christian Tradition', pp. 59, 71).

9.   The latter half of this chapter will emphasize the utility of this concept for application.

integrative approach does not in any way detract from the particularity and peculiarity of theological hermeneutics; indeed, the profitability of the latter for application is amplified by the employment of precepts pertaining to general hermeneutics. Anticipating this gain to homiletics, the rest of Chapter 1 will concern itself with general hermeneutics before engaging in special hermeneutics for the balance of this work.

Chapter 1 proceeds from categories broad to narrow, beginning with the wider bracket of *language-games* that encompasses all discourse entities. The discussion will then converge upon *textuality*, the characteristics of the textual species of language-games. The peculiar properties of written discourse (especially the world in front of the text) make it possible for the reader, located away from the event of writing, to apply the text. The explorations in this chapter will then develop an even more constricted focus upon language-games being played in the textual arena, that is, *genres*; their functions and conventionality (their subjection to rules established by convention) will be examined. Subsequently, in yet another narrowing, the particular secondary genre of the biblical text, the *classic* (canon) and its properties, including its future-directedness, will undergo scrutiny.

Language-games

This work employs the concept of language-games as a dominant image of biblical texts. Crucial to the interpretation of these textual sports – or any other kind of game – is the recognition of their rules; in the case of texts, such rules govern both their production and their interpretation. Prior to the consideration of the specific biblical language-games (primary and secondary genre), the general function and rule-based operation of language-games will be surveyed.

Function of language-games

Of the many metaphysical notions that the language philosopher Ludwig Wittgenstein (1889–1951) bequeathed to posterity, perhaps none has had as much import (or been as enigmatic) as the concept of language-games. Wittgenstein employed the analogy of language-games numerous times and in almost all of his writings; however, an explicit definition of the term was never given by him. Seeing language-games as inextricably interwoven with the specific circumstances and particular situations of life, he refrained from establishing the essence of a language-game. According to Wittgenstein, what it is depends on how, where, when and for what reason it is used; meanings are contingent upon language-games and language-games upon the entire context-in-life of the discourse. The function of a language-game depends upon what is being *done* with the composite whole of the discourse that makes up the game. Such a discourse thus comprises not only the words, phrases and sentences of the utterance but also the action that is accomplished by it. Therefore, language, Wittgenstein's concept of the language-game implies, cannot be considered in abstraction from the concrete circumstances and environs of its actual production and deployment. Not merely a system of signs, language is rather a form of life that is firmly embedded in the actuality of living, in the lives of its users, *in situ*.[10] 'The term "language-*game*" is meant to bring into prominence the fact that the *speaking* of language [*das* Sprechen *der Sprache*] is part of an activity, or of a form of life [*Lebensform*].' A language-game, thus, is a verbally performed communicative practice, an integrated universe of language and its enactment.[11]

Such an integrated universe necessarily involves a multitude of language-games corresponding to the specific activities in which humanity engages. Wittgenstein notes the plurality of language-games in the following examples:

> Giving orders, and obeying them –
> Describing the appearance of an object, or giving its measurements –
> Constructing an object from a description (a drawing) –
> Reporting an event –
> Speculating about an event –
> Forming and testing a hypothesis –
> Presenting the results of an experiment in tables and diagrams –
> Making up a story; and reading it –
> Play-acting –
> Singing catches –
> Guessing riddles –
> Making a joke; telling it –
> Solving a problem in practical arithmetic –
> Translating from one language to another –
> Asking, thanking, cursing, greeting, praying.[12]

---

10. Marie McGinn, *Wittgenstein and the* Philosophical Investigations (London: Routledge, 1997), p. 44. Wittgenstein hints at this notion of language-game in one of his earliest works: 'We call something a language game if it plays a particular role in our human life' ('Notes for Lectures on "Private Experience" and "Sense Data"', ed. R. Rhees, *Phil. Rev.* 77 [1968], pp. 275–320 (300); and idem, *Philosophical Investigations* [2nd edn; trans. G.E.M. Anscombe; London: Basil Blackwell, 1958], ¶7). Also notice his other remarks underscoring this theme: 'Every sign *by itself* seems dead. *What* gives it life? – In use it is *alive*'; 'language is an instrument'; 'words are also deeds' (¶¶432, 546); etc. Clearly, one of the major shifts in Wittgenstein's thinking from the earlier period of *Tractatus Logico-Philosophicus* (1920s) to the later days of *Philosophical Investigations* (1950s) was the transference of his focus from semantics to pragmatics (the component of language studies outside the domain of semantics, which deals especially with meaning related to language as action; see below).

11. Wittgenstein, *Philosophical Investigations*, ¶¶7, 19, 23. 'What belongs to a language game is a whole culture' (Wittgenstein, *Lectures and Conversations on Aesthetics, Psychology and Religious Belief* [ed. Cyril Barrett; Oxford: Blackwell, 1966], p. 8). The role of the biblical text in performing actions will be considered later.

12. Wittgenstein, *Philosophical Investigations*, ¶23.

His musings on these particular variations notwithstanding, Wittgenstein considered a wide spectrum of language-based activities, including mathematics, descriptive geometry and other technical uses of language, as language-games in and of themselves.[13] The inclusion of such a medley of different discourses within the broad category of language-games allows for textual enactments to be accommodated therein as well. Though textuality brings with it unique characteristics and tendencies (as will be discussed), for the purposes of its inclusion as a language-game, written discourse is not unlike spoken discourse.[14] In addition, Wittgenstein's acceptance of the descriptions of everyday material objects as language-games also suggests that references to the non-material world, to God, his attributes, his actions and his relationship with his creation would also fall into the same category.[15] Thus, texts that have a God-reference, that deal with matters theological and that are consequential to human life are but inscribed language-games of a particular kind; this work concerns itself with the particular literary games of Scripture, biblical genres.

The existence of a bewildering array of language-games of different kinds, textual and otherwise, with the potential of a veritable infinity of specific instantiations of each, raises the question of how those instantiations may be recognized as belonging to the same species of game.

Rules of language-games

The comparison between language-using activities and games begets the idea of a multiplicity of situations where meaningful speech (or writing) is undertaken; conceivably, similarities exist between these discrete transactions of verbal communication that enable all of them to be categorized as particular games. Despite the heterogeneous manifestations of games – some use balls, others do not; some are played on courts, others on fields, yet others on boards or computers – there is, nonetheless, 'a complicated network of similarities overlapping

13. Ludwig Wittgenstein, *Remarks on the Foundations of Mathematics* (ed. G.H. von Wright; Oxford: Basil Blackwell, 1956), pp. 296, 322, 327, etc.; and idem, *The Blue and Brown Books: Preliminary Studies for the 'Philosophical Investigations'* (2nd edn; ed. R. Rhees; New York: Harper and Row, 1960), p. 81.

14. Indeed, as was noted above, one of Wittgenstein's own explicit examples of language-games is '[p]resenting the results of an experiment in tables and diagrams' – a species of written discourse.

15. Patrick Sherry, *Religion, Truth and Language-Games* (London: Macmillan, 1977), pp. 22–3; also see Wittgenstein, *Philosophical Investigations*, p. 200. Rather cryptically, Wittgenstein has noted: 'Theology as grammar' (*Philosophical Investigations*, ¶373). Fergus Kerr interpreted this to mean 'the patient and painstaking description of how, when we have to, we speak of God' – as good a description of a theological language-game as any other (*Theology after Wittgenstein* [London: SPCK, 1997], p. 147). (*Philosophical Investigations* has both numbered and unnumbered sections; the former is represented with a pillcrow ['¶'] and the latter is referred to by specific page number prefaced by 'p.'.)

and criss-crossing', shared correspondences that Wittgenstein characterized as 'family resemblances'. In other words, language-games form families, sodalities of individuals resembling one another. The homology between games and language that Wittgenstein seems to be drawing attention to is the multiple and almost inexhaustible iterations of each, made possible by the equally inexhaustible variety of contexts in which these games may be played. These infinite iterations in a virtual infinity of contexts are presided over by the rules of each game, implying a degree of conventionality or institutionality in these literary activities. The utilization of the same set of rules clearly determines similitude between members of a single family of language-games. Thus it ought to be possible to enumerate rules that are shared between different texts playing the same language-game (for biblical genres this is accomplished in Chapters 2 and 3).

Needless to say, these rules are not obligatory impositions upon the interpreter. As Wittgenstein declared, 'A rule stands there like a sign-post', with no intrinsic compulsion upon one to abide by the sign.[16] Moreover, no language-game or speech situation can be exhaustively underwritten by rules in order to govern every potential eventuality. As Wittgenstein noted, 'no more are there any rules for how high one throws the ball in tennis, or how hard; yet tennis is a game for all that and has rules too'. To create absolute, airtight regulations that would 'stop up all the cracks' is an impossibility; a comprehensive rulebook that weighed and regulated every conceivable contingency, even if its creation were a possibility, would render any game unplayable.[17] Rules are only required to be practical, not global in scope or governance. Those that govern language-games are also not absolute in precision, but adequate in function, permitting flexibility. That the boundaries of a language-game and the clarity of its rules are, at least to some degree, blurred, Wittgenstein does not doubt: 'For how is the concept of a game bounded? What still counts as a game and what no longer does? Can you give the boundary? No.' Depending on the *aim* of the language activity, there is bound to be different degrees of tolerance of fuzziness in definition. 'Thus the point here is what we call "the goal". Am I inexact when I do not give our distance from the sun to the nearest foot, or tell a joiner the width of a table to the nearest thousandth of an inch?' Despite the fact that most language-games and their rules have indistinct boundaries, there is no question that 'with "blurred edges" and all, we "get along" quite well in saying things to one another'. The rules are indeed sufficient for their

16. Wittgenstein, *Philosophical Investigations*, ¶¶65–7, 84–5; Dallas M. High, *Language, Persons, and Belief: Studies in Wittgenstein's* Philosophical Investigations *and Religious Use of Language* (New York: Oxford University Press, 1967), p. 74. Related to the rule-following aspect of all games is the sense in which each game has a demarcated playing area, literal or conceptual (or linguistic), a *Spielraum* in which games are undertaken. This concept when applied to biblical texts will become important in the designation of canonical boundaries.

17. Wittgenstein, *Philosophical Investigations*, ¶¶68, 84.

purposes.[18] Those proposed for the generic language-games of the Bible will also be found to be adequate for the sermonic move from text to praxis.

Language-games thus function as linguistic performances – discrete communicative practices of discourse that include those that are textual in nature, related by family resemblance, and governed by particular rules that provide broad and adequate direction for the playing of those games. Here and in subsequent chapters of this work, this notion of textual language-games (genres) and their rules of conduct will be seen to be essential in depicting the world projected in front of the biblical text, the key entity for securing validity in the passage from Scripture to sermon.

Textuality

Language-games have been surveyed as linguistic sports with inherent rules and family resemblances. The examination of this broad category of communicative practices will now be followed by a focus on the concept of texts as language-games. Inscription is distinct from utterance in both performance and consequence, but writing, nevertheless, shares with speech many of the properties of a communicative act; it is a particular kind of 'saying'.[19] This work sees texts, including biblical pericopes, as performing 'speech' acts: a synthesis of the consequences of textual discourse *contra* spoken utterances, therefore, is necessary. While textuality is kin to orality – both are language-games – the differences between the two are substantial and have significant ramifications for textual interpretation, especially for biblical hermeneutics. The unique character of textual discourse in its distanciation and referentiality makes it a perfect medium for the language-games of Scripture, enabling its message to endure the speaker–hearer disjunction and generating the potential for a creative rehearing by a distant reader.

Consequences of textuality

Though the writing of Scripture was preceded by the utterances of the lawgiver, the storyteller, the seer, the songwriter, the teacher and the oral discourses of Jesus himself, it was the inscripturated word that was recognized by the Christian community as the canonical word of God. All subsequent Christian

18. Wittgenstein, *Philosophical Investigations*, ¶¶68–9, 88, 499; High, *Language, Persons, and Belief*, p. 90.

19. While Wittgenstein's concept of language-games originated in his thought-experiments with speech, it is clear that he would have no hesitation considering textual discourse as a linguistic game as well. Also see Mary Louise Pratt, *Toward a Speech Act Theory of Literary Discourse* (Bloomington, IN: Indiana University Press, 1977), pp. 79–200; and Sandy Petrey, *Speech Acts and Literary Theory* (New York: Routledge, 1990), pp. 71–85, for vigorous defences of writing as a 'speech' act.

theology was captioned as a 'theology of the word', according the word pre-eminence in Christian faith and practice.[20] Such a lofty regard for the text is based on the assumption that 'this kind of discourse is not senseless, that it is worthwhile to analyse it, because something is said that is not said by other kinds of discourse' – its reference to God and his relationship to his creation.[21] In addition to this singular quality, the word written – distinct from the word spoken and the Word incarnated – generates a peculiar set of exigencies.

The first and fundamental trait of any discourse, spoken or scripted, is that it is an event of communication wherein somebody says something to somebody else about something in some manner. In this, an inscribed discourse is no different from that which is spoken: they are both communicative actions and, as such, both participate in language-games. However, in distinction to a speech-event, a text is a discourse that is fixed, preserved, archived and disseminated by writing.[22] It is a locus of meaning, one that has undergone significant upheavals in its passage from speech to script. This convulsive transition must be taken into consideration in any account of hermeneutics. In all discourse, there is an implicit dialectic between the *event* of the utterance and the *meaning* thereof, between the act of saying and what is said. In spoken discourse, there is an intimate association between these two poles with each getting adequate emphasis. However, at the moment of inscription of an utterance, a radical breach is created between utterance event and meaning, between the 'saying' and the 'said', by means of a distanciation. Texts have been estranged from their authors, their intended audiences, and their original circumstances of composition. Writing has rendered the text autonomous, an orphan.[23]

20. Acknowledging the primacy of their written scriptures, the Qur'an refers to Christians and Jews as *ahl al-Kitāb* (أهل الكتاب, 'people of the Book'; *Surah al-Ma'idah* 5.77, and elsewhere). Judaism, in like fashion, refers to Jews as עם הספר.

21. Paul Ricoeur, 'Philosophy and Religious Language', *JR* 54 (1974), pp. 71–85 (71).

22. Paul Ricoeur, *Hermeneutics and the Human Sciences: Essays on Language, Action and Interpretation* (ed. and trans. John B. Thompson; Cambridge: Cambridge University Press, 1981), pp. 145, 147.

23. Paul Ricoeur, *Hermeneutics and the Human Sciences*, pp. 134, 139–40. Socrates warned Phaedrus about the ostensible untrustworthiness of writing (Plato, *Phaedr.* 275de): '[Written words] seem to talk to you as though they were intelligent, but if you ask them anything about what they say, from a desire to be instructed, they go on telling you just the same thing forever. And once a thing is put in writing, the composition, whatever it may be, drifts all over the place, getting into the hands not only of those who understand it, but equally of those who have no business with it; it doesn't know how to address the right people, and not address the wrong.' Textuality entails that the writer, his antecedents and his ideology are usually unknown to the reader. No less problematic, the reader is invisible to the author. In the same dialogue, Socrates has just emphasized the importance for an orator of knowing the audience directly: 'Since the function of oratory is in fact to influence men's souls, the intending orator must know what types of soul there are.' The distanciation effected by writing exacerbates this lack of audience analysis on the part of the author and, to that extent, according to Socrates, this deficiency

Distanciation is a critically important textual property. Neither a vestige of vocality, nor an epiphenomenon of inscription, it is, rather, a constitutive element of the enacted transaction of writing. Radical though it might appear – and it indeed is – distanciation is a necessary condition for the preservation of meaning, necessitating at the same time the enterprise of interpretation. The decontextualization of the discourse by distanciation 'becomes a condition for all subsequent interpretation for in preserving the text it also keeps it open for new interpretations. In other words, it makes possible the subsequent recontextualization of its message.' Thus, distanciation is essential for any participation in the meaning of the text by readers outside the text's originary circumstances.[24] The emancipation of the text from the oral situation, however, is not without consequences for the affiliations between message and medium, author, hearer, code and referent of textual discourse.

Message and medium
The medium of writing is clearly different from that of speech, and this mutation 'irradiates in every direction, affecting in a decisive manner all the factors and functions' of discourse.[25] What this change accomplishes is the fixation, not of the *saying* (the event), but of the *said* (the meaning) – the 'noema' of the act of speaking. Ricoeur's observation is apt: 'The human fact [and face!] disappears. Now material "marks" convey the message.'[26] With distanciation and the accompanying alteration in medium comes the rupture between message and speaker, and message and hearer, exploding the dialogical situation and enabling, even in the absence of the author, repeated examination of, and thoughtful reflection upon, the message. From an oral-aural world, it has irrupted into a new sensory world of vision that transforms and indeed

renders writing of questionable legitimacy when compared to speech (271d, 276a). 'Dead discourse', he labelled it, that only implants forgetfulness in human souls and causes the neglect of memory (275a, 276a). The irony, of course, is that Plato *did* commit his own discourses to writing, maintaining the immortality of those 'dead' words. Indeed, in *Phaedrus* he even compliments Isocrates (436–338 BCE) as a promising rhetorician, sharpening the irony, for this educator of orators, because of his own frailty of voice and qualms about public speaking, never executed his remarkable written orations; instead he used them as compositions for his students to analyse, or as speeches for others to deliver (278e–79a; on Isocrates, see James J. Murphy and Richard A. Katula, *A Synoptic History of Classical Rhetoric* [2nd edn; Davis, CA: Hermagoras, 1994], pp. 44–50).

24. Ricoeur, *Hermeneutics and the Human Sciences*, p. 147; also see David Pellauer, 'The Significance of the Text in Paul Ricoeur's Hermeneutical Theory', in *Studies in the Philosophy of Paul Ricoeur* (ed. Charles E. Reagan; Athens, OH: Ohio University Press, 1979), pp. 98–114 (107).

25. Paul Ricoeur, 'Writing as a Problem for Literary Criticism and Philosophical Hermeneutics', in *A Ricoeur Reader: Reflection and Imagination* (ed. Mario J. Valdés; Hertfordshire: Harvester Wheatsheaf, 1991), pp. 320–37 (322).

26. Paul Ricoeur, *Interpretation Theory: Discourse and the Surplus of Meaning* (Fort Worth, TX: Texas Christian University Press, 1976), p. 26.

restructures consciousness. Achieving semantic autonomy, the text is now free to reach a new audience and be applied afresh.[27]

Message and author

The liberation of meaning from event, accomplished in the act of writing, proclaims the escape of the text's career from the finite horizons of its author. This, however, does not imply a total loss of tethering of text to authorial meaning. On the one hand is the intentional fallacy of elevating the psychological event of authorial intention as the criterion for valid interpretation, belittling the semantic autonomy of the text. On the other hand is the opposite fallacy of the absolute text, baptizing it as an authorless entity and discounting the fact that a text is a communicative action between interlocutors, a generator and a receiver. This work advocates a *via media*. Though there is, in writing, some degree of freedom of message from the author, it is not a complete severance that would make authorial guidance unavailable for interpretation.[28] Distanciation does not render the text utterly autonomous, for the text bears with it, to some extent at least, artefacts of the event of writing and traces of the author in its script, medium, content, arrangement, etc. Authorial fingerprints can be detected in the inscription; such residues of intent are essential for interpretation, and are sufficiently present in most texts to establish the writer's intention and purpose.[29]

27. Paul Ricoeur, *Interpretation Theory*, pp. 26–9; Walter J. Ong, *Orality and Literacy: The Technologizing of the Word* (London: Routledge, 1982), p. 85. Lawrence Lessig put it pungently: 'Texts are transportable. They move. Because written, they are carried. Because carried, they are read – in different places and at different times. Nothing (save the loss of the original language or the original text) can stop this semiotic peripateticism. If you write it, it will roam' ('The Limits of Lieber', *Cardozo L. Rev.* 16 [1995], pp. 2249–72 [2249]).

28. Authorial meaning becomes a dimension or facet of the text such that Ricoeur can refer now to the 'intention' of the text as he accords hermeneutic privilege to the concept of an originating intent of the author – the 'main characteristic of discourse' (Ricoeur, *Interpretation Theory*, p. 30; also see Kevin J. Vanhoozer, *Is There a Meaning in This Text? The Bible, The Reader, and The Morality of Literary Knowledge* [Grand Rapids: Zondervan, 1998], p. 216). In a similar vein, Francis Watson stresses the human agency in writing: 'Like speech, writing bears within it an essential reference to its origin in human action, and without this it cannot be understood' (*Text and Truth: Redefining Biblical Theology* [Grand Rapids: Eerdmans, 1997], p. 98). As Northrop Frye has noted, '[O]ne has to assume, as an essential heuristic axiom, that the work as produced constitutes the definitive record of the writer's intention' (*Anatomy of Criticism: Four Essays* [Princeton: Princeton University Press, 1957], p. 87). Meaning, it must be noted, is sought not in the act of authorial intending but in its object and product, the text; 'meaning is sourced in intention [the act] but it is found in the symbol [object – text or speech]' (Ramesh P. Richard, 'Selected Issues in Theoretical Hermeneutics', *BSac* 143 [1986], pp. 14–25 [23 n. 8]).

29. Even the determination by a reader of the language of the written composition is a concession to intentional authorial choice (Steven Knapp and Walter Benn Michaels, 'Against Theory 2: Hermeneutics and Deconstruction', *CI* 14 [1987], pp. 49–68 [55–7]). The phenomenon of 'false friends' illustrates this eloquently: should 'g-i-f-t' be read in English or in German (= 'poison')? The decision is always based upon an assumption of what language the author chose to write in,

Message and hearer

The disruption caused by distanciation in writing also affects hearers, turning them into readers. Though writing may be addressed to a particular individual, this specification is less precise than in oral communication. The reader is, more often than not, beyond the physical vicinity of the author and unknown to him or her. Anyone who can read and is willing to volunteer for the role of addressee may undertake the reading of that particular text; such volunteers open themselves up to the designs of the author.[30] This potential universalization of the audience is one of the more radical effects of written communication. Yet, even when the identity of the reader is not stipulated and the possibility exists for a universal readership, the text may be directed towards an implied (and authorially intended) consumer belonging to a particular community and perhaps even sharing the same authorial concerns that motivated the production of the text in the first place.[31] This is, of course, pertinent to the interpretation of the Bible within a congregation that recognizes that body of writings as its Scripture.

Distanciation also generally assures the physical absence of the writer at the point of reception of the text by the reader: no longer does the scenario of dialogue operate in the transformed mode of the discourse that is writing/reading.[32] Often, in such cases, an interpreter may be recruited as mediator for the writer, especially when the texts in question are those of material importance to life, as is the Bible. The practice of introducing a go-between has much to recommend itself: the interpreter, distanced from the author in time and space, may have a better perspective on the referents of the text; the proximity of such an interpreter to hearers may also enable the former to recontextualize effectively the message of the text for the latter.[33] This is the role of the theologian-homiletician in the Church, an intermediary between author and listeners.

Message and code

Another consequence of distanciation is the form written discourse takes: a secondary code (writing) is superimposed upon the primary one (speech). Neither

a choice manifest in the text. In a published work, the signs of the event of inscription are evident in the details of the edition, printing and publication of the text. Authorial data, acknowledgments and prefaces, frequently included with such works, also provide information on the writer and the event of the writing. Letters and wills, for instance, are always regarded as bearing the intentional presence of their authors or testators.

30. Watson, *Text and Truth*, pp. 99, 102.

31. Ricoeur, *Interpretation Theory*, p. 31.

32. The combination of authorial and readerly absence from the event of reading and the event of writing, respectively, Ricoeur calls a 'double eclipse' (*Hermeneutics and the Human Sciences*, pp. 146–7). The exclusion of the author–reader dialogue is what renders texts 'inherently contumacious', for there is no way to refute a text directly – it always says exactly the same thing as before. 'This is one reason why "the book says" is popularly tantamount to "it is true". It is also one reason why books have been burnt' (Ong, *Orality and Literacy*, p. 79).

33. Watson, *Text and Truth*, pp. 102–3.

simply pictures of objects, nor mere representations of things, texts as surrogates for utterances can be generated and explicated only with an appropriate conventional code. Such an encoded form of communication enables extended and enriched literary compositions, rendering possible a variety of consistent and coherent plots and sub-plots – a striking difference in literary potential between written discourses and those that are orally performed or pictorially symbolized.[34] The secondary code of inscription, comprising the schemas of linguistic and writing conventions, as well as the sub-code of the particular genre, generates what is rightly called a 'work', signifying its kindred with production and labour. Discourse thereby becomes a *praxis* or *techne*, and the author an artisan of the text that is 'wrought'.[35] What is wrought – a text created as a specific instance of a generic type – projects a world, a referent of the text.

Message and referent

The transformation of the referential function of discourse is another momentous legacy of distanciation. Ricoeur explains:[36]

> In oral discourse, face-to-face interlocutors can, in the final analysis, refer what they are talking about to the surrounding world common to them. Only writing can by addressing itself to anyone who knows how to read, refer to a world that is not there between the interlocutors, a world that is the world of the text and yet is not in the text … This issue of the text is the object of hermeneutics. It is neither behind the text as the presumed author, nor in the text as its structure, but unfolded in front of it. This same consideration applies to biblical texts. God, who is named by the texts held open by my desire to listen, is … the ultimate referent of these texts. God is in some manner implied by the 'issue' of these texts, by the world – the biblical world! – that these texts unfold.

The role of this *world in front of the text* in theological hermeneutics, and its significance for the faith and practice of the Christian community – specifically, its importance for sermonic application – is the major consideration of this work.

The world in front of the text

Philip Wheelwright asserted that religious and poetic discourses make 'a kind of trans-subjective reference', pointing to an extratextual dimension.[37] Aristotle would agree. Poetic discourse (ποίησις, including most literary works), he affirmed, tends towards general truth and what could conceivably happen or gen-

---

34. Ronald E. Clements, *Old Testament Prophecy: From Oracles to Canon* (Louisville: Westminster/John Knox Press, 1996), p. 205.

35. Ricoeur, 'Philosophical Hermeneutics and Theological Hermeneutics', p. 8; idem, *Interpretation Theory*, p. 33.

36. Paul Ricoeur, 'Naming God', *USQR* 34 (1979), pp. 215-27 (217).

37. Philip Wheelwright, *The Burning Fountain: A Study in the Language of Symbolism* (rev. edn; Bloomington, IN: Indiana University Press, 1968), p. 4.

erally happens (τὰ καθόλου, the universal); history, in contrast, relates particular facts focusing on what actually happened (τὰ καθ᾽ ἕκαστον). Even if representing historical actuality, the poet's discourse is no less poetic, 'for there is nothing to prevent some actual occurrences from being the sort of thing that would probably or inevitably happen'.[38] All manner of literary compositions, thus, are 'poetic' and make extratextual references, inviting their readers to occupy the place of those limned in the text and to partake of their experiences, for these represented experiences are likely to be τὰ καθόλου. Such discourses, therefore, promote identification, confrontation and an emotional reaction, eliciting a response from the reader.[39] The text is not an end in itself, but the means thereto, an instrument of the author's action of 'manipulating language and structure to incorporate ... a larger, more complex vision' – the world projected by the writer.[40]

Clifford Geertz's commentary on Balinese cockfights is an illuminating analogy of the use of texts as instruments to depict worlds; in his account, the instrument is culture – an 'assemblage of texts'.[41] This grim sport is a metanarrative, a story that sets in perspective all other individual stories of that community. The cockfight refers beyond itself to portray a greater reality, another world – a 'meta-world'. One does not participate in this wrangle of roosters merely to observe a fight between fowl, but rather to see 'what a man, usually composed, aloof, almost obsessively self-absorbed ... feels like when, attacked, tormented, challenged, insulted, and driven in result to the extremes of fury, he has totally triumphed or been brought totally low'.[42] The Balinese cockfight goes beyond the world *of* the culture – the birds, the breeders, the bets, the battles – to project a world *in front of* the 'text' of culture. In like manner, literary texts, too, are referential phenomena. One also does not attend, for instance, a performance of *Macbeth* to acquire knowledge of the history of Scotland; instead, one goes to the play to learn what it is to gain a kingdom and lose one's soul.[43] Thus the text not only tells the reader about the world *of* the text (characters, timeline, plot,

---

38. *Poet.* 9.1–4, 9–10.

39. Literary works such as novels bear 'links of possibility' between characters and reader that enable poetic representations of universal value and relevance; readers thus recognize that story as their own, though the particular details of the novel may differ greatly from those of their own lives. See Martha C. Nussbaum, *Poetic Justice: The Literary Imagination and Public Life* (Boston: Beacon, 1995), pp. 5, 31.

40. Charles Altieri, 'The Poem as Act: A Way to Reconcile Presentational and Mimetic Theories', *Iowa Rev.* 6.3–4 (1975), pp. 103–24 (107–8).

41. Clifford Geertz, *The Interpretation of Cultures* (London: Fontana, 1993), p. 448 (see 412–53 for the entire account). '[C]ultural manifestations must be read as texts are read.' Indeed culture has its own 'grammar' (Morton W. Bloomfield, 'Allegory as Interpretation', *NLH* 3 [1972], pp. 301–17 [303]).

42. Geertz, *Interpretation of Cultures*, p. 450.

43. Northrop Frye, *The Educated Imagination* (Bloomington, IN: Indiana University Press, 1964), pp. 63–4.

settings, rhetorical exigency, etc.), it also projects another world *in front of* the text that bids the reader inhabit it. Such language-games portray a view of life, projecting for the reader a world beyond the confines of the text. Rather than being simply *presented* by a text, life is always *represented* as something, inviting the reader to see the world in one way and not another.[44] Ricoeur's notion of the world in front of the text thus provides a conceptual category for the fruitful readerly transaction of interpretation that can culminate in application.[45]

Discourse is the mediator between mind and world, the 'power of indefinitely extending the battlefront of the expressed at the expense of the unexpressed'.[46] Textuality is a particularly effective means of expressing what is unexpressed; with its attendant properties, it lends itself well to the important task of repairing the rift wrought by distanciation between speaker and hearer. Biblical discourse is even more special, for it is based on an assumption that this divine discourse is unique and worthy of serious consideration. In that it is historically situated, this unique and worthy discourse needs the gap of distanciation to be bridged, for Scripture is intended to be employed far from its originating circumstances. It is to be applied to the faith and practice in the contemporary time, and all times, of those who accept the Bible as Scripture. This is where what is considered to be Ricoeur's most important contribution to interpretation theory, the world in front of the text, achieves notability, for by means of this projected world distanciation is neutralized. In appropriating this world in front of the text, the reader brings to proximity what is far, makes familiar what is foreign, and takes as one's own what is another's.[47] The entire operation of hermeneutics, for Ricoeur, is conducted with this undergirding: the task of

44. Martha C. Nussbaum, *Love's Knowledge: Essays on Philosophy and Literature* (New York: Oxford University Press, 1990), p. 5.

45. This work appropriates Ricoeur in a distinctive way, integrating his philosophy of symbol, metaphor and the world in front of the text to address the specific issue of moving from text to praxis in a sermon. Ricoeur's own philosophical perspectives on these and other issues were generally more latent than concrete, works still in progress at his demise. He confessed: '[W]hen I happen to look backward to my work, I am more struck by the discontinuities of my wanderings than by the cumulative character of my work' (Paul Ricoeur, 'Reply to Lewis S. Mudge', in *Essays on Biblical Interpretation* [ed. Lewis S. Mudge; Philadelphia: Fortress, 1980], pp. 41–5 [41]). Also see Dan R. Stiver, *Theology after Ricoeur: New Directions in Hermeneutical Theology* (Louisville: Westminster/John Knox Press, 2001), p. 248, for his views on canvassing Ricoeur's hermeneutical concepts for theological purposes.

46. Paul Ricoeur, 'Word, Polysemy, Metaphor: Creativity in Language', in *A Ricoeur Reader: Reflection and Imagination* (ed. Mario J. Valdés; Hertfordshire: Harvester Wheatsheaf, 1991), pp. 65–85 (69).

47. Ricoeur, *Hermeneutics and the Human Sciences*, p. 143; idem, 'Existence and Hermeneutics', in *The Conflict of Interpretations* (trans. Kathleen McLaughlin; ed. Don Ihde; Evanston: Northwestern University Press, 1974; repr. 2004), pp. 3–24 (16); also see Kevin J. Vanhoozer, *Biblical Narrative in the Philosophy of Paul Ricoeur: A Study in Hermeneutics and Theology* (Cambridge: Cambridge University Press, 1990), p. 88.

interpretation is the explication and appropriation of this projected world. The definition and semantic modelling of the *world in front of the text* occupied a considerable amount of Ricoeur's philosophical output; this crucial notion was chronologically developed through his work on sense and reference, and symbol and metaphor.[48] To these concepts, particularly second-order reference, attention will now be directed, in order to further define world projection.

Second-order reference

Utilizing Gottlob Frege's distinction between *Sinn* and *Bedeutung*, Ricoeur distinguished between the 'sense' and 'reference' of an utterance.[49] The *sense* is the propositional content of the sentence and is immanent in discourse; the *reference* relates the language to the world, reaching reality, and is thus transcendent. A discourse thereby is an instrument that links its immanent sense to a transcendent reference, its linguistic propositional content to an extralinguistic concept.[50] However, in the transformation of discourses that is effected by writing, referents often become elusive; distanciation potentially affects the ostensive (first-order) referents – those that can be shown, pointed out, labelled, or otherwise indicated by virtue of the collocation in time and space of speaker and hearer. In writing, the 'orphaned' text, dislodged from its generating agent and event, no longer supports the shared temporo-spatial situation between bygone author and bystanding readers. Yet, no discourse fails to link with reality. Nexus with reality is maintained at an additional level *beyond* the first-order referent: a second-order referent is freed, the world in front of the text. This second-order referent, the projected and proposed world, is a world the reader can inhabit, yet one which is still 'bound' in some fashion to the text

---

48. At diverse places in his prodigious productions on matters hermeneutical, Ricoeur has referred to this world as either the 'world of the text' or as the 'world in front of the text'; they are synonymous for him, and are used in the same essay (see Ricoeur, *Hermeneutics and the Human Sciences*, pp. 141–2). He has also, on occasion, employed 'world before the text' (idem, 'Philosophical Hermeneutics and Theological Hermeneutics', p. 17). In this work, the ascription *world in front of the text* will be consistently employed – '*la chose du texte, à savoir la sorte de monde que l'oeuvre déploie en quelque sorte en avant du texte*' ('the thing of the text, namely the kind of world which the work deploys, as it were, in front of the text'). See idem, *Du texte à l'action: Essais d'herméneutique, II* (Paris: Seuil, 1986), p. 168.

49. See Gottlob Frege, 'On *Sinn* and *Bedeutung*', in *The Frege Reader* (ed. Michael Beaney; Malden, MA: Blackwell, 1997), pp. 150–80 (152). Ricoeur does admit that his appropriation of Frege's distinction, especially his use of extralinguistic reference, was a 'very free' adaptation of Frege (Ricoeur, 'Word, Polysemy, Metaphor', p. 68). For the most part, this work will employ 'reference' to denote the action of generating a 'referent'.

50. Ricoeur, *Interpretation Theory*, pp. 19–22. Ricoeur sees this movement operating with *every* textual utterance: 'Our working hypothesis is that the Fregean distinction holds in principle for all discourse' (idem, *The Rule of Metaphor: Multi-disciplinary Studies on the Creation of Meaning in Language* [trans. Robert Czerny, with Kathleen McLaughlin and John Costello; London: Routledge & Kegan Paul, 1978], p. 256).

in question, and which is part of the text's surplus of meaning. Such a world is peculiar to that text and derived from the particular features inherent to it and proposed by it: '[f]or every unique text there is such a world' proper to it.[51] The splitting of reference into first- and second-order – a consequence of textuality and distanciation – renders it essential for the interpreter to attend to the secondary referent, for this is the intermediary that links text and application.[52] The world in front of the text is a world that retains the potential of being inhabited by the reader upon appropriation. In other words, this world is the text's direction for application in the future; it is a horizon of potential experience and possible inhabitation not exhausted by the first-order elements represented in the text.[53]

This world in front of the text may also be depicted using symbolic and metaphoric transactions of language. A symbol is a structure of signification in which a direct, primary referent designates another indirect, secondary referent that can only be apprehended through the former. Thus there is inherent in the symbol an excess of content, with the second-order referent constituting a surplus of meaning in addition to the first-order referent – a 'double intentionality'. A symbol, while referring to one thing, also refers to another at the same time; in other words, the symbol 'provides a meaning by means of a meaning'.[54] For instance, 'body and blood', in an ecclesial context, refers to the physiologi-

51. Ricoeur, 'Philosophical Hermeneutics and Theological Hermeneutics', pp. 11–12; idem, *Hermeneutics and the Human Sciences*, pp. 140–2.

52. It is important to note that Ricoeur suggests that reference is 'split' rather than abolished or eliminated (despite his occasional use of the concept of 'dissolution' of reference): *both* first- and second-order referents are preserved. See Paul Ricoeur, 'The Narrative Function', *Semeia* 13 (1978), pp. 177–202 (194); and Fodor, *Christian Hermeneutics*, p. 155. This work, while emphasizing the role of the second-order referent for application, strongly affirms the utility of the first-order referent upon which the projected world supervenes. The primary referent of the text remains the sole means of access to the surplus of meaning; that is, the discernment of the secondary referent 'rests upon "clues" contained in the text itself'. In this, symbol differs from allegory. In allegory, the nexus between the first- and second-order referent is tenuous; the former is usually eliminated in allegorical interpretation, while both are retained in the interpretation of symbols (Ricoeur, *Interpretation Theory*, pp. 55–6; idem, *Hermeneutics and the Human Sciences*, p. 175).

53. Charles E. Reagan and Paul Ricoeur, 'Interviews: Châtenay-Malabry, June 19, 1982', in Charles E. Reagan, *Paul Ricoeur: His Life and His Work* (Chicago: The University of Chicago Press, 1996), pp. 100–9 (107). Future-directedness, bound up with the projected world, is dealt with below.

54. Thus, Ricoeur can say that '*[l]e symbole donne à penser*' ('[t]he symbol gives rise to thought') (*The Symbolism of Evil* [trans. Emerson Buchanan; Boston: Beacon, 1967], p. 348). Also see idem, 'Existence and Hermeneutics', p. 12; idem, 'Structure and Hermeneutics', *The Conflict of Interpretations* (trans. Kathleen McLaughlin; ed. Don Ihde; Evanston: Northwestern University Press, 1974; repr. 2004), pp. 17–61 (28); and idem, 'The Hermeneutics of Symbols and Philosophical Reflection: I', in *The Conflict of Interpretations* (trans. Denis Savage; ed. Don Ihde; Evanston: Northwestern University Press, 1974; repr. 2004), pp. 278–314 (286).

cal elements of the incarnated Christ; however, a second-order reference to a reality beyond the corporality of Christ is generated in parallel – the atonement and its consequences are encompassed thereby. While not abolishing the first-order referent, interpretation for application involves the identification of the second-order referent, that is, moving from the world *of* the text to a world *in front of* the text.[55]

In addition to the concepts of symbolic operations, Ricoeur utilized the theory of metaphor as a paradigm to examine the functioning of secondary references and surplus significations in works of literature. The relation, in a metaphor, between its literal and figurative meanings (first- and second-order referents) is 'an abridged version ... of the complex interplay of significations that characterize the literary work as a whole'. In engaging in such hermeneutical transactions with a surplus of meaning, texts mimic metaphors. For both, it is discourse-in-context, an event, that creates new meaning, transferring text and metaphor to new interpretive domains; both text and metaphor display the polarity between their first- and second-order referents. Thus, understanding a text is homologous to understanding a metaphor: both project new meanings, new worlds.[56]

Ricoeur fruitfully explores the concepts of symbol and metaphor as he comes to terms with the existence of the world in front of the text. Symbol and metaphor are seen as models for the way in which texts create worlds and yield productive second-order referents as they offer their readers a new world of values and possibilities, a new way of living. For the purposes of application of a text, such a notion is of critical importance. Interpretation cannot cease with the elucidation of the essential elements of textuality, but must proceed further to discern the world in front of the text, in order that valid application of the text may be generated. Grounded upon the text in question, this projected world which readers are invited to inhabit forms the intermediary between inscription and application that enables one to respond to the text. Though distanciation brought about by writing decontextualizes the text from its originary circumstances, this phenomenon is not without benefit: decontextualization enables the projection of a world in front of the text that becomes the condition and

55. Aquinas similarly argued that the things signified by words in Scripture can themselves act as signs, signifying further designations at a second-order level, a level that is based upon and presupposes the original textual sense: 'The author of Holy Writ is God, in whose power it is to signify his meaning, not by words only (as man also can do), but also by things themselves. So, whereas in every other science things are signified by words, this science has the property, that the things signified by the words have themselves also a signification' (*Summa* 1.1.10). In asserting that there is something 'non-semantic' in the interpretation of symbols, Ricoeur implicitly acknowledges the role of pragmatics – the field that concentrates on those aspects of meaning not accounted for by semantic theory (see below) (*Interpretation Theory*, p. 45).

56. Ricoeur, *Interpretation Theory*, p. 46; and idem, *Hermeneutics and the Human Sciences*, pp. 167–70.

basis for all subsequent recontextualization – the counterpart of distanciation. Distanciation (leading to decontextualization) and world-projection (enabling recontextualization) are but two sides of the same interpretive coin; both are essential for application of the text to be consummated.[57]

The essence of a literary work, from the point of view of its application, is its ontological import, the potential and inhabitable world in front of the text, by which the author attempts to bring a new shareable experience through language to readers. 'What is communicated, in the final analysis, is, beyond the sense of a work, the world it projects and that constitutes its horizon'. Calling it the 'issue' of the text, Ricoeur points to this world as the object of hermeneutics.[58] The Christian community also claims that through its canonical Scriptures, such a new world is proclaimed and projected – a world that is significant and singular, a world into which God's people are beckoned to enter. The textual corpus *in toto* projects the world in front of the text; thus Scripture as a whole projects a canonical world. In this schema, individual texts within the canon depict facets or segments of that canonical world, with genres providing, as it were, windows to the world that is projected, framing ways of comprehending the world, and directing ways of responding to that world.[59] Thus, for application purposes, the world in front of the text represents a possible world, a world that could very well become the world of the reader, if one were to align oneself to that world. This projected world is therefore a significant concern of the sermonic endeavour leading to application; the world in front of the text is the locus of the rendezvous between hermeneutics and homiletics.[60]

Pragmatics, speech-act theory and projected worlds
The interpretation of the world in front of the text is a non-semantic operation, properly belonging to the domain of pragmatics, the analysis of what discourses (or speakers/authors) *do*. Wolfgang Iser observes that 'the time has surely come to … replace ontological arguments with functional arguments, for what is important to readers, critics, and authors alike, is what literature

57. Ricoeur, *Hermeneutics and the Human Sciences*, pp. 139, 143; idem, 'Biblical Hermeneutics', *Semeia* 4 (1975), pp. 27–148 (71).

58. Paul Ricoeur, *Time and Narrative*, 3 vols. (trans. Kathleen McLaughlin and David Pellauer; Chicago: The University of Chicago Press, 1984), I, p. 77. Ricoeur acknowledges his debt to Hans-Georg Gadamer in the adaptation of the latter's phrase *die Sache des Texts* (Ricoeur, 'Philosophical Hermeneutics and Theological Hermeneutics', p. 17).

59. The next section of this chapter will introduce the role of genres in world projection. Subsequently, Chapters 2–3 will detail the rules of specific biblical genres that enable the portrayal of such a world; Chapter 4 will explore the utility of all these concepts for developing application.

60. Paul Ricoeur, 'Dialogues with Paul Ricoeur', in *Dialogues with Contemporary Continental Thinkers: The Phenomenological Heritage* (ed. Richard Kearney; Manchester, UK: Manchester University Press, 1984), pp. 15–46 (45).

does'.[61] Thus, while semantics is the theory of *sentence* meaning, pragmatics may be considered the theory of *discourse* meaning. Quite frequently in communication, spoken or written, there is a disjunction between sentence and discourse meanings that semantic theory alone is unable to account for. The prime example of the disjunction between these two categories is the employment of metaphor and irony: in addition to producing sentence meaning, the speaker/author simultaneously generates discourse meaning. It is the non-literal nature of the latter that is the business of pragmatics.[62]

The distinction between semantics and pragmatics has also been made by genre theorists, albeit in a different way. Peter Seitel observes that 'theme' in an utterance refers to two kinds of content, one that is explicit and another that is implicit or inferred. First, there are themes that are the *explicit* topics of an utterance; the explicit themes of a Hollywood western movie, for instance, include panoramic vistas, horses, outlaws, sheriffs and the narrative of their interactions. This is equivalent to the semantics of the utterance. A second, *implicit*, to-be-inferred kind of theme refers to 'the way depicted actions embody, instantiate and/or formulate ethical knowledge and values' – equivalent to the pragmatics of the utterance. The Hollywood film genre of the western, which depicts a particular society in the western United States of the late nineteenth century, implicitly projects a world with the themes of individual rights, responsibilities and codes of honour in the face of evil. Such pragmatic themes are always facets of implied ethical value; they are especially evident in proverbs and maxims. 'Birds of a feather flock together' semantically makes a statement about avian social behaviour; pragmatically, the theme concerns guilt by association, a warning to the reader to eschew questionable company. The determination of both the semantic and pragmatic value of an utterance is therefore integral to the undertaking of hermeneutics, with the projection of the world in front of the text being the essential object of pragmatic analysis.[63]

---

61. Wolfgang Iser, *The Act of Reading* (Baltimore: Johns Hopkins University Press, 1978), p. 53. 'The speaker is a *doer*' (Kevin J. Vanhoozer, *Is There a Meaning in This Text? The Bible, the Reader, and the Morality of Literary Knowledge* [Grand Rapids: Zondervan, 1998], p. 209).

62. Stephen C. Levinson, *Pragmatics* (Cambridge: Cambridge University Press, 1983), pp. 12, 17; Daniel Vanderveken, 'Non-Literal Speech Acts and Conversational Maxims', in *John Searle and His Critics* (eds Ernest Lepore and Robert Van Gulick; Cambridge, MA: Basil Blackwell, 1991), pp. 371–84 (372). The debate as to what constitutes pragmatics and what semantics is ongoing; no doubt, there is a degree of overlap between the two fields. See Stephen C. Levinson, *Presumptive Meanings: The Theory of Generalized Conversational Implicature* (Cambridge, MA: MIT Press, 2000), pp. 9, 168; and François Recanati, *Meaning and Force: The Pragmatics of Performative Utterances* (Cambridge: Cambridge University Press, 1987), pp. 1–27.

63. Peter Seitel, 'Theorizing Genres – Interpreting Works', *NLH* 34 (2003), pp. 275–97 (285–6).

An important notion in the comprehension of the pragmatics of utterances is that of speech acts.[64] The trichotomous composition of a speech act – locution, illocution and perlocutionary intent – constitutes an ordering of increasing complexity, in which illocutions supervene (and are built) upon locutions, and perlocutions, in turn, upon illocutions; the superior elements in this taxonomy are dependent upon, but not reducible to, those below.[65] Though these components are not discrete in the action of communication, they are distinguishable in the analysis thereof. Meaning is apparently 'multi-dimensional', and texts are complex communicative processes with hierarchies of locution, illocution, and perlocutionary intent. The primary unit of meaning in a speech act is the illocution – what the speaker (or writer) is *doing* in/with what is being said (or written), the pragmatics of the utterance. Discerning those illocutions, therefore, is to be the main focus of the interpreter.[66] There can, however, quite frequently be more than one illocution that is being generated – an *indirect* illocution supervenient upon a *direct* one.[67] When *A* tells *B*, 'You are standing

64. Language philosopher J.L. Austin propounded the speech-act theory, distinguishing three discrete acts that are performed with words: locution – the utterance or the action *of* saying something; illocution – the action performed *in* saying something; and perlocution – the action that is brought about *by* saying something (*How to Do Things with Words* [2nd edn; eds J.O. Urmson and Marina Sbisà; Cambridge, MA: Harvard University Press, 1975], pp. 99–100, 109). Austin's proposals have been freighted in multiple directions. John R. Searle's analysis stands as the best exposition of speech acts as a full-fledged schema of communication, as he carries forward (and adapts) Austin's concepts, eliminating the term 'locution', instead introducing 'utterance acts' and 'propositional acts' (see his *Speech Acts: An Essay in the Philosophy of Language* [Cambridge: Cambridge University Press, 1969]; and *Expression and Meaning: Studies in the Theory of Speech Acts* [Cambridge: Cambridge University Press, 1979]. For the purposes of this work that deals with the interpretation of larger volumes of text than a sentence or a snippet of conversation, Searle's finer distinctions need not be of concern.

65. Kevin J. Vanhoozer, 'From Speech Acts to Scripture Acts: The Covenant of Discourse and the Discourse of the Covenant', in *After Pentecost: Language and Biblical Interpretation* (eds Craig Bartholomew, Colin Greene and Karl Möller; Grand Rapids: Zondervan, 2001), pp. 1–19 (29).

66. This work will follow Recanati in holding that '[i]llocutionary force is in fact an aspect of utterance [discourse] meaning, namely, the *pragmatic meaning* of the utterance' (*Meaning and Force*, p. 14). For example, 'John, come' and 'John will come' appear to be distinct illocutionary acts, a command and an assertion, respectively. It is evident, however, that these assignations of illocutionary force are speculative: when uttered with the appropriate inflections, 'John, come' may very well be an entreaty, and 'John will come' may equally be an interrogation. In other words, the determination of the kind of illocution an utterance performs is often (though not always) based upon non-literal and contextual aspects of the speech act; hence the relegation of illocutions to the province of pragmatics.

67. Recanati, *Meaning and Force*, pp. 254–8; Searle refers to these entities as 'indirect speech acts' (*Expression and Meaning*, pp. 30–57). Also see Kent Bach and Robert M. Harnish, *Linguistic Communication and Speech Acts* (Cambridge, MA: MIT Press, 1979), pp. 70–6, although they differ from Searle in the nuances of what constitutes an indirect speech act.

on my foot', the direct illocution (*sentence* meaning) asserts the spatial location of *B* upon the lower limb of *A*, while the indirect illocution (*discourse* meaning) requests *B* to relocate from that traumatic situation. The similarity of this utterance bearing a surplus of meaning beyond the literal sense with those utterances carrying second-order referents is obvious. Both are concerned with the same hermeneutical goal, the generation of a discourse meaning over and above a semantic meaning, that is, pragmatics in addition to semantics. Moreover, in performing that speech act, *A* was implicitly portraying in front of the 'text' a world where no one would be stationed upon *A*'s lower extremities. *A*'s perlocutionary intent, then, was for *B* to be aligned with such an ideal world by alleviating the burden upon *A*'s foot. In and with the projection of this world, *A* was, in fact, expressing a 'transhistorical intention' that goes beyond a current application for *B*, the one directly addressed. Via the projected world, this intention would be applicable to anybody anywhere – *no one* ought to be standing on *A*'s foot (transhistorical intentions and such future-directedness of discourse will be considered in the next section).

Allegories, parables and moral fables are also examples of utterances supporting indirect illocutions or second-order referents. By the telling of a tale, a point is made, a world is projected. That, however, is not a property of fiction alone; Ricoeur sees *all* non-ostensive references as projecting worlds. All literary texts function in this pragmatic manner and may be considered poetic, where 'poetic', rather than designating a literary form, reflects the projection of a world: world projections are characteristic of poetic texts. Thus, all poetic discourses, including biblical texts, help bring to language 'aspects, qualities, and values of reality that lack access to language that is directly descriptive' and that can only be discoursed by means of a second-order referential function that metaphorically projects a world in front of the text.[68] This is 'perhaps the most pervasive and important of the actions' that literary artists perform by means of their textual artefacts; a text, as an artefact projecting a world, serves as an

---

68. Ricoeur, *Time and Narrative*, I, pp. xi, 80; idem, 'Naming God', pp. 218, 225; and idem, 'Writing as a Problem', p. 331. The indirect nature of such communication may call for extra processing effort on the part of the readers, but this is offset by the advantages of procuring textual effects not achievable directly. Information theory, according to Levinson, has demonstrated the relative slowness of discourse encoding; he calls the process 'a bottleneck' in the system, applicable to both phonetic articulation and alphabetic inscription. This communicational impediment is removed by letting not only the content but also the metalinguistic properties of the utterance (its form, genre, etc.) bear some of the speaker's meaning, creating 'a way to piggyback meaning on top of meaning'. For Levinson, making pragmatic inferences of this sort is more efficient than attempting, by an extended discourse, to encode *all* the 'layers' of meaning exclusively in semantic fashion. Correspondingly, from the receiving end of the reader, decoding of such second-order meanings is more efficient if accomplished by pragmatic inference rather than by a meticulous unpacking of semantic codes (*Presumptive Meanings*, pp. 6, 29).

instrument of that action.[69] In other words, a communicative action with a particular direct illocutionary force may simultaneously be the carrier for another indirect illocutionary force, just as a second-order referent is produced by the agency of a first-order referent. In both cases, the success of the former element of each pair is linked to the success of the latter. The first-order direct operation is seminal, the seed for the subsequent, second-order referents or indirect illocutions that are generated.[70]

Ricoeur's projection of a world in front of the text and speech act theorists' indirect illocution, both arriving at the level of second-order reference in similar fashion, attest to the fact that there is more to discourses than is apparent on the surface. There is more to a text than the semantics thereof. As a function of their pragmatic capability, texts also project worlds and, as will be seen, genres enable the perception of such worlds, framing their apprehension and directing their appropriation. The elucidation of such worlds is, therefore, to be an essential transaction of hermeneutics. It is this surplus of meaning that generates potential for application, and apart from the pragmatic ('poetic') operation of language-games projecting worlds, this potential cannot be attained. Such world-projection is particularly pertinent for religious discourse. Unlike other forms of utterances, the text of Scripture is unique in its subject matter: it names God. It is this 'God-talk' – discourses upon God and his relationship with his creation – with its ramifications for application – that is projected as the world in front of the text. Therefore, a key task of biblical interpretation that intends to culminate in application is to unpack the manifold implications of this second-order reference.[71] How this may be accomplished by the theologian-homiletician is the burden of this work.

In summary, the 'speech' act transacted by textuality has major consequences: distanciation affects the relationships between message and medium, speaker, hearer, code and referent. None of these sequelæ preclude understanding and application: the medium has become more definable and per-

---

69. Nicholas Wolterstorff, *Art in Action: Toward a Christian Aesthetic* (Grand Rapids: Eerdmans, 1980), pp. 122, 124. Examples are legion: 'It is cold in here', while being an astute observation of the thermal situation in the room, could, undoubtedly, also be a request to shut the open window or adjust the thermostat. In the same way, 'Could you pass the salt?' is hardly an interrogation of the addressee's capacity to transfer the shaker; it is in fact a request to do so. One discourse generates another – two levels or orders of discourses being related in a generative manner. Also see Raymond W. Gibbs, Jr., 'Nonliteral Speech Acts in Text and Discourse', in *The Handbook of Discourse Processes* (eds Arthur C. Graesser, Morton Ann Gernsbacher and Susan R. Goldman; Mahwah, NJ: Erlbaum, 2003), pp. 357–93 (358–61).

70. See Nicholas Wolterstorff, *Works and Worlds of Art* (Oxford: Clarendon Press, 1980), pp. x, 107; idem, *Divine Discourse: Philosophical Reflections on the Claim that God Speaks* (Cambridge: Cambridge University Press, 1995), pp. 212–13.

71. Ricoeur, 'Naming God', p. 219; idem, 'Philosophy and Religious Language', pp. 83–4; idem, 'Philosophical Hermeneutics and Theological Hermeneutics', pp. 15–16.

during; the writer is 'present' and recognizable through the pragmatics of the text, enabling a subsequent recontextualization of the message; and a potential universe of readers is available and willing to take on their interpretive responsibilities. Especially germane to this work, distanciation also affects the referential function of the discourse: a second-order referent is generated in addition to the first-order component, and a world is thereby projected in front of the text – a function of the pragmatics of discourse. Such worlds are framed and their appropriation governed by the language-games played by texts, namely, genres. To these textual language-games, therefore, attention will be directed next. The focus of Chapter 1 has narrowed from language-games to textuality. Another convergence now follows, this time to investigate the notion of genres – specific rule-governed language-games that texts play to aid world projection.

Genres

An examination of the generic language-games played by texts is a necessary preamble to the discussion of specific biblical genres, primary and secondary (in Chapters 2 and 3, respectively). Biblical texts clearly qualify as language-games, linguistic 'sports' of particular kinds. From the consideration of a specific text as an instantiation of a *genus* to the conception of the text's *genre* as the language-game in question is more than just an etymological leap.[72] A genre (with its rules) constitutes the language-game that is actualized by a specific text, analogous to the way a specific match played with ball and racquet on a court with a net belongs to that particular genre of games called 'tennis'. A text, then, is an instance of a generic language-game, played in accordance with, and while abiding by, the rules of that game. The corollary to this notion is that interpretation of the text involves the utilization of those rules as well.[73] If literary works are rule- and convention-bound, then their rule-boundedness makes them 'verbalized habits' of writing/reading, textual practices that may be expounded using those same rules.[74] This section will survey the property of the

72. The origin of the word 'genre', from its various Latin roots *genus, genre, gignere*, gives the sense of class and division (Ralph Cohen, 'History and Genre', *NLH* 17 [1986], pp. 203–18 [203]).

73. 'Literary genres are language games, each with its own set of rules for making sense' (Kevin J. Vanhoozer, 'Exegesis and Hermeneutics', in *New Dictionary of Biblical Theology* [eds T. Desmond Alexander and Brian S. Rosner; Downers Grove: InterVarsity, 2000], pp. 52–64 [59]). In the inimitable words of C.S. Lewis, 'The first qualification for judging any piece of workmanship from a corkscrew to a cathedral is to know *what* it is – what it was intended to do and how it is meant to be used', that is, the 'genre' and 'rule' of the object (*A Preface to Paradise Lost* [rev. edn; London: Oxford University Press, 1960], p. 1).

74. Kevin J. Vanhoozer, 'From Canon to Concept: "Same" and "Other" in the Relation between Biblical and Systematic Theology', *SBET* 12 (1994), pp. 96–124 (113).

rules (governance by convention) and the general roles of genre before moving
on to the specific biblical categories of these games.

Rules of genre

As a literary genus, a textual genre is a rule-governed social behaviour: it is
an institutional convention of literature.[75] Genres are themselves products of
institutions, and those institutions may be considered reading situations specific
to their particular literary genres – courts of law, the Church, legislature, aca-
demia, etc.[76] Not only do they help the author conceptualize and rhetorically
enact ('play') the game of discourse, genres also help the reader experience
and interpret those plays. It is by means of their rules that they serve these
crucial communicative functions; one might go so far as to say that genres are
collections of rules for the efficacious production of meaning. These text-types
have 'ruling power' because they are socially sanctioned modes of creating and
comprehending written discourse.[77] For this reason, it is misleading to speak
of texts as autonomous entities, self-existent and self-sufficient. Rather, they
are discourses that have meaning only with respect to a particular system of
genre conventions utilized by the author and recognized by the reader. So much
so, the operation of different conventions of play would potentially render the
meaning of a given text different. 'When language-games change, then there is
a change in concepts, and with the concepts the meanings of words change.'[78]
Even at the very basic unit of textual structure, a single sentence can have different meanings depending on the genre it adopts. 'Love all!' in a compendium
of moral maxims means something quite different than when it is located in the
reportage of a tennis match.

Genres thus further communication in societies in which they flourish by
virtue of their rule-dependent institutionality. Indeed, for effective communication to be transacted between author and reader, genres are essential, for 'a
text which bears no similarities of structure, content, or the like with anything

---

75. '[T]he study of genres has to be founded on the study of convention' (Frye, *Anatomy of
Criticism*, p. 96). 'There is probably no better single word than "convention" to embrace the
entire system of usage traits, rules, customs, formal necessities and proprieties which constitute a
type of verbal meaning – genre' (Hirsch, *Validity in Interpretation*, p. 92).

76. Werner G. Jeanrond, *Text and Interpretation as Categories of Theological Thinking* (trans.
Thomas J. Wilson; New York: Crossroad, 1988), pp. 98–9. René Wellek and Austin Warren
called literary genres 'institutions' (*Theory of Literature* [3rd edn; New York: Harcourt Brace
Jovanovich, 1977], p. 226).

77. Anis Bawarshi, 'The Genre Function', *CE* 62 (2000), pp. 335–61 (341).

78. Ludwig Wittgenstein, *On Certainty* (eds G.E.M. Anscombe and G. H. von Wright; trans.
Denis Paul and G.E.M. Anscombe; San Francisco: Harper & Row, 1969), ¶65; also see Jonathan
Culler, *Structuralist Poetics: Structuralism, Linguistics, and the Study of Literature* (London:
Routledge & Kegan Paul, 1975), p. 116.

previously written cannot be understood by a reader'.[79] In other words, without the rules of genre a text is incomprehensible. Thus genre is the consummate bridge that links writer to text and text to reader by means of rules derived by convention – the shared expectation of goals and the shared means of achieving those goals. If genres are critical to felicitous and successful communication, Mikhail Bakhtin was surely right in considering them 'form-shaping ideology', schemata that give rise to the form of texts. They are prerequisites for the conveyance of meaning, and their mediatory rule-based function in the text-linguistic transportation of concepts, opinions and ideas from one mind to another cannot be underestimated.[80] An examination of the rules of biblical genres in later chapters will be equally crucial in elucidating the communicative action of Scripture and – this is the thrust of this work – in making the hermeneutical and homiletical move from text to praxis.

Roles of genre

No longer serving as pigeonholes in which to stuff the various structural components that make up the textual universe, genres are 'generative devices', conventionalized rhetorical ways of communication.[81] An adjunct to a genre's text-generating function is its equally significant utility as an interpretive tool. Genres, therefore, are both *genetic* – they play significant roles in the creation of texts – and *heuristic*, with equally weighty roles in the interpretation of those materials. These genetic and heuristic roles are grounded upon their substratum of rules, the conventional and recognizable modes of operation in particular rhetorical environments.[82] In these environments where interpersonal human

79. Tremper Longman III, 'Form Criticism, Recent Developments in Genre Theory, and the Evangelical', *WTJ* 47 (1985), pp. 47–68 (50–1). As Jacques Derrida asserted, '[A] text cannot belong to no genre, it cannot be without or less a genre … there is no genreless text' ('The Law of Genre', trans. Avital Ronell, *CI* 7 [1980], pp. 55–81 [65]). Mikhail Bakhtin, dealing with orality, concurs: 'If speech genres did not exist … if we had to originate them during the speech process and construct each utterance at will for the first time, speech communication would be almost impossible' ('The Problem of Speech Genres', in *Modern Genre Theory* [ed. David Duff; Essex, UK: Pearson, 2000], pp. 82–97 [90]).

80. Moreover, this essential and intrinsic text-forming function of genres cannot be totally reduced to a set of propositions; nor are they 'transcribable with no residue' into other literary forms. See Gary Saul Morson and Caryl Emerson, *Mikhail Bakhtin: Creation of Prosaics* (Stanford, CA: Stanford University Press, 1990), p. 307.

81. Ricoeur, *Interpretation Theory*, p. 33.

82. Lloyd F. Bitzer perceptively notes: 'From day to day, year to year, comparable situations occur, prompting comparable responses; hence rhetorical forms are born and a special vocabulary, grammar, and style are established.' These forms of discourse become programmatic and dependable, with a rhetorical power of their own ('The Rhetorical Situation', *P&R* 1 [1968], pp. 1–14 [13]). Also see Kevin J. Vanhoozer, 'Language, Literature, Hermeneutics, and Biblical Theology: What's Theological about a Theological Dictionary?', in *New International Dictionary of Old*

relationships are transacted, by means of genres, discourses are generated, their interpretations propounded and their application proposed. The fundamental role of genres in aiding and abetting these social interactions and communicational goals gives them the status of Wittgensteinian language-games. As repeatable patterns of written discourse that enable both the transmission of information and the reception thereof, literary genres are not simply communicative *forms*. They are also, perhaps primarily, communicative *practices* governing textual meaning; particular texts that instantiate a genre are specific communicative *acts*.[83] Thus, every act of communication is generic. Biblical acts of communication are no different, for their language-games are genre based as well.

Author and reader in genre function

The role of genres may be scrutinized from the aspect of the author, as well as from the vantage point of the reader. The performance of the language-game (the inscription of a text in that genre) is guided by the *purpose of the author* that not only dictates the choice of genre but also how adjustments are made to a chosen genre as it is adapted for the specific aims of the writer.[84] This authorial purpose, therefore, is the presiding principle in the selection and shaping of the genre into a specific text to perform a specific communicative act intended to have a specific effect on specific readers.

If texts are the literary products of communicative agents (authors), then the intended response of the communicative subjects (readers) must also be an important consideration in interpretation. The *response of the reader* begins with an expectation of the text-in-its-genre. Indeed, it was in anticipation of what the reader might expect that that genre was chosen by the author in the first place; therefore genre is the cipher key to decoding the text. It is the conventional and institutional system of these rule-bound language-games that leads the reader to peruse expectantly.[85] A text does not make an appearance as an absolutely new

---

Testament Theology and Exegesis, vol. 1 (ed. William VanGemeren; Grand Rapids: Zondervan, 1997), pp. 15–50 (38).

83. Discussing Pierre Bourdieu's theory of practice, John B. Thompson notes that habitus, a disposition that generates practices, gives individuals a sense of how to act and respond in daily life. 'It "orients" their actions and inclinations without strictly determining them. It gives them a "feel for the game", a sense of what is appropriate in the circumstances and what is not, a "practical sense" (*le sens pratique*).' By extension, this work considers genre as a communicative practice, a *literary* habitus – *sens pratique et littéraire* (John B. Thompson, 'Editor's Introduction', in Pierre Bourdieu, *Language and Symbolic Power* [trans. Gino Raymond and Matthew Adamson; ed. John B. Thompson; Cambridge: Polity, 1991], pp. 1–31 [13]).

84. The flexibility of literary genres (addressed at greater length in Chapter 2) reminds one of the equally flexible and non-peremptory nature of their rules.

85. This 'notion of effect presupposes modes of reading which are not random or haphazard' – readers are already clued in by the genre as to the kind of response the text expects of them (Culler, *Structuralist Poetics*, p. 116).

entity in an informational vacuum but, predisposing the audience to a particular kind of reception, genre 'evokes for the reader (listener) the horizon of expectations and rules familiar from earlier texts'.[86] By creating expectations in readers and instructing them how to read, genres shape the response of readers to the text; they are directions for viewing the world.

Genres may therefore be seen as 'meta-information', supplementing semantics with pragmatic value.[87] In other words, the particular language-game determines how both author and reader should participate in the playing of that game. It controls the meaning of the text as purposed by the author, and it directs how the text is to be responded to by readers.[88] The genetic role of genres serves as a filter for the author through which the writer's idea passes from conception to inscription. The heuristic role of genres, in contrast, is as a filter for the reader through which inscription must pass on its way to comprehension and subsequent response.[89] Straddling both the authorial and readerly banks of the textual stream, the generic filter also serves as a bridge. The negative effects of the distanciation breached by the act of writing is to some extent mitigated by the literary context of genre that is shared between author and reader. Genre transports the cargo of past resources, serving as the organ of literary memory and facilitating the efficacious portrayal of the text's projected world.[90]

By making it possible for the text to transcend the concrete circumstances of its composition, genres promote interpersonal activity between author and reader. All communication is likely to embody such cooperation. The privileges and responsibilities of those participating in such cooperative, social intercourse are best conceived of in covenantal terms: a genre is a covenant of discourse. Both author in inscription and reader in interpretation implicitly execute generic agreements of what is written and what is expected to be read and acted upon, respectively. Such covenantal or contractual obligations superintended by rules – commitments that authors and readers are called to honour – are

---

86. Hans Robert Jauss, *Toward an Aesthetic of Reception* (trans. Timothy Bahti; Brighton, UK: Harvester, 1982), p. 23.

87. Seitel, 'Theorizing Genres – Interpreting Works', p. 290; Carolyn R. Miller, 'Genre as Social Action', *QJS* 79 (1984), pp. 151–67 (159).

88. 'Knowing the genre means knowing not only…how to conform to generic conventions but also how to respond appropriately to a given situation' (Amy J. Devitt, 'Generalizing about Genre: New Conceptions of an Old Concept', *CCC* 44 [1993], pp. 573–86 [577–8]). Here the issue of 'competence' becomes significant: only competent authors can achieve their purposes with the deliberate utilization of such language-games, and only competent readers can respond appropriately and adequately to the text. These competent ones are those who are capable of discerning generic conventions and bringing to the discourse an implicit understanding of the operations of that genre, whether in the creation of a text or in its reception. Generic competence is therefore a critical aspect of communication.

89. Richard A. Burridge, *What Are the Gospels? A Comparison with Graeco-Roman Biography* (2nd edn; Grand Rapids: Zondervan, 2004), p. 48.

90. Morson and Emerson, *Mikhail Bakhtin*, p. 288.

essential for the production and reception of meaning and, indeed, for maintaining societal relationships. This is why in the absence of a generic concept (a literary lawlessness) communication is nigh impossible: '[a]ll understanding of verbal meaning is necessarily genre-bound'. Genres thus work to establish an author–reader covenant in order to make certain expectations operative in the transaction.[91] Such expectations involve a specific manner of viewing the world in front of the text.

Genres and world projection

The fundamental components of 'poetic' discourse, according to Ricoeur, are textuality (the autonomy and distanciation of the text), genres (the shaping of discourse through text-types) and the world in front of the text – 'the world intended beyond the text as its reference', the object of hermeneutics.[92] Genres of all kinds – a motley assemblage of literary forms including drug prescriptions and parking tickets, to-do lists and theses, journals and junk mail – enable the reader to envisage a world or a specific facet thereof. In the sense that genres represent aspects of reality in their particular ways, they may be compared to maps: both are cognitive strategies for viewing worlds; different maps and different genres provide different views of the world.[93] Each genre plays a distinct language-game; each one enables a unique view of the world projected by the text and directs a response to such a vision. Just as grammatical codes help the reader in the heuristic analysis of a sentence, literary generic codes also perform a heuristic function, enabling the reception of and reaction to a text by the reader.[94] Genre, as a code governing reading, appears to be exhorting the reader: *Receive the text this way, to generate this meaning and to respond in this fashion.* In other words, genres beckon the reader to look at the world in a specific way, as recommended by the author.[95] Creating the framework for the reader's experience of the world so portrayed, the generic form significantly contributes to textual meaning and facilitates the subsequent appropriation of that world by the reader, that is, application. The perspective of the world framed

91. Hirsch, *Validity in Interpretation*, p. 76; also see Heather Dubrow, *Genre* (London: Methuen, 1982), p. 31; and Culler, *Structuralist Poetics*, p. 147. Vanhoozer, too, tends to see all communicative action in covenantal terms ('From Speech Acts to Scripture Acts', p. 18). This covenantal view of language is especially germane to the function of biblical texts in the ecclesial setting, and will be explored further in Chapter 4.

92. Paul Ricoeur, 'Toward a Hermeneutic of the Idea of Revelation', in *Essays on Biblical Interpretation* (ed. Lewis S. Mudge; Philadelphia: Fortress, 1980), pp. 73–118 (99–100).

93. Seitel, 'Theorizing Genres – Interpreting Works', p. 277; Vanhoozer, 'Language, Literature, Hermeneutics, and Biblical Theology', p. 39; Morson and Emerson, *Mikhail Bakhtin*, p. 282.

94. Linguistic codes, similarly, play a heuristic role: 'p-a-i-n' by the code of English language means one thing; in French, it means entirely another.

95. See Ricoeur, 'Philosophy and Religious Language', p. 74.

by a genre is ultimately what enables the text to transcend the particularities of the circumstances of its inscription, aiding readers located at a distance in time and space from the author to comprehend the text and to apply it to their own specific situations. Facilitating such application is a part of the work of genre, and an operation integral to textuality.[96]

In sum, genres preside over the author's purpose and, offering a way of apprehending the world of the text, help put forth a linguistic vision of how the reader ought to respond. A comprehensive description of a communicative act of writing, therefore, necessarily includes an account of the work of the genre and the world thus projected by the text – a work begun by the author in projection and completed by the reader in application. In the enumeration of the Rules of Genre in Chapters 2 and 3, it will be shown how primary and secondary biblical genres work to depict the world in front of the text. Prior to this undertaking, however, the unique properties of the secondary genre of Scripture will be discussed in the remainder of this chapter. The singular characteristics of this generic entity are crucial for the future-directedness of the biblical text and, therefore, for its application in the lives of readers.

Secondary genre: the canonical 'classic'

Progressively developing a narrower focus of attention – from language-games in general, through textuality, to genres – a specific category of genres, that of the canonical 'classic', and its properties will be examined next.

Routinely, in written discourse, primary literary genres are assimilated into a larger work: commonplace dialogues and unexceptional letters, for example, are introduced into novels and they retain their significance in the fresh setting in a different dimension, that of the literary event. The novel, here, is the new context that constrains the interpretation of the primary genres it has annexed.[97] However, with regard to the Bible, which also incorporates a variety of primary genres, there is another broader and more pertinent secondary genre category that prevails, not one that merely engulfs primary genres. This secondary bibli-

---

96. The unique nature of writing, 'transferred from the *Sitz im Leben* to a *Sitz in Schrift*, assures the destiny of the message as able to reach other receivers than those intended by the original speech act' (Paul Ricoeur, 'Sentinel of Imminence', in *Thinking Biblically: Exegetical and Hermeneutical Studies* [eds André LaCocque and Paul Ricoeur; trans. David Pellauer; Chicago: The University of Chicago Press, 1998], pp. 165–83 [167]). Literary genres, as elements of textuality, begin 'the process of "decontextualization" which opens the message to fresh reinterpretation according to new contexts of discourse and of life' (idem, 'Biblical Hermeneutics', p. 71).

97. Bakhtin also made a similar distinction between primary (simple) and secondary (complex) genres, the latter being the assimilation of various primary genres that, as a consequence, may undergo alteration and assume a special character when incorporated into the more complex category ('Problem of Speech Genres', pp. 84–5).

cal language-game is the genre of the canonical classic; applied to Scripture as a whole, this genre governs and regulates the reading of the primary genres it comprises. Superimposed upon those primary components, secondary genre favours the biblical text with some unique properties, especially in the generation of potential for future application. Neither primary nor secondary genres are transformed in the process of such an overlaying; both categories remain intact and functional, though new significances are generated, as discussed below. The interpretive task, then, must include an examination of the biblical text in *both* its genres, primary and secondary. Two levels of language-games are being played in Scripture, and the employment of the rules of both is critical to interpreting the world in front of the text.[98]

The secondary genre of the Bible claims a game status of its own, with its own particular rules. Scripture is in a unique 'class': it is a classic, unlike other secondary, complex genre amalgamations, and it is inimitable in its canonical and classic properties. The genre of the classic is unusual in that the text's membership in this elite category is conferred by its community of readers subsequent to its composition, in recognition of its unique attributes. That this bestowal of *classic* status upon Scripture harmonizes with the affirmation of its *canonical* status is not coincidental; the overlap between the categories of canon and classic is considerable. The nature of the Bible as divine discourse plays no small part in both its canonicity and its disposition as a classic. Perhaps one could establish that its intrinsic canonical standing is chronologically prior to its conferred classic status. For the purposes of this work, they are treated as coextensive categories encompassed within the single entity of the secondary genre. The biblical canon will be considered as an example *nonpareil* of the category of the classic: each of the features of the classic achieves the zenith of its expression as it is exemplified in this particular classic, the Bible. Indeed, it is by virtue of its overlapping characteristics as both canon and classic that Scripture promulgates a peremptory call: 'Read and apply!'

Characteristics of classics

Michael Levin suggests five criteria that make a classic. Though he deals with works in the field of political science, the characteristics are apposite to the biblical canon as well: (1) philosophical quality; (2) original content; (3) influence on events; (4) the foremost example of a certain category of thought; and (5) extended relevancy beyond their own time of publication to the present, even to provide judgements of universal application.[99] The Bible succeeds in meeting every one of these criteria. However, the peculiar features of this sacred classic

---

98. The Rules of Primary Genre will be attended to in Chapter 2; the Rules of Secondary Genre, in Chapter 3.

99. Michael Levin, 'What Makes a Classic in Political Theory?', *Pol. Sci. Q.* 88 (1973), pp. 462–76 (463).

surpass the qualities of secular classics, particularly with regard to the future-directedness of Scripture. The characteristics of the biblical canon with potent repercussions for future application and, thus, for the life of the Christian community are its prescriptive nature, its perennial standing and its portage of a plurality of significance.[100]

Prescriptivity. David Tracy declares that, by labelling something a classic, 'we recognize nothing less than the disclosure of a reality we cannot but name truth' – truth that is so compelling as to be normative. Hans-Georg Gadamer would agree: 'the most important thing about the concept of the classical…is the normative sense'.[101] That it is divine discourse renders the Christian canon prescriptive in a manner that other classics can never be. This prescriptive corpus, the Bible, makes itself binding upon the faith and practice of the community that recognizes it as Scripture and owns it as such. It is by the application of the text in the circumstances of its hearers/readers that this prescriptivity is actualized. That is precisely why the preaching of the Scriptures with a view to expounding its application is essential for the life of the Church. Given this prescriptivity – its normative status for believers – theological hermeneutics is to be occupied by unfolding the perennial and plural significance of the Bible.

Perenniality. The abiding nature of the classic indicates the unlimited durability of the work as it imbues its receivers with 'a consciousness of something enduring, of significance that cannot be lost and which is independent of all the circumstances of time – a kind of timeless present that is contemporaneous with every other present'; not that it is without the bounds of time, but that it is within the frontiers of *all* time.[102] The reason for the immediacy of Scripture is its unique penetrability: dealing as it does with matters of critical importance to mankind, it remains vital and potent across the span of time. The perennial standing of a classic is not just an a priori assumption. Rather, it demonstrates itself to be relevant and material in every new generation, addressing the present

100. Sandra M. Schneiders, 'The Paschal Imagination: Objectivity and Subjectivity in New Testament Interpretation', *TS* 46 (1982), pp. 52–68 (64). David Tracy agrees that classic texts 'bear a certain permanence and excess of meaning' ('Creativity in the Interpretation of Religion: The Question of Radical Pluralism', *NLH* 15 [1984], pp. 289–309 [296]).

101. David Tracy, *The Analogical Imagination: Christian Theology and the Culture of Pluralism* (New York: Crossroad, 1981), p. 108; Hans-Georg Gadamer, *Truth and Method* (2nd rev. edn; trans. Joel Weinsheimer and Donald G. Marshall; London: Continuum, 2004), p. 288. '"Classic" or "canonical" status means that a work is borne along into a future of indefinite duration by a communally-authoritative tradition which has found in the work a claim to normative significance' (Watson, *Text and Truth*, pp. 49–50).

102. Gadamer, *Truth and Method*, p. 288. He stresses that it is not that the truth claim is 'suprahistorical', but that the classic suggests 'a specific way of *being* historical' – its timelessness is a 'mode of historical being' (287, 290).

('every present') as if it were its only audience or readership.[103] The canonical classic that the Bible is has proven its perenniality over the millennia of its reading and exposition within the community of believers.

Plurality. Not only are the truths of a classic perennial, they are also carried in a surplus or plurality of understanding, 'the richness of the ideal meaning which allows for a theoretically unlimited number of actualizations, each being somewhat original and different from others'.[104] The fact that classics are those texts that transport an excess *and* permanence of meaning is paradoxical on the surface. They appear to be stable in their textual fixity and timeless contemporaneity (perenniality), yet 'unstable' in their plurality, as readers in an infinite variety of situations and settings appropriate those truths in an equally wide variety of ways into their own lives.[105] Such a conception of simultaneous perenniality and plurality is an essential property of Scripture; its classic status reflects its possession of a surplus of meaning that crosses the bounds of time and goes beyond the needs of any one generation of its readers.[106] The fact that the biblical classic, with its property of plurality, has provided the basis of infinitely varied application throughout the history of the Church ensures its utility into the future and its continued standing as a classic *sui generis*.

Not only are classics piercingly *truth-telling*, they are also *truth-forming* within the community of readers as the truth told is actualized in life as truth formed. Those truths that a classic propounds as it discloses a new world,

103. Gadamer, *Truth and Method*, p. 290. Webster suggests that the perennial nature of the Bible, bridging the gap between past witnesses and present hearers, is determined by the omnitemporal and universal 'presence and activity of Jesus, the "revealedness" of God', a self-communicative presence that is prevenient in all readings and hearings of Scripture. '[T]his means that the little fragment of historical action which we call the church's reading of the Bible is what it is because, in the power of the Holy Spirit, Jesus makes it contemporary with himself, commissioning it as a sphere of his presence and speech' (Webster, *Word and Church*, pp. 69–70). Such a transaction of 'presence' across the hermeneutical gap – an activity directed by the Holy Spirit – enables the classic of Scripture to maintain a kind of perenniality unmatched by any other classic.

104. Schneiders, 'Paschal Imagination', p. 64. Including future actualization (or appropriation) within his concept of 'meaning', Gadamer asserts that '[n]ot just occasionally, but always, the meaning of a text goes beyond its author' (*Truth and Method*, p. 296). Such a 'layering' of meaning that includes future application will be considered in the next section.

105. David Tracy, *Plurality and Ambiguity: Hermeneutics, Religion, Hope* (San Francisco: Harper and Row, 1987), pp. 12, 14. The re-engagement of later generations with the truths of the classic renders those truths anew and in different ways, as fresh perspectives, concerns and situations are brought into an encounter with the text.

106. Frank Kermode affirmed that 'the only works we value enough to call classic are those which, as they demonstrate by surviving, are complex and indeterminate enough to allow us our necessary pluralities'. Yet he conceded that there is, in classics, 'a substance that prevails' unchanging. See 'A Modern Way with the Classic', *NLH* 5 (1974), pp. 415–34 (418, 429, 434); and idem, *The Classic* (London: Faber & Faber, 1975), p. 133.

those verities it proffers for consideration, have the potential to enrich its readers – their lives and their destinies. Tracy sees the Bible, the Christian classic, as presenting permanent and essential possibilities for human existence: 'When we read any classic ... we find that our present horizon is always provoked, sometimes confronted, always transformed by the power exerted by that classic's claim.' It is this power to provoke, confront and transform that led Gadamer to declare, 'I am convinced of the fact that, quite simply, we need to learn from the classics.' This was a fundamental presupposition of his magnum opus, *Truth and Method.*[107] Prescriptive, perennial and plural in character, the canonical classic of Scripture demands to be read. And it is only in readers' volunteering to be challenged by the claims of this text that it can become a classic for them, as its transformative properties are brought to bear upon those volunteers. One might go so far as to say that this willingness to read and be changed is the mark of a member of the community that affirms Scripture as its canon. 'A Christian must apply the Bible' is an accurate statement of the obligation laid upon such a one by this classic. The primary task of interpreters of this text, therefore, is to apprehend its truth-claims and illuminate the possibilities for its application in the present, in contexts different from that of the author, the writing-event and from that of all prior readers and their reading-events.[108]

The prescriptive nature of the Bible renders it profitable for application in the life of its readers; its perennial standing projects its relevance across the span of time; its plurality enables recontextualization in any number of specific circumstances in the future. The canonical classic is, indeed, a language-game that demands to be played.[109] The critical and irreducible attributes of this secondary genre imply that, for the biblical canon, a degree of future-directedness is an intrinsic property of its textuality and its referent (the world it projects). Indeed, it is by means of this futurity that the canon is endowed with a reach that extends beyond the immediate space–time realms of its composition. Such an orientation to the future enables readers to deploy the biblical text for application in times and circumstances distant from, and dissimilar to, its originary context(s) of inscription. How the secondary genre embodies future-directed intentions will be the focus of the rest of Chapter 1.

107. Tracy, *Analogical Imagination*, pp. 110, 134; Gadamer, *Truth and Method*, p. 537.

108. Watson, *Text and Truth*, p. 50. Also see Tracy, *Analogical Imagination*, p. 105. In this act of transformative reading and hearing, the role of the Holy Spirit must not be underestimated. A proper and fitting reading of this classic emphasizes 'both the overruling and redirecting activity of the Spirit in the reader ... and also the reader's own invocation of the Spirit'. Neither must be forgotten the attitude of the reader to this 'demanding' text: a faithful hearing exhibits a 'self-forgetful reference to the prevenient action and presence of God ... the Christian reading is a kind of surrender' (Webster, *Word and Church*, pp. 43, 82–3).

109. Krister Stendahl, 'The Bible as a Classic and the Bible as Holy Scripture', *JBL* 103 (1984), pp. 3–10 (6, 8).

The futurity of classics

The 'literature of knowledge', which only makes first-order references, becomes outdated as the distanciation of the text creates a breach between the event of writing and the event of reading. It is the 'literature of power', making in addition second-order references, that never grows outdated. Its referentiality persists into an indefinite future.[110] Authors of such literary compositions, conscious of the future-directedness of their work, typically intend meanings to go beyond what is attended to at the moment of writing; the effects of classic texts are indefinitely extended in space and time. However, this future-direction need not be explicitly acknowledged by the writer; it is, rather, an inherent property of textuality, particularly of classics. Such works of legal and religious literature, the *US Constitution* or the Bible, for instance, appear to require that meaning go beyond what a historical author could possibly have willed.[111] It is in the text's projection of a world (its second-order referent) that it achieves this futurity and counters the impact of distanciation. The elucidation of this projected world is therefore an essential task of the interpreter, for by this intermediary valid application is derived.[112] How may this future-orientation be detected in the text?

Transhistorical intention and exemplification. Hirsch extended the idea of the 'meaning' of a text beyond original textual sense to encompass what might conceivably lie in the realm of that text's future use, for literature is typically an instrument designed for 'broad and continuing future application'.[113] Meaning, in light of this future-directedness, includes a *transhistorical intention*, a conceptual entity with a defined boundary that can comprise one or more future exemplifications (applications). What an author intended to convey was therefore not necessarily limited to what the writer was actually conscious of; instead, what was sought to be imparted in addition was a transhistorical intention encompassing every possible future exemplification of the text.[114] For instance, while

110. E.D. Hirsch, Jr., 'Past Intentions and Present Meanings', *Ess. Crit.* 33 (1983), pp. 79–88 (88).

111. Psalm 102.18 explicitly points to the future: 'This will be written for a generation to come' (also see Deut. 31.19; Rom. 15.4; and 1 Cor. 10.11). See Hirsch, *Validity in Interpretation*, pp. 121–2.

112. Chapter 4 will consider this projected world as the theology of the text; application, both of religious and legal classics, will be dealt with there, as well.

113. 'Original textual sense' should not be confused with Frege's 'sense'. Hirsch's term, as it will be used in this work, includes propositional sense *and* ostensive, first-order referents.

114. E.D. Hirsch, Jr., 'Meaning and Significance Reinterpreted', *CI* 11 (1984), pp. 202–25 (209); idem, *Validity in Interpretation*, pp. 51, 65; idem, 'Past Intentions and Present Meanings', p. 82; and idem, 'Transhistorical Intentions and the Persistence of Allegory', *NLH* 25 (1994), pp. 549–67. This relationship between transhistorical intention and exemplification resembles that between type and trait; in fact, those were the terms Hirsch employed in his earliest work, *Validity*

the Metropolitan Police Act of 1839 makes it an offence to repair a carriage on a street in England, it is reasonably certain that the transhistorical intention of the original textual sense of 'carriage' went beyond a horse-drawn buggy. A world was being projected in which no one would be impeding traffic by repairing road-using vehicles on a public street; thus, what was being intended by 'carriage', in a transhistorical and future-directed sense, was *vehicle using the road*. Though the Act was legislated at a time when automobiles were unknown, this transhistorical intention borne by the projected world encompassed not only 'carriage' (original textual sense) but also 'car', 'truck', 'motorcycle', etc. (exemplifications). Indeed, such a reading is reflected in the fact that more than a century later, in an amendment to the original statute, the Act was formally construed as including motor vehicles.[115] In other words, the transhistorical intention of a text is not historically bounded, but can transcend known possibilities of the contemporaneous time of its inscription, thereby even including within its scope exemplifications not explicit in the utterance or text, or even conceived of by its author. The writer would be conscious of the broad transhistorical intention and its boundaries, but not necessarily of every one of the exemplifications falling within them. Exemplifications in the future, that were unconscious to the author in the past, would nonetheless be valid, provided that they lay within the boundary of the transhistorical intention of the text.[116]

What is fixed for the future in the past event of writing, then, is the transhistorical principle of deriving future exemplifications. Wittgenstein's analogy

---

in Interpretation (1967). In the span of almost three decades since, Hirsch managed to generate an array of labels for his notions. However, the concepts indicated by the diverse designations are remarkably consistent across time. Therefore, rather than demonstrate the chronological development of these various terms, for the sake of clarity this work will keep the nomenclature consistent, even if this involves occasionally attributing to that writer an anachronistic designation.

115. 'Every person shall be liable to a penalty ... who, within the limits of the metropolitan police district, shall in any thoroughfare or public place ... to the annoyance of the inhabitants or passengers ... repair any part of any cart or carriage, except in cases of accident where repair on the spot is necessary' (Metropolitan Police Act 1839 [c. 47], s. 54 [1]; for the amendment, see Road Traffic Act 1972 [c. 20], s. 195). See Stephen Guest, *Ronald Dworkin* (Stanford, CA: Stanford University Press, 1991), pp. 183–4.

116. Hirsch, 'Past Intentions and Present Meanings', pp. 82–3; idem, *Validity in Interpretation*, pp. 48–51. Hilary Putnam warns against confusing *metaphysical* necessities (for instance, the nature or composition of substances – here, what is 'contained' in the transhistorical intention), with *epistemological* necessities (the author knowing those components) (*Mind, Language and Reality* [vol. 2 of *Philosophical Papers*; Cambridge: Cambridge University Press, 1975], p. 240). Authors deliberately endow their works not only with the original textual sense but also with 'intentional potentials' (transhistorical intentions) for exemplifications in the unforeseen future. 'Thanks to the intentional potential embedded in [classics], such works have proved capable of uncovering in each era ... ever newer aspects of meaning' (Mikhail Bakhtin, *The Dialogical Imagination: Four Essays* [trans. Caryl Emerson and Michael Holquist; ed. Michael Holquist; Austin, TX: University of Texas Press, 1981], p. 421).

in this connection is illuminating: he imagines a student being taught to continue a series of numbers begun by the teacher (= original textual sense) by observing the rule '+2', the addition of 2 to each successive number in the series (= transhistorical intention). The pupil has been guided in creating the sequence up to the number 1000, and then asked to take over without help. Wittgenstein posits the situation where such a pupil produces the set 1000, 1004, 1008, 1012, etc., imagining the instructor to have meant by '+2' that one is to add 2 only up to 1000, but 4 thence to 2000, and 6 thence to 3000, and so on. While it seems obvious that the teacher meant the student to arrive at 1002 after 1000, one could ask in what sense this was 'meant'. Was '1002' actually thought of? Indeed, an infinite series of +2 numbers that followed 1000 (= exemplifications) could certainly not have been conceived of or 'meant'. Wittgenstein responds that when the instructor 'meant' (or 'knew') the sequence of numbers that the student was supposed to come up with, all that was 'meant' (or 'known') was that 'if I [the instructor] had then been asked what number should be written after 1000, I should have replied "1002"'.[117] This 'meaning' (or 'knowing') is not necessarily a matter of the teacher actually thinking of the specific number '1002', but of being able to generate the sequence of such exemplifications by recognizing the transhistorical principle involved. Wittgenstein's answer thus implies an embedding of a necessary principle-of-extension within the stated rule that makes possible any number of unstated future iterations or applications that are consonant with that rule. The comprehension of this future-directed principle-of-extension, that is, the transhistorical intention, makes subsequent exemplifications possible. Indeed, one would be able to generate all possible future answers to the problem without necessarily apprehending in one's mind the exact circumstances and finer details of the exemplification *before* one began the task. 'A future-directed intention is an explicit plan with areas of inexplicitness.'[118] The distanciation achieved by writing generates this phenomenon of unfixed future-directedness; the transhistorical intention of the text enables all its possible future exemplification(s) to be derived from the fixed past meaning.

In light of the fact that the communication intentions of texts, particularly of classics, are future-directed, their 'meaning' can, therefore, be said to extend beyond the original textual sense, to the level of transhistorical intention *and* also to future exemplifications. Exemplifications in the new readerly situation are true to the original textual sense and congruent to it, insofar as they remain within the bounds of the transhistorical intention. Indeed, many different future exemplifications of a single transhistorical intention could be considered to belong to the same meaning. If one thinks of one's spouse, *A*, while reading a Shakespearean love sonnet, and another thinks of another's own, *B* (both *A* and *B* being exemplifications derived from the same original

---

117. Wittgenstein, *Philosophical Investigations*, ¶¶185–7.
118. Hirsch, 'Meaning and Significance Reinterpreted', pp. 203–4, 206.

textual sense that yields the same transhistorical intention – 'one's beloved'), that does not make the meaning of the poem necessarily different for each of the readers. The world of spousal romantic bliss projected in either reading bears the same transhistorical intention. However, readers understand that 'the text's meaning is not limited to any particular exemplification but rather embraces many, many exemplifications'. Such applications in the future that fall within the perimeter of the transhistorical intention of that text are, thereby, part of the meaning of the text.[119] Those not so bounded, Hirsch labelled 'significance'; these applications are not part of textual meaning but, instead, 'meaning-as-related-to-something-else' (as for instance, when, in light of the Metropolitan Police Act, one decides to subscribe to a towing service for stranded vehicles). Application is thereby split between exemplification (within 'meaning') and significance (outside 'meaning'). The Hirschian triad of meaning, thus, comprises original textual sense, transhistorical intention, and exemplification(s).[120]

FACETS OF MEANING			
Original Textual Sense	*Transhistorical Intention*	Exemplification	Significance
		FACETS OF APPLICATION	

Now the interpreter can move from original textual sense ('carriage') to exemplification ('car') by way of the transhistorical intention ('road-using vehicle') which serves as a bridge between the original textual sense in the past and the exemplification of the future. This transhistorical intention is part of the world in front of the text, the second-order referent (in the case of the Metropolitan Police Act, this is a world wherein traffic on English streets remains totally unimpeded by disabled vehicles of any kind whatsoever). The determination of the projected world is thus critical in the navigation from text to praxis, for it bears the transhistorical intention. Genres and their rules play a key role in this transaction.[121]

In sum, the validity of an application in a future reading situation is contingent upon its falling within the boundaries of the transhistorical intention of the text. This latter unchanging component of the inscription is conceptual, creating a vast and virtually infinite potential of exemplifications that may be realized in a myriad of future reading contexts. It is this transhistorical entity, borne by the projected world, that gives the classic its future-directedness – its

119. Hirsch, 'Meaning and Significance Reinterpreted', pp. 207, 210. Hirsch is 'very much in agreement with Gadamer's idea that application can be part of meaning' (210, 212). Also see idem, *The Aims of Interpretation* (Chicago: The University of Chicago Press, 1976), p. 80.

120. These aspects of meaning will be explored further in Chapter 4 for their utility in the interpretation and application of biblical texts.

121. See Chapters 2 and 3 for the Rules of Genre that perform this function for biblical texts.

perenniality and plurality. This work proposes that for biblical pericopes as well
the world in front of the text is the conceptual entity that implicitly bears the
transhistorical intention; this world projection enables the generation of future
exemplifications that may not have been envisaged by the author. It is the mediating world in front of the text bearing a transhistorical intention that facilitates
a valid move from Scripture to sermon.

Identity of original textual sense and exemplification. A link between original textual sense and different exemplifications is preserved if the latter are
instances subsumed by the transhistorical intention borne by the projected
world; those exemplifications so linked are, by definition, part of meaning. In
other words, there is evidently a preservation of some kind of correspondence
between original textual sense and exemplifications that makes the latter legitimate. Vanhoozer's discussion of the concepts of identity is illuminating in this
regard.[122] What is similar between original textual sense and exemplification is
not *idem*-identity, 'sameness' that is governed primarily by permanence in time
(or superimposable numerical or qualitative identity). This kind of identity only
tends to become weaker as the time between the two entities that are being compared stretches longer, just as, for instance, the present physical identification of
a particular person as being the same (idem) as in the past is less certain when
that interval between past and present is considerable. Indeed, so is the case
with a classic text that has survived the ebb and flow of time. The *idem*-identity
between a text written then and an application wrought now becomes harder to
maintain. Instead, the correspondence that can be discerned between a text and
its future exemplification(s) is Ricoeur's notion of identity in the sense of *ipse*,
a 'selfness' discrete from any concrete characteristic that perdures, but which
is dependent, rather, upon a narrative identity that remains constant. Ipseity is
exemplified in the keeping of one's word – an expression of dynamic, narrative self-constancy in the faithfulness to a promise, a oneness that transcends
changes of outer circumstances or inner feelings.[123] Not too far removed from
that notion of faithfulness is the theologian-homiletician's pursuit of fidelity in
keeping God's inscripturated word constant across the relentless passage of time,
between text and praxis. Thus, *ipse*-identity, a selfness persisting through time,
is contrasted to *idem*-identity, the 'mere permanence or perseverance of things'
or immutability.[124] The maintenance of *ipse* likeness between application and

122. Kevin J. Vanhoozer, *The Drama of Doctrine: A Canonical-Linguistic Approach to Christian Theology* (Louisville: Westminster/John Knox Press, 2005), pp. 126–9.

123. Paul Ricoeur, *Oneself as Another* (trans. Kathleen Blamey; Chicago: The University of
Chicago Press, 1992), pp. 2–3, 116–19, 123–4, 266. This 'description of the identity of the narrative text as a *dynamic* identity may help bridge the gap between the work's world and the reader's
world' (idem, 'The Text as Dynamic Identity', in *Identity of the Literary Text* [eds Mario J. Valdés
and Owen Miller; Toronto: University of Toronto Press, 1985], pp. 175–86 [184]).

124. Ricoeur, *Oneself as Another*, pp. 267, 318. Also see idem, *The Course of Recognition*

original textual sense is rendered possible by the dynamic entity of the world in front of the text (and its transhistorical intention).[125] Both being subsumed by this projected world, original textual sense and application display *ipse*-identity with one another; thus, future application has been rendered faithful to its text. It is in this fashion that the gap between text and praxis is spanned.

Textuality was designed to overcome the time-and-space restrictions imposed by orality. Implicit in the very nature of texts, then, is the splicing of two historical worlds – the world of the writing event and the world of the reading/hearing event. Interpretation is, therefore, Janus-faced, looking in two directions, because it is always an affair involving at least two discrete times, two separate places and two independent consciousnesses. Though it is especially true for classics, this bidirectional nature of interpretation is inherently part of the human endeavour of reading, irrespective of what is read. A nexus between the past and present is necessarily native to textuality and the act of written communication. The bond between the event of inscription and the event of interpretation is consolidated in the world in front of the text, a product of the referentiality of literature. Any intent to refer to something in the future must resort to this world and its transhistorical intention, whereby a written discourse may be validly translated from the situation of inscription to that of interpretation.[126] This operation is particularly important for the biblical canon: it is the transhistorical intention borne by the projected world that enables the theologian-homiletician to navigate from Scripture to sermon with fidelity. 'That texts in the secular as well as the sacred canon may exhibit this transhistorical core meaning is, I think, a root assumption of responsible interpretation.'[127] Such responsible interpretation that leads to application is the product of a fruitful interlocution between hermeneutics and homiletics, a conversation that has commenced in this chapter.

Summary: language-games, textuality and genres

The goal of this work is the assessment of validity in the move from text to praxis in a sermon on a biblical periscope. To this end, hermeneutics is engaged in dialogue with homiletics. Chapter 1 has addressed the general hermeneutical

(trans. David Pellauer; Cambridge, MA: Harvard University Press, 2005), p. 101. Vanhoozer refers to the *idem* species of identity as 'hard' and to the *ipse* as 'soft' (*The Drama of Doctrine*, p. 127).

125. It will be shown in Chapter 4 that the task of the theologian-homiletician is not to produce, in application, an 'uncritical, uninformative, and unimaginative repetition of the past' that retains the wooden sameness of *idem*-identity with the textual sense. Instead, the mandate is to 'improvise' application while maintaining selfness (*ipse*-identity) with the original textual sense (Vanhoozer, *Drama of Doctrine*, p. 127).

126. E.D. Hirsch, Jr., 'Counterfactuals in Interpretation', in *Interpreting Law and Literature: A Hermeneutic Reader* (eds Sanford Levinson and Steven Mailloux; Evanston: Northwestern University Press, 1988), pp. 55–68 (57–8); idem, 'Past Intentions and Present Meanings', p. 92.

127. Idem, 'Counterfactuals', p. 61.

aspects of the undertaking: the focus of this chapter narrowed itself from the broader arena of language-games to the narrower field of textuality to alight – and encamp hereafter in Chapters 2 and 3 – upon the specific locus of genres, both primary and secondary (classic).

In brief, genres are the language-games played by texts. The nature of these language-games and, particularly, the distanciation effected by textuality make possible the application of texts in situations distant from that of the author. The language-games played by texts, genres, are of particular interest to this work. These linguistic sports, operating by rules, are conventional rhetorical devices from the author's point of view: they are genetic in function. From the reader's perspective, genres are critical for interpretive purposes: they are heuristic in function. Genetic and heuristic, genres facilitate the projection of a world in front of the text, a second-order reference that is the consequence of textuality. It is this projected world that can neutralize distanciation and enable future application of those texts authored in the past.

The literary games of genre are played on two tiers – primary and second-ary; the latter, the secondary genre of the canonical classic, in concord with the Bible's status as divine discourse, renders Scripture prescriptive in status, with perennial and plural significance for its readership. The intrinsic future-directedness (the transhistorical intention) of this secondary genre is carried by the world in front of the text; the classic is thus endowed with a unique futurity, extending its scope beyond the temporo-spatial environs of its composition. This property of the biblical classic creates the potential for an infinite variety of exemplifications of the text by subsequent readers. These exemplifications (a subset of application) are bounded by the transhistorical intention of the text, and thereby maintain *ipse*-identity with the original textual sense. Such a cor-respondence, it is proposed, legitimizes the homiletical navigation from text to praxis, rendering the latter faithful to the former.

The utilization of general hermeneutical principles in this first chapter has paid significant dividends: the foundation has been laid for deriving sermonic application. Chapter 1 identified two categories of biblical genres, primary and secondary (the canonical classic), that help provide the framework for the deter-mination of the world in front of the text. Chapters 2 and 3 will detail the rules of genres that enable the discernment of that projected world. In Chapter 4, this secondary referent of textual discourse (the world in front of the pericope with its implicit transhistorical intention) will be found to play a key role in gen-erating valid application by mediating between text and praxis. The dialogue between hermeneutics and homiletics has hereby begun: general hermeneutics has been considered; specific biblical hermeneutics, with a view to its fruitful-ness for homiletics, will be discussed in the following two chapters. Thus, the first three chapters will have prepared the ground for the employment of all of these hermeneutical concepts in the fourth and final chapter; the derivation of valid praxis from a biblical text will then be well under way.

2

PRIMARY GENRE

In the consideration of general hermeneutics as a prelude to the focus of this work on biblical interpretation, Chapter 1 brought to the fore the notion of language-games, a metaphor to be employed in the rest of this work that seeks to determine how a valid move from text to praxis may be undertaken. *Language-games*, both oral and written, and the nature of their rules – extensile and flexible – were addressed. *Textuality* as a broad category of language-games that are characterized by distanciation was also considered. The major consequence of inscription is that, by means of the world projected in front of the text (the second-order referent), recontextualization of the distanciated discourse is now rendered viable in a new readerly milieu. The role of *genres* (textual language-games) in this recontextualization was surveyed, with special attention focused upon their capacity to frame the worlds projected by texts. These rule-bound discourse-events were broadly divided into two categories, primary and secondary genre, the latter being the genre of the *classic*. As a peerless classic, the biblical canon is charged with significances of a peculiar nature – prescriptive, perennial and plural – mandating readers of all time to 'read and apply'. Its potential for future application, intrinsic to the status of Scripture as a canonical classic, was seen to be a function of the transhistorical intention borne by the world in front of the text. This future-directedness of the Bible drives the quest to generate legitimate application in the sermonic undertaking. This work, engaging hermeneutics and homiletics in dialogue, expects to provide a basis for gauging the validity of application – its faithfulness to the text and its appropriateness for the congregation.

In this pursuit, an examination of the Rules of Genre is essential, for these rules govern the projection and perception of the world in front of the text, the key intermediary between inscription and application. In facilitating the portrayal and discernment of this world and its transhistorical intention, these rules enable the derivation of valid application. The Rules of Genre, therefore, play a central role in the hermeneutical and homiletical endeavour that takes the preacher from Scripture to sermon.[1]

---

1. Such rules, it must be borne in mind, are not hard and fast; neither are they peremptory. Instead, these rules serve as Wittgensteinian 'signposts', directing rather than dominating,

Chapters 2 and 3 enumerate the Rules of Primary Genre and Secondary Genre, respectively, paying particular attention to their framing of the world in front of the text. Before proposing the Rules of Primary Genre in this chapter, the fundamental issue of the classification of biblical literary genres will be addressed, utilizing the NT Epistles and Gospels as case studies, and considering the problem from the discrete vantage points of author and reader. Subsequently, four of the predominant primary genres of Scripture will be examined and their rules listed.

Types of primary genre

When considering the genres of Scripture, one is immediately faced with the difficulties of taxonomy. With what degree of precision is it possible to demarcate a text as belonging to a particular genre? For the purposes of this work, it will not be necessary to undertake a definitive disposition and arrangement of all the genres in the Bible. Rather, the goal of this exercise will be to generate a more panoramic vista of genres as 'works' capable of successfully accomplishing the textual interaction between author and reader. It will be concluded that the concept of genre, though somewhat nebulous at the edges, is sufficiently serviceable for the broad classification of biblical texts. The idea of primary generic classes thus retains its utility for interpretive purposes. Indeed, an understanding of the ordering of these biblical text-types is essential in the move towards application, for each individual language-game performs the work of world-projection in its own specific fashion, under the stewardship of its own specific rules.

The problem of classification

Specific genres undoubtedly do exist, but it will be maintained in the tradition of Wittgenstein that imprecision abounds in the categorizations thereof and particularly in the earmarking of texts as they are allocated to generic classes. The complexity of the task of defining primary genres and locating texts in such categories, especially when those texts and categories are ancient, is daunting.

The NT Epistles exemplify the difficulty of rigorous and scrupulous classification. Though Paul's writings in Scripture are incontrovertibly letters and, as such, part of the extended Graeco-Roman epistolary genre, 'consensus ends here, since ancient letters come in various shapes and sizes, making it

---

persuading rather than prevailing upon the reader (Ludwig Wittgenstein, *Philosophical Investigations* [2nd edn; trans. G.E.M. Anscombe; London: Basil Blackwell, 1958], ¶¶85, 198). Hirsch considers such rules 'rules of thumb'; Pavel calls them 'effective recipes', 'good artistic habits', and 'practices of the trade'. See E.D. Hirsch, Jr., *Validity in Interpretation* (New Haven: Yale University Press, 1967), p. 93; and Thomas Pavel, 'Literary Genres as Norms and Good Habits', *NLH* 34 (2003), pp. 201–10 (209–10).

difficult to place Paul's letters in their precise cultural setting'.[2] Based on the characteristic trio of elements in Graeco-Roman letters (*salutation* – identification of sender(s) and addressee(s), and thanksgiving; *body* – background information and message; and *subscriptions*, including conclusions), the NT Epistles are generally considered as belonging to the category of official literary communiqués, guiding particular communities on specific theological or moral issues. Such letters were rhetorically conceived and often involved the intermediary of couriers who could also orally supplement the dictates and biddings of their senders. In all these respects, the Epistles conformed to the sub-genre of the official letter. The adaptation of this form gave Paul's communications a degree of formality and authority as it furthered his apostolic status as a commissioned representative of Christ.[3] Yet, at the same time, these missives retained similarities with the occasional, non-literary form of Graeco-Roman epistolography in the personal touches visible, in the naming of particular individuals and in the depiction of the sender's personal concern for the reader(s). The incorporation of the elements of a personal letter declared Paul's identification with, and commitment to, his readers, as well as his pastoral concern for the body of believers. Softening the seeming imperialism and the relative detachment of the magisterial, official form of communication, personalization enabled the letter to touch not only the minds but also the hearts of God's people, persuading them to respond and to align their lives to the world projected in front of the text.

Therefore, rather than considering letters as either literary or non-literary, official or personal, it is more helpful to recognize the existence of a whole spectrum of forms between these two poles. In other words, flexibility appears to be an integral property of this genre (and, indeed, of every other). Paul, it appears, tailored the genre into a form of Christian communication for his own purposes, introducing into the non-literary version elements of the higher, literary style such as chiasmus, allegory, metaphor, ellipse, etc. He successfully utilized and modified an existing form to address theological issues in the context of matters of daily life. Such a move to elevate an occasional letter is not without precedent: both Cicero (first century BCE) and Pliny the Younger (first and second centuries CE) did exactly that; Seneca (first century CE) combined philosophical treatises and the casual epistle.[4] Clearly the flexible form of the genre was adaptable to the needs of the creative letter-writer.

2. Jeffrey T. Reed, 'Using Ancient Rhetorical Categories to Interpret Paul's Letters: A Question of Genre', in *Rhetoric and the New Testament: Essays from the 1992 Heidelberg Conference* (eds Stanley E. Porter and Thomas H. Olbricht; Sheffield: JSOT, 1993), pp. 292–324 (292).

3. M. Luther Stirewalt, Jr., *Studies in Ancient Greek Epistolography* (Atlanta: Scholars Press, 1993), pp. 9–10.

4. See E. Randolph Richards, *The Secretary in the Letters of Paul* (Tübingen: J.C.B. Mohr, 1991), pp. 214–16; and Stirewalt, *Studies in Ancient Greek Epistolography*, pp. 1–26. In both length and style, Paul appears to flout the recommendations of Demetrius for informal letter-writing (*Eloc.* 4.226, 228; first century CE).

The NT epistolary sub-genre was thus a specific communicative form intentionally chosen for the purpose of convincing readers/hearers of the stance of
the writer on the subject at hand. The specific adaptations of this category of
letters were integrally linked to the particular purposes of the letter-writers,
the malleability of the form providing authors with a literary shape that
could be accommodated to their own specific needs.[5] Precise classification of
epistles, therefore, is not necessary; neither is it a facile endeavour. Pseudo
Demetrius (Τύποι 'Επιστολικοί, from third century BCE to third century
CE), for instance, identifies twenty-one types of official letters, and Pseudo
Libanius ('Επιστολιμαῖοι Χαρακτῆρες, from fourth to sixth century CE),
forty-one. Indeed, one epistolary style noted by the latter is the mixed (μικτή)
type, attesting to the plasticity of these categories.[6] This is also clearly the
case with the NT Epistles. In keeping with his theological purposes, Paul's
'mixed' letters incorporate a variety of literary forms within them: autobiog-
raphy (Phil. 1.12-14); apocalyptic material (1 Cor. 15.12-28); catalogues and
lists (Gal. 5.19-23); catechesis (specific accounts of teaching on Christian
holiness: 1 Thess. 4.1-12); confessional statements (Rom. 10.9); hymns (Col.
1.15-20); kerygma (proclamations about Christ: 1 Cor. 15.1-7); and prophetic
denouncements (Rom. 1.18-32).[7] Such diversity underscores the fact that the
epistolary genre, like other genres, was finely tuned to achieve the author's
purpose in writing. Form, content, context and audience factors were inextricably intertwined in the achievement of authorial goals, contributing to a
substantial degree of inexactness in the classification of text-type.

However, this is not at all a paralysing deficit for interpretation: despite the
variety generated by the mélange of constituent elements, sufficient family
resemblance is maintained between texts for their demarcation into one primary
genre or the other. An identifiable combination of characteristics or portfolio
of features marks a text as belonging to a particular genre. At the same time,
the very imprecision of generic boundaries highlights the attribute of genres
as 'works', instruments that are adapted, shaped and deployed by authors to
accomplish their purposes and to elicit specific responses from their audiences.
Genres work to project a world with a transhistorical intention and, thereby, to
facilitate future application of the text by hearers and readers. The composite
product of the institutional and conventional elements of textuality, a genre is
'the instrument whereby the author "encodes" and the reader "decodes" the

---

5. Calvin J. Roetzel, *The Letters of Paul: Conversations in Context* (4th edn; Louisville:
Westminster/John Knox Press, 1998), pp. 55–65; and Stanley K. Stowers, *Letter Writing in
Graeco-Roman Antiquity* (Philadelphia: Westminster, 1986), pp. 22–3.

6. See John L. White, *Light from Ancient Letters* (Philadelphia: Fortress, 1986), pp. 189–90,
203.

7. Charles B. Puskas, Jr., *The Letters of Paul: An Introduction* (Collegeville, MN: The Liturgical Press, 1993), pp. 10–11.

communication'.[8] Indeed, this encoding and decoding by author and reader presumes a duality in the manner in which genres may be conceived: from the author's vantage point, and from the reader's outlook. Such a distinction between authorial and readerly perspectives of text-type will be demonstrated in the following discussion of the Gospels, members of the broad generic category of narrative.

Author and reader in the classification of primary genres

An examination of the Gospels reveals the purposeful and response-focused employment of this sub-genre; it also demonstrates the problematic nature of categorization. The literary form of the Gospel will illustrate the role of genre in the cooperative interaction of the author–genre/text–reader triad. Genre, exercising its pragmatic function (discussed in Chapter 1), frames the text's projected world and, via the transhistorical intention of the text, facilitates the derivation of valid application.[9] Thus both the purpose of a writer in the text and the response of a reader to the text are directed by the genre that is adopted. In this section, the genre of the Gospels will be explored from the viewpoints of author and reader: from the authorial side, Richard Burridge's labelling of the Gospels as *bioi*, and, from the readerly side, Hans Frei's caption, 'realistic narratives'. This scrutiny will shed light on how these two poles on the interpretive spectrum function flexibly and freely to tag the Gospels within the commodious literary landscape of narrative.

Author and the classification of primary genres

Genres serve to objectify the author's purpose in the particular text that instantiates that language-game; they enable the author not only to *say* something, but also to *do* something with what is said – the projection of a world, the pragmatic component of discourse. 'The unifying and controlling idea in any type of utterance, any genre, is the idea of purpose' – that of the author as embodied in and performed by the text.[10] The classification of Gospels as *bioi* serves as an example of such a textual representation of the writer's purpose. A flexibility in the genesis of genres is readily apparent as the author shapes the text for his purpose, giving genres the character of 'works'.

The Gospels: similarities among bioi. It appears safe to conclude that the Gospels fit into the Graeco-Roman category of *bios*, a type of writing generated within communities that sought to follow after a particular leader. One must concede, however, that, while existing within the larger genre category of narrative, the

---

8. Richard A. Burridge, *What Are the Gospels? A Comparison with Graeco-Roman Biography* (2nd edn; Grand Rapids: Zondervan, 2004), p. 107.

9. The concept of sermonic application is developed in Chapter 4.

10. Hirsch, *Validity in Interpretation*, pp. 79, 99.

bios itself encompassed a spectrum of literature with historical writings at one end and encomiastic productions at the other, with moral philosophy, polemic, story and novel falling in between – all of them borrowing from each other. Indeed, boundaries of all generic classes are porous and pliant; genres are not petrified compartments into which texts may be squeezed. Rather, these flexible text-types have efficiency and functionality as major considerations, and their deliberate choice and moulding are intended to serve authors' goals.[11] In their portrayals of Jesus' life, the Gospel writers achieved their theological purposes in a manner unique to the sub-genre of *bioi*, teaching, influencing and persuading readers by means of a narrative centred upon the person and work of Jesus Christ. This enactment of authors' purposes was accomplished in and with the major elements that constituted the genre. The combinatorial possibilities and permutations of its various components aided in the adaptation of the genre to the writers' own communicational needs and aims. In a *bios*, such standard genre elements included opening features, subject, external features and internal features; these will be surveyed briefly, comparing the Gospels with specific Graeco-Roman *bioi*.

Opening Features. Matthew begins by addressing his subject's ancestry (1.1-17), as does Plutarch in *Cato Minor* (c. 96 CE); Mark, like Xenophon (*Agesilaus*, c. 360 BCE), commences his account with a single introductory statement (1.1).[12] Both these evangelists include the name of their protagonist at the very beginning, as do most Graeco-Roman *bioi*. Luke, in contrast, has a more formal preface with his central character prominently named only as the main narrative emerges (3.23; 4.1) – comparable to Isocrates' *Evagoras* (the writer mentions the birth of his protagonist at line 12 and proceeds with a genealogical discourse on the gods, before winding his way back to Evagoras' birth in line 21; c. 464–375 BCE) and Tacitus' *Agricola* (who appears only in 4.1; c. 98 CE).

Subject. In the Synoptic Gospels, Jesus is the subject of about a quarter of the verbs; another fifth is located in his own utterances, approximating the statistics for Satyrus' *Euripides* (subject of verb, 26 per cent; verb in subject's words, 18 per cent; third century BCE). The Synoptics compare well with ancient *bioi* in their allocation of textual volume to the last days and death of their main subject: from 15 to 20 per cent (*Cato Minor* allots 17 per cent).[13]

External features. The Gospels are prose narratives of medium-length category, similar to writings of that period. Matthew and Luke are equivalent in size

---

11. Burridge, *What Are the Gospels?*, pp. 62–4.

12. Of Agesilaus, Xenophon writes (1.2): 'Now concerning his high birth what greater and nobler [testimony] could be said than this, that even today the line of his descent from Heracles is traced through the roll of his ancestors, and those no simple citizens, but kings and sons of kings?'

13. Burridge, *What Are the Gospels?*, pp. 160, 191–2, 312, 318–20.

to the longest of Plutarch's *Lives*; Mark's 11,242 words correspond to Plutarch's average for his *bioi* (from 10,000 to 11,000). The NT narratives' chronological framework, though perhaps less distinct than the precisely sequenced lives of the military commanders Agricola and Agesilaus, is more structured than the loose collection that composes Lucian's *Demonax* (second century CE). Pronouncement stories, common in the Synoptics, are found as often in *Demonax*. In addition, prefaces to *bioi* frequently mentioned their sources (for example, Philo's *Moses*, c. first century BCE to first century CE), as did Luke (1.1-4).[14]

Internal features. Settings of all *bioi* centre around the main character. Descriptions of the subject's ancestry and depictions of his last days are common; the Gospels of Mark and John, to be sure, do not detail the birth of their subject, but neither does *Agesilaus, Cato Minor* or *Demonax*. Despite some Semitic influence, the style of the Gospels in their internal features remains similar to that of Graeco-Roman *bioi*. The evangelists, as did Plutarch, eschewed the archaic Attic style, retaining a literary form of the Koiné. In tone, the serious and respectful ambience of the Gospel accounts is reminiscent of the atmosphere of *Agricola* and *Moses*.[15] As in other *bioi*, the Gospels, too, contain material that is encomiastic, exemplary, didactic and apologetic.

This is not to indicate that there is nothing at all new about the Gospels. The very fact that the Gospels were considered *euangelia*, rather than *bioi*, suggests that a significant distinction between the two had been consciously made by the early Church (see Clement of Alexandria, *Strom.* 1.21; and Irenaeus, *Haer.* 3.11.7).[16] While demonstrating considerable similarity with the contemporary category of *bios*, the Gospels nonetheless assert their own individuality as they exhibit the flexibility inherent in the notion of this text-type. The goal of the writer dictated the manner in which generic elements were mixed and matched. These elements of genre, in turn, serve the interpreter in determining the author's purpose implicit in the text: 'a genre does not exist to

14. Burridge, *What Are the Gospels?*, pp. 164, 194. Philo's opening remarks (1.1.1-4) are strikingly similar to Luke's in his Gospel: 'I have conceived the idea of writing the life of Moses, who, according to the account of some persons, was the lawgiver of the Jews, but according to others only an interpreter of the sacred laws, the greatest and most perfect man that ever lived, having a desire to make his character fully known to those who ought not to remain in ignorance respecting him'. Philo claims to be narrating the events of Moses' life, 'having learnt them both from those sacred scriptures which he has left as marvellous memorials of his wisdom, and having also heard many things from the elders of my nation, for I have continually connected together what I have heard with what I have read, and in this way I look upon it that I am acquainted with the history of his life more accurately than other people'.

15. Agricola, Tacitus notes, was born in an 'ancient and respectable' colony; his grandfather served a 'trust of importance'; his father, 'distinguished by his eloquence', was a 'man of merit'; his mother was 'respected for the purity of her manners'; his own disposition was 'ingenuous', and his temperament 'happy'; etc.; see 4.1.

16. Justin Martyr explicitly calls the apostles' memoirs εὐαγγέλια (*1 Apol.* 66).

project a subject matter ... but an attitude underlying it, the writer's purpose or emotion'.[17] One can detect in the Gospel narratives both a restraint (they appropriate the characteristic features of *bioi*) and a release (they are freely tailored for their authors' purposes and in being so modified, vary from *bioi*), a dualism common to all rule-bound language-games of genre.

The Gospels: differences among evangelists. Though specific features of the *bios* are shared among the Gospels, and though all four share a common subject and protagonist, the individual writings display significant differences in choice of content, arrangement of material and style of writing, as the authors undertook to achieve their specific purposes in and with their compositions. Their pragmatic goals were different. The disparity of content, arrangement and style (reflecting the three main canons of classical rhetoric – *inventio, dispositio and elocutio*) point to the theological purposes of their authors and how these texts frame, in their own manner, the projected world.

Content. The *bioi* focus on their main subject, and the Gospels therefore concentrate on Christ, but in a variety of ways. Mark generally tends to maintain the 'messianic secret', whereas Matthew identifies Jesus clearly at the start – 1.1, 1.21; 2.2, 11; etc. Luke does so as well, albeit following a prolonged birth and baptism narrative; John explicitly names Jesus as the divine Word. The differing emphases of the four evangelists may also be recognized in their narratives of the resurrection of Jesus. Matthew's account depicts his concern to answer Jewish charges of body theft by the disciples of Jesus (27.57-66; 28.11-15); Mark highlights the fear and silence of the women who visited the empty tomb (15.47–16.8); John 20 contains a multiplicity of verbs denoting sight – in the context of darkness (20.1, 19) – culminating in a forthright declaration of the focal purpose of that Gospel directed towards readers in posterity unable to *see* the evidence physically (20.29-31).

Arrangement. In the ordering of their material, *bioi* tend to be quite chronological and so do the Gospels. Among the latter, however, differences remain. Matthew has an extended introduction and contains five main discourses alternating with narrative – each discourse is concluded by the summary statement: 'And when Jesus had finished these words...' (Mt. 7.28-9; 11.1; 13.53; 19.1; 26.1). Mark is characterized by a unidirectional movement from Galilee to Jerusalem underscoring his focus on a journey of discipleship ἐν τῇ ὁδῷ. Luke provides a formal preface and introduction, and depicts a geographical organization that continues in Acts (Galilee, Samaria, Jerusalem, Judaea–Samaria and Rome). John's sublime prologue is followed by two major sections of Jesus' ministry, involving signs and discourses (1.19–10.42), and the Last Supper, passion and resurrection narratives (chapters 12–20), with both these sections being arranged around a pivot, the interlude at Bethany in chapters 11–12.

17. Robin Magowan, 'A Note on Genre', *Coll. Eng.* 30 (1969), pp. 534–8 (536).

Style. The respectful voices of the Gospels reproduce the deferential tone of *bioi*; yet the Gospels are distinct from each other and maintain their individuality and divergence from their Graeco-Roman forebear. In Mark, 88 sections begin paratactically with καί, and there are 19 examples of asyndeton – all in the context of a culture that prized period and conjunction. Matthew's language is purer, but includes Semitisms. Luke, after the classical Greek of his preface, opts for a Septuagintal style, reflecting OT stories and connections. John's idiolect combines both Semitisms ('Rabbi', 'Cephas', 'Messiah', etc.) and Hellenisms typical of contemporary non-literary Koiné; a repetitive vocabulary – 'love', 'truth', 'life', etc. – stresses his theological purposes and emphasizes his main themes.[18]

In sum, *bios*, like other categories and sub-categories of genre, is malleable and extensible, existing within a continuum of language-games. A certain degree of imprecision prevails in any categorization of genres; therefore, fine distinctions are probably neither achievable nor necessary. Generic form is not inviolate; rather genres are in 'a constant state of flux, shifting and regrouping as features alter and as new works are written'.[19] Though the particular thrusts of other biblical genres are different from those of *bioi*, this property of purposefulness and adaptability is shared by all text-types, as they function in their individual ways as literary devices focused on achieving the goals of authors – the projection of the world in front of the text.

Reader and the classification of primary genres

While attending to authorial purpose has always been a prominent goal of interpreters, approaches concentrating on readers and their responses to the text have not, until recently, generated much interest. In the case of the Gospels, the rise of form criticism in the early twentieth century rendered Matthew, Mark, Luke and John collectors and tradition-transmitters, emphasizing how the sub-units of their literary productions (incidents, parables, etc.) were orally relayed within the community before the composite accounts of those writers were inscribed as the Gospels. While the evangelist's role as an author was thereby eclipsed – he was no more than 'a mere stenographer at the end of the oral tunnel' – the focus, nonetheless, remained upon the compositional and authorial end of the literary

18. See Richard A. Burridge, 'The Gospels and Acts', in *Handbook of Classical Rhetoric in the Hellenistic Period 330 B.C.–A.D. 400* (ed. Stanley E. Porter; Leiden: E.J. Brill, 2001), pp. 507–34 (514–27).

19. Idem, *What Are the Gospels?*, p. 43. Good writers both conform to existing genres and transform them; rather than inventing genres, they 'enter into other men's labours' (René Wellek and Austin Warren, *Theory of Literature* [3rd edn; New York: Harcourt Brace Jovanovich, 1977], p. 235). Accommodation (adaptation of an old genre to a new, current purpose) and assimilation (adaptation of the new purpose to an old genre) occur simultaneously as the author produces the text (Tzvetan Todorov, *Symbolism and Interpretation* [trans. Catherine Porter; Ithaca, NY: Cornell University Press, 1982], p. 27).

enterprise.[20] The development of redaction criticism in the middle of the twentieth century began to see the evangelists as creative compilers, as compositional
analyses examined the ways in which these editors shaped and moulded their
source materials to export their theological agendas. Consideration here was
given to the originality of the authors as they manipulated their raw data. Later,
along with literary criticism, these writers' capabilities and skills – artistic and
pragmatic, aesthetic and functional – were increasingly appreciated. Even in
these shifts of foci, authors continued to attract most of the attention. Only with
the advent of reader-centred approaches in the latter half of the last century did
the third entity in the stratagem of communication that involves author, genre/
text and reader come into prominence: the reader was now recognized as an
active participant in the triad.[21] Frei takes advantage of the vantage point of this
player of the game, the reader, as he delineates an 'anachronistic' model for the
sub-genre of the Gospel within the wider bounds of the narrative genre. Where
Burridge sought to place these texts in a category contemporaneous with, or
antedating, their authors (*bioi*), Frei located the Gospels within a text-type more
contemporaneous with the reader than with the author ('realistic narrative').
Flexibility of genres is again evident, here from the heuristic vantage point of
the reader, as these literary forms are classified.

The Gospels as realistic narrative. A particular view of the Gospels as belonging to the sub-genre of 'realistic narrative' propels Hans Frei's reception of,
and response to, the stories of Jesus.[22] With his view of the textual world as
self-sufficient for interpretive transactions, and of language as perspicuous and
intelligible, comes his commitment to discover meaning in the text and nowhere
else.[23] Frei argues vigorously against the kinds of interpretation that open up a
lacuna between the text and its meaning (or referent); such an approach, he
claims, eclipses the literal sense. Instead, Frei's understanding of the literary

20. Burridge, *What Are the Gospels?*, p. 12.

21. The broad brushstrokes used here do not deny the multiplicity of stances along the spectrum of reader-response approaches, all the way from a conservative position that sees readers
as subservient to texts and authors, to a radical one that promotes meaning created *ex libris* by
the reader. This degree of diversity holds true for the practices of form, redaction and literary
criticism as well. See Kevin J. Vanhoozer, *Is There a Meaning in This Text? The Bible, the Reader,
and the Morality of Literary Knowledge* (Grand Rapids: Zondervan, 1998), p. 148.

22. Though he patterns his form upon the realistic narrative literature of eighteenth- and
nineteenth-century England and Germany, Frei observes that the concept of realistic narratives
pervades the biblical text, suggesting its implicit presence even before its formal manifestation
towards the end of the second millennium in Western Europe (Hans W. Frei, *The Eclipse of Biblical Narrative: A Study in Eighteenth and Nineteenth Century Hermeneutics* [New Haven: Yale
University Press, 1974], pp. 15, 142–54).

23. Idem, 'The "Literal Reading" of the Biblical Narrative in the Christian Tradition: Does It
Stretch or Will It Break?', in *The Bible and the Narrative Tradition* (ed. Frank McConnell; New
York: Oxford University Press, 1986), pp. 36–77 (66–7).

independence of the text sees the *sensus literalis* as being generated intratextually, with no recourse to extratextual references. He observes that there is an analogy between biblical material and a novel; in both cases the authors assert: 'I mean what I say. It's as simple as that: the text means what it says.'[24] Extending this comparison, Frei claims that Gospel narratives exhibit 'a realistic or history-like (though not necessarily historical) element'; thus he includes them within the sub-genre of realistic narratives. Biblical realistic narratives are autonomous and self-referential, and the proper reception of these accounts ought simply to be the observation of the story itself – its structure and shape – to render it intelligible on its own terms. Meaning, for Frei, is linguistic through and through, and, therefore, in his bounded literary universe of textuality, the reception of a text does not involve the appropriation of any external referent.[25] However, his resistance, it appears, is only to the *reversal* of the relationship between text and world, to the notion that 'a world comes into being *apart from* that which the biblical texts project', and to which the texts must adapt.[26] Thus, even Frei's notion of realistic narrative seems to be open to the possibility that a text can portray a world, so long as that world is constrained by the text itself and not by the caprices of the reader.

At first blush, this particular class of text, as defined by Frei, seems to violate the custom of genres cooperating with readers to perform work and project worlds – it simply means what it says and no particular reception-stance is called for on the part of the reader. However, these realistic narratives, like other genres, do have an authorial purpose: to render the singular figure of Jesus of Nazareth present to the reader, 'truly manifest as Jesus, the risen Christ'.[27] Such an authorial purpose necessarily implies a particular readerly response as a corollary. In fact, Frei's account does require a reader capable of responding to the narrative by experiencing the presence of the narrated Jesus Christ. 'Just as Christ's presence and identity cannot be con-

---

24. 'There is no gap between the representation and what is represented by it' (Hans W. Frei, *The Identity of Jesus Christ: The Hermeneutical Bases of Dogmatic Theology* [Philadelphia: Fortress, 1975], p. xiv). Also see idem, *Eclipse of Biblical Narrative*, pp. 119, 280; and idem, 'Response to "Narrative Theology: An Evangelical Appraisal"', *TrinJ* 8 (1987), pp. 21–4 (22).

25. James Fodor, *Christian Hermeneutics: Paul Ricoeur and the Refiguring of Theology* (Oxford: Clarendon Press, 1995), pp. 267, 296; Frei, *The Eclipse of Biblical Narrative*, pp. 10, 13–14; idem, *The Identity of Jesus Christ*, pp. 37, 87. Gary Comstock calls Frei's approach 'pure narrativism', a modus operandi that sees these stories as immediately intelligible to the reader and irreducible to external referents ('Truth or Meaning: Ricoeur versus Frei on Biblical Narrative', *JR* 66 [1986], pp. 117–40 [120–1]).

26. Francis Watson, *Text, Church and World: Biblical Interpretation in Theological Perspective* (Grand Rapids: Eerdmans, 1994), p. 22 (italics added). Chapter 1 of the present work, in agreement with Frei, detailed how the conception of the world in front of the text is surely and securely dependent upon the text.

27. Frei, *Identity of Jesus Christ*, p. 138.

ceived apart, factual affirmation of him and commitment to him cannot be conceived apart either.'[28] That an actual response to the textually manifested Jesus and the significance of his story – the projected world – is appropriate and, indeed, an essential condition for correct interpretation is affirmed by Frei: 'The shape of the story being mirrored in the shape of our life is the condition of its being meaningful for us.'[29] Such an existential apprehension of the Gospels' protagonist and the world of his salvific activity ('shape of the story'; the world that depicts God's *modus* of salvation) is a pointed response on the part of the reader, a response necessary for the full realization of the meaning of the realistic narrative. Therefore, even for Frei, the sub-genre of realistic narrative creates the expectation of a response from the reader; and, without such expectation guided by genre, the meaning of the story would neither be comprehended nor its significance appropriated. Frei also appears to concede in his later writings that the autonomous meaning of the story is available only to certain kinds of readers – competent ones, that is, competent enough to respond. He noted that the literal sense 'belongs first and foremost into the context of a sociolinguistic community, that is, of the specific religion of which it is part, rather than into a literary ambience'. It is in such a community that the narrative may be competently read as a 'determinate code' and responded to.[30] Thus, realistic narrative (like the *bios*) may be seen as rendering a hermeneutic code that functions by convention: it appears to be projecting a world, and it appears to require a response from the reader. Indeed, the very label 'realistic narrative' assumes that the genre will be responded to as one would to a realistic narrative.[31]

Both authorial *and* readerly activities are operating in and through Frei's category just as they were with the *bios*: the purpose of the author with/in the

28. Frei, *Identity of Jesus Christ*, p. 156.

29. Frei, *Identity of Jesus Christ*, pp. 170–71. Comstock observes that the story's meaning is thus located 'between' the text and the reader – in front of the text ('Truth or Meaning', pp. 125–6).

30. Frei, 'The "Literal Reading" of the Biblical Narrative', pp. 67, 70–1. This directional shift appears to be the result of Frei's suspicion that his category of realistic narrative is itself an extratextual, general hermeneutical category superimposed on the Gospels (ibid., p. 66).

31. One particular readerly response to this sub-genre – '[w]henever possible use the literal sense' – is voiced by Frei as being fundamental to the interpretation of realistic narrative (Hans W. Frei, *Types of Christian Theology* [eds George Hunsinger and William C. Placher; New Haven: Yale University Press, 1992], p. 14). Interestingly, for precritical readers of Scripture there existed another parallel convention: 'if it seemed clear that a biblical story was to be read literally, it followed automatically that it referred to and described actual historical occurrences'. That is to say, a literal reading of narratives has traditionally acknowledged salient historical (extratextual) references. Yet Frei has consistently been unclear about the factuality of the biblical narrative (especially the accounts of the resurrection), thus threatening 'to eclipse not the biblical narrative, but biblical claims to truth' (Frei, *Eclipse of Biblical Narrative*, p. 2; see also Watson, *Text, Church and World*, pp. 23–9, 224, for a critique of Frei).

genre is closely identified with the reception of, and response to, the realistic narrative by the reader. In fact, such an identification is the only one possible in the interaction between author and reader via the text – an interaction wherein purpose and response coincide in the world in front of the text. Thus, despite Frei's protestations to the contrary, readerly expectations governed by generic conventions are integral to interpretation and to the realization of authorial purpose; realistic narratives also perform 'work' like other genres, projecting worlds in front of their texts for their readers to inhabit – a rule-governed labour. The author–genre/text–reader triad remains fully operational even in Frei's conception of the realistic narrative.

Thus, on the one hand, there is Burridge who recognizes the Gospels as sub-genres from the vantage point of the *author*: determining how the Gospels were composed or created, *bioi* are seen as the paradigmatic form of the text, a form that antedated or was contemporaneous with the Gospels. On the other hand, there is Frei who perceives the Gospels as particular text-types from the station of the *reader*: his generic model is the realistic narrative, one that obviously post-dated the production of the Gospels. While both forms belong to the major genre of narrative, the one sub-genre asserts *this is how the Gospels came about*; the other exhorts *this is how the Gospels must be read.* The flexibility of these text-types appears to resolve this dilemma quite diplomatically, offending neither faction. Both modes of approach are valid and indeed necessary, for there are indeed two entities involved in the production and reception of a text, the author and the reader; genres generate rules that direct the literary activities of both. For the author, genre determines the genesis of the text, the representation of authorial purpose and the projection of the world in front of the text. For the reader, genre determines the 'heuresis' of the text; aided by the Rules of Genre, the projected world is discerned and valid application derived therefrom. The world in front of the text and its transhistorical intention is the textual embodiment of authorial purpose; the future-directed intention governs the reader's subsequent response to the text. This work holds that authorial purpose and readerly response conceptually co-localize in the world projection, irrespective of the nuances of generic categorization.

Thus far, the examination of primary genres has noted the looseness of genre compartmentalization. This is certainly not a hindrance to interpretive activity; neither does the plasticity of the form preclude the formulation of the Rules of Genre. While absolute precision and rigorous exactitude may not be possible, there is an adequacy of classification that, even as it restrains, also permits release. Within the broad bracket of narrative, whether one employs *bios* or realistic narrative to slot the Gospels, the rule-governed work of the genre is evident and recoverable – the purpose of the author directing the response of the reader, by means of the world in front of the text. For the Gospels, both genetic and heuristic transactions are governed by the particular world projected: the Christian 'eucatastrophe' – the complex of historical events portraying the person and redemptive work of Jesus Christ – that has 'cataclysmic beneficial effects'.[32] Despite the inexactness of generic borders, the same flexibility that gave authors at the proximal end of inscription free rein to adapt the generic forms for their purposes also allows readers, at the distal end of interpretation, the freedom to extend the reach of the text into their own futurity, by means of the projected world and its transhistorical intention. It is to further such a future-directed endeavour culminating in application that the Rules of Genre will be employed in the rest of this work.

For the consideration of the Rules of Primary Genre in the latter part of this chapter, broad categories of genre will be handled – narrative, prophecy, law and hymnody. The choice to inventory the rules of only four primary genres is, as will be seen, a practical one. However, this is not to deny the presence of a multiplicity of genres and sub-genres in the canonical Scriptures. As Heb. 1.1 declares, biblical speech acts are 'polygeneric': God spoke to his people πολυμερῶς καὶ πολυτρόπως πάλαι, utilizing a variety of generic language-games. Moreover, these genres often interlace in a 'transgeneric' fashion, when a larger work (book) in a single genre contains smaller texts (pericopes) in a variety of other genres (see below).[33] These multilayered interactions among the heterogeneous language-games of the Bible have important ramifications for the interpretive endeavour and, therefore, before the Rules of Primary Genre are proposed, the polygeneric and transgeneric nature of Scripture will be examined.

Polygeneric and transgeneric Scriptures

It is the multiplicity of primary genres that are enfolded within the secondary genre of the biblical canon that makes it polygeneric. This feature of Scripture predicts that texts in different genres display different facets of the projected world of the Bible, for each of the literary forms framing such worlds is itself theologically significant and deliberately employed: '[n]ot just any theology may be attached to the story form' or any other genre, for that matter.[34] Ricoeur

---

32. Kevin J. Vanhoozer, 'From Canon to Concept: "Same" and "Other" in the Relation between Biblical and Systematic Theology', *SBET* 12 (1994), pp. 96–124 (113).

33. Idem, 'God's Mighty Speech-Acts: The Doctrine of Scripture Today', in *A Pathway into the Holy Scripture* (eds P.E. Satterthwaite and D.F. Wright; Grand Rapids: Eerdmans, 1994), pp. 143–81 (173).

34. Genres are not merely decorations for ideas: 'literary genres of the Bible do not constitute a rhetorical facade which it would be possible to pull down in order to reveal some thought content that is indifferent to its literary vehicle'. See Paul Ricoeur, 'Toward a Hermeneutic of the Idea of Revelation', in *Essays on Biblical Interpretation* (trans. David Pellauer; ed. Lewis S. Mudge; Philadelphia: Fortress, 1979), pp. 73–118 (91). 'Literary form is not separable from philosophical content but is itself a part of content – an integral part of the search for and the statement of truth' (Martha C. Nussbaum, *Love's Knowledge: Essays on Philosophy and Literature* [New York: Oxford University Press, 1990], p. 3).

sees five distinct genres in Scripture – prophetic, narrative, prescriptive, wisdom, and hymnic discourses – as he deals primarily with the OT. In contrast, Goldingay assigns four: witnessing tradition (narrative), authoritative canon (law), inspired word (prophecy) and a less-specific category of experienced revelation (psalms, apocalypses, wisdom literature and epistles).[35] Whereas Burridge and Frei inclined towards extrabiblical categories to locate the genres of Scripture (*bioi* and realistic narratives serving as their respective models for the Gospels), both Ricoeur and Goldingay conduct their investigations with intrabiblical categories, generating classes of texts based primarily upon internal features. The fruits of the labour of neither pair are incompatible with the other. Depending on the breadth of literary entities (extrabiblial or intrabiblical) within which the interpreter seeks to locate the text of interest, a specific text may ostensibly be categorized differently. The scope is synchronic in the case of Burridge and Frei, restricting themselves, for the most part, to a text pattern belonging to a particular time frame: Graeco-Roman or eighteenth- and nineteenth-century Europe. It is diachronic in the case of Ricoeur and Goldingay who confine their analyses and classifications to the fully developed corpus of the canon. The flexibility of genres, as has been noted earlier, enables this freedom, and in no way inhibits productive interpretive activity.

Any number of other classifications and sub-classifications that generate genres and sub-genres might equally well be employed in the examination of the primary language-game. However, the recognition of, and respect for, a broad differentiation of text-types is more than sufficient for the successful interpretive move from text to praxis. Every categorization of primary genre, whether it be the fivefold compartmentalization of Ricoeur or the fourfold conception of Goldingay, will have as much imprecision about its boundaries as any other. The precise division of genres and the accurate disposition of texts therein, while quite a formidable undertaking, is not a particularly fruitful enterprise. The gain in genre specificity is not necessarily accompanied by an increase in hermeneutical productivity. For the discernment of the world in front of the text and its transhistorical intention, a broad classification is quite adequate. Acknowledging the polygeneric aspect of the Scriptures, the following account of primary genres will seek to enumerate the rules of a representative sample of the commonly accepted subsets of texts – narrative, law, prophecy and hymnody. Without making any claim to comprehensiveness in the consideration of generic categories, these are employed simply to demonstrate the operation of the Rules of Primary Genre and their utility for the discrimination of the world in front of the text.

A foundational contribution of the polygeneric aspect of Scripture is the manner in which God is named – the depiction of the ultimate referent of the

---

35. Ricoeur, 'Toward a Hermeneutic of the Idea of Revelation', pp. 73–95; and John Goldingay, *Models for Interpretation of Scripture* (Grand Rapids: Eerdmans, 1995), pp. 1–2, 4.

world projected. Each biblical genre works to name God in a particular fashion, and the author, employing that genre, utilizes this inherent propensity to advantage. In narrative, God is the omnipresent actor in the founding events of the community of faith; in prophecy, as omniscient authority, he appears as the voice beyond the prophet; in law, he is the sovereign one who legislates. God, in other genres, is often hidden and transcendent (wisdom writings), or personal and immanent (hymnic literature), and comprehensible and communicable (the Epistles). This multidimensional reflection of God's dialectical relationship to his creation (the projected world) is an integral part of the representative work performed by the polygeneric Scriptures. Corresponding to the multiplicity of genres in the Bible, there is thus a complex and polyphonic 'en-titlement' of God. At this very general level of depiction, then, God as the protagonist interacting with mankind is viewed in particular ways by each genre. The canon is thus a 'complex simplex', a chorus of diverse voices testifying to the same multifaceted world of God and his relationship to his creation. Each text therein projects a different aspect of that world.[36]

As may be expected, such an imbrication of genres within the polygeneric text has momentous theological consequences. Not only does each genre, in its own fashion, frame the world projected by particular biblical texts, another peculiar feature of this phenomenon is the manner in which genres 'interact' when placed in textual proximity within a single book. Such generic interactions sharpen the focus on the projected world and clarify its particular facets. Indeed, Ricoeur observed, '[a]n exhaustive inquiry, if this were possible, would perhaps reveal that all the forms of discourse together constitute a circular system and that the theological content of each of them receives its meaning from the total constellation of the forms of discourse'.[37] A unique organization of time is manifested when narrative and non-narrative genres are interwoven and juxtaposed. These intercalations give rise to theologically significant tensions that serve both to express and to explicate matters of importance to Christian faith and practice. The nuanced details of the projected world, shaped by interacting genres, contribute to the composite, plenary world portrayed by Scripture.[38] The temporal relationship between narrative and each of the other genres will be considered briefly below, within the discussion of the Rules of Primary Genre.

36. Paul Ricoeur, 'Naming God', *USQR* 34 (1979), pp. 215–27 (217–22, 225); Kevin J. Vanhoozer, *The Drama of Doctrine: A Canonical-Linguistic Approach to Christian Theology* (Louisville: Westminster/John Knox Press, 2005), p. 287.

37. Paul Ricoeur, *From Text to Action: Essays in Hermeneutics, II* (trans. Kathleen Blamey and John B. Thompson; Evanston: Northwestern University Press, 1991), p. 92.

38. Idem, 'Philosophical Hermeneutics and Theological Hermeneutics: Ideology, Utopia, and Faith', in *Protocol of the Seventeenth Colloquy, 4 November 1975* (ed. W. Wuellner; Berkeley: The Center for Hermeneutical Studies in Hellenistic and Modern Culture, 1976), pp. 1–28 (9–10). Also see idem, 'Biblical Time', in *Figuring the Sacred: Religion, Narrative, and Imagination* (trans. David Pellauer; ed. Mark I. Wallace; Minneapolis: Fortress, 1995), pp. 167–80.

While the fastidious and meticulous taxonomy of texts into genres is itself impractical, it seems nigh impossible when one examines the variety of pericopal forms that usually constitute the larger categories of texts. For instance, a specific biblical book, characterized at the *macro* level as belonging to a particular primary genre, quite often comprises a multiplicity of discrete genres at the *micro* level of the pericope.[39] This is the 'transgeneric' property of Scripture – a larger work or text considered to be in a single genre assimilating within itself pericopes in a plurality of primary genres. For instance, the book of Daniel contains pericopes of apocalyptic writing as well as narrative; the Gospel of Luke contains parabolic literature and poetry in addition to the proper content of the *bios*; the Epistles, as was noted earlier, contain pericopes in a diversity of literary forms; the post-Pentateuchal prophetic books contain narratives; etc.[40] Therefore, though one might be handling a particular genre at the broader level of the book, when the focus converges upon the narrower scope of the pericope, standard genre assignments may need revision. In other words, panoramic taxonomies are unsustainable when zooming in upon the specific terrain of basic, functional textual units. This, of course, is not to deny that there is considerable value in broad generic divisions, especially for the enumeration of their rules, as is undertaken below. However, a comprehensive and exhaustive inventory of texts into specific types is ultimately an unmanageable task, given the transgeneric interweaving and amalgamation of language-games.

The particular texts chosen for the elaboration of the Rules of Primary Genre in the next section will themselves demonstrate this transgeneric property: the rules for narrative are illustrated with a text properly consigned to the prophetic section of the canon, the book of Jonah; the rules for prophecy are acquired from two narrative vignettes of the prophet Nathan, wherein the man of God exercises his prophetic office; the rules for law are drawn from the reading of a NT imperative, among other texts; and the rules for hymnody are exemplified in a portion of the Pentateuch – the Song of the Sea, a victory psalm celebrating the exodus. Such a transgeneric approach underscores the commingling of various genres, reflecting the impracticality of a rigid differentiation of texts in the biblical canon. Nevertheless, this work holds that, when working with

---

39. Pericopes, in this work, are considered the fundamental and essential units of text – irrespective of genre – that are utilized in ecclesial and homiletical settings (see Chapter 4).

40. The pattern of poetry following immediately upon prose within the same biblical book is an especially intriguing example of the 'cross-pollination' between genres; these transgeneric texts are not rare in Scripture: Judges 5, containing the song of Deborah and Barak celebrating the victory over Sisera, follows the prose account in Judges 4; and Hannah's song in 1 Sam. 2.1-10, rejoicing in the birth of Samuel, interprets the events of 1 Samuel 1. Perhaps the *Magnificat* could be seen in the same light, Lk. 1.46-55 rendering in poetry the significance of the narrative in 1.26-38 of Mary's annunciation and conception. See below for an analytical comparison of the prose and poetic accounts of the exodus (Exodus 14 and 15, respectively) to derive the rules of hymnody.

pericopes of Scripture, a broad breakdown of genres and an enumeration of their cardinal rules is not only possible but also adequate for the discovery of the world in front of the text.

Rules of primary genre

As has already been stated, the rules propounded here partake more of the nature of convenient principles that guide interpretation, rather than of categorical precepts that govern it. A fairly relaxed understanding of genre boundaries, *à la* Wittgenstein, contributes to the malleability of the rules and their tractable disposition. Flexible and adaptable, generic rules aid the activities of the theologian-homiletician seeking to comprehend the biblical text for application purposes. Their primary utility is for hermeneutic transactions that attempt to educe the world projected in front of the text, and to this end these rules are tailored. For the most part they are descriptive rather than prescriptive, predictable principles rather than *de novo* concoctions – signposts, as Wittgenstein was wont to refer to them.[41] This work holds that the Rules of Genres herein discussed are widely – if not universally – instantiated in reading practices of Christian interpretive communities. This also means, of course, that there are instances of significant local variation in the application of these rules; there might very well be communities and schools of reading practices wherein some or all of these rules are neglected entirely. However, the fairly broad deployment of these rules qualifies them as worthy of attention.

While these guidelines are derived from a phenomenology of reading, it is obvious that such phenomenological description is to some degree determined by the standpoint of the describer. That, of course, is not to disparage the apprehension of phenomena from the particular perspective of a given observer. As Watson notes,

> [t]o appeal for an autonomous 'description' is to ignore the fact that there is no such thing as a pure description of a neutral object; description always presupposes a prior construction of the object in terms of a given interpretative paradigm.[42]

With regard to those rules that specifically pertain to, and are brought to bear upon, the biblical text, the bias of this work towards a Protestant, evangelical mode of interpretation may at certain points be apparent. This is likely to be most evident in the discussion of the Rules of Secondary Genre (see Chapter 3), where the canonical corpus under examination has a composition that is materially affected by the particular Christian tradition to which the interpreter belongs. Nevertheless, even as a bias is acknowledged, an attempt has been

---

41. Wittgenstein, *Philosophical Investigations*, ¶85; also see Frederick Schauer, *Playing by the Rules: A Philosophical Examination of Rule-Based Decision-Making in Law and Life* (Oxford: Clarendon Press, 1991), pp. 1–3.

42. Watson, *Text, Church and World*, pp. 32–3.

made there to express those Rules of Secondary Genre in a reasonably broad and 'generic' fashion. In contrast, in the present chapter, where the Rules of Primary Genre are to be discussed, the issue of personal perspective, though still active, is considerably less visible. This, no doubt, reflects the fact that what is considered under primary genre are textual schemata and literary forms that are widely utilized across a variety of literary traditions, both religious and otherwise. The Rules of Narrative, for instance (the Rules of Plot and Inter-action), are applicable to texts both biblical and extrabiblical. However, even with the Rules of Primary Genre, biblical genres, it will be seen, merit special consideration. For instance, with prophecy, the stance adopted will reflect the understanding of the Christian tradition that prophetic genre is unique to divine discourse. Nonetheless, even for this unique genre, the statement of its particular rules (Rules of Anticipation and Correction) are enunciated in a broadly applicable fashion that recognizes their wide instantiation within the larger Christian community.

To reiterate, these rules are intended as guidelines. As they prompt and promote reading in a particular manner, the interpreter is beckoned to attend to specific foci of the text – foci that must not be neglected if the reader is to recognize the pragmatic elements of the pericope. Drawing notice to such elements, the rules usher the reader towards the destination of the projected world.

The following listing of rules for each primary genre is not exhaustive: there may be more rules that could be proposed for every genre. If one takes sub-genres into consideration, one might very well expect an overwhelming proliferation of such guidelines. Rather than attempt to create a comprehensive compendium of rules to cover every aspect of every text in every genre, the more distinctive rules of the prominent language-games will be elucidated, particularly those rules that aid the interpreter in the discernment of the world in front of the text. The limitation of this examination to four primary genres is justified in that it not only enables an adequate consideration of the major categories of texts but also keeps the enumerative and descriptive task within manageable limits, without being inattentive to the practical needs of the theologian-homiletician. Such a one would be ill-served by the unmindful multiplication of prescriptions and prohibitions, caveats and cautions. The essential goal of this enterprise is to illuminate the operation of the Rules of Primary Genre in the depiction of the world in front of these texts; for this purpose the exploitation of the four basic categories and the more dominant rules of each will suffice.

Rules of Genre: narrative

Narrative creates the most visible scaffolding of time in the canon.[43] Inasmuch as narrative penetrates and weaves its way through all the other genres of Scripture – indeed, all its genres may be said to subsist within narrative – its emplot-

---

43. Ricoeur, 'Biblical Time', p. 179.

ted time influences the thrust of every other genre. Through this interweaving complementarity of genres (the transgeneric property of Scripture), God is named and time is structured. Redemption is wrought and hope is restored. Fixed in time, the events of narrative give temporal structure to all the other genres of Scripture, making the whole Bible, in this sense, a narrative – one magnificent story from Genesis to Revelation.

Every historical narrative, Hayden White declared, 'has as its latent or manifest purpose the desire to *moralize* the events of which it treats', thus creating a '*moral* drama'.[44] This moralizing impulse might have led to the innovation of biblical narrative as a form of prose art rarely seen before in the ancient Near East. The coherent and sequential emplotment of the events in the life of God's people and the interactions of its various characters (including the divine protagonist) makes the projection of the world in front of the text comprehensible, and the appropriation of such a world in the future circumstances of readers persuasive.[45] In the rhetoric of forensic discourse, Quintilian noted that 'narrative [*narratio*] was not invented simply to acquaint the judge with the facts, but rather to ensure that he agrees with us' – a moralizing impulse, indeed (*Inst.* 4.2.21).

The story that gets told in a particular fashion in narrative instantiates one of the many ways the selected events and interpersonal encounters could have been represented; the path actually chosen by the narrator was one that would effectively project the world in front of the text and culminate in application for the reader. This ethical objective is accomplished primarily by way of the plot and the purposeful interaction of its characters; these two predominant features mark the primary genre of narrative and generate its two rules, the Rule of Plot and the Rule of Interaction. From the author's 'genetic' point of view, plot

---

44. Hayden White, 'The Value of Narrativity in the Representation of Reality', in *On Narrative* (ed. W.J.T. Mitchell; Chicago: The University of Chicago Press, 1981), pp. 1–23 (11, 14, 19–20). He asks rhetorically, 'Could we ever narrativize *without* moralizing?' (23). Indeed, 'narrative has the power to teach what it means to be *moral* beings' (idem, 'The Narrativization of Real Events', in *On Narrative* [ed. W.J.T. Mitchell; Chicago: The University of Chicago Press, 1981], pp. 249–54 [253]).

45. Robert Alter, *The Art of Biblical Narrative* (New York: Basic Books, 1981), pp. 24–7; and Dale Patrick and Allen Scult, *Rhetoric and Biblical Interpretation* (Sheffield: Almond, 1990), pp. 37–8, 41. 'It is this power to capture the universal in the particular that made their stories live on and continue to teach long after the persons and their fates were of no practical concern to the reader' (67). Roberts calls such texts 'constitutive narratives', those that give an account of persons and events, in the matrix of a particular moral outlook. Constitutive narratives go beyond displaying virtue: the persons and events depicted constitute the 'very grammar of those virtues' they prescribe, making up what is distinctive about them. This concept also reminds the reader that though the focus, for applicational purposes, is on second-order referents, the neglect of first-order referents – those constitutive aspects of narrative – will only impoverish the interpretation, to the detriment of the Church. See Robert C. Roberts, 'Narrative Ethics', in *A Companion to Philosophy of Religion* (eds Philip L. Quinn and Charles Taliaferro; Cambridge, MA: Blackwell, 1997), pp. 473–80 (478–79).

and character interaction enable the narrator to broadcast the projected world. From the reader's heuristic vantage point, they enable, in turn, the discovery of that world. It is when confronted by this world (and the transhistorical intention it bears) that the reader is directed to make a response. The determination of this projected world, therefore, is of great significance to the theologian-homiletician expositing Scripture. In such an interpretive endeavour that deals with narrative, the Rule of Plot and the Rule of Interaction assume critical roles. An examination of the plot and character interactions in the book of Jonah will exemplify the workings of these rules of the primary genre of narrative and explain how they aid in identifying the world in front of the text.

Rule of Plot
The Rule of Plot prepares the interpreter of biblical narrative to attend to the structured sequence of events emplotted in the text, in order to apprehend the world projected by that text.

A plot is a sequence of causally related events. Aristotle's conception of the plot of tragedy gave it 'a beginning and middle and end'. He argued that 'well-constructed plots must not therefore begin and end at random'; instead, they are to follow a deliberate scheme founded upon the moral framework underlying the emplotment.[46] Narratives, thus, have an ideology – 'the system that governs the conceptual vision of the world in all or part of the work'; such a moral fabric in the scriptural narratives is, in essence, a theocentric vision.[47] Therefore the plotted series of scenes and episodes is not displayed in haphazard fashion; the selection, ordering and rhetorical representation of those events is a function of the trajectory of the narrative – the world the narrator wishes to project in front of the text.

The Rule of Plot uncovers Jonah's story as a satirical account with a theological 'sting' that reveals, in its moral framework, a particular facet of the larger world in which God relates to his creation.[48] Interestingly, this prophet also made a showing in 2 Kgs 14.23-7, prophesying during the reign of Jeroboam II over the Northern Kingdom in the early eighth century BCE. The thrust of

46. *Poet.* 7.3-7. The author of the Fourth Gospel, for instance, explicitly remarks upon the selection made of incidents in Jesus' life, with the theological and moral goal of bringing readers to a belief in Christ for life in his name (Jn 20.30-1).

47. See Paul Ricoeur, *Time and Narrative* (3 vols; trans. Kathleen McLaughlin and David Pellauer; Chicago: The University of Chicago Press, 1984–8), II, pp. 93–4; idem, 'On Narrative', *CI* 7 (1980), pp. 169–90 (171); and J.P. Fokkelman, *Reading Biblical Narrative: An Introductory Guide* (trans. Ineke Smit; Louisville: Westminster/John Knox Press, 1999), pp. 77–8. Also see Seymour Chatman, *Story and Discourse: Narrative Structure in Fiction and Film* (Ithaca, NY: Cornell University Press, 1978), pp. 43–7; and idem, *Reading Narrative Fiction* (New York: Macmillan, 1993), pp. 18, 20–26.

48. Ernst R. Wendland, 'Text Analysis and the Genre of Jonah (Part 1)', *JETS* 39 (1996), pp. 191–206 (198).

that message was to demonstrate God's willingness, despite the wickedness of the king, to help Israel in her affliction. It is that same compassion of God that is in view here as a major component of the ideology of this prophetic book. The world projected through the plot is one in which God still resolves to save people, despite evil abounding; furthermore, it is a world in which God expects his agents and his people to reflect the same compassion that he exhibits.

As Jonah attempts to flee the call of God to proclaim the fate of Nineveh, his getaway vehicle, a ship, is caught in a threatening storm. The sailors cast lots (Jon. 1.7) to discover on whose account this evil (רע) had come upon them; it was רע that had triggered the whole story in the first place (1.2; 3.8) – Nineveh's evil that had come up before Yahweh. This theme of 'evil', apparent at the very commencement of the plot, threads its way through the entire narrative, tying the story coherently together.[49] The evil (רע) that Yahweh threatened the pagan nation with (in 3.10) had, indeed, befallen pagans, but the wrong ones – these seafarers. The plot continues to link these discrete events: a way of escape is discovered, but from an unexpected source, the captain of the ship. 'Call (קרא) upon your god', he exhorts the sleeping Jonah, 'so that we will not perish (ולא נאבד)' (1.6). Another pagan leader, the Ninevite king, would issue an identical command in 3.8-9 (also using קרא and ולא נאבד). These parallels between the sailors and the Ninevites and their perilous estates are purposefully introduced: the response of the former to their imminent maritime רע adumbrates the response of the latter to their own impending doom of רע. Jonah, the plot implicitly informs the reader, should have been warned that the next set of pagans he would encounter would also turn to God. In a pointed act of irony, the writer has the ship's crew cry out to none other than Yahweh; they explicitly confess his sovereignty as well (1.14). Unaware of all these nuances, the prophet, in contrast, can only make a hypocritical confession to the boatmen: he is fleeing from the God he has just acknowledged as omnipotent and on the very sea that he has just affirmed Yahweh created (1.9). Upon being offered by Jonah the option to remove physically the problem from their midst, the sailors, curiously enough, have mercy upon this Hebrew and attempt to row harder. The Rule of Plot thus makes no attempt to be subtle about the moral thrust of the narrative and what acceptable behaviour is; the pagans are exhibited in a far better light than the man of God. When Jonah finally gets ejected overboard, the turbulence subsides, and the prophet is swallowed by a great fish appointed by God.

The nature of the plot has now become evident: it is a satire. Jonah 1 conspicuously displays its characteristic features: the fantastic (great storms that calm in an instant and great fish that swallow humans), the grotesque (pagans who worship Yahweh while Yahweh's prophet attempts to escape him) and the absurd (slumbering prophets and supplicating pagans). Satires have definite targets – in this case it is the self-centred and hypocritical prophet; satirical

---

49. See Jon. 1.2, 7, 8; 3.8, 10 (×2); 4.1, 2, 6.

assaults are typically indirect – Jonah is unmasked for what he is when he is compared with the other personæ of the story; satire flays hypocrisy; and satire tends to emphasize events from the external vantage point of actions and their effects, rather than by depicting internal thoughts and contemplations.[50] This satirical narrative of Jonah, like other thinly veiled literary productions of the same order, adopts a prominent ethical stance, pointing to an implicit moral framework underlying the narrative: a world in which certain attitudes and actions are deemed appropriate and others not. With sharp irony, this theological undergirding is manifest even in Jonah's prayer within the belly of the fish; on display is his ethnocentric prejudice as he derides the pagan sailors as idolaters who forsake faithfulness (חֶסֶד, 2.8). Yet it was precisely those 'worthless' ones who were truly loyal and whose behaviour was implicitly lauded by the writer. In fact, it is Jonah who later slights the חֶסֶד of Yahweh (even as he cites Exod. 34.6 in 4.2), deprecating the grace of a God who deigns to spare Nineveh. The satire continues unremittingly for the rest of the narrative. While God seeks to show mercy by averting the prophesied reprisal for the רַע of Nineveh, Jonah is scandalized by Yahweh's forgiveness (רַע, according to the prophet; 4.1).

The Rule of Plot thus presides over the satirical narrative, aiding the projection of a world in front of that text; it portrays a God who is gracious, and deprecates Jonah as a hypocritical foil for God's plans, one who apparently lacks any compassion whatsoever towards unbelievers. The sailors, in their turn, are depicted as ironic foils for the disgruntled prophet, displaying both mercy and the fear of God; these attitudes in the projected world, the narrator implicitly suggests, should be exhibited by God's people.

Rule of Interaction

The Rule of Interaction directs the interpreter of biblical narrative to attend to the interpersonal transactions of the characters as represented therein, in order to apprehend the world projected by the text.

While one might conceive of a narrative or recount a story that focuses solely upon a single human character, such a concept is virtually unknown in biblical texts. God is always present, explicitly or implicitly. He is one character that cannot be eliminated and, therefore, biblical narrative has at the very minimum a two-way interaction of its actants, mankind and God. In the world framed by the Rule of Interaction, isolation is impossible; Jonah's attempts to escape Yahweh are truly in vain. Encounters in word and deed between prophet and God exemplify the Rule of Interaction throughout the book.

Such interpersonal transactions in narrative are not purposeless; the confrontations between characters are neither random nor capricious. Rather, they are rendered with purpose, serving to depict the goals attributed to agents and,

---

50. John C. Holbert, ' "Deliverance Belongs to Yahweh!": Satire in the Book of Jonah', *JSOT* 21 (1981), pp. 59–81 (62, 68–70).

on a broader canvas, to portray the world in front of the text. The core of such
character interactions in narrative is conflict. Biblical narratives are no exception; conflicts abound therein: God vs. Satan, good vs. evil, discipleship vs.
rebellion, the way of God vs. the way of man, etc. These conflicts and their
resolutions enable the projected world to be enacted and visualized in concrete
relationships between God and man, and between man and man.[51] Thus, in and
through these interpersonal dealings, the Rule of Interaction, acting in concert
with the Rule of Plot, furthers the narrator's projection of the world in front of
the text.

Though the purpose of the book is not explicitly stated, Jonah, as was noted,
is clearly a foil for God and his plans, an anti-hero whose own schemes collide
with Yahweh's designs. This is the main conflict of the narrative generated
by the interactions between these two protagonists.[52] At the very onset of the
story, set in motion by Yahweh's commission to the prophet, a complication is
encountered. While divine summons routinely elicited protestations from the
ones called (Moses, Gideon, Isaiah and Jeremiah, for instance), Jonah does not
even deign to debate; he decamps. The conflict is evident with the prophet's
very name: he is Jonah *ben Amittai* (בֶּן־אֲמִתַּי), 'the son of faithfulness'. Surely
one could have expected only obedience from him in his relationship with
Yahweh? Why Jonah decides to abscond is not immediately obvious; his goal
in avoiding any possible interaction with God – a futile enterprise when dealing
with omnipresent deity – is yet to be clarified.

The conflict between Yahweh and Jonah continues with the latter being
ejected overboard and being swallowed by a fish sent by the former. Jonah 2, set
in the belly of the beast, does not advance the narrative, but simply recollects
Jonah's prayer in the fish – another dialogical interaction between God and man.
The key word in the original command of Yahweh to 'call' (1.2) reappears in
this encounter (2.1). The prophet is certainly calling out; however, it is neither
for God nor against Nineveh that he does so, but for himself; the entire prayer
emphasizes the first-person singular. Compounding this self-centredness, Jonah
immediately proceeds to blame God for his predicament, accusing the latter of
having cast him into the deep, conveniently forgetting that it was he, himself,
who had requested to be thrown overboard (2.3; see 1.12).[53] Though couched
in prayer, this accusatory (unilateral) interaction between Jonah and Yahweh
is another exercise in hypocrisy. The prophet's traumatic experiences on the
water and in the fish do not appear to have taught him that it was always in
his own best interests to align his goals with those of God; the two are still at

51. Grant R. Osborne, *The Hermeneutical Spiral: A Comprehensive Introduction to Biblical
Interpretation* (Downers Grove: InterVarsity, 1991), pp. 158–9.

52. Elmer Dyck, 'Jonah among the Prophets: A Study in Canonical Context', *JETS* 33 (1990),
pp. 63–73 (63).

53. Holbert, ' "Deliverance Belongs to Yahweh!" ', pp. 71, 74.

cross-purposes. The Rule of Interaction thereby draws attention to the conflict between the characters even in Jonah's rendezvous with God in prayer. The prophet ends his 'psalm', claiming a superior ground, promising to sacrifice to God and fulfil his vows (2.9). Remarkably, those sailors whom he had cavalierly dismissed in his prayer (2.8) had already done both (1.16); Jonah, for his part, would do neither in this book. Even in the absence of the sailors in this chapter, and despite the fact that they are but a 'backdrop', their composite and corporate character is in stark contrast with the prophet: while Jonah is a foil for Yahweh, the sailors are a foil for Jonah. Their behaviour, especially their dealings with Yahweh (1.14), should have been a model for the prophet. Jonah, instead, is one whose conflict with God marks him as a rebel unwilling to see things God's way. A seemingly grand declaration concludes Jonah's prayer: 'Salvation belongs to Yahweh' (2.9). Jonah's attitude, however, was constantly gainsaying this creedal affirmation.[54]

The interaction between Jonah and God resumes in Jonah 3 after the latter is regurgitated on to terra firma, with Yahweh attempting to reanimate his original strategy. Jonah is therefore confronted, once again, with his commission (3.1-2). This time, the prophet acquiesces; on the surface, one might surmise that Jonah has finally gotten his act together and harmonized his goals with those of God, eliminating all conflict. That, however, turns out not to be the case: Jonah goes to Nineveh and half-heartedly executes his commission, uttering just five words (in Hebrew), the shortest prophetic oracle on record.[55] The entire city, amazingly, is transformed (3.5-9), a conversion of epic proportions that involved attitudes of repentance and acts of penitence undertaken not only by the human populace but by the land's beasts as well! Salvation, indeed, belongs to Yahweh. By the Rule of Interaction, the intended outcome of God's design, the goal of his business with Jonah and Nineveh, is finally revealed: he had desired the Ninevites' repentance all along and that desire is consummated (3.10). At this juncture the misalignment between the goal of Jonah and that of God becomes most pronounced and acute. In response to God's magnanimous act of mercy towards Nineveh, Jonah becomes enraged; he even sees 'it' (Nineveh's repentance?

54. 'It is no wonder that immediately after Jonah shouts, "Deliverance belongs to Yahweh!" the big fish throws up!' (Holbert, ' "Deliverance Belongs to Yahweh!" ', p. 74).

55. R.J. Lubeck considers Jonah's sermon to be a contaminated version of what God had probably commanded him to proclaim. Quite uncharacteristic of the spirit of other biblical oracles of judgement, Jonah proclaims an inexorable and inescapable fate: there is no reason propounded, no repentance proposed, no hope proffered, no remnant preserved (see the Rules of Prophecy, below). Also, one cannot but notice the absence of the modifying phrase 'according to the word of Yahweh' with the verb of proclamation (קרא, 3.4). It is significant that this phrase qualified the two other key verbs in 3.2-3 (קום and הלך, 'arise' and 'go'); these verbs, along with קרא, constituted the core of Jonah's original commission from God in 1.2 ('*Arise, go* to Nineveh the great city and *cry* against it') ('Prophetic Sabotage: A Look at Jonah 3.2–4', *TrinJ* 9 [1988], pp. 37–46).

Yahweh's repentance?) as 'great evil' (וַיֵּרַע ...רָעָה גְדוֹלָה, 4.1). The quintessence
of the conflict between prophet and deity is now unveiled: all along Jonah had
feared Yahweh would relent and not give the Ninevites their due. In fact, in
Jonah's eyes, Nineveh was not very different from Sodom and Gomorrah, cities
that Yahweh overthrew (הָפַךְ, Gen. 19.21, 25, 29; the same word was used by
Jonah in his prophetic threat to Nineveh in 3.4).[56] God's mercy went against
Jonah's self-righteous and hypocritical grain. Quite strangely, the pagan sailors
– unpretentious, self-deprecating, merciful, and loyal – and even the Ninevites,
appeared to be more aligned with God's purposes than the prophet was. While
God's חֶסֶד directed his actions, Jonah's anger and self-righteousness drove his.
The conflict between the two characters is carried on in their interactions in
chapter 4. Yahweh questions Jonah's right to be angry (4.4) and proceeds to
give the prophet an object lesson utilizing a shade-bearing plant that grows and
withers within a matter of hours, raising and dashing Jonah's petty hopes (4.6-7).
Narrative closure is achieved with Yahweh's final rhetorical question (4.11): how
could Jonah who had compassion on a plant that was there one day and gone the
next begrudge Yahweh's compassion for 120,000 humans ... and many animals?
Even in this final remonstrance, the Rule of Interaction and the conflict between
the two main personages of the story point to a world wherein it is expected of
God's people that they will be merciful themselves.

In sum, through the representation of the mutual dealings between the characters of the narrative, the Rule of Interaction helps project a world in which
God's lovingkindness and mercy are extended towards those who repent, even
Gentiles, even pagans. God's compassion and Jonah's utter lack of appreciation
thereof, while even the 'ungodly' sailors and Ninevites respond to Yahweh, are
the driving forces of the conflict in the mutual interactions of these protagonists.
Moreover, the projected world is not only one where the grace of God shines
brilliantly, it is also one where God's people potentially reflect and display those
same characteristics.

As they frame the world projected by the narrative text, the Rule of Plot and
the Rule of Interaction implicitly call for a response. The narrative closed with
Yahweh's query, and Jonah's response remains unrecorded. Indeed, the silence
of the narrator at this finale is a significant element of the narrative design: the
plot reaches its assigned ending with a concluding verbal interaction, though
one-sided, between God and the sulking prophet. Both rules converge at this
terminus in a query that continues to echo in the ears of readers: *Will you be*
merciful like the God who called you? Thus the narrative, by means of the Rules
of Plot and Interaction, is portraying a world wherein the attitudes and actions
of God's people are commensurate with and reflect God's own magnanimity
and grace; this is a call to inhabit the displayed world in alignment with God's

---

56. David M. Gunn and Danna Nolan Fewell, *Narrative in the Hebrew Bible* (Oxford: Oxford
University Press, 1993), p. 139.

values. The projected world is thus a 'thick description' of the communicative act represented by the text and framed by the genre through its Rules of Plot and Interaction, a secondary level of reference that facilitates the homiletical move from text to praxis.[57]

Rules of Genre: prophecy

The prototypic case of the 'word of God', this genre depicts the prophet speaking in the name of deity – 'the speech of another behind the speech of the prophet'.[58] Prophecy is the paradigmatic scriptural genre for God's explicit second-person address to listeners. Not only in the direct nature of its divine discourse but also in its manœuvres with time prophecy maintains a singular rank in the canon. The starting point of the prophet was the future he was called to proclaim. Prophecy may therefore be considered as history from the vantage point of the future. However, though the future was the launching pad of prophecy, this genre invoked both the past and the present in its utterances, usually focusing upon the misdeeds of its audience. The entire spectrum of time thus makes an appearance in prophetic oracles for, in espying the eschatological future, prophecy understands that 'the Coming One is no other than he who has already dealt with Israel in past history and has spoken to it, and to whom the present Israel is therefore responsible'. It is the narrative constancy and consistency of God that unites time in prophecy: the 'work' (מַעֲשֶׂה) of God denotes his activity in the future (Isa. 5.19), in the past (5.12; 28.21) and, indeed, represents the whole compass of his exertions (10.12).[59]

As are other genres, prophecy, too, is rooted in narrative; the prophets address the same situations and presuppose the same structures as does the

57. In a classic description of intentionality, contrasting a wink and an involuntary eyelid twitch, Gilbert Ryle introduced the notion of 'thick description' ('a many-layered sandwich') – the characterization of actions so as not to lose their intentionality (Gilbert Ryle, *Collected Essays* [vol. 2 of *Collected Papers*; New York: Barnes and Noble, 1971], pp. 480–96). Vanhoozer effectively adopted this metaphor for textual interpretation: 'A description is sufficiently thick when it allows us to appreciate everything the author is doing in a text' (*Is There a Meaning in This Text?*, p. 284 [italics removed]). An adequate interpretation of a text is, thus, a matter of offering a thick description of what the author has done by means of the discourse, that is, both first- *and* second-order referents. A thick description thus explicates the world in front of the text that, implicitly bearing the transhistorical intention, prepares the way for the move to application.

58. Ricoeur, 'Toward a Hermeneutic of the Idea of Revelation', p. 75. Nicholas Wolterstorff reminds the reader that God did not bypass human authors; prophets were his spokesmen, and their utterances his 'deputized discourses', the phenomenon of 'speaking in the name of', akin to the official pronouncements of an ambassador commissioned to represent a head of state (*Divine Discourse: Philosophical Reflections on the Claim that God Speaks* [Cambridge: Cambridge University Press, 1995], pp. 43–4).

59. Hans Walter Wolff, 'The Understanding of History in the Old Testament Prophets', in *Essays on Old Testament Interpretation* (trans. Keith R. Crim; ed. Claus Westermann; London: SCM Press, 1963), pp. 336–65 (337–8, 341).

primary history in which their oracles are enfolded. Traditionally, the 'narrativization' of prophecy has been specifically marked by including the books of
history from Joshua to 2 Kings within the division 'Former Prophets'.[60] The
interaction between the prophetic genre and that of the narrative in which it is
embedded is a dialectical process that contributes to the larger story of the OT.
While the prophets depict the disruption of the flow of narrative by retribution,
they are also quick to augur the irruption of relief in the streams of the future.
Future hope glimmers amid the gloom of present hopelessness: 'narrative when
touched by prophetic eschatology liberates a potential of hope'.[61] From such
a bifid purpose – reprisal and rehabilitation – arises the two rules of prophetic
genre: the Rule of Anticipation and the Rule of Correction.

For the demonstration of these two rules that are closely related to each other,
the prophet Nathan's two appearances before King David in 2 Samuel 7 and 12
will be treated as exemplars.[62] The choice of the Nathan Oracle and the Davidic
Debacle as models of the prophetic voice is justified by the transgeneric nature
of Scripture: these prophetic snapshots lie within the narrative genre of their surrounding texts (the 'narrativization' of prophecy). Both incidents were precipi-
tated by God's sending of Nathan (2 Sam. 7.5; 12.1). Both pronouncements by
the prophet were punctuated by assertions that it was indeed Yahweh, himself,
who was speaking (7.5, 8, 11; and 12.7, 11). Each message had its origin in the
particular circumstances of the present, but both looked to the past and the future
as well. The king was reminded of what had been, what is and what would be.
Both words, one of anticipation and the other of correction, emphasized God's
demand for faithful conduct from the addressee: a response was sought from
the reader by means of the projected world framed by these rules.[63]

Rule of Anticipation
*The Rule of Anticipation affirms that, in the interpretation of prophetic texts,
consideration must be given to the eschatological thrust of the prophecy to
discern the projected world of hope wherein a sovereign God's purposes for his
people are ultimately fulfilled.*

60. 'Who are the former prophets? – R. Huna said: They are David, Samuel and Solomon'
(*b. Soṭah* 48b). The references in the book of Zechariah to the 'former prophets' (1.4; 7.7) also
lend this distinction credibility.

61. Ricoeur, 'Biblical Time', p. 176.

62. Nathan's third cameo in 1 Kings 1 is markedly different from his role as Yahweh's spokesman in 2 Samuel 7 and 12; absent in the account in 1 Kings is any attribution of his counsel as a
word from God.

63. Ronald E. Clements, *The Conscience of the Nation: A Study of Early Israelite Prophecy*
(London: Oxford University Press, 1967), pp. 16–17. Also of significance are the other elements
of similarity between 2 Samuel 7 and 12: God's appointment of David (7.8; 12.7); 'house' (7.16,
18; 12.8, 10); 'will never depart' (God's lovingkindness, 7.15; the sword, 12.10); God's raising up
(a descendant, 7.12; evil, 12.11); and 'I will do/make' (עשׂה, 7.11, 25; 12.12). See Michael Avioz,
Nathan's Oracle (2 Samuel 7) and Its Interpreters (Bern, Switzerland: Peter Lang, 2005), p. 60.

'Surely the Lord GOD does nothing, unless he reveals his secret counsel to his servants the prophets' (Amos 3.7). Whether it was the promise of restoration or the proclamation of retribution, the prophets provided a glimpse of the future as the word of God came to them. The Rule of Anticipation, however, focuses on the restorative aspects of such prospective previews; the warnings of future doom, intended to rectify current behaviour, will be considered as belonging to the Rule of Correction. While every prophetic book, taken as a whole, is undoubtedly anticipatory in this fashion, not every pericope therein may proffer this word (and world) of hope. To illustrate the Rule of Anticipation in prophecy, a specific oracle is chosen that exemplifies the hopefulness of this important category of biblical language-games. Indeed, this particular passage, 2 Samuel 7, with its messianic overtones, in one way or another forms the underpinning of the optimism that is discernible in every other prophetic text.

The Oracle of Nathan in 2 Sam. 7.1-17 was a key text in the eschatological conceptions of Israel, for in it the eternal destiny of the house of David was heralded.[64] The narrator, after a brief introduction and a transition (7.1-4, 17–18a), turns over the verses that remain to the (in)direct speech of Yahweh (7.5-16) and David's subsequent response (7.18b-29). Nathan, too, though God's mouthpiece, is barely present in the whole episode. He is simply recorded as having spoken everything 'in accordance with all these words [of God] and all this vision' (7.17). The doubling of the word 'all' underscored Nathan's total obedience to the word that came from Yahweh. It is as if Nathan were not even on the scene, except to give, initially, the wrong advice to his regent (7.3)![65] Instead, a complex, multilayered discourse structure is visible in the oracle: the narrator of the account (7.4) quotes God (7.5a) quoting Nathan (7.5b) quoting God (7.5c-7a) quoting himself (7.7b) – 'free indirect discourse'. This intense degree of specificity in the instructions of God to Nathan and the virtual absence of the prophet exemplify the core of prophecy – divine discourse: 'Thus says the LORD'.[66] All through the oracular section, God's activity and sovereignty

64. This account of 2 Samuel 7 is paralleled in 1 Chron. 7.7-14, as well as in similar elements echoed in Pss. 89.2-4, 19–37; 110; 132; and 2 Sam. 23.1-7. Of note also is the Qumran treatment of this text (4Q174, Florilegium); see Y. Yadin, 'A Midrash on 2 Sam. vii and Ps. i–ii (4QFlorilegium)', *IEJ* 9 (1959), pp. 95–8; and D. Flusser, 'Two Notes on the Midrash on 2 Sam. vii', *IEJ* 9 (1959), pp. 99–109.

65. In a misconceived acquiescence to his liege, Nathan advised David to 'do all that is in your mind'. That was not to be. Not David's inclinations but Yahweh's purposes were what would come to pass. Nathan may have been speaking to 'the king', but God was speaking to his 'servant' (2 Sam. 7.3-5) – there was no question as to who was in charge. See J.P. Fokkelman, *Throne and City (II Sam. 2–8 & 21–24)* (vol. 3 of *Narrative Art and Poetry in the Books of Samuel*; Assen, The Netherlands: Van Gorcum, 1990), p. 230.

66. Keith Bodner, 'Nathan: Prophet, Politician and Novelist?', *JSOT* 95 (2001), pp. 43–54 (46–7); also see Kenneth M. Craig, Jr., 'The Character(ization) of God in 2 Samuel 7:1–17', *Semeia* 63 (1993), pp. 159–76 (167–8).

governs its anticipatory element, especially marked in 7.12-16 with its cascade of first-person assertions (promises). The independent pronoun 'I' (אָנִי) that opens Yahweh's announcement (7.8) emphasizes his initiative in bestowing favour upon David and his house. God is the causal agent and the one in control of history as its prospective particulars unfold in the future of the Davidic dynasty. The Rule of Anticipation keeps its focus upon God's sovereignty in accomplishing his ultimate purposes, helping project a world of hope wherein God is in control of the future.

This hope is not just for the head of state; despite the emphasis in the initial proceedings upon the king, God's voice consistently highlights the people of Israel (7.6, 7, 8, 10, 11). Indeed, Yahweh's concern in prophecy is never solely for patriarch, patrician or prophet, but for the community as a whole. The establishment of the dynasty does not serve as an end in itself; it simply ensures and empowers God's own righteous rule of his people – the goal of the eschatological kingdom. Twice in 2 Samuel 7, the prophetic declaration claims that Yahweh gave David rest from his enemies (7.1, 11); the word 'rest' in the hiphil of נוח is practically a technical term in Deuteronomic writing for Yahweh's blessing upon the people of Israel, rest from enemies in the promised land (Deut. 12.10; 25.19). By the Rule of Anticipation, that ancient hope is revived in 2 Samuel 7 through David for the entire nation in the eschaton. Israel, the people, is thereby 'superimposed' upon David, its king. The latter is in the service of the former and God's dealings through his regent are meant to extend God's blessings to his people.[67] In its essence, then, prophecy is intended primarily for the community; the Rule of Anticipation makes possible the projection of a world in which God's people find ultimate hope.[68] Sirach 49.10 reflects on this anticipatory ministry of the prophets: 'May the bones of the Twelve Prophets send forth new life from where they lie, for they comforted the people of Jacob and delivered them with confident hope' (NRSV). The Rule of Anticipation enables the interpreter to focus upon God's ultimate purpose for his people. Even in prophetic utterances that dealt

---

67. Dennis J. McCarthy, 'II Samuel 7 and the Structure of the Detueronomic History', *JBL* 84 (1965), pp. 131–8 (132–3); Craig, 'Character(ization) of God', p. 172.

68. Though בְּרִית is not explicitly used in the oracle of 2 Samuel 7, covenant implications are evident in 7.14-15; defection from the obligations thereof promised to bring discipline (בְּרִית, it must be noted, is used in the parallel texts, Ps. 89.3, 28, 34; and 2 Sam. 23.5). See Gwilym H. Jones, *The Nathan Narratives* (Sheffield: Sheffield Academic Press, 1990), p. 88. Also of interest are the correspondences between 2 Samuel 7 and Genesis 15 (the making of the covenant with Abraham). Both incidents involve the 'word of Yahweh' and nocturnal visions (Gen. 15.1, 12; 2 Sam. 7.4, 17); both concern a 'house' and 'your seed' and 'one who will come forth from your body' (Gen. 15.2-4, 18; 2 Sam. 7.12). The presence of the Rephaim and the Jebusites in the list of Canaanites (Gen. 15.15) is also suggestive in light of David's military endeavours against the same peoples (2 Sam. 5.6, 8, 18, 22). Thus, the Davidic covenant 'becomes the counterpart, and the fulfilment, of the first covenant made with the patriarch'. See Fokkelman, *Throne and City*, p. 230.

with specific historic agents and entities, hope is being proffered to all God's faithful for the future.

A redemptive thrust is also clear in the Rule of Anticipation: that things will not be the same as they have been 'formerly' (2 Sam. 7.10), suggests a contrast with the centuries of Israelite bondage (7.6; 'since the day I brought up the sons of Israel from Egypt'). Evidence of early Christian understanding of this redemptive focus of Nathan's oracular promise to David can be detected in Paul's Antioch sermon in Acts 13. Not only did Paul's opening statement connect the exodus with God's bringing to Israel a Saviour, Jesus (13.17, 23), the whole complex of OT citations in 13.33-7 demonstrated how Jesus' resurrection fulfilled God's promise of an eternal dynasty to David in 2 Samuel 7, guaranteeing final redemption.[69] In interpretation of prophecy, by the Rule of Anticipation, the theologian-homiletician must therefore keep in focus the redemptive scope of divine activity, the transformation of current conditions in light of a brighter future – a world in which God's sovereign purposes are fulfilled for his people, bringing them a Messianic hope. Such a projected world, depicting the culmination of God's plans for his creation, is intended to elicit a response. The specific response to the Rule of Anticipation that is depicted in the 2 Samuel account suggests what the transhistorical intention might be in the world projected. In the grand scheme of God's operations, David was but an element. His were not the goals that would be achieved, but God's. David's response is telling: God is affirmed, his purposes acquiesced to, and his ultimate designs acknowledged; after repeating God's name over 25 times in the span of 12 verses, the earthly king concludes his prayer declaring, 'O Lord GOD, Thou art God, and Thy words are truth' (1 Sam. 7.28).

Rule of Correction
The Rule of Correction asserts that, in the interpretation of prophetic texts, consideration must be given to the remedial thrust of the critique that threatens retribution for rebellion and promises restoration for repentance.

What had been a promising start to the story of Israel with the call of Abraham and the exodus appeared to have degenerated into an ethos of disobedience ensuing in an era of punishment. Hosea 11.1-2a condensed this phase of the narrative: 'When Israel was a youth I loved him, and out of Egypt

---

69. The parallel elements are unmistakable – God's promise: ἀπαγγελεῖ (2 Sam. 7.11b LXX) / ἐπαγγελίαν (Acts 13.23, 32); David's death: κοιμηθήσῃ (2 Sam. 7.12) / ἐκοιμήθη (Acts 13.36); God's raising up: ἀναστήσω (2 Sam. 7.12b) / ἀναστήσας, ἀνέστησεν (Acts 13.33, 34); David's seed: σπέρμα (2 Sam 7.12c) / σπέρματος (Acts 13.23a); God's son: μοι εἰς υἱόν (2 Sam. 7.14a) / υἱός μου εἶ σύ (Acts 13.33b); God's lovingkindness: ἔλεός μου (2 Sam. 7.15a; MT, חַסְדִּי) / τὰ ὅσια (Acts 13.34b; MT of Isa. 55.3, which is being cited here, has חַסְדֵי); and the dynasty's endurance: πιστωθήσεται (2 Sam. 7.16a) / τὰ πιστά (Acts 13.34b). See Dale Goldsmith, 'Acts 13.33–37: A *Pesher* on II Samuel 7', *JBL* 87 (1968), pp. 321–4 (321–2).

I called my son. The more they [the prophets] called them, the more they [the people] went from them.' The Rule of Correction is thus the primary focus of the pre-exilic prophets. Israel's wickedness and waywardness called for action on the part of hearers in the form of repentance, and, should that not be forthcoming, retribution from God would be certain, the prophets warned. While living in the midst of tribulation (or expecting it in the future), the prophets' ordained task was to alert their audiences to the calamitous consequences of covenantal disobedience, to locate God's purposes for his people in the midst of their trials, and to enable them to respond adequately to God, so that, ultimately, in and through Israel's correction, the work of God would be accomplished.[70] And it is to this dramatic *telos* that the seers' thundering declamations are launched – the work of prophecy embodied in the Rule of Correction. The prophets were the consciences of God's people, and so theirs was an anomalous narrative, a narrative of the future: what will, or might be, based upon one's behaviour in the past or present, and, importantly, how one could escape that future. A response from the reader was indubitably being sought, for prophecy was a rhetoric of repentance and return.[71] The projected world portrays, by the Rule of Correction, the inevitability of punishment for transgression in the community of God. A moral framework is clearly depicted; however, unlike the similar, but indirect, ethical structure laid down in narrative, in prophecy the requirements of God are sharply and starkly formulated in stinging, second-person critique.

The role of the prophet Nathan, in the aftermath of David's sin with Bathsheba, models this Rule of Correction (2 Sam. 12.1-25). The authoritative 'sending' (שלח) of the prophet Nathan to the iniquitous king by Yahweh (12.1) is clearly an overturning of the tables on the adulterer and murderer who, until then, had been doing all the sending, symbolic of his regal power now gone corrupt (the verb שלח appears 23 times in 2 Samuel 10–12, mostly with the king as its subject; see Chapter 4 for an analysis of 2 Samuel 11). David's sin and crime had not gone unnoticed by God who was now taking the initiative as he pursued the situation to a conclusion. The divine discipline (Rule of Correction) is applied by means of a juridical parable recounted by Nathan (12.1-6). In that denunciatory fiction, the poor man's lamb would eat (אכל) of his bread and drink (שתה) of his cup and lie (שכב) in his bosom (12.3). Earlier, in response to David's urging that Uriah go home – an attempt by the king to hide his own paternity of Bathsheba's illegitimate child – that soldier had indignantly replied, 'Shall I then go to my house to eat [אכל] and to drink [שתה] and to lie

---

70. See Goldingay, *Models for Interpretation of Scripture*, p. 193.

71. שוב ('return') echoes throughout the prophets: Isa. 6.10; Jer. 3.7, 10, 12, 14; Hos. 3.5; 5.4; Zech. 1.3, 4; Mal. 3.7; etc. The hope was being extended that, as a result of the people's return, perhaps God himself would 'return' to them (מִי יוֹדֵעַ יָשׁוּב – 'who knows if he will return', Joel 2.14; also see Jonah 3.8-10, where the Ninevite king expresses the same sentiment).

[שׁכב] with my wife?' (11.11). David, the prophet implies, was as callous as the parabolic rich man who slew the poor man's favourite pet. Flying into a rage over Nathan's narrative, the king unwittingly passed sentence on himself: the rich man deserved to die and he was to make restitution for his callousness fourfold (12.5-6).[72] The Rule of Correction points the divine finger directly at the sinner: 'You are the man!' (12.7). A world is thus depicted where sin is not tolerated but condemned outright.

Then follows the verdict against David in Yahweh's own words delivered by the prophet ('thus says the LORD', 12.7) – again, the Rule of Correction in operation. God had given David power as king; he had abused it. God had given David escape from death at the hands of Saul; he had killed another. God had blessed him with much (house, wives, nations) and would have given him more had he asked; David had not asked, he had stolen. God had given David his word; he had despised it. Indeed, he had despised Yahweh himself (12.7-10, בזה). Earlier, Yahweh had declared: 'Those who honour me I will honour, and those who despise [בזה] me will be lightly esteemed' (1 Sam. 2.30). There was no excuse for the king; he stood accused of having done evil 'in Yahweh's sight' (2 Sam. 12.9; also 11.27), and the Rule of Correction threatened punishment commensurate with the sin.[73] Yahweh would take David's wives 'in his sight' and they would be lain with 'in the sight' of the sun (12.11; see 16.21-2 for Absalom's fulfilment of this curse, upon the same roof whence David had commenced his contemptible conspiracies).[74] The scorning of Yahweh and his word is a heinous crime indeed, and that not by a private individual but by

---

72. The 'traveller' in the parable (הֵלֶךְ, 2 Sam. 12.4) likely alluded to David's initial action of walking on his roof (הָלַךְ, 2 Sam. 11.2), those idle steps that launched the whole egregious episode. Ecclesiastes 6.9 pictures the 'wandering' (הָלַךְ) of desire. Of interest is R. Robert Polzin's view that the identity of David in the parable changes with the scope of the narrative: (1) God, the rich man, taking the wives of Saul, the poor man, and giving them to David, the traveller (2 Sam. 12.7-8); (2) God, the rich man, taking the wives of David, the poor man, and giving them to his sons (12.11-12); and (3) David, the rich man, taking the wife of Uriah, the poor man. Indeed, Polzin considers Nathan's parable paradigmatic of the entire history of Israel from Deuteronomy through 2 Kings: Yahweh dispossesses the nations and gives the land of Canaan (the ewe lamb) to Israel (the traveller/sojourner). See Robert Polzin, *David and the Deuteronomist* (part 3 of *A Literary Study of Deuteronomic History [2 Samuel]*; Bloomington, IN: Indiana University Press, 1993), pp. 120–30.

73. This assessment by Yahweh of the malignity of David's misdeeds was diametrically opposed to David's own assertion of the benignity of his activities; see 2 Sam. 11.25 where, upon hearing the news of the fatalities on the battlefield that resulted from the sinister plot to execute Uriah, David placates Joab: 'Do not let this thing be evil in your eyes'. This is immediately followed by 11.27, where the narrator counters: 'But the thing that David had done was evil in the eyes of the LORD.'

74. Yahweh would take (לקח, 2 Sam. 12.11) David's wives, reminding David how he had taken (לקח) Bathsheba (11.4; 12.9, 10), just as the rich man had taken (לקח) the poor man's ewe lamb (12.4).

Yahweh's anointed himself, the king of God's chosen people (Israel/Judah is mentioned five times in 12.7-15). The repercussions of David's sin and crime – a rebuke to Yahweh and a reproach to the people – were felt far beyond the confines of bedroom and palace. The entire nation, therefore, would witness the punishment: 'before all Israel' (12.12). The fact that these nefarious affairs had given occasion for the enemies of Yahweh to blaspheme him (12.14) could not be forgotten either (Rom. 2.23-4 underscores the seriousness of such an accusation). The Rule of Correction portrays a world wherein recompense in kind and measure is threatened upon the one rebelling against Yahweh, and who, wantonly and selfishly wielding power and authority, disregards what is good 'in the eyes of the LORD', disparaging God's word and dishonouring God's name.

The Rule of Correction also implies a conditionality. A remedial thrust is inherent therein: if the ones being corrected were to repent and seek forgiveness, it would be granted them. David's response to correction is a helpful pointer to that called for in a reader. He confesses: 'I have sinned against the LORD' (2 Sam. 12.13b). The rule intends that the hearer return to God; this is essentially its purpose, a rehabilitation of the sinner: 'I will go away and return to my place until they acknowledge their guilt and seek my face; in their affliction they will earnestly seek me' (Hos. 5.15). The prophetic word of correction is but an instrument of history, seeking to bring about a change of heart in readers and hearers, and thereby the *non*-fulfilment in the future of the dire consequences threatened.[75] This is visible in the continuing story of David the repentant sinner. While 2 Sam. 12.15b-25 resumes the narrative with Bathsheba continuing to be referred to as 'Uriah's wife' (12.15), at the end of the section she is mentioned as 'his [David's] wife' (12.24) and she conceives. David's sins take their tragic and traumatic toll, but with this change in Bathsheba's ascription and the birth of Solomon the accusatory unit ends positively. Once again Yahweh 'sends' (שׁלח), and once again it is Nathan, but this time with a message of tenderness: the child would be 'beloved of Yahweh' (12.24). Forgiveness had been achieved, though the consequences of sin would remain. In and through these human failures and all-too-mortal misdeeds, Yahweh inexorably would work out his sovereign purposes. The Messianic line, through Solomon, would be preserved; God's ultimate purposes would not be thwarted.[76] In sum, the Rule of Correction facilitates the portrayal of a world in front of the text that depicts particular facets of the

75. Wolff, 'Understanding of History', p. 340.

76. Thus, along with the Rule of Correction, the Rule of Anticipation appears to be operating implicitly and simultaneously. 'The message of doom serves ... to explain the past, in the manner of a theodicy, to warn and admonish the present, since Israel is seen to be living under the consequences of its past experiences of judgment, and to provide a groundwork of hope for the rich and glorious future.' See Ronald E. Clements, *Old Testament Prophecy: From Oracles to Canon* (Louisville: Westminster/John Knox Press, 1996), p. 214.

rebellion of humankind against God, the potential consequences thereof, and the possibility of restoration at the hands of a just, yet gracious, God.[77]

In dealing with prophecy, the task of the theologian-homiletician is to translate the thrust of such texts – the world projected by them and the transhistorical intentions they bear – into legitimate application for a new generation of hearers. Acts 3, recording Peter's speech at Pentecost, emphasizes not only the unity and coherence of the prophetic message, but its futurity as well: 'all the prophets who have spoken, from Samuel and his successors onward, also announced these days' (3.24). It may be assumed, then, that application of OT prophecy in NT times was not a foreign hermeneutic but an operation already inherent in the genre – the extension of the original meaning of prophetic discourses and the expansion of their spheres of operation to times and places in the future.[78] To this end, the Rules of Anticipation and Correction enable the interpreter to discern how the world in front of the prophetic text is framed.

Rules of Genre: law

Law, at the core of Israel's defining story, causes it to be placed at the commencement of the nation's overarching narrative. Embedded for the most part in a texture of narrative, law is dependent upon the surrounding text for the marking of time; the fixture of the Mosaic law in the Pentateuch sustains the organic connection of the founding events of the nation of Israel with their law.[79] When narrative intersects law in the Pentateuch, both genres are affected: ethics is 'narrativized' and narrative is 'ethicized'. This 'narrativization' of ethics makes law a memorable and narratable event in itself, giving this genre a distinct temporality; the 'ethicization' of narrative frames the story in a matrix of obedience and disobedience. It is significant that this imbrication, almost seamless, was such that narrative in the OT was not considered a separate genre; there was only the law, prophets and writings. Historiography was moralized throughout as the annals of disobedience, for the most part an indictment of the Israelites for their ethical lapses.[80] For this censure, law formed the basis and, therefore, the actual content and context of the promulgated laws are to be an important focus of the interpreter in the determination of this world in front of the text – the Rule of Directive. However, the transgeneric nature of Scripture, in this case the intertwining of law and narrative, adds yet another dimension to the genre of law: the remarkable presence of motive clauses reflecting upon the broad rationale for those laws has significant ramifications for application

77. In this case, David's sin involved the abuse of power in the service of immoral self-indulgence, resulting in his despising God's word and reputation.

78. Clements, *Old Testament Prophecy*, pp. 193–4.

79. Ricoeur, 'Toward a Hermeneutic of the Idea of Revelation', p. 82.

80. Idem, 'Biblical Time', pp. 171–3; James W. Watts, *Reading Law: The Rhetorical Shaping of the Pentateuch* (Sheffield: Sheffield Academic Press, 1999), p. 85.

of those texts. This generates the Rule of Rationale. The combined deployment of these two rules enables the hermeneut to visualize the world that is projected in front of biblical texts of law.

Rule of Directive

The Rule of Directive calls upon the one interpreting biblical law to attend to the particular content of that law and its literary context, in order to discern the world the text projects.

The actual content of the law and its textual milieu directs the interpreter to the world in front of the text. Legal content and literary context frequently offer clues to the projected world. In the sense in which this rule is framed, it resonates with the Rule of Correction (a rule of prophetic genre): both make divine demands upon the reader: one preemptively (Rule of Directive), the other punitively, after the law has been broken (Rule of Correction). An examination of the NT command to honour the emperor (1 Pet. 2.17) demonstrates that this Rule of Directive operates also upon imperatives of Scripture not located in the corpus of law.

First Peter 2.13–3.7 is considered a *Haustafel*, a household duty code, a list of the obligations of members of a household, one to another. However, there is not that symmetry as is found in the *Haustafeln* of Eph. 5.22–6.9 and Col. 3.18–4.1. Only half of each of the pairs is intact – wives, not husbands (the men do get a mention, but only in a single verse, 1 Pet. 3.7); and slaves, not masters; children and parents are not addressed at all. In this 1 Peter text, a new directive, the obligations of Christians to those *outside* the believing community is introduced – to the emperor and those in authority; upon this directive the rest of the duties of the *Haustafel* are built. This responsibility might have been at the root of its very asymmetry, for the list thereby emphasizes its outward gaze: Peter assumes the situation of Christian subjects under pagan rulers, Christian wives living with non-Christian husbands, and Christian slaves serving unbelieving masters. This would also explain the omission of parental and filial responsibilities, for in such relationships there rarely is the imbalance of belief confronting unbelief.[81] The pericope (2.13-17) bearing the imperative of interest (2.17, 'honour the emperor') commences the *Haustafel*, setting the focus squarely upon those without the community, and on how the Christian should behave towards them. This is the thrust of the imperative, the Rule of Directive in operation: this is how the projected world looks.

In 2.13-14, readers are required to undertake the specific action of submitting to governmental authorities, for they are all worthy of respect διὰ τὸν κύριον.[82]

---

81. J. Ramsey Michaels, *1 Peter* (WBC, 49; Dallas, TX: Word, 1988), pp. 122–3.

82. When Peter requires submission 'for the Lord's sake', he is also anticipating the paradigmatic behaviour of Jesus in the face of opposition from the rulers of the realm – the Jewish religious leaders and the Procurator of Judea (1 Pet. 2.21-5).

This clause to submit 'for the Lord's sake' reminds believers that, though they are free from the darkness of their unbelieving past (2.9), they are now bond-slaves of God (2.16); attention is drawn to the one who is truly in authority. Therefore, it is as slaves of God that believers are to abide by the injunction of the pericope. In 2.17, with a series of four pithy maxims provided in asyndetic fashion and forming an *inclusio*, the passage is summarized: though all men are to be respected and honoured, to the community the believer has a duty to demonstrate love; though God alone is the ultimate authority, worthy of reverential awe and fear, the emperor also is due respect.[83] Paralleling 'honour *all* people' (2.17), the directive to respect the emperor thus makes this ruler 'an example of the particular stations and people to be given deference by the Christians'.[84] From 'all people' to 'emperor' is a convergence also found in 1 Tim. 2.1-2. Moreover, 1 Pet. 2.13-14 has just clarified that those entities to whom honour is due include 'every human institution, whether to an emperor ... or to governors', that is, all those who wield power to punish evildoers and praise 'well-doers'. In other words, from the pericope itself (the legal content and the literary context), it becomes obvious that the emperor is but one in a series of civic authorities, all of whom as representatives of the heavenly sovereign are due honour.[85] This is the divine demand borne by the text. The Rule of Directive, enjoining the specific action prescribed in the pericope and providing contextual clarification of the imperative, succeeds in framing the world projected by the text, one where Christians live lives marked by well-doing, submitting to God-ordained authorities of civic societies whoever they may be, regarding them all worthy of respect. The consequences of this projected world for application by those living within governmental structures and hierarchies that are not monarchical are obvious. The Rule of Directive thus facilitates the projection of the world in front of imperative texts, rendering future exemplifications possible in circumstances and situations vastly different from those in which the ancient text was composed.

Rule of Rationale
The Rule of Rationale prompts the one interpreting biblical law to give due consideration to the justification and motive behind the particular law in order to discern the world that the text projects.

---

83. Jews, for the most part, were respectful to their Roman rulers, even sacrificing and praying for them (see Philo, *Embassy* 23.157; Josephus, *J.W.* 2.10.4; and *Ag. Ap.* 2.6). Christ, too, adjured his followers to abide by this pattern (Mt. 22.21).

84. Barth L. Campbell, *Honor, Shame, and the Rhetoric of 1 Peter* (Atlanta: Scholars, 1998), p. 120.

85. While Jn 19.15; Acts 17.7; and Rev. 17.9 (as well as Josephus, *J.W.* 5.13.6) indicate that βασιλεύς refers to the Roman Emperor, Rom. 13.1; 1 Tim. 2.1-2; and Tit. 3.1-2 remind the reader of Scripture that a king is only one of many who exercise authority under the sovereignty of God. Also see Michaels, *1 Peter*, p. 126.

A singular characteristic of the biblical genre of law, as opposed to other ancient Near Eastern legal compilations, is the presence of motive clauses linked to many commands. For the most part, such rationales were associated with the historical traditions of the nation and enunciated in response to issues that arose in those narratives.[86] Comparing the laws of the OT with legal collections of Israel's *Umwelt*, it is evident that motive clauses, including paraenetic exhortations, were a peculiarity of the laws of Israel. Such clauses made up 45 per cent of the laws in the Decalogue (Exodus 20 and Deuteronomy 5) and about 50 per cent of the laws in Deuteronomy and Leviticus. On the other hand, motive clauses were found only in 6 per cent of the Laws of Hammurabi and in 5 per cent of the directives of Middle Assyrian Law. It appears that legal motivation was not characteristic of cuneiform law.[87] The Rule of Rationale, respecting this general biblical tendency to provide justification for its imperatives, seeks to discover the motive and purpose of the law as a means to framing the world projected by these legal texts. Especially in a reading of the law intended to culminate in its application for situations far removed from the text's originary circumstances, an understanding of the law's justification enables the interpreter to discern the kind of world the law intends to oversee and govern. Such a hermeneutic is intrinsic to the genre of law as a whole for, even as canonically inscribed, the biblical law code clearly did not cover every contingency of Israelite life, leaving much to extensions and implications of those laws already promulgated.[88] Highly selective as the code was, it may well have been that the particular laws included in the Pentateuch were intended 'less as a source for legal action...than as a statement of legal policy', less as a fountain of specific information on community governance, than as an instrument for the depiction of the world the text projects.[89] The rationale of the laws is thus a key generic

86. For instance, the prohibition of the oppression of strangers is yoked with the Israelites' own experience as aliens: 'You shall not wrong a stranger or oppress him, for you were strangers in the land of Egypt' (Exod. 22.21). See Calum Carmichael, *The Spirit of Biblical Law* (Athens, GA: University of Georgia Press, 1996), pp. 176–7 n. 14; also see Jon D. Levenson, 'The Theologies of Commandment in Biblical Israel', *HTR* 73 (1980), pp. 17–33 (27–8).

87. Rifat Sonsino, *Motive Clauses in Hebrew Law: Biblical Forms and Near Eastern Parallels* (Chico, CA: Scholars, 1980), pp. 86–93, 155–73. Also see B. Gemser, 'The Importance of the Motive Clause in Old Testament Law', in *Congress Volume: Copenhagen* (VTSup, 1; Leiden: E.J. Brill, 1953), pp. 50–66 (52).

88. Paul's application of Deut. 25.4 in 1 Cor. 9.9 and 1 Tim. 5.18 exemplifies such an operation of moving from original textual sense to application beyond what was likely to have been conceived of by the author. How this move may be conducted in sermons today will be addressed in Chapter 4.

89. Carmichael, *Spirit of Biblical Law*, p. 27. The selectivity of the laws included in the corpus is telling. For instance, the 'statute of the law which the LORD has commanded Moses' as referred to by Eleazar (Num. 31.21) is not found elsewhere in the Pentateuch. Perhaps not every law given to Moses was included in the collection. This is also suggested by the observation that the number of laws, 611, is the numerical equivalent of תורה; the traditional enumeration of 613 considers,

feature to be elucidated by the interpreter as the world projected by the text is discerned. Admittedly, not all laws have motives that may be ferreted out. For some laws, the rationale may simply be the imitation of God (Exod. 22.27; Lev. 11.45; Deut. 10.17-19; etc.). On occasion, there may even be multiple rationales for a given regulation: for instance, the observance of the Sabbath was based upon the *imitatio Dei* (Exod. 20.8-11); it was a sign of the covenant (31.12–17); it had a humane rationale that considered the plight of servants (Deut. 5.14); and it was also a memorial to the exodus (5.15). While the presence of motive clauses within the text is significant, even in their absence, according to the Rule of Rationale, due effort must be expended to discern the possible purpose of the law when interpreting this genre for contemporary application.

The commandment in Deut. 22.12 requiring the wearing of tassels on the four corners of the Israelite's cloak serves as an example of the utility of the Rule of Rationale for discovering the world projected by an imperative text. The tassel, as an extension of the garment hem – usually the most ornate part of a Near Eastern garment – was considered an important social statement, 'the "I.D." of nobility', signifying the special status of the wearers as gods or kings. The blue colour of the affixture required by the law made this undertaking quite exclusive, for the production of this dye was extremely expensive.[90] However, even a poor Israelite could afford to have four threads of blue in the tassel as mandated in the regulation; it was possible for everyone in the community of God to be tagged by the badge of honour. This appendix to clothing, therefore, was to serve as a reminder to the children of the Hebrew nation, one and all, of their unique standing before God on the basis of their redemption, and the resulting obligation to obey him; this was the rationale implied in the law. The tassel commandment that is also found in Num. 15.37-41, in fact, makes this explicit, linking the Israelites' distinctive position as those redeemed from Egypt by Yahweh with the demand for obedience to him ('I am the LORD your God who brought you out from the land of Egypt to be your God').[91] Thus, by

in addition, the Shema (Deut. 6.4) and Exod. 20.2 ('I am Yahweh your God'). It would seem that the very embedding of law within narrative was intended 'to give the reader an understanding of the nature of the Mosaic Law and God's purpose in giving it to Israel' (John H. Sailhamer, *The Pentateuch as Narrative: A Biblical-Theological Commentary* [Grand Rapids: Zondervan, 1992], pp. 63–4).

90. See Jacob Milgrom, 'Of Hems and Tassels', *BAR* 9 (1983), pp. 61–5. He also suggests that the blue tassel denoted elements of the priesthood as well, in accordance with God's declaration that Israel was a kingdom of priests (Exod. 19.6).

91. Stephen Bertman, 'Tasseled Garments in the Ancient East Mediterranean', *BA* 24 (1961), pp. 119–28 (128); David A. Dorsey, 'The Use of the OT Law in Christian Life: A Theocentric Approach', *EvJ* 17 (1998), pp. 1–18 (13–15). Indeed, it appears that obedience to all the commandments of Yahweh was inextricably bound up with this privileged station of the children of Israel as God's possession redeemed from the land of Egypt: see Exod. 19.4-6; Deut. 4.20; 7.6-8; 26.16-18; etc.

the Rule of Rationale, the world framed by this genre depicts those in God's community, those redeemed by God, constantly bearing upon their person a reminder of their high status before God and of the priority of a lifestyle commensurate with that privilege. The Rule of Rationale sees this projected world as the basis for any subsequent application of the text.[92]

Wenham argues that obedience to rules was not a sufficient definition of OT ethics, but that much more was expected from covenant members. The law simply established a minimum standard of acceptable behaviour (the floor), the transgression of which attracted sanction; it did not prescribe ideal conduct (the ceiling). Ethics was, and is, much more than keeping the letter of the law. Merely avoiding the worship of false gods, for instance, may have precluded reprimand and retribution, but the ethical goal was far more comprehensive and, involving matters of mind and heart, impossible to legislate. Wrapped up in the worship of God and God alone was not only demonstrable (external) loyalty to God (Deut. 5.6-10) but also the intangible love for him with all of one's being (6.4-5).[93] The prohibition of murder based upon the rationale of the *imago Dei* (Gen. 9.6) is a similar example. The Rule of Rationale facilitates the projection of a world wherein not only is murder condemned (the floor), but all that is implied in the concept of man as God's image-bearer demands respect (the ceiling). It is the combination of the Rule of Directive and the Rule of Rationale that, by pointing to the pragmatic scope and breadth of the law, can help determine the ethical space for obedience. This is the projected world that the people of God are called to inhabit.

Rules of Genre: hymnody

Dealing with collections of non-narrative biblical texts, such as the Psalms, wherein the intersection of different genres is not particularly significant, the interpreter must, nevertheless, consider their 'narrativizing', the implicit manifestation of a more expansive biblical time in those texts. These non-narrative texts, though 'outside' time, are still contemporary to the whole canonical story. The individual psalms, as prime examples of hymnody in the Scriptures, depict a keen awareness of people's confrontations with ageless and timeless issues, as they seek to portray God and engender a proper perspective on life in their readers. It is in this manner that such texts gain a universal and ahistorical character, for what they express and exhort reflect the concerns of humanity of all times and in all places.[94] Life experience that has been reflected upon

92. Consequently, for contemporary application, based upon the world the text projects, such a reminder of position and responsibility could be any number of tangible objects, not necessarily restricted to blue threads in a tassel on a cloak.

93. Gordon Wenham, *Story as Torah: Reading Old Testament Narrative Ethically* (Grand Rapids: Baker, 2000), pp. 79–80, 82–3.

94. Mark I. Wallace, 'Ricoeur, Rorty, and the Question of Revelation', in *Meanings in Texts*

constitutes hymnody: good is celebrated and evil is complained against; victory is remembered and vindication is sought. Hymnody, thus, is narrative remembered, an anthology of religious experience, 'reactualizing' and recapitulating in the present time of worship all the past temporalities of narrative, prophecy and law.[95] This is exactly why this genre, unlike all others, is characterized by an immediacy and a lack of distance, spatially, temporally and culturally. With its contemporaneous present-tense and frequent first-person discourse it addresses both readers and God with directness – praising, supplicating, lamenting, complaining, exhorting, thanking or admonishing – as it intersects with, and intimately touches, hearers' lives.[96] The material of all other genres is fodder for hymnody which transfigures their content, imbuing it with pathos to impact both heart and mind. Moreover, this category of texts directs the reader to move purposefully from the projected world that depicts the relationship between God and man to the immanent significance of this relationship for daily living under the hand of God. It is this dialectic from which is derived the two rules of hymnody, the Rule of Portrayal and the Rule of Perspective.

In hymnody, where the truths of narrative, law and prophecy are comprehended in a new way, its texts have already commenced the move from narrative to reflection as they (re-)project, in another genre, and often couched in poetry, the world that had once been displayed by narrative. An examination of the poetic account of the Israelites' deliverance from Egypt (the Song of the Sea, in Exod. 15.1-21, reflecting upon the experience recounted in the narrative of Exodus 14), is particularly illuminating in this regard. The poetic 'depth language' account – evaluative, emotive and evocative – clearly succeeds in conveying more than the prosaic 'steno language' description (the language of plain sense).[97]

---

and Action: Questioning Paul Ricoeur (eds David E. Klemm and William Schweiker; Charlottesville, VA: University Press of Virginia, 1993), pp. 234–54 (245).

95. Ricoeur, 'Biblical Time', p. 179. He observes that 'celebration elevates the story and turns it into an invocation', for 'to recount the story is one aspect of celebration'. One might say that the celebration is a crucial aspect of the event or story itself. Often the particular event of narrative and the celebration of that event in hymnody are almost superimposable, the latter being integral to the former, reminiscent of the way the first Passover was actually part of the event of deliverance. It is experience that has been reflected upon in this fashion that enables the reader to comprehend the fuller ('thick') meaning of those events. See J. Gerald Janzen, 'Song of Moses, Song of Miriam: Who is Seconding Whom?', *CBQ* 54 (1992), pp. 211–20 (218); and Ricoeur, 'Toward a Hermeneutic of the Idea of Revelation', pp. 88–9.

96. Fokkelman, *Reading Biblical Narrative*, pp. 177–8.

97. The poetic language often prominent in such texts makes a kind of 'trans-subjective reference'. One significant feature of such reference is its 'plurisignation' – the bearing of more than one connotation, with its constituent 'monosignative' components together yielding 'an integral meaning that radically transcends the sum of the ingredient meanings' (second-order referent and world projection). See Philip Wheelwright, *The Burning Fountain: A Study in the Language of Symbolism* (rev. edn; Bloomington, IN: Indiana University Press, 1968), pp. 4, 15, 81.

The prose and poetry renditions in Exodus 14 and 15 share themes and vocabulary, emphasizing the sea, wind and water, army and chariots, officers and pursuit, the Israelites' escape and the Egyptians' doom. Marked differences exist between the two accounts, however. The prose narrative provides a more comprehensive background to the story, including a confession of the Israelites' terror, the hardening of Pharaoh's heart and the particulars of his martial array, the assurances of God, angelic intervention, and Moses' role in the miracle. In contrast, the poetic account is graphic, with emotion running high, and visual imagery abounding in the free use of hyperbole.[98] Exodus 15 offers a highly metaphorical description of the escape from Egypt: God hurled the Egyptians into the sea (15.1, 4–5, 21); the enemies ('chaff') are consumed by the fiery wrath of God (15.7); they are destroyed as the blast of his nostrils releases a torrential flood (15.8, 10); and the Egyptians are swallowed by the earth as God extends his right upper extremity (15.12). Only in the song is the enemy quoted in direct speech (15.9; and those are the only humans depicted in any active role in the psalm). The Egyptians' cascade of threats brings to the fore the malevolence of their pursuit, and thereby, implicitly, highlights the magnificence of the deliverance wrought by Yahweh. While the prose account indicates the sea being cast on the Egyptians (14.26-8), it is the Egyptians who are cast into the sea in the poetic version (15.4). Pharaoh's order that the Hebrew babies be thrown into the Nile (1.22) is thus recapitulated – poetic justice, no doubt! Clearly, poetry succeeds in projecting a different facet of the world in front of the text than does prose; the transhistorical intention of each is different.

Rule of Portrayal
The Rule of Portrayal invites the interpreter of biblical hymnody – that characteristically focuses upon, and often directly addresses, God – to discover how God is depicted in the text, a significant component of the world projected in front of hymnic literature.

The portrayal of God is, of course, not restricted to the category of hymnody. Nevertheless, in a unique and direct way, this genre transcends the temporality of narrative, the prescriptivity of law and the futurity of prophecy, to present God through the world the text projects. This makes the Rule of Portrayal a cardinal rule of the primary genre of hymnody. In a sense, hymnody distils the essence of other genres into its own discourse, the secondary product of reflection upon a first-hand experience of God. All these poetic reservoirs of

---

98. This song appears to be a victory psalm, the characteristic features of which are a focus on the specific name of Yahweh, ascription of praise to him, description of Yahweh's use of the forces of nature over his enemies, the mocking of the foes and an account of the enemy's downfall (Richard D. Patterson, 'Victory at Sea: Prose and Poetry in Exodus 14–15', *BSac* 161 [2004], pp. 42–54 [47–9]).

reflected experience assume the presence and activity of a God who personally relates to his people and promulgates specific ethical values.

The Song of the Sea is unwaveringly focused upon God and what he has done: the divine name appears 13 times in the space of 21 verses; God is also addressed in the second person (Exod. 15.6-18), as is often the case in hymnody. Not surprisingly then, Moses is completely invisible in the poem, and all the historical details of Israel's active involvement are subordinated (the Israelites, themselves, are hidden until 15.13). This is a redemption effected by Yahweh alone. The Israelites are told to stand still (הִתְיַצְּבוּ) and watch (14.13); Yahweh then makes the water stand still (נִצְּבוּ, 15.8). Where the narrative has Moses stretch out (נטה) a hand to divide the sea and make it return (14.16, 21, 26, 27), the psalm has Yahweh stretching out a right hand (נטה ימן) to make the earth swallow his enemies (15.12).[99] Here is the Rule of Portrayal in action – Yahweh is depicted in all his might and power. The identity of Yahweh in Exodus had already been an issue for Moses and the Israelites, as well as for Pharaoh and the Egyptians (3.13-15; 5.2; 7.5, 17; 14.4, 18). Who he is is finally clarified in this Song: Yahweh is the sole, mighty agent of salvation. In overpowering his enemies, he had justified his superiority over all other gods and redeemed his claim to be the exclusive object of worship for the Israelites (15.11). As a matter of fact, for the first time in Scripture, a new dimension to God's nature is discovered and extolled: 'The LORD is a warrior; the LORD is his name' (15.3). The fresh revelation of this divine characteristic was not a random utterance by the celebrants; it had a purpose, and this distinct portrayal of God would have ramifications for the future (see the Rule of Perspective, below).

The Rule of Portrayal detects in Exodus 15 yet another significant facet to the character of Yahweh: he is also the promise-keeper. His pledges to deliver the Israelites from Egypt were linked in Exodus to his guarantees to them regarding the promised land (3.17; 6.6-8; 13.3-4). In its depiction of the nation's victory by the sea (15.1-12) and its conquest of the land (15.13-18), the Song of the Sea celebrates the fulfilment of this bipartite promise of deliverance from Egypt and delivery into Canaan. What Yahweh promised in 6.6 ('I will redeem you with an outstretched arm') is 'literally' accomplished in 15.12 (also see 15.13, 16). Yahweh does, indeed, keep his promises.[100]

---

99. James W. Watts, *Psalm and Story: Inset Hymns in Hebrew Narrative* (Sheffield: JSOT, 1992), p. 46. There is also a subtle shift in focus from the end of the narrative to the beginning of the song. In Exod. 14.31, the people are located on one side of the verb 'believed in', while Moses and Yahweh, on the other side, are the objects of this belief. However, in the song (15.1), Moses is with the people, located on the subject side of the verb 'sang'; together, leader and followers sing to Yahweh, the focus of the psalm (Janzen, 'Song of Moses, Song of Miriam', p. 213).

100. Watts, *Psalm and Story*, p. 48. The promise of God appears to be gazing even farther ahead as it adumbrates the institution of the temple and the establishment of Mount Zion in 15.17.

The Rule of Portrayal thus enabled a specificity of description of deity that was invisible in the prose of the preceding chapter. Yahweh was the mighty deliverer, the one who fights for his people and keeps his word. Comprising a crucial part of the world in front of the text, this portrayal of God by hymnody has significant repercussions for the movement from text to praxis. The reader's response to the hymnic text is to be contingent upon the depiction of God in that passage. Hymnody's vivid and vigorous representation of God, often in direct address, is intended to govern the perspective of the reader on life and how it is to be lived. Therefore the Rule of Portrayal leads to the second rule of hymnody.

Rule of Perspective
The Rule of Perspective urges the interpreter of biblical hymnody to elucidate the direction offered by the text on how the complexities of life and the intricacies of daily living ought to be viewed.

The Rule of Perspective is clearly connected to the preceding rule, the Rule of Portrayal; indeed the former is a consequence of the latter: readers' outlook on life and living is grounded upon their conception of God. What the Rule of Portrayal affirms forms the basis of what the Rule of Perspective exhorts. Who God is and how he relates to his creation is to direct one's perspective on life – the world in front of the text. This, subsequently, leads to application as that projected world is inhabited.

Of interest in Exodus 15 is the fact that, from the point in time of the singers of that psalm, the conquest of the promised land is still in the future. The portrayal of Yahweh's promise-keeping is partly proleptic: only the exodus from Egypt has been achieved; the entry into Canaan is yet to happen. The poem looks back on the events of the past, but it also confidently anticipates what the future will be, on the basis of what had already happened. Thus, 15.13–18 'depicts' the victorious entry of Israel into the Promised Land.[101] The people's 'passing over' (יעבר, 15.16) is echoed in the later report of their crossing the Jordan (Josh. 5.1, using the same word יעבר).[102] The vocabulary used to describe the Canaanites' fear of Israel in Exod. 15.14-16 is also recycled in the accounts of the actual conquest – רגז ('to tremble') and חיל ('anguish') reappear in Deut. 2.25; מוג (niphal, 'to melt away') and אימה ('terror') return in Josh 2.9. Such a prospective future victory in Exodus 15, achieved by Yahweh over his and the Israelites' enemies, is a transaction of the Rule of Perspective. This warrior God and this promise-keeping God (as depicted by the Rule of Portrayal) is worthy of trust for the future, the Song affirms; he can be relied upon for troubles

---

101. Peter C. Craigie, *The Problem of War in the Old Testament* (Grand Rapids: Eerdmans: 1978), p. 67; Brevard S. Childs, *Exodus: A Commentary* (London: SCM Press, 1974), pp. 249–51.

102. See also Num. 33.51; Deut. 2.4; Josh. 24.17; etc.

and trials yet to be encountered. The present perspective on life, especially as future days of tumult and turbulence are anticipated, is to be characterized by trust in the God who had already done great things in the past. So much so, the mighty deeds of God in the future can be celebrated in *advance* of their fulfilment (a 'flash-forward'). Praise for Yahweh's deeds was simply that – a celebration of his acts, both past *and* future; those in the future were as good as done! Watts, showing the predilection of ancient Near Eastern narratives to close with psalmody, suggests that hymnic reflective poetry at the conclusion of a story invites its readers to celebrate the greatness of the God it portrays. Such a triumphant commemoration was intended to create in the celebrants a perspective on life grounded upon faith in the one who enables them to triumph over all the vicissitudes of life in a sin-ridden world.[103]

While the Rule of Portrayal depicts a world in which Yahweh is the mighty deliverer of his people, the Rule of Perspective envisages a world in which the attitude of God's people, in all manner of adverse circumstances, is one of trust, based on who God is. Together, the two rules of hymnody make possible the appropriation of the truth of the song for readers anytime and anywhere, for in its lyric expression is the timelessness of poetry. A world is projected that mediates the application of the text for the particular contexts and situations of the readers; this is the work of hymnody governed by its rules. Time and trial have elicited thoughtful treatises in hymnody of various kinds (lament, praise, supplication, thanksgiving, etc.). Notwithstanding this diversity, all sub-genres in this class address the issue of the perspective on life the believer should have, given the portrayal of God in the world in front of the text. The Rule of

---

103. James W. Watts, 'Song and the Ancient Reader', *PRSt* 22 (1995), pp. 135–47 (139, 143–4). Underlying the text of Exodus 15 is also a subtle polemic against the myth of Baal, a Canaanite cosmology that outlines the process of creation with the sequential motifs of conflict (caused by the chaotic Yamm – 'Sea'), restoration of order, establishment of kingship and palace-construction. The song employs the same motifs: conflict between God and Egypt (15.1-12), with the sea, here, in contrast to its role in the pagan narrative, used as an instrument to *restore* order (15.4-6, 10); proclamation of kingship and supremacy (15.11); and, after future enemies are vanquished (15.14-16), establishment of God's palace and eternal regency (15.17-18). This drama is therefore more than simply a poetic account of the escape of the Israelites from slavery. Paralleling the myth of Baal's creative operation, Exodus 15 is announcing, at the level of its secondary referent, a new act of divine creation. Whereas Genesis 1 proclaims the creation of a new *world*, Exodus 15 celebrates the creation of a new *people*, Israel – an event of extraordinary significance in Scripture. The associations go further. In the Exodus version of the Decalogue, the Israelites are mandated to observe the Sabbath in response to God's creation (Exod. 20.11); in the Deuteronomic version (5.15), abiding by the fourth commandment is a commemoration of the exodus, a new 'creation' accomplished by Yahweh. The two reasons for keeping the Sabbath are not unrelated. See Peter C. Craigie, *Ugarit and the Old Testament* (Grand Rapids: Eerdmans, 1983), pp. 88–90; also see Martin L. Brenner, *The Song of the Sea: Ex 15:1–21* (BZAW, 195; Berlin: de Gruyter, 1991), pp. 98–9, 101–2.

Portrayal and the Rule of Perspective thus enable the theologian-homiletician to move from text to praxis by means of this projected world.

Summary: primary genre

The language-game of primary genre was considered in this chapter, and its types and rules were examined. The classification of primary genres was noted to be an uphill task. It was acknowledged that the boundaries of individual genres are less than precise and the taxonomy of these text-types far from perfect; the categorization of the Epistles exemplified the struggles of this endeavour. This imprecision, however, is not at all an impediment to successful interpretation. Rather, it underscores the vital nature of primary genres as 'works' being fitted and adapted for their authors' purposes, to frame projected worlds and thereby to elicit appropriate responses from their readers. From *bioi* to realistic narrative – from Graeco-Roman categories to late second-millennium European forms – the Gospels, it was shown, handle their variety of labels remarkably well. Within the broad category of narrative, these ascriptions and allotments function adequately in elucidating authorial purpose and readerly response. The world in front of the text can be determined well enough to enable the sermonic move from text to praxis.

Rules for the language-games of primary genres were also propounded in this chapter, rules that are fairly obvious and recognizable by a phenomenological analysis of reading; these guidelines are accepted widely enough (though not universally endorsed) for them to be utilized with profit by the interpreter. This work undertook to scrutinize four broad genre categories – narrative, law, prophecy and hymnody – in order to list the potential rules by which these individual language-games operate to frame the world projected in front of their texts. These guidelines point to specific foci of textual interpretation that must not be neglected by the hermeneut, if one is to identify the pragmatic element of the text, the segment of the world projected.

The Rules of Primary Genre govern in a paradoxical manner, by restraint and release (also discernible in the Rules of Secondary Genre, the language-game of canon; see Chapter 3): *restraint* grounds the interpretive operation upon the original textual sense; *release*, in contrast, expands the scope of meaning beyond this sense to the world projected by the text and the trans-historical intention it bears, enabling future application (for which, see Chapter 4). Where restraint focuses the interpreter upon the inscribed literary discourse (the *revealed* will of God), release, instead of generating interpretive chaos, guides the reader in that life-transforming move from history to contemporaneity, from the context of the author to the context of the reader (the *relevant* will of God). How the revealed will of God in any of the primary genres of Scripture translates into the relevant will of God for the believer today is at the crux of this work's undertaking.

Biblical texts are instruments of action employed by their authors, both human and divine, to project worlds. Hermeneutics must therefore involve explicating texts both as objects and as instruments of authorial action. The primary genres of Scripture facilitate the projection of the world in front of particular texts; the canon as a whole projects the plenary, cumulative world comprising all the individual textual projections. To extend the cartographic analogy, the secondary genre of the canon may be considered an atlas, a collection of maps of various kinds and particularities (primary genres) that enable the representation of a single world in all its variegated fullness.[104] The polygeneric nature of Scripture is perfectly suited to represent the various levels of complexity in reality, for biblical genres are geared to frame world-projections in discrete ways. Thus some genres befit certain aspects of that reality more than others; those aspects are best manifest by that particular text-type. In other words, genres have essential epistemological significance. The world-perspective provided by a genre and its rules enables the text to transcend the particularities of the circumstances of its inscription, neutralizing distanciation and enabling readers located at a distance in time and space from the author to apprehend the text, and to apply it to their own specific situations. Making possible such application via the projected world is part of the work of genre. A comprehensive description of the communicative act, therefore, necessarily includes an account of this work of world-projection, an interpretive task performed under the guidance of the Rules of Primary Genre. This is a task commenced by the author in the text and completed by the theologian-homiletician in the move from text to praxis.

In sum, biblical genres preside over the author's purpose and the reader's response as they depict a world, a linguistic vision of God and his relationship to his creation. For the discernment of this world, the Rules of Primary Genre are crucial aids to the theologian-homiletician. Chapter 3 will continue in the same vein, proposing the Rules of Secondary Genre. Together, these two chapters will have completed the examination of the Rules of Genre, in preparation for the final phase of the dialogue between hermeneutics and homiletics in Chapter 4.

---

104. Vanhoozer, *The Drama of Doctrine*, p. 294.

3

SECONDARY GENRE – THE CANON

In seeking to help the preacher move from inscription to application in a valid manner, this work mediates a dialogue between hermeneutics and homiletics. Broadly, Chapters 1, 2 and 3 concentrate on the hermeneutical aspects of this colloquy. Chapters 2 and 3 inventory the rules that govern language-games played by biblical texts – primary and secondary genres – rules that help these genres frame the world in front of the text. The rules proposed, it must be noted, are more like 'rules of thumb' than like inviolate and unassailable 'rules of nature'.[1] They are more descriptive rather than prescriptive, promulgating an arbitrary mandate. While not universally applied, these rules will be seen to have had wide custom through the history of the Church in guiding the interpretation of the foundational text of that believing community. With the enumeration of these rules, the field is thus prepared for generating legitimate application, the final move from Scripture to sermon. The discussion of application in Chapter 4 will constitute the homiletical contribution to the dialogue.

The goal of the theologian-homiletician is to proceed from text to praxis such that sermonic application derived from Scripture reflects the authority of those ancient writings and is relevant to the circumstances of contemporary auditors. Chapter 1 provided the general hermeneutical bases for such an endeavour. Application that is faithful to the text, it was proposed, is that which is subsumed by the transhistorical intention of the text's projected world. The determination of the world in front of the text is therefore a critical aspect of interpretation. Chapter 2 propounded the Rules of Primary Genre, focusing upon narrative, prophecy, law and hymnody, and how these generic rules, directing the reading of biblical texts, enable the interpreter to discern the world they project. Chapter 3 continues this line of inquiry into the operations of language-games, listing the rules of the entity that forms the secondary genre of Scripture – the canonical classic.

The Rules of Secondary Genre, as were the Rules of Primary Genre, are found to exercise simultaneously a restraint and a release upon the interpretive

---

1. See Frederick Schauer, *Playing by the Rules: A Philosophical Examination of Rule-Based Decision-Making in Law and Life* (Oxford: Clarendon Press, 1991), pp. 1–3.

exercise: the *restraint* designates the boundaries within which the interpretation must remain; the *release* enables recontextualization of the text for application, in contexts remote from those of the text's originary circumstances. Recontextualization, an operation necessitated by the distanciation characteristic of textuality, is facilitated by the world in front of the text. This operation effectively neutralizes distanciation and its consequences, and valid application is now rendered viable. It is in aiding the discovery of that projected world, the crucial intermediary in the move towards sermonic application, that the Rules of Primary and Secondary Genre have their greatest utility. Therefore, with the conclusion of Chapter 3, this work, having enumerated the Rules of Genre, will have set the stage for the strategy that transports the theologian-homiletician from text to praxis in a manner faithful to Scripture and pertinent to auditors.

Rules of secondary genre

The content of faith in the biblical texts, it has been asserted previously, is inseparable from the forms of their discourse, the primary genres that the texts adopt.[2] These rule-bound conventions of inscription, however, play their games within the broader context of another rule-bound linguistic 'sport', the secondary genre of Scripture. This secondary language-game, the canonical classic, serves as the literary setting for primary genres and their interactions (the polygeneric and transgeneric nature of the canon). Moreover, secondary genre imbues the corpus with its own peculiar properties – prescriptivity, perenniality and plurality of meaning – making a significant contribution to the projection of the world in front of the text. Chapter 3 will give an account of the Rules of Secondary Genre by which the canon governs these hermeneutical transactions.

In the first two centuries of the Church, as well as in the NT itself, κανών signified nothing more than a 'rule' or standard of living, in accordance with right doctrine.[3] It was not until the late second century that the word began to designate the table of doctrine that regulated the faith and practice of the early Church; in the mid-fourth century it was applied to Christian writings. By that time, κανών had acquired the formal status of a designation for the collection of books considered authoritative in the Church: the Council of Laodicea demarcated books that were ἀκανόνιστα from those that were κανονικά (*Can.* 59; 363 CE).[4] Thus, over a period of time, the 'rule' of doctrine became

---

2. Paul Ricoeur, 'Philosophical Hermeneutics and Theological Hermeneutics: Ideology, Utopia, and Faith', in *Protocol of the Seventeenth Colloquy, 4 November 1975* (ed. W. Wuellner; Berkeley: The Center for Hermeneutical Studies in Hellenistic and Modern Culture, 1976), pp. 1–28 (9).

3. See Gal. 6.16 ('those who will walk by this rule') and 2 Cor. 10.13 (κατὰ τὸ μέτρον τοῦ κανόνος); also see *1 Clem.* 1.3 ('rule of obedience'); and 7.2 ('rule of our holy calling').

4. Athanasius, in *Decr.* 5 (No. 18; soon after 350 CE), dockets *The Shepherd of Hermas* as μὴ ὢν ἐκ τοῦ κανόνος, and, in his Easter Letter of 367 CE (*Ep. fest.* 39.4-5), lists Christian

co-identified with the canon that gave those doctrines authoritative status. The individual texts were collated and codified into one corpus under the aegis of that authoritative canon which became a genre of its own, playing a unique language-game.

As are all games, and language-games in particular, the game of the canonical classic is also regulated by rules; it is a rule-bound operation that projects a world in front of the biblical text, the canonical world. This chapter outlines some of the more significant of the Rules of Secondary Genre, rules that have been in wide use for the reading of Scripture throughout the history of the Church. This is illustrated in the historical examples of the use of each rule. However, as was noted for the Rules of Primary Genre (see Chapter 2), it must be reiterated here that broad employment of the rules does not equate to their universal application. Neither should the set of rules enumerated in Chapters 2 and 3 be considered monolithic codes. Each collection, in all likelihood, has never functioned as a single unified statute-book. Local variations certainly abound among communities that use some or all of these rules to varying degrees, exploiting their nuances to varying extents, and applying them variably to discrete texts within the canon. Examples surely exist that demonstrate a disregard for, or negation of, individual rules.[5] Nonetheless, most of these rules have been widely instantiated as the historical citations will demonstrate.

This work attempts to state rules – for both primary and secondary genre – in as broad a form as possible, in order to describe their individual operations and to render them widely applicable. Inevitably, any act of description is biased. In that the Rules of Primary Genre deal with biblical literary forms that are also found outside the Bible, observer bias may be less noticeable in Chapter 2 than in the following enumeration of the Rules of Secondary Genre; here, the perspective of the operator may be more evident. The corpus that is being considered for these latter rules is the Christian canonical classic, the Bible. With its peculiar properties of prescriptivity, perenniality and plurality

---

writings that are κανονιζόμενα. The clearest instance of κανών for the whole assemblage of sacred writings occurs in a poem by Amphilochius, bishop of Iconium (c. 380 CE), where, after listing the books of the Old and New Testaments, he declared it the most reliable κανών ... τῶν θεοπνεύστων γραφῶν. For the first time, κανών τῆς καινῆς διαθήκης occurs in Macarius Magnes' *Apocriticus* (4.10; c. 400 CE). See Bruce M. Metzger, *The Canon of the New Testament: Its Origin, Development, and Significance* (Oxford: Clarendon Press, 1987), p. 292; and Harry Y. Gamble, *The New Testament Canon: Its Making and Meaning* (Philadelphia: Fortress, 1985), pp. 15–17.

5. Footnotes to each rule will direct the reader's attention to such contrasting material. While this work acknowledges the breadth of acceptance of these rules across the span of Christian traditions and over much of Christian history, the qualifications registered provide a necessary counterpoint, in order to generate a realistic view of the scope and transactions of these rules.

of meaning, with its character as divine discourse and all that that ascription entails, the Rules of Secondary Genre are more specific to this particular religious text than are the Rules of Primary Genre. A descriptive bias reflecting a Protestant and evangelical tradition may therefore be discernible in the application of the rules of canon. However, that does not rule out their validity *tout court*. First, the particular assumptions held in this work, while broadly evangelical, are shared with other Christian traditions as well; the prescriptivity, perenniality, and plurality of Scripture, for instance, are widely accepted. Second, a perspectival description is not necessarily for that reason alone rendered unviable; the fact that a description is motivated does not disqualify it, 'since an unmotivated description independent of any interpretative frame or purpose is impossible to imagine'.[6] Indeed, an explicitly confessed frame of reference that enables observation from a particular point of view enables one 'to see the events considered from one's own ... perspective as capable of a different, but not necessarily inaccurate and usually complementary portrayal'.[7] No single frame of reference can capture every aspect of the phenomenon being observed; the contribution of this work is therefore made from a vantage point that is unique, and, hopefully, the description of rules provided here will complement those made by other observers from a variety of traditions. Indeed, illustrative material from an eclectic variety of sources is utilized with the exposition of each rule to complement the perspective from which this work is composed.

These rules, in concert with the Rules of Primary Genre, enable the identification of the world in front of the text. While the ramifications of this projected world for application will await examination in Chapter 4, this chapter will explore the significance of these rules for the description of such a world.

The Rules of Secondary Genre are classified here by the part they play in presiding over the text's structure, function and content. These three categories obviously do overlap; nevertheless, the tripartite division forms a convenient infrastructure for examining the rules they comprise, and for comprehending the role of these rules in framing the text's projected world.

Rules of Structure

The Rules of Structure point the interpreter to the final form of the canonical text that is the object of interpretive activity (Rule of Completion), emphasize the character of the texts as an integral unity (Rule of Singularity) and take note of the ordering of its divisions – testamental, literary and chronological (Rule of Organization).

---

6. Francis B. Watson, *Text, Church and World: Biblical Interpretation in Theological Perspective* (Grand Rapids: Eerdmans, 1994), p. 37.

7. Sidney Ratner, 'Presupposition and Objectivity in History', *Phil. Sci.* 7 (1940), pp. 499–505 (504).

Rule of Completion
The Rule of Completion affirms that the final form of the canonical text should
be considered the object of interpretation for applicational purposes.

This Rule designates the final form of the text of Scripture as the basis and
context for the undertaking of interpretation that leads to application. The
confession of the canon by Christians affirms this corpus alone, moulded in
this way, as authoritative for their faith and practice. Enshrined in the canon is
the account of the unique relationship between God and his people, the text's
completed form giving this particular anthology of discourses normative status
for believers. The synchronic view of the Rule of Completion espoused here
is opposed to the diachronic bias of the historical-critical tradition.[8] Francis
Watson criticizes this latter movement for being insensitive to the complex
unity that is the text's final form, and for 'dissipating its energies on speculative
reconstructions that serve only to distract attention from the texts themselves'.
It is the integrated function of the text in its relatively stable shape, rather than
discrete functions in hypothetical precursors, that is to be accorded precedence.[9]
It therefore behoves readers to align themselves to the text after the fashion of
the community that calls the canonical Scriptures its own, a community that
has continued to use the final form of the canonical text, considering that form
of the text alone as having utility for applicational purposes. Generating valid
sermonic application from the completed form of the canon is the burden of
the theologian-homiletician. To this end, the Rules of Primary and Secondary
Genre are deployed to discern the world in front of this final form of the text.
Legitimate application derived from this projected world is what ultimately
maintains a right relationship between God and his people.[10]

The structuring of individual psalms within the canonical Psalter gives evidence of the significance of the final form of that larger corpus in which they
appear. For instance, the close connection between Psalms 1 and 2 enables them
to serve jointly as the introduction to the compilation. On the one hand, in these
psalms, are the 'just' – those whose lives are moulded by the Torah, whose ways
are known to Yahweh, and whose allegiance is to Yahweh's anointed; their happy
lot is announced in 1.1 and 2.12 (they are 'blessed', אַשְׁרֵי). On the other hand are
the 'wicked,' the 'sinners,' the 'scoffers,' and others of the same rebellious ilk;
their doom is proclaimed in 1.6 and 2.11-12 (they will 'perish', אָבַד).[11] Indeed,

---

8.   Brevard S. Childs, *Introduction to the Old Testament as Scripture* (London: SCM Press,
1979), p. 75. In distinction to the traditional historical-critical approach, Childs's canonical
modus operandi for interpretation is concerned with the theological shape of the text in its final
form (Stephen Fowl, 'The Canonical Approach of Brevard Childs', *ExpTim* 96 [1985], pp. 173–6
[174]).

9.   Watson, *Text, Church and World*, pp. 16–17, 35.

10.   See Chapter 4 for the significance of this homiletical transaction in the ecclesial context.

11.   Joseph P. Brennan, 'Psalms 1–8: Some Hidden Harmonies', *BTB* 10 (1980), pp. 25–9
(25–6).

the joint nature of the prologue, linking Psalms 1 and 2, is echoed in the variant reading (D) for Acts 13.33, where Psalm 2 is cited with the words ἐν τῷ πρώτῳ ψαλμῷ γέγραπται. This notable inauguration of the Psalter is renewed and revived in Psalm 149, where ultimate victory over the unrighteous is achieved. The 'nations', 'peoples', 'kings', and 'nobles' – the insurrectionists in 2.1-2 – become the objects of Yahweh's retribution in 149.7-9. The locus of the king's anointing, Yahweh's holy mountain, Zion (2.6), evolves into the parent whose children rejoice in their king (149.2). The subjugation of the riotous ones with a 'rod of iron' (2.9) also reappears in 149.8, where the seemingly same horde is bound with 'fetters of iron'. All of this signals a careful and systematic effort to organize the entire collection of Psalms, evidence of which is visible in both its opening and closing sections. The final canonical form of the book thus appears to have been deliberately collated to perform its integral theological role within Scripture; a particular facet of the canonical world is thereby projected.

In Judaism, the estimation of the final form of the text as sacred is evident in the system of *kethibh* and *qere*. The latter marginal reading registers those locations in the text where the traditional recited version of the Hebrew text would entail a different set of graphic signs than those of the traditional written version. James Barr has suggested that the person reciting the text usually did so from memory and therefore did not need the *qere* instructions for reading purposes. What the system was designed to preclude, instead, was the error of a scribe who, misled by the remembered recitation tradition, might record the wrong graphic signs. The *qere*, therefore, may have served not as a correction of the *kethibh* and a prompt to readers and interpreters but, rather, as a rendition of the reading tradition intended to prevent scribes from erroneously lettering the text that way – a clear case of respect for the final form, the *kethibh*, of the text.[12]

The Rule of Completion takes the judgement of the process of canonization as authoritative and perpetuates this authority in the final disposition of the text. In this decisive role in the language-game of canon, the Rule establishes and fixes the profile of each individual text of the Bible. This is, of course, not to deny any imprecision of what exactly constitutes the completed form. As stated, the rule simply sees a fixity of text form as bearing the most utility for the community that recognizes the text as such; the rule itself does not recommend what that final form should look like for any given tradition. For James Sanders, contra Childs, the final form is not much of a consideration at all: the hermeneutics of the canon focuses not so much on the delimited form the corpus finally achieved, but rather on the *operation* of canonization. This process of

12. James Barr, 'A New Look at *Kethibh-Qere*', in *Remembering all the Way ...* (Oudtestamentische Studiën, 21; ed. B. Albrektson; Leiden: E.J. Brill, 1981), pp. 19–37 (36–7); and John Barton, *The Spirit and the Letter: Studies in the Biblical Canon* (London: SPCK, 1997), pp. 123–4.

reaching the final form, Sanders holds, is itself instructive. Demonstrating a species of hermeneutics, it should serve as a model for all subsequent interpretive practices.[13]

Text-critical issues notwithstanding, in the spirit of Wittgensteinian rule-making, the Rule of Completion asserts its importance despite the blurring of the borders of its object, the final canonical form. Fuzziness at the edges does not render a given text unrecognizable or unusable. As the plethora of modern translations of the Bible and their widespread utilization amply attest, the final form, as far as it is attainable, is adequate for the faith and practice of the Church, as it has indeed been for over two millennia. Both Eusebius (*Quaestiones ad Marinum* 1) and Jerome (*Ep. ad Hedybiam*), for instance, discuss the variant endings of Mark, entertaining more than one option without questioning the Gospel's utility on the basis of that uncertainty. Imprecision is no bar to application.[14] A certain degree of inexactness is acceptable, and does not render application of biblical texts to daily life impossible. For homiletical purposes, the final form of the text is sufficiently capable of projecting a canonical world with enough precision and detail to enable a valid movement from text to praxis. Thus the Rule of Completion, establishing the form of the canonical text, is a critical foundational principle that helps determine the shape of the world in front of the text.

Rule of Singularity

The Rule of Singularity calls the interpreter to consider the canonical text as a single unit for applicational purposes – an integral whole, intrinsically related in all its parts.

Though comprising individual language-games, the canonical whole, is, in and of itself, one specific language-game *sui generis*. The Bible has traditionally been perceived and comprehended as a unity. It is as a unity that this classic

13. See James A. Sanders, *Canon and Community: A Guide to Canonical Criticism* (Philadelphia: Fortress, 1984), pp. 21–45; and Robert W. Wall, 'Reading the New Testament in Canonical Context', in *Hearing the New Testament: Strategies for Interpretation* (ed. Joel B. Green; Grand Rapids: Eerdmans, 1995), pp. 370–93 (374). This work is positioned closer to Childs than to Sanders, while acknowledging that within the canon itself one can detect the practice of hermeneutics. This intracanonical operation – the reinterpretation and recontextualization of antecedent texts – is a potential model for deriving contemporary application.

14. See James A. Kelhoffer, 'The Witness of Eusebius' *ad Marinum* and Other Christian Writings to Text-Critical Debates concerning the Original Conclusion to Mark's Gospel', *ZNW* 92 (2001), pp. 78–112. Even today, the same issue of where Mark 16 concludes generates practices that are unique; the example, admittedly extreme, of serpent-handling prevalent among certain sects of Pentecostalism in the southeastern USA is to a significant extent dependent upon Mk 16.18. See W. Paul Williamson and Howard R. Pollio, 'The Phenomenology of Religious Serpent Handling: A Rationale and Thematic Study of Extemporaneous Sermons', *JSSR* 38 (1999), pp. 203–18.

has fired literary imaginations and stoked artistic dreams, and it is as a unity that the Church has utilized the Scriptures as the norm for its faith and practice.[15] This singularity is also evidenced in the common practice of prefacing a biblical quote with, 'The Bible says...', evincing a widespread conception of the Scriptures as *one* book, a unified corpus.[16] At the same time, the singularity attested here affirms that the canon is a complex, not a simplex; it is a *singularity*, not a *simplicity* in the sense of being unanalysable, indivisible or uncompounded. Such a property is reflected in NT references to the general tenor and content of OT writings; these citations construe the latter as a single book as, for instance, in the 'anonymized' formulae introducing the citations in Mt. 26.24; Mk 9.13; and 14.21 (καθὼς γέγραπται) or in Lk. 18.31; 21.22; and 24.44 (τὰ γεγραμμένα).

This unity, a wholeness comprising discrete parts, is manifested in the structure of the canon with a beginning, middle and end (also see Rule of Organization), and reflected in the harmony of its doctrine and its depiction of a single trajectory of divine purpose. While one must acknowledge that the Bible does not have the kind of unity and coherence one might expect of the literary product of a single human author, there is, nevertheless, a unity between the various parts of the canon that bespeaks a singularity.[17] Individual texts and sections of the canon recognize the history of preceding parts and portions, and cumulatively add to what has gone on before. Genesis through 2 Kings constitutes the story from creation to the exile; 1 and 2 Chronicles cover the same ground, utilizing an extended nine-chapter genealogy to represent the period from Adam to David. The replication of the last two verses of 2 Chronicles (36.22-3) at the beginning of Ezra (1.1-3a) also signifies the continuity of the historical narrative. In the NT, the account of Jesus and the apostles is considered the sequel to the OT story of Israel. The genealogy of Matthew 1 retells, in structural and formulaic fashion, the biblical story thus far, indicating the providential design of

15. Northrop Frye, *The Great Code: The Bible and Literature* (New York: Harcourt Brace, 1982), p. xiii.

16. The seismic move from scroll to codex in the compilation of the Christian canon also enabled a 'singular' reading technology; now a reader could go back and forth within and between books with great ease – 'a crude form of hypertext' that recognizes and employs the corpus as a single unit. See George Aichele, *The Control of Biblical Meaning: Canon as Semiotic Mechanism* (Harrisburg, PN: Trinity, 2001), pp. 48–9.

17. Confounding factors militating against this rule include potential contradictions within the canonical corpus. Is the OT God of war (Exod. 15.3) the same as the NT God of peace (Rom. 15.33)? Is one justified by faith (Rom. 3.28) or by works (Jas 2.24)? The 400-year gap in the narrative history of Israel, the intertestamental period between the Old and New Testaments, also points to a less than completely cohesive and tight story. Further, the juxtaposition of multiple genres within the Bible (the polygeneric and transgeneric nature of Scripture) makes for a very unusual kind of 'singularity'; thus, a certain disjointedness with regard to textual form might offset the unity proclaimed by this rule. Nonetheless, Christian tradition has generally chosen to privilege unity and singularity over potential contradictions and seeming diversities.

the terrain of Israelite history between the major landmarks – Abraham, David and the exile. The periodic summaries in both Testaments attest to the unity and integrity of the biblical narrative as found in the entirety of the canon.[18] Moreover, in the demarcation of history 'from Abel to Zechariah' (Mt. 23.35), Jesus encompasses all the OT martyrs, from the one in the first book to the one in the last (Genesis to 2 Chronicles in the Jewish ordering of the canon). Therefore, the acknowledgement of the Bible's overall unity and authority, *in tota scriptura*, is to legitimize it as a single metanarrative – the Christian world-view articulated and established by a coherent and comprehensive perspective – and to interpret it as such.[19] In other words, a single canonical world is projected in front of the biblical text.

To assert that the Bible is 'God's book', is not to say that it is a collection of books authored by God, 'God's *opera omnia*'; rather, it is to declare that the Bible is '*one* book of God' – the Rule of Singularity in operation. 'The entire Scripture is one book and was revealed by the one Holy Spirit' (Cyril of Alexandria, *Commentary on Isaiah*, on Isa. 29.11-12). That this singularity is a reflection of a divine intentional act justifies the ascription 'divine discourse' to the canonical text.[20] One consequence of the divine act of communication and the reciprocal human construal of that act as being such (canonization) is that the constituent texts, written to specific groups of people in particular time periods, become, in the singularity of the canon, potentially applicable to *all* believers for *all* time, with prescriptivity, perenniality and plurality (also see

18. These summaries are located in Deut. 6.20-24 (exodus to occupation of the promised land); 26.5-9 (settlement in Egypt to occupation of the land); Josh. 24.2-13 (Abraham to occupation of the land); Neh. 9.6-37 (creation; Abraham to return from exile); Psalm 78 (exodus to David); Psalm 105 (Abraham to occupation of the land); Psalm 106 (exodus to exile); Ps. 135.8-12 (exodus to occupation of the land); Psalm 136 (creation; exodus to occupation of the land); Acts 7.2-50 (Abraham to Solomon); and Acts 13.17-41 (patriarchs in Egypt to the resurrection of Christ). See Richard Bauckham, 'Reading Scripture as a Coherent Story', in *The Art of Reading Scripture* (eds Ellen F. Davis and Richard B. Hays; Grand Rapids: Eerdmans, 2003), pp. 38–53 (40–2).

19. Also see Rule of Congruence, below, a consequence of this Rule of Singularity.

20. Nicholas Wolterstorff, *Divine Discourse: Philosophical Reflections on the Claim that God Speaks* (Cambridge: Cambridge University Press, 1995), p. 53; also see idem, 'The Importance of Hermeneutics for a Christian Worldview', in *Disciplining Hermeneutics: Interpretation in Christian Perspective* (ed. Roger Lundin; Grand Rapids: Eerdmans, 1997), pp. 25–47. John 10.35 uses 'word of God' in parallel with 'Scripture'; also see Mk 7.9-13, where 'commandment of God', what 'Moses said', and 'word of God' are interchangeably employed, all attesting to the singularity of the corpus as divine discourse. This divine communicative action does not contravene, but supervenes upon the human communicative action, those intentions of the texts' individual human authors (Kevin J. Vanhoozer, 'From Speech Acts to Scripture Acts: The Covenant of Discourse and the Discourse of the Covenant', in *After Pentecost: Language and Biblical Interpretation* [eds Craig Bartholomew, Colin Greene and Karl Möller; Grand Rapids: Zondervan, 2001], pp. 1–49 [37]).

Rule of Applicability, below). The singularity of the canon results in a singularity of its function as well; the unified goal of these writings is to proclaim the presence of God among his people, uniformly and with one voice. Despite their diversity, the component texts of the canon thus 'function ensemble' to direct the life of the Church, maintaining the identity of the community of God as a single, united and integral organism.[21]

The implication of the Rule of Singularity for interpretation is that the context for the hermeneutical undertaking has now become the unified canon of divine discourse, the individual and discrete texts of which are interpreted as constituent parts of *one* book. It is at the level of the canon that the illocutions and secondary referents of its divine author are borne and are particularly discernible. Thus it is also at the canonical level that the world in front of the text (the canonical world) becomes a distinct entity.[22]A particular pericope, part of the extended discourse of the canon as a whole, frames only a segment or facet of this comprehensive and plenary world projected by the canon. Therefore, though individual books and smaller texts within the Bible have their own integrity and identity, the interpreter must consider them in the singular context of the entire canon.[23] Thus the Rule of Singularity, asserting the unity and univocity of the canon, helps project a singular and plenary world in front of the canonical text, facets of which are framed by the individual texts comprising Scripture.

21. David H. Kelsey, *The Uses of Scripture in Recent Theology* (Philadelphia: Fortress, 1975), pp. 91, 106.

22. See Kevin J. Vanhoozer, *First Theology: God, Scripture and Hermeneutics* (Downers Grove: InterVarsity, 2002), p. 292. Paul R. Noble argues that meanings at the canonical level (illocutions and second-order referents) are themselves strong evidence that the present shape of the canon was 'intentionally produced, and produced, moreover, by an author who *intended* its final form to have these meanings – a few happy accidents aside, there is no other rational explanation as to how it *could* have such meanings' (Paul R. Noble, *A Canonical Approach: A Critical Reconstruction of the Hermeneutics of Brevard S. Childs* [Leiden: E.J. Brill, 1995], p. 199).

23. Yet, such a consideration must not result in those individual voices being 'outshouted by God', thus denying the reality of the distinct utterances that compose the canon. See Charles M. Wood, *The Formation of Christian Understanding* (Philadelphia: Westminster, 1981), p. 74; also see Wolterstorff, 'Importance of Hermeneutics for a Christian Worldview', pp. 45–6. What the human authors say does not become invalid the moment these writers are commissioned as God's spokesmen; neither does what God says cease to be his words in the presence of a human intermediary. While there is no hesitation in affirming that what the human author intended to say is part of the divine author's meaning, it is another matter to ask if the latter's meaning is exhausted by that of the former. The nature of divine discourse raises the possibility that the divine author might conceivably have intended more than what the human author could have appreciated. The 'prophecy' of Caiaphas in Jn 11.49-52, where, as high priest, he communicated a message from God that clearly went beyond anything he could have consciously intended, is an instance of this phenomenon. There can conceivably be a surplus of meaning to texts 'playing' in the canonical *Spielraum* – a surplus that may not have been circumscribed by the original textual sense of the human utterance, but which is within the boundaries of its projected world and the transhistorical intention it bears (see Chapter 1).

Rule of Organization
The *Rule of Organization* calls the interpreter using the biblical texts for applicational purposes to be attentive to the structuring of the bipartite canon, to the
ordering of books within each Testament and to the chronological unfolding of
the metanarrative resulting therefrom.

Organization of the Testaments. The canon of Scripture is not a random agglom-
eration of discourses, but a text with a particular shape, a pivotal core and two
distinct corpora that circumscribe that one focal point.[24] It is the centrality of
the redemptive life of Jesus Christ, foretold in the Old Testament and fulfilled
in the New, that consolidates the two collections into a unified whole, providing the foundation that regulates all subsequent hermeneutical movements of
reading and interpretation (see also the Rule of Primacy, below). The discrete
specification of these two parts, in terms of covenant/testament terminology,
came into practice, according to Eusebius, in the late second century with
Melito, bishop of Sardis (c. 170–190 CE), who mentioned a list of 'the books of
the old covenant'. Clement of Alexandria (writing in c. 180–200 CE) noted that
the term 'covenant' was applied to *both* Jewish and Christian Scriptures. His
successor, Origen (c. 185–254 CE), appears to have conceded that διαθήκη was
the common way to refer to parts of the canon; he spoke of 'what we believe
to be the divine Scriptures both of the Old Testament, as people say, and of
the New [Testament], as it is called'.[25] Such a juxtaposition was not simply
an attempt to ratify a historical continuity between Israel and the Church, but
rather an affirmation of the dealings of the selfsame God with his people on
either side of Pentecost, while at the same time acknowledging a discontinuity
between what was old and what was new.[26] In announcing this dialectic of continuity and discontinuity in the canon, the Church claimed the Jewish Scriptures
for itself and, yoking its new writings to it, canonized into one the Old and New
Testaments as divine discourse essential for its faith and practice.

Does the Rule of Organization (and that of Singularity) change the role of
the erstwhile Jewish Scriptures upon their incorporation and reshaping into the
Christian canon? Theologians and biblical scholars for the better part of the
last two millennia have considered the OT an adumbration of Christ that gave
significance to his life, death and resurrection, but which also, in turn, derived
its own significance from those same epochal events and their representation in
the NT.[27] Thus, the earlier writings acquire new shades of meaning in the light of

---

24. Francis Watson, *Text and Truth: Redefining Biblical Theology* (Grand Rapids: Eerdmans,
1997), p. 122.

25. Eusebius, *Hist. eccl.* 4.26.12-14; Clement of Alexandria, *Strom.* 1.9.44; 3.11.71; 4.21.134;
5.13.85; etc.; Origen, *Princ.* 4.1.1. Also see Gamble, *The New Testament Canon*, pp. 20–1.

26. See Brevard S. Childs, *Biblical Theology of the Old and New Testaments: Theological
Reflection on the Christian Bible* (London: SCM Press, 1992), p. 74.

27. Watson considers the important implications of the terminology 'Old' and 'New' as

their concatenation with the later texts; the incorporation of both together into a new canon not only alters the significance of what is within but also governs how what is within is organized, and thereby nuances the shape of the world in front of the text.[28]

Organization of the books. There is ample evidence of Christian redactional activity in the absorption of the Hebrew Bible into the canon of the Church. The tripartite division of that older corpus (*Torah, Nevi'im* and *Kethuvim*), for instance, was abandoned in favour of an arrangement consisting of the Pentateuch, books of history, wisdom literature and the prophets – an ordering that best reflected the Church's new, Gospel-oriented understanding of the Hebrew Scriptures.[29]

At the same time, in the original ordering of the OT, history was subsumed by the prophetic collection, with the canon ending with Chronicles. This placement appears to have been deliberate, separating the last book (located in the Writings) from the similar account of the Kings (located among the Prophets). The beginning of Chronicles contains a genealogy that proceeds from Adam (1 Chronicles 1–9), and the ending has a brief account of the return of Israel from

applied to the two Testaments: first, the polarity between oldness and newness indicates that the Christian Bible is 'irreducibly twofold'; the fact that all biblical texts fall on one or the other side of the dividing line between the two Testaments is essential rather than accidental. Second, there is a dialectical relationship between the two Testaments: without the Old there would not be the New, and vice versa. Third, this newly located relationship between the Old and New Testaments, within the circumscription of the canon, 'takes the form of a preceding and a following'. What has come before 'points forward to the moment that will retrospectively establish that its reality consists in whatever is implied by "oldness"'. Fourthly, oldness and newness are more than chronological in orientation – they are qualitative descriptions as well of an absolute kind. 'That which is new is always new. It cannot be superannuated, and it resists every attempt to convert its newness into oldness by [further supplementation].' Fifth, 'in so far as the old is constituted as old by the new it is relativized'. The new is assigned a certain degree of priority over the old, though maintaining with the latter a 'mutually constitutive relationship' (Watson, *Text and Truth,* pp. 179–80).

28. In opposition to the Rule of Organization concerning the two Testaments stands Marcion's rejection of the OT altogether. Less extreme, but operating in the same mould were Schleiermacher, who recommended the OT simply be an appendix to the New (*The Christian Faith* [eds H.R. Mackintosh and J.S. Stewart; Edinburgh: T. & T. Clark, 1928], p. 611), and Adolf von Harnack who declared that keeping the OT canonical in the nineteenth century was 'a consequence of religious and ecclesiastical crippling' (*Marcion: The Gospel of the Alien God* [trans. John E. Steely and Kyle D. Bierma; Durham, NC: Labyrinth, 1990], 134). These extreme and rare cases notwithstanding, the widespread tendency towards a de facto underutilization of the OT may also reflect a devaluing of that Testament.

29. Childs, *Biblical Theology of the Old and New Testaments,* p. 75. The physical organization of the canon, the codex, contributed to a fixity of sequence, for the ordering of the books was now 'inside' the Scriptures themselves, intrinsic to the collection (Aichele, *Control of Biblical Meaning,* p. 49).

exile (2 Chron. 36.22-3). This arrangement of the book, depicting the history of the nation from Adam through to the exile, makes it a recapitulation of the entire canon.[30] Jerome describes this closing volume of the Hebrew Scriptures as what 'we may more expressively call a chronicle of the whole of the sacred history'.[31] Perhaps it was the experience of the Babylonian exile that was decisive in this organizational predilection and the reiterative mode of the concluding book: the path to community renewal appeared obstructed, and unanticipated institutional developments had fragmented the religious leadership into competing parties. The trauma of the ejection from the land of promise and the destruction and loss of all that was valuable to the Israelites could conceivably have fostered this anamnestic focus in the rehearsal of history. However, in the midst of this despair there appeared Jesus of Nazareth. That remarkable intervention called for a reassignment of the prophets to the end of the OT (in the new Christian canon) to herald the imminent coming of this promised Messiah.[32]

The Christian OT thus concludes with a proleptic vision of wrathful judgement but softens the intensity thereof with a reminder of Moses and the giving of the law (thereby jogging its readers' memory of the redemption of the children of Israel), and with the reassuring promise of the return of Elijah and the reconciliation of Israel with God (Mal. 3.1; 4.1-6). The end, Janus-faced, looks back to the past as well as forward into the future. The NT that follows immediately reiterates originary events (Matthew's genealogy of Jesus Christ reaches back to Abraham, and Luke's to Adam; John goes even further back – $\dot{\epsilon}\nu$ $\dot{\alpha}\rho\chi\hat{\eta}$), links the final promise of the Old Testament with the contents of the New (e.g., Mt. 11.9-14; and Mk 1.2-7, that unite John the Baptist with Elijah), and ultimately takes the reader to the final consummation of history with Revelation and its visions of the heavenly city and the *Endzeit*. The organization of books thus creates the infrastructure upon which is projected the world in front of the text.[33]

30. Roger Beckwith, *The Old Testament Canon of the New Testament Church* (London: SPCK, 1985), pp. 139, 151, 158. This facet of the Rule of Organization is countered by the Septuagint, wherein Chronicles does not conclude the Hebrew canon as it does in the Masoretic order of books; instead, this particular corpus follows and supplements Kings, designating the former as the 'things left out' ($\pi\alpha\rho\alpha\lambda\epsilon\iota\pi\acute{o}\mu\epsilon\nu\alpha$). Such an observation is not to disregard the considerable common ground in the ordering of books between the Masoretic Text and the Septuagint.

31. Jerome, *Prefaces to the Books of the Vulgate: Samuel and Kings*, NPNF, Series II, vol. 6, pp. 489–90.

32. John W. Miller, *The Origins of the Bible: Rethinking Canon History* (Mahwah, NJ: Paulist, 1994), pp. 162–3.

33. Undoubtedly elements of scribal practice other than theological considerations could also have contributed to the rationale of the arrangement of the biblical texts, especially those of the Hebrew canon, including linkage of themes and theme words, arrangement in descending order of size, manner of storage of papyrus rolls, the justifiably parsimonious practice of copying multiple books on a single scroll, etc. Such considerations, pragmatic rather than theological, may conceivably dilute the force of the Rule of Organization.

Organization of time. '[The Bible] begins where time begins, with the creation of the world; it ends where time ends, with the Apocalypse, and it surveys human history in between' – truly an awe-inspiring narrative.[34] The Christian canon may therefore be considered to possess a tripartite shape in its essential 'plot' – a beginning (the purpose and action of God in creation), a middle (redemption) and an end (consummation).[35] Genesis to Revelation, in this reorganized depiction of time, outlines a trajectory of human history that begins in a verdant garden containing the tree of life (Gen. 2.8-17) and ends in a glorious city that also contains a tree of life (Rev. 22.1-2). The garden at the commencement of the story served as the place where man engaged in עָבַד ('cultivation', Gen. 2.5, 15). This word later acquired strong liturgical connotations and came to be used regularly for the service of worship (as in Num. 3.7-8; 8.25-6; 18.5-6; etc.), hinting at the kind of activity Adam had actually been engaged in, in that primeval agricultural paradise. It is no coincidence, then, that the δοῦλοι of the Lamb, in the restored garden that is the heavenly city, will also be 'serving' (Rev. 22.3; from λατρεύω, also used frequently of worship as, for example, in Heb. 10.2; 13.10; Rev. 7.15; etc.). Eden was the garden of God, with God's presence its central and dominating feature (see Isa. 51.3; and Ezek. 28.13); quite appropriately, the Rule of Organization has the canon end with another divine sanctuary, the New Jerusalem wherein is stationed 'the throne of God and of the Lamb' (Rev. 22.3).[36] The recurring motifs delineate the high degree of organization of time, from the opening act to the closing one, a structuring both deliberate and precise.

However, it is not only the beginning and the end of the story that is emphasized in the canon. Indeed, the 'middle' takes an unusual prominence in the fourfold retelling of the story of Jesus and the account of his redemptive work (also see Rule of Primacy). In their foundational stance at the commencement of the NT, the Gospels resemble the inaugural and fundamental books of the Pentateuch; that one of the texts in the former category opens with the same words as the first book of the latter reinforces the similarity. Justin equates the 'memoirs of the apostles' with the 'Gospels' (*1 Apol.* 66–7), perhaps the first Christian occurrence of the word in the plural, indicating a multiplicity of these *bioi*. Nonetheless, these remarkable multiple iterations of the life of the protagonist of the NT are all subsumed under a single heading of 'the gospel'. Each individual *bios* is designated as the Gospel 'according to' (κατά) its presumed author, demonstrating a unity of theological meaning in a diversity of witnesses

34. Frye, *Great Code*, p. xiii.

35. Joel B. Green, 'Reading the Gospels and Acts as Narrative', in *Narrative Reading, Narrative Preaching: Reuniting New Testament Interpretation and Proclamation* (eds Joel B. Green and Michael Pasquarello III; Grand Rapids: Baker, 2003), pp. 37–66 (51–2).

36. William J. Dumbrell, 'Genesis 2:1–17: A Foreshadowing of the New Creation', in *Biblical Theology: Retrospect and Prospect* (ed. Scott J. Hafemann; Downers Grove: InterVarsity, 2002), pp. 53–65.

– a *fourfold* gospel.[37] While this unity does not preclude the presence of four discrete Gospels, none of the Gospels is *the* gospel, but together the four – unity in diversity – ensure that this one Lord of whom they speak 'transcends not only those witnesses but also all subsequent Christian theological and ethical positions and decisions'.[38] The Muratorian Canon (late second century) asserted that 'though various elements may be taught in the individual books of the Gospels, nevertheless this makes no difference to the faith of believers, since by the one sovereign Spirit all things have been declared in all [the Gospels]'. In the same vein, Irenaeus observed that 'He who was manifested to men, has given us the Gospel under four aspects, but bound together by one Spirit' (ἐνὶ πνεύματι συνεχόμενον; *Haer.* 3.11.8).[39] The early Church, therefore, resisted both Marcion's exclusive use of one Gospel (Luke) as well as Tatian's harmonizing approach (the *Diatessaron*), maintaining that the goal of each individual account was to tell the story of this particular person, Jesus Christ, in a particular way.[40] In other words, the very acceptance of the fourfold gospel by the early Church attested to its consideration of these works as not merely histories, but also as crucial theological witnesses to Jesus Christ.[41] His story remains the

37. 𝔭[66] and 𝔭[75] (from the second and early third centuries) provide these superscriptions to the Gospels.

38. Robert Morgan, 'The Hermeneutical Significance of the Four Gospels', *Int* 33 (1979), pp. 376–88 (385, 387). It is quite likely that the early Christian predilection for the codex, rather than the scroll, was the result of the co-location of the four Gospels; Christian papyri, unlike non-Christian ones, are almost all fragments of codices (T.C. Skeat, 'The Origins of the Christian Codex', *ZPE* 102 [1994], pp. 263–8). Also see Graham N. Stanton, 'The Fourfold Gospel', *NTS* 43 (1997), pp. 317–46 (330, 337).

39. Origen, likewise, claimed that the unity of Christ proclaimed by the evangelists was reflected in the gospel which 'though written by several hands, is, in effect, one' (*Comm. Jo.* 5.4). For the Muratorian canon see Metzger, *The Canon of the New Testament*, pp. 305–7.

40. However, it must be conceded that Tatian and Marcion introduce complicating factors into the application of this aspect of the Rule of Organization, once again demonstrating that, while this rule was widely applied, it clearly has not been universal in acceptance. Produced in c. 175 CE, the *Diatessaron* was the standard gospel text in the liturgy of Syrian Christians for over two centuries, generating at least one commentary based on that harmonization of the Gospels (by Ephrem the Syrian, c. 306–373 CE – *Saint Ephrem's Commentary on Tatian's Diatessaron* [trans. C. McCarthy; Oxford: Oxford University Press, 1993]).

41. Stanton, 'The Fourfold Gospel', pp. 343–4. Respecting this decision of the community of God that recognized the canon, Burridge cautions that the common practice of harmonizing Gospel passages, especially during the seasons celebrating the birth and passion of Jesus, should be undertaken with judicious restraint. Matthew's account of the wise men carries particular theological emphases such as kingship, worship and the coming of powerful Gentiles to Jesus; Luke's settings with the shepherds introduces the theme of Jesus' identification with the lowly. Mark portrays the forsakenness of Jesus on the cross with the cry in 15.34; John, in contrast, announces victory in the final declaration of Jesus (τετέλεσται, 19.30). The world portrayed by each account depicts Jesus in a particular relation to God's creation: the theological purposes of the individual authors are borne by such unique world projections (Richard A. Burridge, *Four*

heart of the Scriptures, the fulcrum about which the canon pivots, sustaining the weight of both Old and New Testaments, and generating the force of their impact on the lives of believers. This four-faceted structure of the 'middle' of the plot gives the organization of canonical time a unique emphasis, shaping the projected world in front of the text.

Thus, the Rule of Organization has radically redesigned the reading frame of the individual texts, reorganizing the contents of the canon – the Testaments, the books and their time: 'there is hermeneutics in the Christian order'.[42] In and through these organizational characteristics, the canon works to project a world, respecting the sequential movement from Old to New, both in biblical history and in time (see also the Rule of Sequentiality, below).

Together the Rules of Completion, Singularity and Organization (the Rules of Structure) undergird the literary projection of the world in front of the canonical text. The final form of the text forms the source material for the world, the colours and pigments that authors (artisans) employ to paint an integral, singular and organized 'structure'. This world in front of the text, in its canonical form, is a composite of the projections of each of its constituent pericopes, a plenary world that depicts the activities of God and his relationship with his creation.

Rules of Function

The Rules of Function point the interpreter to the operations of the language-game of canon: what it permits within its membership (the Rule of Exclusivity); which texts in the canon may be employed for application and for whom such application is relevant (Rule of Applicability); the manner in which it mandates its own reading (Rule of Congruence); and the appropriate locus of its interpretive processes and practices (Rule of Ecclesiality).

Rule of Exclusivity

The Rule of Exclusivity determines that only those books included in the canon may be utilized for applicational purposes.

This rule discriminates between what is acceptable for inclusion in the canon and what is not. In effect, the canon is an ancient form of 'copyright', protecting the corpus as a whole from distortion and deformation.[43] For the purposes of interpretation, then, the Rule of Exclusivity demarcates what textual discourses may (or may not) function in the edification of the community. It restricts authority to particular texts; only these selected writings may be preached from

Gospels, One Jesus? A Symbolic Reading [London: SPCK, 1994], pp. 164–5). See also Chapter 2 for the importance of the authorial purpose in determining the trajectory of each text and the world it projects.

42. Paul Ricoeur, 'Preface to Bultmann', in *The Conflict of Interpretations* (trans. Peter McCormick; ed. Don Ihde; Evanston: Northwestern University Press, 1974), pp. 384–401 (384).

43. Aichele, *Control of Biblical Meaning*, p. 20.

and applied.[44] The inclusion of certain books within the canon renders those books, and those books alone, authoritative for the faith and practice of the Church. The language-game of the canon commissions such texts to be utilized repeatedly in the community to bring its corporate life and the lives of the individuals it comprises into line with the will of God.

Through a reflective evaluation of its literary heritage, the early Church in the second century construed as canonical a set of authoritative writings. It realized that without a written norm, its station in time was too distant from the apostolic age for it to be able to guard the purity of what had been handed down. This *principle* of a canon was an acknowledgement by the community of believers that thenceforth, every subsequent tradition would be submitted to the control of the authoritative apostolic tradition that constituted the Church, a tradition that was fixed in, and bounded by, the canon. Such a settled and stable body of literature was deemed an adequate norm, sufficient for regulating the teaching office of the Church, and upon which norm such office would be dependent.[45]

The act of canon recognition was not a random process, but one that appealed to certain principles that, however, were not employed with great rigor or consistency; rather, the determination of the canon rested essentially upon 'a dialectical combination of historical and theological criteria'. The primary yardsticks that served in the assessment of texts for inclusion in the canon were traditional usage (including catholicity) and orthodoxy of the candidate volumes.[46] Authorship and inspiration, for the recognition of books as canonical, played a more indirect role. However, in the face of attacks on the canon by Marcion and others, when forced to justify its acceptance of some books and not others, the Church employed apostolic authorship of those texts as a condition for their inclusion within the canon. Tertullian declared as of primary importance 'that the evangelical Testament has apostles for its authors, to whom was assigned by

44. As with the Rule of Completion that does not specify the actual final form to be employed, this Rule of Exclusivity also does not mandate the canonical composition of books that must be accepted. No one list of the books of the canon is preferred by this rule over others. The rule as stated implies that applicational practices of the community will be contingent upon the boundaries of the canon that they submit to. The belief in purgatory, for instance, may depend on whether the tradition includes within its canon the deuterocanonical books of Maccabees; *The Catechism of the Catholic Church* (2nd edn; New York: Doubleday, 2003), ¶1032, asserts that the teaching of purgatory is partly based upon 2 Macc. 12.45.

45. Oscar Cullman, *The Early Church* (London: SCM Press, 1956), pp. 90–1. John Webster notes that the Church's act of canonization was 'an act of faithful *assent* rather than a self-derived judgment' – a confessional act, one of submission to the authority of the Holy Spirit present in the Church. By this act of submission, the Church also pledged itself to abide by the norm of the canon in all its beliefs, speech, and activities (*Word and Church: Essays in Christian Dogma* [Edinburgh: T. & T. Clark, 2001], pp. 38–40).

46. Metzger, *Canon of the New Testament*, p. 254; Gamble, *New Testament Canon*, pp. 67–8.

the Lord himself this office of publishing the gospel' (*Marc.* 4.2).[47] Moreover, while according the Jewish Scriptures the status of inspired writings, similar claims for the newer Christian writings were also made by the early Church. Clement of Rome, for instance, acknowledged that Paul wrote 'with true inspiration' (*1 Clem.* 47.3).[48] The increasing practice of reading those Christian texts alongside the Hebrew Scriptures inevitably resulted in the assignment of equal *gravitas* to both collections. Nonetheless, as F.F. Bruce noted, 'inspiration is no longer a criterion of canonicity: it is a corollary of canonicity'.[49]

By utilizing the criteria of traditional usage and orthodoxy, the early Church drew a perimeter with quite a lengthy – but not indefinite – radius, implicitly propounding a Rule of Exclusivity that demarcated those texts deemed canonical. The canon, thus, allows the interpreter to work with a variety of primary genres, composed by a variety of authors, dealing with a variety of theocentric matters and issues, assuring the interpreter of a full range of discourses or 'God-talk' that successfully projects the canonical world in front of the text.

Traditional usage. Traditional usage of a document was, perhaps, one of the most important elements for deciding upon the canonicity of a text. This principle pertained primarily to the (then) current practices of the Church, rather than to the intrinsic character of the writings themselves. The texts included in the canon were, for the most part, those that had consistently enjoyed pre-eminence in the Church because they had been deemed the most useful in the nurture, sustenance and promotion of the faith of the first Christian communities.[50] Formal accep-

47. Likewise, the Muratorian Canon also adduced the personal qualifications of the authors, either as eyewitnesses or as apostles, as grounds for the canonicity of several of the NT books (translated in Metzger, *Canon of the New Testament*, pp. 305–7).

48. Some of the writers of the canonical texts understood the inspired nature of their own writings: the author of the Apocalypse, for instance, denoted his writing as 'the words of this prophecy' (Rev. 22.19). The readers of the seven letters in Revelation 2–3 were adjured, in each of those epistles, to 'hear what the Spirit says to the churches', again implying that those texts had a divine imprimatur (also see 2 Tim. 3.16; and 2 Pet. 1.21).

49. F.F. Bruce, *The Canon of Scripture* (Downers Grove: InterVarsity, 1988), p. 268. Metzger concludes similarly: 'A writing is not canonical because the author was inspired, but rather an author is considered to be inspired because what he has written is recognized as canonical, that is, recognized as authoritative in the Church' (Metzger, *Canon of the New Testament*, p. 257). Nevertheless, the Bible's own claim to being inspired (2 Tim. 3.16) must be respected. To make sense of the Bible on its own terms and upon its own claims, one need not believe in inspiration or, indeed, even the rules of grammar, but one *must* postulate both. See Meir Sternberg, *The Poetics of Biblical Narrative: Ideological Literature and the Drama of Reading* (Bloomington, IN: Indiana University Press, 1987), p. 81.

50. Gamble, *New Testament Canon*, pp. 70–1. He observes that some writings that met the criterion of traditional usage were excluded (*The Shepherd of Hermas, 1 Clement, Didache*); others that were not as widely utilized were included (James, 2 Peter, 2 and 3 John). Whether or not the books were edifying also played a significant part in determining their traditional usage

tances of such recognized books were quite early events in the life of the Church; Paul credits the Thessalonians, for instance, with having received his word as the word of God (1 Thess. 2.13). The designation of Luke's Gospel as 'Scripture' also affirms its canonical reception by the Church from early days (1 Tim. 5.18 labels it as such, citing Lk. 10.7; also see 2 Pet. 3.15-16). In this connection, Jerome assured Dardanus, the prefect of Gaul, that, no matter who the author of Hebrews was, it was constantly read in churches as the work of a churchman (*ecclesiastici viri*).[51] Traditional usage was also closely linked to the catholicity of the documents: to be deemed authoritative, a document had to be relevant to the community of God's people as a whole. For instance, despite the particularity of the Epistles, addressed as they were to specific individuals and congregations, the early Church recognized their broad appeal and utility. Tertullian could therefore ask rhetorically: 'But of what consequence are the titles [of the letters], since in writing to a certain church the apostle did in fact write to all?' (*Marc.* 5.17). The goal of the criterion of traditional usage and catholicity was to preclude idiosyncratic, esoteric and sequestered documents of limited relevance and utility from entering the canon; passing muster, in contrast, were texts that were widely accessible and generally approved of as bearing perennial significance for edification.[52] Augustine asserted that the Christian interpreter of the Scriptures should prefer those texts 'accepted by all catholic churches to those which some do not accept' (*Doctr. chr.* 2.8.12). Traditional usage and catholicity thus marked those documents that finally found inclusion within the canon.

Orthodoxy. Another fundamental gauge of canonicity was the text's consistency and congruence with apostolic teaching, the orthodoxy (and, perhaps, orthopraxy) of the Church. If the canon was ultimately the product of divine authorship, then what was asserted in the candidate document, were it truly canonical, would be in concord with the instruction of the apostles. The appli-

---

(Heb. 4.12; 2 Tim. 3.17). This ambiguity of the status of certain books is a countervailing force upon the applicability of the Rule of Exclusivity that adduces traditional usage as evidence for its employment.

51. Jerome, *Ep. ad Dardanum*, *Sancti Hieronymi Epistulæ* (Paris: Société d'Edition 'Les Belles Lettres', 1961), pp. 160–1 (161).

52. For instance, the Colossians are asked to have their letter passed on to other Christian assemblies (Col. 4.16). Revelation 1.3 also assumes a wider readership than the seven churches to which John wrote; the Muratorian Canon says of Revelation that 'John also in the Apocalypse, though he writes to seven churches, nevertheless speaks for all' (see its translation in Metzger, *Canon of the New Testament*, pp. 305–7). Vanhoozer's observation is worth noting: 'That the church recognizes the canon authenticates the church rather than the canon, which needs no ecclesial approval to be what it is: the Word of God. Canonicity is the criterion of catholicity, not vice versa' (Kevin J. Vanhoozer, *The Drama of Doctrine: A Canonical-Linguistic Approach to Christian Theology* [Louisville: Westminster/John Knox Press, 2005], p. 150 [italics removed]). Nevertheless, there is a sense in which catholicity (and traditional usage and orthodoxy) helped identify those texts that would formally be included in the canon.

cation of the criterion of orthodoxy was, therefore, a symbiotic process, with Scripture shaping apostolic tradition and apostolic tradition helping to recognize canonical material (also see Rule of Congruence). The 'apostolic deposit', over the decades and centuries of the Church, became the core of the authoritative literature of the NT, by which standard the doctrine of the books vying for canonical inclusion was gauged. Regarding disputed books, Eusebius wrote: 'And further, the character of the style is at variance with apostolic usage, and both the thoughts and the purpose of the things that are related in them are so completely out of accord with true orthodoxy that they clearly show themselves to be the fictions of heretics' (*Hist. eccl.* 3.25.7).[53] Orthodoxy, along with traditional usage and catholicity, thus demarcated those texts deemed worthy of being accorded canonical status.

The early Church, implicitly employing the Rule of Exclusivity in the evaluation of candidate documents vying for inclusion in the canon, accepted certain texts as worthy of reading even before those writings were formally acknowledged as being members of the circumscribed corpus of the canon. In other words, while critics determine *what ought to be* appreciated, readers determine *what actually is* appreciated.[54] In applying the Rule of Exclusivity, the Church was asserting that the world projected by the canon should be constituted by the contributions of a selected coterie of texts; such texts alone, making up the canon, were to be authoritative for the depiction of the canonical world and, thereby, for application.

Rule of Applicability
The Rule of Applicability asserts that every text in the canonical Scriptures may be utilized for applicational purposes by the Church universal.

Totality of Scripture. All the biblical writings are to be utilized in the life of the Christian community for the determination of its faith and the coordination of

53. The very existence of contradictory claims regarding certain books indicates that the Rule of Exclusivity was not an absolute mandate universally applied. Eusebius' distinctions between texts that were *homologoumena* (recognized), *antilegomena* (disputed), *notha* (spurious) and heretical suggests that all was not being smoothly administered by this rule (see *Hist. eccl.* 3.5.5-7; 3.25.1-7). However, one must admit that contested books form only a fraction of the total canonical content; there is considerable agreement as to what constitutes the remainder.

54. George Steiner declared that '[t]he critic prescribes a syllabus; the reader is answerable to and internalizes a canon' (' "Critic"/"Reader" ', *NLH* 10 [1979], pp. 423–52 [445]). On the other hand, a major factor that positively influences the trust of future readers in written discourse, especially literature, is the selection pressure those documents have undergone at the hands of publishers and critics – editings and reviews that decide on its printability, that adjudicate between other competing texts and that chaperone the 'winning' text to its final shape and form. The analogy with the process of finalizing the canon is obvious (Elizabeth Closs Traugott and Mary Louise Pratt, *Linguistics for Students of Literature* [New York: Harcourt Brace Jovanovich, 1980], p. 261).

its practices 'because the power of God's kingly rule graciously shapes human identity and empowers new forms of life in persons through Scripture'. The divine discourse that is the canon renders it efficacious for the transformation of the individual and community into the will of God – the 'ground of its authority *de jure*'.[55] The canon asserts the right of every one of its constituent parts to be heard: *all* Scripture is profitable for application (2 Tim. 3.16). Neither did Paul hesitate to confirm, in Rom. 15.4, that 'whatever was written' in earlier times was written for the instruction of the contemporary reader. The canon mandates application of all Scripture because all Scripture is efficacious, and all Scripture is efficacious because it is divinely empowered; thus is begotten the Rule of Applicability that expresses itself as the potential for application of all Scripture.[56]

The Rule of Applicability expects that no text included in the canon will be disregarded for the purposes of application. If the canon projects a world in front of itself, and individual texts portray facets thereof, then for the discernment and appropriation of the plenary world all texts must be utilized. It is the totality of the canonical package – the diverse forms of its communicative action that constitute the interpretative framework for understanding God and his relationship with his creation – that governs the activities of the people of God.[57] However, Gamble's assertion that 'the creation of the canon had a levelling effect upon its contents' may not be historically sustainable. It seems, instead, from the early days of the Church, that ecclesial practice utilized some books of the corpus more than others: Genesis, Psalms and the prophecies of Isaiah appear to have had more currency than other canonical texts. A complete literary work presumes the thematic and formal relevance of all its constituent details, but that is not to say that all those details are equally relevant; rather, 'to identify the structure of a work is to construct a *hierarchy* of relevance that makes some of its details central and others peripheral. No detail, however, can be completely irrelevant.'[58] Despite the potential variation in degree of rel-

---

55. David H. Kelsey, 'The Bible and Christian Theology', *JAAR* 48 (1980), pp. 385–402 (395).

56. Reading the Bible is, therefore, to be a moral and spiritual endeavour aided by God, not merely a cognitive exercise. In any account of the hermeneutics of Scripture the role of the Holy Spirit in illuminating the interpreter must be considered. Accordingly, Webster denotes Christian reading as a prayerful activity that constitutes and accompanies such reading (Webster, *Word and Church*, pp. 78, 82–3).

57. Vanhoozer, *Drama of Doctrine*, pp. 149–50.

58. Gamble, *New Testament Canon*, p. 75; Gary Saul Morson, *The Boundaries of Genre: Dostoevsky's* Diary of a Writer *and the Tradition of Literary Utopia* (Austin, TX: University of Texas Press, 1981), p. 42. This hierarchy of relevance may, in practical terms, be equivalent to a contravention of this Rule of Applicability for, over a period of time, when certain books are preached from more often than others, those less-preached texts are effectively relegated to some degree of insignificance and neglect.

evance between texts, every individual portion of the canon must be construed as contributing, in its own fashion, to the projection of the world in front of the text.

Universality of relevance. While acknowledging the importance of discerning the original setting of God's address to his people, the canon creates a situation where the whole is greater than the sum of its parts: a unique canonical context is superimposed upon the contexts of the individual texts and discourses. A consequence of this superimposition is that the canonical text attains 'a form which has erased, to a greater or lesser extent, most of the particularities of its circumstances of origin'.[59] From the perspective of the canon, this erasure, seen as an intentional action, is of critical importance to the congregation of future readers. The consolidation of heterogeneous writings into a single normative canon created a new reading frame for its component texts, a playground (*Spielraum*) for those language-games. The canon, thus, recontextualizes the texts incorporated therein, redeploying them as parts of a new literary whole in a new hermeneutical context. Such a transaction generates for those texts prescriptive, perennial and plural significance, and enables another subsequent recontextualization in the individual circumstances of its many and varied readers. This hermeneutical shift prompted by the canon, *in nuce*, was a move to render the will of God accessible for future generations, and that move, already begun, is consummated in a further move for future members of the community of faith by the preaching of Scripture. The Rule of Applicability thus renders the canon potentially relevant for every believer in every era. Chrysostom declared that what was written in the Bible was written 'for us' and, therefore, worthy of diligent attention (προσέχετέ, παρακαλῶ, μετὰ ἀκριβείας τοῖς παρ' ἡμῶν λεγομένοις). In like manner, asserting the universality of the canon's relevance and readership, Gregory the Great asked rhetorically: 'For what is sacred Scripture but a kind of epistle of Almighty God to His creature?'[60] The Talmud, citing Exod. 13.8, also declared the relevance of the Scriptures for all: 'It is therefore incumbent on every person, in all ages, that he should consider it as though he had personally gone forth from Egypt' (*m. Pesaḥ.* 10). Such an acceptance of the universal relevance of the historic text emphasizes the significance of the Rule of Applicability.[61]

59. Watson, *Text, Church and World*, p. 40.

60. Chrysostom, *Hom. Gen.* 2.2 (PG 53, 27); Gregory the Great, *Ep. ad Theodorum medicum* (PL 77, 706 A). The Bible itself consistently affirms the relevance of its message for future generations. The words of the Mosaic Law, for instance, were expressly intended to transcend the immediate audience: in Deut. 29.14-15, Yahweh explicitly establishes his covenant not only with those Israelites present but also with 'those who are not with us here today'. Also see Deut. 6.6-25; 31.9-13; 2 Kgs 22–23; Neh. 7.73b–8.18; Ps. 78.5-6; Mt. 28.19; Rom. 15.4; 1 Cor. 9.10; 10.6, 11; 2 Tim. 3.16-17; etc.

61. While the emphasis on universality of relevance in the Rule of Applicability may be widely

The concern for recontextualization and application of the canonical Scriptures was clearly visible with the return of the Jews to their homeland after the Babylonian exile. With that experience came the need for precision in matters of daily behaviour regulated by the Scriptures. The domain of commentary that governed such matters evolved into the *halakah*, the collective corpus of biblical laws 'interpreted, fleshed out, and even supplemented', and later codified in the *Mishnah*.[62] Expositional application became a fixture of synagogue worship. Philo observed that on the Sabbath, a day of learning for all, Scripture is read and 'some of those who are very learned explain to them what is of great importance and use, lessons by which the whole of their lives may be improved'.[63] This Jewish orientation of reading for application was retained in the hermeneutics of the Church. Justin Martyr's description of a second-century worship service in Rome noted that, after the reading of the Gospels, 'the presider verbally instructs, and exhorts to the imitation of these good things' (*1 Apol.* 67).

The exuberant production of texts and sermons on every portion of the canon throughout the centuries of the Church's existence also attests to the crucial nature of application for the community (as well as to the crucial nature of the subjects addressed in the Bible; see the Rule of Substantiality below). Augustine took pains to emphasize this practical aspect of interpretation: 'So anyone who thinks that he has understood the divine Scriptures or any part of them, but cannot by his understanding build up this double love of God and neighbour, has not yet succeeded in understanding them.' Of an expositor of the Scriptures, he wrote that the aim to be pursued by such a one was 'to be listened to with understanding, with pleasure, and *with obedience*'. This church father also borrowed from Cicero, on the goal of the orator: 'instructing is a matter of necessity, delighting a matter of charm, and *moving them* a matter of conquest'.[64] Application of Scripture was to be the culmination of the move

---

accepted in principle, large tracts of Christendom do not necessarily agree that every portion of the canon can be applied to everyone, everywhere. The fact that the NT declares that the Mosaic Law is no longer in force upon those of the new covenant (Rom. 6.14; 10.4; Eph. 2.15) raises the question of whether this rule is too broadly stated. Christian Reconstructionists (theonomists) would demur: biblical law, for them, ought still to be applicable today. See William S. Barker and W. Robert Godfrey (eds), *Theonomy: A Reformed Critique* (Grand Rapids: Zondervan, 1990). Nonetheless, the Mosaic code remains firmly entrenched in the Christian Bible, and lectionaries continue to draw from it, assuming that the Pentateuch can be treated like other biblical material.

62. *Halakah* comes from Neh. 10.29, לָלֶכֶת בְּתוֹרַת הָאֱלֹהִים, 'to walk in God's Torah'. James L. Kugel and Rowan A. Greer, *Early Biblical Interpretation* (Philadelphia: Westminster, 1986), pp. 67–72.

63. *Spec. Laws* 2.15.62. Also see *Hypoth.* 7.13.

64. *Doctr. chr.* 1.36.40; 4.15.32; and 4.12.27 (from Cicero, *Or. Brut.* 21) (italics added). Augustine decried the futility of persuading hearers of the truth, or delighting them with style, if the learning process did not result in action (*Doctr. chr.* 4.13.29). Also see Quintilian, *Inst.* 3.5; and Cicero, *De or.* 2.115, 121, 128; *Brut.* 185, 276.

from text to praxis. Such a notion of applicability was based upon the stance of therapeutic opposition assumed by the canon as it declares that readers, in the sight of God, are not who they are tempted to think they are, and that they should act otherwise than they are naturally inclined, in order to abide by the demands of God's word.[65] That matter of 'acting otherwise', and the discernment of how one might actually do so, is the burden of interpretation that seeks to arrive at valid application.

The Rule of Applicability testifies to the prescriptive, perennial and plural significance of the biblical canon for the faith and practice of the Church, asserting the universal relevance of this canonically recontextualized colligation of documents. This is a text that must be applied by those who acknowledge that corpus as their Scripture. In such application, readers inhabit the world in front of the text, thus moulding the community of God of all time and in all places into the will of God. How this is accomplished through the agency of preaching will be considered in the next chapter.

Rule of Congruence
The Rule of Congruence bids interpreters assume broad coherence and consistency among the constituent texts of the canon, for applicational purposes.

The Rule of Congruence in this secondary language-game, closely related to the Rule of Singularity and a consequence thereof, calls for an assumption of coherence and consistency among the various texts within the canon. The construal of the canon as a single unified discourse forms the basis for attributing congruence between the discrete texts of the corpus. For biblical interpretation, not only is such a rule the reflection of canonical unity, it is also a fundamental precept of charitable reading, the first reflex of the reader that accords the text the benefit of such an assumption of congruence.[66] Indeed, all reading operates upon such a starting assumption of intratextual coherence and consistency. While the Rule of Singularity urged that the canon be considered an integral

65. John Goldingay, *Models for Interpretation of Scripture* (Grand Rapids: Eerdmans, 1995), p. 125. 'God's address is interceptive; it does not leave the hearer in neutrality, or merely invite us to adopt a position vis-à-vis itself and entertain it as a possibility. It allows no safe havens; it *judges*' – a response to the text *must* be made (Webster, *Word and Church*, p. 75).

66. Barton, *Spirit and the Letter*, p. 139; Kevin J. Vanhoozer, *Is There a Meaning in This Text? The Bible, the Reader, and the Morality of Literary Knowledge* (Grand Rapids: Zondervan, 1998), p. 32. Understanding involves a starting assumption, an 'initative trust, an investment of belief', which is an act of charity towards author and text. 'We venture a leap: we grant *ab initio* that there is "something there" to be understood, that the transfer will not be void.' George Steiner calls this a 'radical generosity' (*After Babel: Aspects of Language and Translation* [London: Oxford University Press, 1975], p. 296). To begin with doubt, Booth warned, 'is to destroy the datum' – the material and subject of interpretation; a primary act of assent and surrender is the essential first step in approaching a text (Wayne C. Booth, *The Company We Keep: An Ethics of Fiction* [Berkeley, CA: University of California Press, 1988], p. 32).

whole, by the Rule of Congruence a charitable approach to Scripture is adopted that assumes that the canonical writers do not contradict themselves or each other; the burden of proof is upon the interpreter to demonstrate otherwise. No one place in this unique discourse may be so expounded 'that it be repugnant to another' (Art. 20, *The Thirty-Nine Articles*, 1563).[67] The Rule of Congruence calls for a reading that respects the complementarity of the texts comprising the canon; underlying the workings of this guideline is the notion of the 'rule of faith'. Complementarity and the rule of faith will be considered here.

Complementarity. The Rule of Congruence of the canonical Scriptures yields the notion of complementarity of the different parts of the text, one to another. A hermeneutical construct by design, the canon not only bestows upon Scripture organization, coherence and unity but also promotes the reading of each text in the light of all the others. The language-game of canon is itself, thus, a locus of meaning.[68]

Complementarity by the Rule of Congruence is reflected in, and implied by, several of the principles (*middoth*) of rabbinical exegesis that were attributed by the Talmud to Rabbi Hillel (c. 70 BCE–10 CE).[69] One of them, *binyan 'ab mišenê ketûbim* (בנין אב משני כתובם = 'building up a family from two texts'), constructs a leading rule from two passages: for example, from the commands to unmuzzle the working ox (Deut. 25.4) and to give temple priests a share of the sacrifices (Deut. 18.1-8), one reasonably infers the right of ministers to earn a living (1 Cor. 9.9, 13). Another, *kāyoṣēʾ bô bemāqôm ʾahēr* (כיוצא בו במקום אחר = 'something similar in another place'), solves a

67. In W.H. Griffith Thomas, *The Principles of Theology: An Introduction to the Thirty-Nine Articles* (London: Longmans, 1930), p. 281.

68. Gamble, *New Testament Canon*, p. 79. The existence of multiple editions of 'Study Bibles' besprinkled with cross-references testifies to the importance of the Rule of Congruence (complementarity) for the Christian community. Frances Young finds that, in patristic exegesis, cross-references were frequently made in order to discern the sense intended by the authors, the whole approach to the text being shaped by 'well-rehearsed assumptions that Scripture was a unity, and that the wording was intended to point beyond itself to the underlying meaning or overall truth being expressed' (Frances Young, 'The "Mind" of Scripture: Theological Readings of the Bible in the Fathers', *IJST* 7 [2005], pp. 126–41 [133–4]).

69. *'Abot R. Nat.* 37; and *t. Sanh.* 7.11. Also see E. Earle Ellis, 'Biblical Interpretation in the New Testament Church', in *Mikra: Text, Translation, Reading and Interpretation of the Hebrew Bible in Ancient Judaism and Early Christianity* (ed. Martin Jan Mulder; Philadelphia: Fortress, 1988), pp. 691–725 (699–702), for the examples cited. The imprecision of the Talmud's attributions of these notions to first-century rabbis notwithstanding, the *middoth* of Rabbi Hillel offer valuable insights into the Jewish conception of hermeneutical principles in the first three centuries of this era. That early Christian interpretive precepts could have been drawn from antecedent and contemporary notions of Jewish hermeneutics should come as no surprise; not only did Judaism and early Christianity have scriptural texts in common, but also the reading thereof and the principles that guided those readings were likely shared as well.

difficulty in one text by analogy and comparison with another: for example, the covenant at Sinai (Exodus 19–31; Lev. 26.9-12) is shown to be inadequate and temporary by a subsequent and similar passage (Jer. 31.31-4) in which a new covenant is broached (Heb. 8.7-13). The rule of *gezērâ šawâ* (גזירה שוה = 'equivalent regulation') allows the interpreter to draw an inference from analogous expressions elsewhere: for example, David, who received the kingdom from God, was blameless when he and his associates violated the Law in eating the consecrated bread (1 Sam. 21.6); the Son of Man, who also received a kingdom from God (Dan. 7.13), is equally blameless when those with him violate the Sabbath law under similar circumstances (Lk. 6.1-5). It is the assumption of complementarity of the various parts of the canon that makes possible the employment of these rabbinical principles.

The concord between the texts of the canon may be further demonstrated in Daniel's acceptance of Jeremiah's prophecy (Dan. 9.2 citing Jer. 25.11-12 on the seventy-year length of the Babylonian captivity) and the grounding of his own revelatory vision in the שָׁבְעִים שִׁבְעִים (seventy sevens/weeks, Dan. 9.24). Another example of the operation of the Rule of Complementarity is the identity of the serpent of Gen. 3.1-5 that has traditionally been understood as being disclosed in Rev. 12.9 ('the serpent of old, who is called the devil and Satan'; also see Rev. 20.2). The Rule of Congruence thus respects the multivocal nature of the canon with regard to any given topic. Irenaeus wisely noted (*Haer.* 2.28.3):

> [A]ll Scripture, which has been given to us by God, shall be found by us perfectly consistent; and the parables shall harmonize with those passages which are perfectly plain; and those statements the meaning of which is clear, shall serve to explain the parables; and through the many diversified utterances [of Scripture] there shall be heard one harmonious melody in us, praising in hymns that God who created all things.

This sentiment resonates with the attribution to the canon the characteristics of a polyphonic musical composition with multiple and contrapuntal melodic lines blending into a harmony.[70] The Rule of Congruence is thus exemplified in the complementarity of the constituent parts of the canon, a congruence that is the consequence of the Bible being divine discourse.[71] In Justin's *Dialogue with*

---

70. Richard B. Hays, *The Moral Vision of the New Testament: Community, Cross, New Creation: A Contemporary Introduction to New Testament Ethics* (San Francisco: HarperSan-Francisco, 1996), p. 188, calls the NT 'a complex polyphonic choral composition *scored by God* and performed by human voices under the direction of the Holy Spirit'. It is incumbent upon the interpreter not to have the individual vocal lines drowned out by the polyphony. The agendas and intentions of each authorial voice must be respected, while at the same time acceding to the Rule of Congruence (see also the Rule of Singularity).

71. One danger of carrying the concept of this simultaneous multivocality too far is the inevitable synoptic readings, especially of the Gospels (for instance, the valiant attempts to harmonize the multiple cock crowings at the time of Simon Peter's denial of Christ). Complementarity by the

Trypho (65.2), he rebukes the latter for having attempted to cast doubt on the consistency of the Scriptures: 'I am entirely convinced that no Scripture contradicts another'. Granted this mutual relationship between portions of the corpus, another hermeneutical maxim emerges, that of *regula fidei* (rule of faith).

Rule of faith. The language-game of the canon provides the field for this principle to operate. *Regula fidei* in the days of the early Church was considered the central and clear teachings of Scripture seen as a whole, the construal of Scripture as a unified and congruent narrative. Summarizing the fundamentals of the faith, Tertullian observed that the rule of faith was taught by Christ and 'wherever it shall be manifest that the true Christian rule and faith shall be, there will likewise be the true Scriptures and expositions thereof, and all the Christian traditions' (*Praescr.* 13, 18).[72] The proliferation of accounts postulated to be penned by apostles during the early centuries of the Church necessitated the recognition of a précis of truths common to the genuine texts. The rule of faith, akin to a creed, 'was a kind of apostolic *résumé* of the books of the New Testament, as it were a rule of apostolic interpretation of all the very different books'.[73] Irenaeus defends the divinity and humanity of Jesus Christ, affirming this doctrine 'as he himself the Lord does testify, as the apostles confess, and as the prophets announce' – an indication of the utility of such epitomes of scriptural truth in apologetic disputations (*Haer.* 3.17.4). These secondary formulations of core doctrines in creeds and other compendia expanded *regula fidei* to subsume those theological encapsulations as well.[74]

Rule of Congruence is also frustrated by other attempts to reconcile the descriptions and events in the Gospels: Matthean and Lucan genealogies of Jesus Christ; the Sermon on the Mount (in Matthew 5–7) and the Sermon on the Plain (in Luke 6); the number of 'Temple Cleansings' and trips to Jerusalem undertaken by Jesus; etc. However, the very existence of the fourfold gospel indicates that Church as a whole does not hold that the Gospels be harmonized at all costs.

72. 'The overarching story enshrined in the Rule of Faith provided the framework, the core of revelation to which scripture universally testified' (Frances Young, 'Allegory and the Ethics of Reading', in *The Open Text: New Directions for Biblical Studies?* [ed. Francis B. Watson; London: SCM Press, 1993], pp. 103–20 [115]).

73. Cullmann, *Early Church*, p. 95.

74. Vanhoozer, *Drama of Doctrine*, p. 204; Charles H. Cosgrove, 'Toward a Postmodern *Hermeneutica Sacra*: Guiding Considerations in Choosing between Competing Plausible Interpretations of Scripture', in *The Meanings We Choose: Hermeneutical Ethics, Indeterminacy and the Conflict of Interpretations* (ed. Charles H. Cosgrove; London: T. & T. Clark, 2004), pp. 39–61 (44–5). Creeds and church councils (and their pronouncements) were certainly not accepted *semper, ubique, et ab omnibus*; Catholics, Protestants and the Eastern Orthodox disagree over which of the ecumenical councils of history are authoritative in laying down a rule of faith; moreover, not every component within the rule(s) of faith was equally shared or strongly held in all quarters of Christendom. The insertion of the *filioque* clause into the Nicene Creed and the subsequent controversy between Eastern and Western Christianity is a case in point that countermines the universality of the Rule of Congruence. The fact remains, however, that even within this creed the controversial clause forms but a small portion of the widely accepted remainder.

Thus, the rule of faith was never independent of Scripture but was intended as an outline of its major themes, a shorthand for what was taught therein, to serve as a standard to which churches could concur and by which heresies could be countered, for, as the Muratorian Canon put it, the Church would not allow 'gall be mixed with honey'.[75] Eusebius observed that Bishop Serapion of Antioch (c. 200 CE), when asked by the church in Rhossus for permission to read *Gospel of Peter* in the church, initially agreed, and then later revoked his permission upon discovering that the work denied the humanity of Jesus. The bishop's rejection, based on the divergence of the text's teaching from what was generally accepted as true, gives evidence of the presence of a *regula fidei* operating in such decisions.[76] The sense of *regula fidei* thus mandated all interpretation to be in line with what was generally considered orthodoxy, especially the key portions of Scripture that serve as the *sedes doctrinae* ('seats of doctrine') of theological assertions, such as Genesis 1–2 (creation), Isaiah 53 (atonement), 1 Corinthians 15 (resurrection), Philippians 2 (incarnation), etc. The recommendation of Augustine is still sound: 'we must consult the rule of faith, as it is perceived through the plainer passages of the Scriptures and the authority of the church'.[77] The latter part of this exhortation deals with the Rule of Ecclesiality, the next rule to be considered.

The Rule of Congruence thus enables the diverse texts of the Bible to project a world in front of the canon in a united and coordinated fashion. The contribution of each text complements that of every other to yield a fully orbed depiction of the canonical world; the particular elements or facets of the world that are projected by individual texts congruently compose the plenary world of the canon.

Rule of Ecclesiality
The Rule of Ecclesiality obligates the reading of Scripture for applicational purposes to be conducted under the auspices of the community that recognizes its canonicity.

The Bible is, without doubt, the Church's book and, therefore, attributing to that book the qualities and properties of Scripture is to acknowledge the pre-eminence of the canon in shaping the life of the Church and of the indi-

---

75. The conception of the 'rule of truth', according to Karl Barth, 'was originally connected with the dogma as well as the constitution of the texts which are recognized to be holy' – the canon (*Church Dogmatics* [trans. G.T. Thomson and Harold Knight; eds. G.W. Bromiley and T.F. Torrance; Edinburgh: T. & T. Clark, 1956], 1.2.473). The term *analogia fidei* is often used coextensively with *regula fidei*. For the Muratorian Canon, see Metzger, *Canon of the New Testament*, pp. 305–7.

76. See Eusebius, *Hist. eccl.* 6.12.3-6.

77. Augustine, *Doctr. chr.* 3.2.2. 'Even if the writer's meaning is obscure, there is no danger here, provided that it can be shown from other passages of the holy Scriptures that each of these interpretations is consistent with the truth [rule of faith]' (*Doctr. chr.* 3.27.38).

vidual believer when it is used in the context of the Christian community.[78] The nature of language-games requires a bounded playing field (Wittgenstein's *Spielraum*), and the canon itself forms a literary playground for the individual texts it comprises, as it delineates a metaphorical space in which the Church is to hear the word of God. However, for its own reading and appropriation, the arena of action is the congregation of God's people of all time. This normative, fixed corpus of religious literature is to be interpreted within the community of faith that acknowledges it as Scripture and affirms its applicability to its life.[79] The hermeneutical significance of the Rule of Ecclesiality is that it calls upon its readers to maintain interpretive solidarity with the Christian community. This rule contends that Christians and local congregations, as part of the one, holy, catholic and apostolic Church must not seek to interpret Scripture as if they were the only ones ever to undertake such an endeavour; the task of biblical hermeneutics must be conducted in concert with the universal community of God, past and present.[80] Implicit in such an assertion is the assumption of the validity of Scripture for God's people of all ages – its perenniality, the transhistorical potential of the text for application. Indeed, the Holy Spirit who invigorates and empowers the body of Christ continues to illuminate readers of the biblical text (1 Cor. 2.12–15); at least two millennia of evidence of this enlightenment is available to the reader today. It is the presence of the Holy Spirit in the Church throughout the ages that makes possible the assertion that the right reading of the canon is the reading of the Church – the *creatura Verbi divini*.

Origen asserted that 'the teaching of the church…is to be accepted as truth which differs in no respect from ecclesiastical and apostolical tradition' (*Princ.* preface), echoing the claim of Scripture itself that the Church of the living God is 'the pillar and support of the truth' (1 Tim. 3.15). It is the responsibility of the Church universal, charged with the custody of the Scriptures, to serve as the conduit and channel for the truth therein. Irenaeus declared that it was the Church that, 'receiving the truth from the apostles, and throughout all the world alone preserving them in their integrity, has transmitted them to her sons' (*Haer.* preface). Such a Rule of Ecclesiality clearly had ramifications for the practices of the early Church, especially with regard to guarding orthodoxy. One of the bases of the rejection of the Arians by Athanasius in the third and fourth cen-

78. Aichele, *Control of Biblical Meaning*, p. 20.

79. Brevard S. Childs, *Biblical Theology in Crisis* (Philadelphia: Westminster, 1970), p. 99; Kelsey, *Uses of Scripture*, pp. 91–3.

80. Stephen E. Fowl, *Engaging Scripture: A Model for Theological Interpretation* (Malden, MA: Blackwell, 1998), p. 205; Webster, *Word and Church*, p. 64. This is, of course, not to deny the interpreter independence or to deprecate pioneering scholarship; it is but the sounding of a caution against idiosyncratic readings of Scripture. Neither does this rule generate an artificial polarity between tradition and Scripture; the Rule of Ecclesiality does not require the interpreter to opt for a stance that pits one against the other.

turies was that the heresy was 'unworthy of communion with the church', and 'although it receive[d] the support of the Emperor and of all mankind, yet it was condemned by the church herself' (*Ep. mort. Ar.* 4). The Rule of Ecclesiality, thus, operated implicitly from the emerging days of the Church.[81]

This rule governs interpretation by keeping it within the constraints of what has generally been considered orthodoxy by the Church universal (also see Rule of Congruence). With regard to texts that appear to support multiple interpretations, Christian communities can at least agree that not *all* interpretations are contextually legitimate.[82] Thus, to acknowledge the canon is to lobby for the use of this body of texts in particular ways for ecclesial faith and praxis. The primary locus for such a mode of reading is the Church, both local and universal, a setting that provides the direction and thrust for its interpretation, as well as the criteria by which the validity of such readings may be judged. In short, there can be no dichotomy between the canon and the community that treasured it. Vanhoozer perceptively comments that 'the church is less the cradle of Christian theology than its *crucible:* the place where the community's understanding of faith is lived, tested, and reformed'.[83] The depiction of the world projected by the canonical text is thus constrained by the hermeneutic arena of the Church, the primary agent of its interpretation and application. The Rule of Ecclesiality, along with the other Rules of Secondary Genre, functions as a guardian of biblical hermeneutics, providing a communal constraint upon the shape and scope of the world in front of the text. At the same time, this rule reminds the preacher stationed within a local ecclesial context to attend to the specificity of the circumstances of that particular body of believers, for application is to be tailored to the unique situation of that assembly of auditors.

Together the Rules of Exclusivity, Applicability, Congruence and Ecclesiality (Rules of Function) regulate the literal, textual source of the projected world and the manner of reading the canonical text to discern that world. While reminding the theologian-homiletician of the interpretive space in which such activities should be conducted, the Rules of Function prompt the hermeneut not to lose sight of the ultimate goal of reading – application. Thus, only those writ-

81. However, one must inject here a note of caution. What is 'ecclesial' is often a matter that is decided in the eye of the beholder. While wide acceptance of the Rule of Ecclesiality laid down the path of what is generally considered orthodoxy, the numerous schisms and secessions that have occurred in the last two millennia – not the least of which was the Protestant Reformation of the sixteenth century when Luther broke away from the established order of the Church – suggest that this Rule may not command universal subscription.

82. Umberto Eco argues that 'any community of interpreters … can frequently reach (even though nondefinitively and in a fallible way) an agreement' about the text under consideration, ruling out readings that are clearly groundless (*The Limits of Interpretation* [Bloomington, IN: Indiana University Press, 1990], p. 41).

83. Vanhoozer, *Drama of Doctrine*, p. 25; also see Childs, *Biblical Theology in Crisis*, p. 99. How Scripture yields 'live' application that is valid will be discussed in Chapter 4.

ings construed as canonical portray this world authoritatively and accurately. However, all constituent texts of the canon are potentially world projecting, and therefore applicable for all readers when interpretation is performed with an assumption of mutual congruence between the discrete texts, and when such readerly transactions are conducted under the ægis of the community that recognizes the biblical canon as its Scripture.

Rules of Content

The Rules of Content focus the interpreter upon the importance of the subject matter of the canon (Rule of Substantiality), the multiplicity of textual echoes within it (Rule of Intertextuality), the temporal progression of God's canonical revelation (Rule of Sequentiality) and the cruciform centre of the normative text (Rule of Primacy).

Rule of Substantiality
The Rule of Substantiality calls upon the interpreter to accord the message of the canonical texts the consideration worthy of the materiality and gravity of Scripture.

Dealing as it does with matters concerning its main character, God, the canon addresses issues of significant moment, both temporal and eternal. That it contains nothing trivial or ephemeral gives it its perennial significance across the span of time and space for all peoples everywhere.[84] As the Bible itself asserts, the consequences are great for one who neglects 'so great a salvation', for the texts of Scripture are the sacred writings that are able to give one 'the wisdom that leads to salvation through faith which is in Christ Jesus'. Their profitability for Christian faith and practice was the reason Timothy was enjoined to 'preach the word' at all times.[85] Athanasius declared that the canonical books were fountains of salvation; 'they who thirst may be satisfied with the living words they contain. In these alone is proclaimed the doctrine of godliness. Let no man add to these, neither let him take aught from these' (*Ep. fest.* 39.6). This kind of Christian discourse as is contained in the Bible, is not senseless, Ricoeur wagered, but worthy of analysis 'because something is said that is not said by other kinds of discourse'.[86] As a consequence of the gravity of the contents of Scripture, the world projected by the text attains supreme priority for the faith and practice of the Church. As will be discussed in Chapter 4, it is this world that is the critical intermediate station in the hermeneutical and homiletical journey from text to praxis.

The reverence and respect that God's people have accorded Scripture and the responsibility with which its exposition has been undertaken over the centuries amply testify to the substantiality of the canonical classic. The innumerable

---

84. Barton, *Spirit and the Letter*, pp. 135–7.

85. Heb. 2.3; 2 Tim. 3.15-16; 4.2.

86. Paul Ricoeur, 'Philosophy and Religious Language', *JR* 54 (1974), pp. 71–85 (71).

commentaries, homilies and tracts that have been developed upon the canon register this pre-eminent quality of the Bible. The '*halakah*' of the early Church was a proliferation of such interpretive tomes on Scripture. By Epiphanius' account (*Pan.* 64.63.8), the prodigious output of Origen included about 6000 writings, falling into three categories – commentaries, homilies (on almost the entire Bible; over 200 preserved) and *scholia* (brief summaries of difficult biblical texts).[87] Equally productive was Chrysostom, who bequeathed over 900 sermons (that is, those that survive), a large proportion of them being homilies on scriptural texts: 55 on Acts, 34 on Hebrews, 15 on Philippians, 16 on 1–2 Thessalonians, etc.[88] No less significant in attestation to the substantiality of the canon is the abundance of manuscript copies extant and the plethora of translations and versions of Scripture that continue to be produced. Ironically, even the myriad controversies that have dogged the Church throughout its existence testify to the substantiality of the corpus. Scripture matters, therefore interpretations matter and are material enough to be vigorously defended, as indeed they were, sometimes even violently.[89]

It is as Scripture and all that that designation implies that the canon is rendered substantial, with perennial, plural and prescriptive significance. Not only the entire collection but individual texts and pericopes as well are non-trivial. In fact, it is the substantiality of the content of the corpus that promotes the serviceability of pericopes in the ecclesial setting: the density of the canonical text, packed as it is with significance and meaning, makes it possible, and even advisable, to engage the Scriptures in smaller segments for regular ecclesial use.[90] In addition, the Rule of Substantiality affirms that no part of the canon is devoid of importance or consequence; for instance, in 1 Cor. 9.9, Paul considers Deut. 25.4, a relatively unimportant text in the OT, as being significant for the 'current' practice of the community of believers. That *nomina sacra* (contracted names in ancient biblical manuscripts: God, Jesus, Son, Christ, Holy Spirit, etc.) were commonly employed by Christian scribes handling both Testaments also suggests the construal of every part of the canon as sacred in the same sense.[91]

---

87. For an ordered list of the works of Origen mentioned in Jerome's *Ep. ad Paula*, see Henri Crouzel, *Origen* (trans. A.S. Worrall; Edinburgh: T. & T. Clark, 1989), pp. 37–9.

88. See Wendy Mayer and Pauline Allen, *John Chrysostom* (London: Routledge, 2000), p. 7; and J.N.D. Kelly, *Golden Mouth: The Story of John Chrysostom – Ascetic, Preacher, Bishop* (London: Duckworth, 1995), pp. 132–3.

89. It can be argued contrariwise that these bellicose polemics and the often irreconcilable dissensions only prove that, while agreement may be wide on the substantiality of the canonical text, what exactly is considered substantial is up for debate; the use of icons, creedal clauses, glossolalia, timing of future events, baptism, indulgences have all been argued over, generating considerable disunity within the Church.

90. See Chapter 4 for the utility of pericopes in the setting of the Church.

91. John Barton, *Holy Writings, Sacred Text: The Canon in Early Christianity* (Louisville: Westminster/John Knox Press, 1997), pp. 122–3.

The canonical language-game is, indeed, a 'sport' of great consequence, and the world in front of it is a significant construct; this text is therefore not to be neglected, but read and applied, its projected world appropriated. The Rule of Substantiality calls for a faithful reading, a surrender to the substantiality of the text and the will of God, a willingness to inhabit the world in front of the text.[92]

Rule of Intertextuality

The Rule of Intertextuality exhorts the reader to attend to citations of, and allusions to, antecedent Scripture within the particular texts being interpreted for applicational purposes.

The phenomenon of intertextuality, by which an earlier text is embedded in a later one, enables the authoritative voice of Scripture to continue resounding in the chambers of those later texts.[93] The new theological context, created by the intentional juxtaposition of the various canonical books, forms a new reading frame that renders textual movement between the different discourses possible (also see Rule of Organization). The significance of the Rule of Intertextuality is that texts from one part of the canon are incorporated within later texts of other parts, a sort of literary simultaneity or multivocality of the members of the canon. In effect, the Rule of Intertextuality proclaims that through the multiple voices simultaneously heard, a single melody, the unified canonical world, is discernible (see Rule of Singularity). Positing a temporal sensibility that connects the present with the past as it enables textual carryovers, the Rule of Intertextuality is a recontextualization of a different kind, as the writers of Scripture appropriate earlier writings into their own work. Thereby, these later texts define and locate their own 'present' time in relation to, and within, the larger ongoing story of God's interaction with mankind, a narrative that stretches from the past into an as yet unconsummated future.[94]

There is a resonance in the canonical space that makes echoes come alive when one text is 'relocated' by intertextuality to another context in the canon. An example of intertextuality within the OT is found in 1 Kgs 19.11, where God warns Elijah that he is about to 'pass by' (עבר), a clear intertextual allusion to Moses' experience in Exod. 33.22. The prophet's location in the cave paralleled Moses' in the 'cleft of the rock' as well. In Elijah's days in the Slough of

---

92. Such a reading by an interpreter is 'an aspect of *mortificatio sui*, a repudiation of the desire to assemble all realities, including texts, including even the revelation of God, around the steady centre of my will' (Webster, *Word and Church*, pp. 43–4).

93. Richard Hays, *Echoes of Scripture in the Letters of Paul* (New Haven: Yale University Press, 1989), p. 14. The critical task, Hays notes, is 'to see what poetic effects and larger meanings are produced by the poet's device of echoing predecessors' (18).

94. These acts of intertextual appropriation were undertaken rather by 'homiletical and prophetic readings' than by 'rigorously exegetical ones' (Hays, *Echoes of Scripture in the Letters of Paul*, pp. 184–5).

Despond, only a vision of the living God in such a dynamic and electrifying fashion as this could have inspired him to don once more the mantle of God's spokesman. As another example of intertextuality, Hosea's statement in 2.15 that the valley of Achor would be turned into a 'door of hope' alludes to that dreadful scene in Josh. 7.24-6 where Achan was stoned after bringing immense grief to the children of Israel. The intertextuality brings out the pathos and poignancy of the source of the allusion and anticipates the dramatic redemptive renewal to be wrought by God in the future of the nation.[95]

Biblical intertextuality, in its essence, consists of the literary interaction between texts; such intersections of discourses and the embedding of one genre within another (the transgeneric nature of Scripture, considered in Chapter 2) create intertextuality.[96] Obvious citations are but the visible evidence of the generally pervasive and implicit phenomenon of intertextuality that also includes allusions to antecedent texts. All of these may be considered extensions of metaphoricity, as this textual transplantation carries the meaning from one level to another. Indeed, '[t]he text interprets before having been interpreted'.[97] In other words, before a contemporary hermeneut undertakes the interpretation of a text, by the Rule of Intertextuality the embedd*ing* text has already performed a hermeneutical operation on the embedd*ed* text as it cites or alludes to the latter. Thus the embedding text, in the final form of the canon, both depends upon, and transforms, the embedded text.

A major operation of intertextuality within the canon itself is the explicit reuse of ancient Scripture: as the New Testament lavishly cites the Old, the latter, by its reinterpretation in the former, enters into a new network of intel-

95. The original setting of the cited text can itself contain echoes of other texts, generating a 'multiverse' of sounds and their networks. Each echo is the product of an interpretive endeavour when it is carried to a fresh textual context within the canon. Schnittjer analyses Jesus' quotation in Mt. 4.4 of Deut. 8.3 ('man shall not live by bread alone ...') that, in turn, is a summary of the events of Exod. 16 and Num. 11 (the provision of manna). The resonant chamber of such biblical echoes is the boundary of the canon, defining 'the universe within which the reader can traverse between narrative worlds'. See Gary Edward Schnittjer, 'The Narrative Multiverse within the Universe of the Bible: The Question of "Borderlines" and "Intertextuality"', *WTJ* 2 (2002), pp. 231–52 (236, 239).

96. Mark I. Wallace calls intertextuality the 'cross-fertilization' between different texts and their respective theological itineraries 'that preserves the polyphony of biblical revelation' (*The Second Naiveté: Barth, Ricoeur, and the New Yale Theology* [2nd edn; Macon, GA: Mercer University Press, 1995], p. 41).

97. Paul Ricoeur, 'The Bible and the Imagination', in *The Bible as a Document of the University* (ed. Hans Dieter Betz; Chico, CA: Scholars, 1981), pp. 49–75 (53–4, 66–7). Ricoeur considers parables as the paradigmatic form of intertextuality and metaphoricity as they exemplify narratives embedded within Gospel narratives. Hays concurs with Ricoeur's understanding of intertextuality as a species of metaphoricity: he observes that intertextuality in biblical texts provides readers with a model of 'hermeneutical freedom', enabling them to appreciate the 'metaphorical relation' between a text and its contemporary reading (*Echoes of Scripture in the Letters of Paul*, pp. 178–92).

ligibility – 'harmony by means of a transfer'. The canon is therefore more than simply an anthology of writings; it is 'a hermeneutical medium which by its very nature influences the understanding of its contents', and significantly shapes the world projected in front of it (also see Rule of Organization).[98] Components of this world are intricately intertwined as they play off one another in the phenomenon of intertextuality. The Rule of Intertextuality demonstrates the kind of reading that must be undertaken in order to discern this world in the fullness of its detail. A comprehensive grasp of what antecedent texts are doing in their original settings and in their newly adopted literary neighbourhoods will enable a nuanced description of the world in front of the text.

Rule of Sequentiality
The Rule of Sequentiality emphasizes the need for interpreters to consider the temporal sequence of inscripturation for purposes of application, as later, progressive revelation develops and clarifies earlier material.

With the exercise of the Rule of Sequentiality, consideration is given to the temporal sequence of revelation: to explain earlier revelation, recourse is sought in later revelation, especially in those texts that carry forward and develop the broad narrative and themes of Scripture. This rule is contingent upon the understanding that God works within time as he accomplishes his purposes for humanity, revealing himself and his plans in gradual and deliberate fashion. The OT, speaking primarily to those within the administrative stewardship of that dispensation, did not see fit to unfold in detail the manner of fulfilment of the prophecies generated therein.[99] The NT, in contrast, speaking primarily to those within the economy of this later covenant, broadens the vistas of prophecy in progressive revelation, enlarging the horizons and boundaries of knowledge.[100]

98. Gamble, *The New Testament Canon*, p. 75; Ricoeur, 'Preface to Bultmann', p. 379. The use of the OT in the NT is, no doubt, a prominent mode of intertextual operation within the canon, but how the citations and allusions function and whether earlier texts were employed 'legitimately' in their later contexts are matters of ongoing debate. Did Isaiah actually mean 'virgin' in 7.14, as Matthew asserts in 1.23? Does Hebrews 10 'fairly' use Psalm 40 in its argument? Did the NT writers 'discover' meaning in OT texts that was not immediately apparent to the original scribes? Is the hermeneutic framework for intertextuality a function of exegesis that is literalistic, midrashic, pesher, allegorical ...? See Richard N. Longenecker, *Biblical Exegesis in the Apostolic Period* (2nd edn; Grand Rapids: Eerdmans, 1999), pp. 6–35.

99. Acts 17.30, for example, attests to Scripture being revelation that progresses beyond 'times of ignorance'. First Peter 1.10-12 makes it clear that the OT prophets did not grasp all the ramifications of their own prophecies; they are stated to have 'made careful searches and inquiries'. Another situation where a prophet appears to have been unaware of the reach of his own prophecy is found in Dan. 12.8, where Daniel confesses, 'As for me, I heard, but could not understand'.

100. Ramesh P. Richard, 'Selected Issues in Theoretical Hermeneutics', *BSac* 143 (1986), pp. 14–25 (20). Indeed, those horizons and boundaries will continue to be enlarged with fresh revelation in the eschaton and beyond (1 Cor. 13.9-12).

Irenaeus recognized the incomplete nature of what was revealed in times past, particularly of the components of the Mosaic Law. He employed the analogy of a seed that sprouts into a fruit-producing plant to depict the transition from partial to complete revelation: 'For the patriarchs and prophets sowed the word [concerning] Christ, but the Church reaped, that is, received the fruit' (*Haer.* 4.16.5; and 4.25.3). God's utterances are, in this sense, 'seminal', containing as they do the inchoate mechanisms of their later development.[101]

The Rule of Sequentiality implies that, for interpretive purposes, earlier statements of God's purposes may be complemented by later assertions. For example, progressive revelation has amplified the details regarding the atoning sacrifice of Christ. The OT mandated continual sacrificial offerings in the court of the temple, twice-daily incense offerings in the outer court and the yearly high-priestly sacrifice in the Holy of Holies. These earlier dictates were fulfilled and supplanted in Christ, as he secured for believers eternal redemption ἐφάπαξ (Heb. 9.1-14). Ephesians 3.4-6 explicitly states that some facets of the divine programme were never grasped by earlier generations simply because these truths were not made known then: specifically, the inclusion of Gentiles among the heirs within the body of Christ, as equal partakers of the divine promise. The supplementation of revelation with time depicts a fuller picture of the subject than what was available previously. Later revelation may thus clarify and develop the 'incomplete' particulars of the world in front of the text discerned from earlier revelation.[102]

The food laws of the Bible also demonstrate this Rule of Sequentiality. What was permitted for Adam and Eve in the garden of Eden (a vegetarian diet, Gen. 2.16) was expanded, after the flood, to include non-vegetarian components (Gen. 9.3-4). Leviticus 11 and Deut. 14.3-21 narrowed down those options

---

101. Vanhoozer, 'From Speech Acts to Scripture Acts', pp. 38–9, n. 76. Darrell L. Bock has propounded a variation of this view labelled 'complementary hermeneutics' that considers the NT as adding, in a complementary fashion, to OT promises. According to this conception 'God can say more in his development of promises from the OT in the NT, but not less. He can also bring in fresh connections in the development of promise as more revelation fills it out.' The NT thus complements the content of the OT (Darrell L. Bock, 'Why I Am a Dispensationalist with a Small "d"', *JETS* 41 [1998], pp. 383–96 [390]). Such a notion, in effect, recognizes the broad perimeter of the projected world and its transhistorical intention; all exemplifications falling within those bounds are equally part of the meaning of the text (see Chapter 1).

102. It must be admitted that there are elements of this rule that are less than clear, particularly with regard to OT law. While the Law is declared to be no longer binding (Rom. 6.14; Eph. 2.15; Heb. 8.13; etc.), paradoxically, it is also said to have been written for all believers (1 Cor. 9.8-10) and, frequently, demands of the Christian made in the NT are grounded upon those same laws (Gal. 5.14; Eph. 6.1-3; 1 Tim. 5.18; Jas 2.8, 11; 1 Pet. 1.15-16; etc.). The Rule of Sequentiality does not expressly provide a resolution to this quandary; a universal application of that rule across the board may be impossible. See David A. Dorsey, 'The Law of Moses and the Christian: A Compromise', *JETS* 34 (1991), pp. 322–34 (322, 330–1); also see Chapter 2 for how this work proposes that the genre of law be handled by an interpreter.

considerably, distinguishing between items 'clean' and 'unclean'. The rationale for such a distinction was indissolubly linked to holiness: the demand that God's people be like God himself, and the need for separation from Gentiles because the Israelites had been chosen 'out of all the peoples who are on the face of the earth' (Deut. 14.2; also see Lev. 11.44-5).[103] Yet these aspects of the Mosaic Law underwent development with the progress of time and revelation. Indeed, in the NT era, the Church, the new creation, admitting those of every tribe and tongue and people and nation, made the food laws that symbolized these distinctions inutile.[104] Significant is Peter's vision in Acts 10 and the accompanying divine declaration, 'what God has cleansed, no longer consider unholy' (10.9-16; also see 1 Tim. 4.4-5). Luke recounts this episode thrice – in Acts 10; 11; and 15; in this last chapter, at the Jerusalem council, a new law was promulgated that, affirming the inclusion of Gentiles within the Church, announced the annulment of the basic food laws.

Therefore, though this is not the first task of interpretation, there is justification for the hermeneutical navigation from an expanded network of progressive revelation back to the texts of either Testament in order to facilitate a thicker reading of those particular texts. By employing the Rule of Sequentiality (and the Rule of Congruence, as well), the plurality of scriptural voices in the singular canonical context are brought to bear upon any biblical theme, expanding the scope of an earlier text's projection of the world. The canonical speech act is heard in its entirety, in the wholeness of its larger polyphonic context, and this significantly narrows the interpretive possibilities of individual texts in the canon. An important consequence of this rule is the disambiguation of meaning, as the breadth of the canon acts as the context and filter for the specific utterances included in its reach.[105] The world in front of the text is thereby more precisely depicted and its details filled out in the temporal progression of revelation.

---

103. Mary Douglas observed that cleanness regulates the structure of both animal and human realms in a similar fashion; there is 'clean' and 'unclean' in both. Of animals (and birds) there is clean and unclean; of the clean there are those that may be sacrificed and those that may not – acceptable ones were sheep and goats, turtledoves and pigeons (Leviticus 1; 5; 12; 27, etc.). This threefold division of animalia is paralleled in the division of mankind: there are two main groups, Jews and Gentiles, and within the former only priests may approach the altar to offer sacrifice. These distinctions reminded the Israelites every mealtime that 'holiness was more than a matter of meat and drink but a way of life characterized by purity and integrity' (see Isa. 59.3; Jer. 2.23; Ezek. 4.14; 43.8; Hos. 5.3; etc.) (Mary Douglas, *Implicit Meanings: Selected Essays in Anthropology* [2nd edn; London: Routledge, 1999], pp. 244–8; also see Gordon Wenham, *Story as Torah: Reading Old Testament Narrative Ethically* [Grand Rapids: Baker, 2000], pp. 139–41, 143).

104. Mt. 15.16-28; Mk 7.18-30; also see Gal. 3.24-5; Eph. 2.15.

105. Acknowledging the polysemy of lexemes, Ricoeur writes: 'The context thus plays the role of filter; when a single dimension of meaning passes through by means of the play of affinities and reinforcements of all analogous dimensions of other lexical terms, a meaning effect is created which can attain perfect univocity, as in technical languages' ('The Problem of Double Meaning as Hermeneutic Problem and as Semantic Problem', in *The Conflict of Interpretations* [trans.

Rule of Primacy

The Rule of Primacy grounds the interpretation of canonical texts for applica-
tion purposes upon the pre-eminent person of Christ who fulfils the will of the
Father in the power of the Spirit.

The canon is the playing field wherein God and his relationship to his creation
are headlined through the language-games that texts play. The Rule of Primacy
points the interpreter to what God has done, is doing and will do in and through
Christ, underscoring the pivotal nature Christology plays in the orientation of
the canon (also see Rule of Organization). This rule therefore subsumes under its
ægis all the discourses in the canon for, in the divine act of communication, Jesus
Christ takes centre-stage: as God, Christ is the sender; as the incarnate Word, he
is the message; as the one who fulfilled God's word, he is the perfect receiver.
Christ's person and work, therefore, forms the foundation for all hermeneutical
operations upon Scripture.[106] What the canon is doing is offering a theologically
thick description of Jesus Christ; this is the content of the world in front of the
canonical text.[107] Biblical history portrays at its focal point the key figure of
Heilsgeschichte, the Lord Jesus Christ, and all interpretation, therefore, must
be a Christotelic application of the Rule of Primacy.[108] Irenaeus declared: 'If
any one, therefore, reads the Scriptures with attention, he will find in them an
account of Christ, and a foreshadowing of the new calling … the treasure hid
in the Scriptures is Christ' (*Haer.* 4.26.1). The incarnated Word is directly or
indirectly portrayed in every part of the inscripturated word; no part of that grand
metanarrative fails to be influenced by the Rule of Primacy. To this depiction

Kathleen McLaughlin; ed. Don Ihde; Evanston: Northwestern University Press, 1974; repr.
2004], pp. 63–78 [69]). Eco would agree: 'A text is a place where the irreducible polysemy of
symbols is in fact reduced because in a text symbols are anchored to their context' (Eco, *Limits of
Interpretation*, p. 21).

106. See Graeme Goldsworthy, *Gospel-Centred Hermeneutics: Biblical-Theological Foundations and Principles* (Nottingham, UK: Apollos, 2006), p. 56.

107. All the communicative actions of Scripture 'are subject to the criteria established by the
speech act that lies at the centre of Christian Scripture, the life, death and resurrection of Jesus
as the enfleshment and the enactment of the divine Word' (Vanhoozer, *Drama of Doctrine*, p. 68;
also see Watson, *Text and Truth*, pp. 121–2).

108. The term 'Christotelic' was employed by Peter Enns in order to preclude the connota-
tions of 'Christological' or 'Christocentric' that sometimes tend to see Christ in nearly every
OT text with the resultant attenuation of the text's own voice. 'Christotelic' proclaims that the
OT is a story that is going somewhere, a narrative that as a whole 'finds its *telos*, its comple-
tion, in Christ', who, after all, is the τέλος of the Law (Rom. 10.4). See Peter Enns, 'Apostolic
Hermeneutics and an Evangelical Doctrine of Scripture: Moving beyond a Modernist Impasse',
WTJ 65 (2003), pp. 263–87 (277). Of all the rules, the Rule of Primacy is perhaps the one that has
had the widest acceptance among Christians. Nevertheless, its mode of application has not won
universal endorsement. What sort of transaction is the interpreter to perform on the OT text to see
Christ therein? Variations in approach (allegorical, typological, redemptive-historical, promise-
fulfilment, etc.) render the application of the Rule of Primacy a somewhat delicate operation.

the Church seeks to be aligned as to a cornerstone, and to this end the Church preaches Christ. This is to say that canonicity gives the Scriptures a foundation upon the Second Person of the Trinity, the Lord Jesus Christ – the fulfilment of the demands of God, the power of God and the wisdom of God, and in whom is the fullness of deity.[109] In proclaiming the canon one cannot, therefore, but preach in a Christotelic manner. However, the fact that the revelation of God is the focus of the Scriptures (Rule of Substantiality) also affirms that the Christotelic theme incorporates the Trinitarian aspect of the Godhead – God the Son fulfilling the doxological purpose of God the Father in the power of the God the Spirit. This interpretive core finds its plenary expression only in the completed canon and the world it projects; it takes the whole canon to fully depict Christ.[110] The Rule of Primacy therefore focuses the theologian-homiletician upon this central component of the world in front of the canonical text.

Indeed, such a focusing is a joint effort on the part of all the Rules of Content. The Rules of Substantiality and Primacy direct the interpretive exercise towards elucidating the nucleus of the world in front of the text: Christ who fulfilled all the demands of the Father in the power of the Spirit. This substantial and primary feature of the projected world is not the product of any one particular pericope or book, but the emerging result of a reading enterprise that discovers an operation of the Rule of Intertextuality (in citations and allusions), as well as a progressive temporal lineage of revelation in the canon (the Rule of Sequentiality), both of which phenomena serve to link the discrete parts of the world so projected into a canonical whole. All of these rules together thus effectively portray the plenary world in front of the canonical text, with all its intricacies of detail.

Role of the rules of secondary genre

The Rules of Secondary Genre surveyed in this chapter brought to the fore the nature of the canon as a secondary language-game and the work it accomplishes by means of its rules – the projection of a world in front of the canonical text. In the history of the Church, these rules have implicitly performed the role of directing the reading of the secondary genre of the canonical classic. They make possible the construal of the canon as a communicative act at the level of the divine illocution and second-order referent, thereby enabling a world projection by Scripture. Rules, by definition, are *restraining*. That they are also *releasing* is the argument that Chapters 2 and 3 make, foreshadowing a future discussion in Chapter 4 of the manner in which the tension between restraint and release serves the theologian-homiletician in the move from text to praxis, as the prescriptivity of the Scriptures and its perennial and plural significance for the hearer are proclaimed with authority and relevance.

---

109. Mt. 5.17; 1 Cor. 1.30; Col. 2.9.
110. Vanhoozer, *First Theology*, p. 286.

The Rule of Substantiality announces that the canon demands reading and application, while the Rule of Ecclesiality calls for such reading and application to be conducted under the auspices of the community of God that acknowledges the canon as its Scripture. In tandem with these rules, the Rule of Applicability focuses the theologian-homiletician upon the importance of rendering the particular texts relevant for the faith and practice of this community. Thus, these rules provide the institutional framework for application of the text. The Rule of Exclusivity limits the interpretive activity to a compilation of particular texts, and the Rule of Completion limits those texts that may be utilized for application to their final form within the canon; the boundaries of the playing field are thus demarcated. The Rule of Singularity prompts the interpreter about the manner in which the canon should be read – as a unified corpus that is structured as directed by the Rule of Organization, and which is broadly consistent in its constituent parts as proclaimed by the Rule of Congruence. In such a reading, interpretive movements between texts are permitted by the Rules of Intertextuality and Sequentiality that attend to citations and allusions, and progressive revelation, respectively. Above all, the Rule of Primacy grounds every reading of the word-in-canon upon the Word incarnate.

The *restraint* of rules notwithstanding, significant freedom is permitted the interpreter in reading – the *release*. The Rules of Substantiality, Ecclesiality and Applicability make it possible for the theologian-homiletician to move beyond the particularities of the text and attend to the context of the hearers, for this is a text that is full of moment and material to the life of the Church, implicitly calling for future recontextualization. The scaffolding provided by these rules enables the preacher to construct application for the Church in a manner that is specifically relevant to that community, that glorifies God and that edifies his people. The Rule of Primacy sets the interpreter free to explore the alignment of any text to the Christotelic focus and thrust of the canon. The Rule of Completion releases the reader from the task of arbitration: one does not have to sit in judgement on what textual vestige or *Vorlage* is authoritative for the life of the community of God's people; by the Rule of Exclusivity, neither does the hermeneut have to vote upon which text is to be welcomed into the canon. The Rules of Singularity, Organization and Congruence, as well as the Rules of Intertextuality and Sequentiality, open out the boundaries of the interpretive transaction from the margins of each individual book to the broader limits of the canonical corpus, generating a lively conversation between the literary components of the canon. The perimeter of the *Spielraum* is thus enlarged; the plenary world in front of the canonical text must also be discovered in the process of interpretation. Coordinated with this canonical projection, the individual segments of the world projected by particular texts make possible, via their transhistorical intentions, the application of Scripture to the specificities of the lives of God's people (see Chapter 4).

It is evident from the rules propounded in this chapter that the Rules of Secondary Genre serve both a direct and indirect role in interpretation. On the one hand, they are simultaneously deployed alongside the Rules of Primary Genre in the actual task of interpretation, where they serve to coordinate the reading of the text with the rest of the canonical material, ensuring the coherence and compatibility of the world framed by the pericope with the world projected by the canon. Particularly employed in this regard are the Rules of Singularity, Organization, Congruence, Applicability, Intertextuality, Sequentiality and Primacy. On other hand, the Rules of Secondary Genre set the stage for, and superintend, in a more general manner, all the interpretive activities centred upon the canonical text – the Rules of Completion, Exclusivity, Ecclesiality and Substantiality. The Rules of Secondary Genre thus regulate the conditions with which the hermeneut must approach Scripture, determine the stance that must be adopted towards it and ascertain the correspondence and correlation of the world projected by the individual text to the plenary world projected by the canon. Together, the Rules of Primary and Secondary Genre carry the interpretive endeavour significantly forwards in the move from text to praxis: by means of their joint operations the world in front of the text is discerned and application is rendered possible.

Summary: secondary genre – the canon

The canonical classic as a language-game, a secondary genre, has been the focus of this chapter. Rules of Secondary Genre, categorized by structure, function and content, were proposed as guidelines for interpretation, with the caveat that these rules, while widely accepted, are not universal in ratification or application. Nonetheless the broad instantiation of these rules in Christian interpretation renders them adequate for the purposes of this work. It is proposed in this work that an essential function of the rules of Genre, both primary and secondary, is to delineate the world projected in front of the text – a canonical world that depicts God and his relationship to his creation in its multifarious facets. These rules aid and abet a practice of reading that operates from the understanding that texts project worlds, and that genres are particular ways of perceiving these worlds that facilitate their appropriation. Therefore, for the theologian-homiletician, the Rules of Genre are invaluable in the navigation from text to praxis.

This work examines the interlocution of hermeneutics and homiletics as it seeks to discover how a sermon may move validly from text to praxis. Chapter 1 dwelt upon aspects of general hermeneutics germane to this undertaking, proposing the concept of the world in front of the text. Chapters 2 and 3, moving into the special hermeneutical arena, demonstrated that biblical texts play the primary language-game of genre and the secondary language-game of the canon, the classic. The rules of these language-games enable the theologian-homiletician to discern the world projected by the canon and the segments thereof projected by individual genres/texts. How the homiletical transaction is consummated in application will be the thrust of Chapter 4, as it builds on the theme of the world in front of the text: application involves the key step of discovering this projected world and inhabiting it. In taking up the sermonic contribution to the dialogue between hermeneutics and homiletics, the final chapter of this work necessarily converges down to the level of particular texts of Scripture – pericopes – that are utilized in the ecclesial setting for the preaching endeavour; Chapter 4 will concentrate on the work of these fundamental units of the biblical text.

4

PERICOPAL THEOLOGY AND APPLICATION

By engaging hermeneutics and homiletics in dialogue, this work seeks to establish a means to validate the move from Scripture to sermon. The metaphor of language-games serves as a foundation for such an assessment. Chapter 1 outlined the language-games played by biblical texts, primary and secondary genre, and explored the manner in which texts project worlds in front of themselves (secondary reference). Chapters 2 and 3 listed the Rules of Genre that help identify this projected world. Rules for Primary Genre were enumerated in Chapter 2: the categories of texts considered there were narrative, prophecy, law and hymnody. Chapter 3 proposed the Rules of Secondary Genre: the Rules of Structure mould and shape the source material for the world projected by the text; the Rules of Function regulate the textual sources of the projected world and their reading; and the Rules of Content highlight the canonical properties of the world in front of the text.[1] Interpretation of the scriptural text is conducted under the auspices of these Rules of Genre, enabling the theologian-homiletician to discern the world in front of the text. The Rules of Primary Genre play a direct and active role in this transaction, discovering the individuality of the various biblical genres in their framing of this projected world; the Rules of Secondary Genre take on the indirect status of umpire and operate on a more general level of supervision, correlating and coordinating the entire interpretive undertaking, and creating the broader context for reading the canonical text.

The final chapter of this work concentrates primarily upon the homiletical contribution to the dialogue between hermeneutics and homiletics. Chapter 4 therefore necessarily deals with the textual object of sermonic focus, the biblical pericope. The utilization of pericopes in an ecclesial setting will be considered first, drawing upon the concept of covenant renewal as a paradigm for the homiletical enterprise. Such a programme, it will be proposed, is mediated by the segment of the world projected by the pericope, to which world readers are bidden to align their lives. Generated as it is by a theological interpretation of

---

1. All such rules, it will be remembered, are of the nature of counsel and caution rather than imperative and injunction. These rules are not creations *de novo*; rather, they are fairly self-evident and reflect the established practices of the Church in reading Scripture.

the text employing the Rules of Genre, this pericopal sector of the canonical world is, in fact, the theology of that particular pericope – *pericopal theology*. This entity will be shown to serve as the intermediary between Scripture and sermon that gives validity to the homiletical transaction. A bipartite transaction is thereby envisaged in exposition: the task of the theologian-homiletician consists in moving from pericope to theology, and subsequently from theology to application. Such a passage from text to praxis via theology is directed by the Rules of Genre; under the governance of these rules, valid application is enabled that retains the authority of Scripture and remains relevant to the audience.

In operating by these Rules of Genre in the homiletical enterprise, the expositor will have accomplished the translation of the rhetorical objective of the text (the *textual* intention), via the *transhistorical* intention borne by pericopal theology, to arrive at the sermonic terminus of application, the response of readers to the text (the *homiletical* intention). Thus this last chapter will complete the construction of the bridge between ancient text and modern audience, a credible causeway that may be crossed confidently by a theologian-homiletician.

Pericopes

'Pericope' (περικοπή = section, passage) refers to a portion of the biblical text that is of manageable size for homiletical and liturgical use in an ecclesial setting. Though traditionally applied to segments of the Gospels, the term in this work will indicate a slice of text in any genre, as it is customarily utilized in Christian worship. It is through pericopes, read and exposited in congregations as fundamental units of the scriptural text, that the community of God corporately encounters the Bible. Indeed, it is impossible to conceive of a communal gathering of the faithful that does not implement such a reading of biblical pericopes.

At first glance, the reason for the serviceability of pericopes might appear simple: the impossibility of grasping the entirety of the magnificent breadth of canonical thought on any single occasion, within the constraints of time spent in the corporate assemblies, dictates the employment of a smaller quantum of text that may be conveniently read and adequately exposited. Justin Martyr reports on a Sunday gathering of Christians where the Gospels and the Prophets were read 'as long as time permits' (μέχρις ἐγχωρεῖ; *1 Apol.* 66), suggesting that a relatively fixed period of time had been allocated for the weekly event. Pericopes are eminently usable, given this temporal restraint.

However, it is not merely the constraint of time that imposes a limit upon the length of the biblical text utilized in the liturgical setting. The function of a pericope as a coherent 'sense unit' must also be taken into consideration. While Scripture is considered as a singularity, exhibiting univocity and congruence in the main, it obviously does not comprise one unbroken, run-on thought. And, while its substantial content is ultimately grounded upon the person and work of Christ, neither is Scripture a serialized and exclusive display of a single topic replicated in variegated fashion in multiple genres and in a multitude of pericopes. Instead, under the banner of the Rules of Singularity, Congruence, Substantiality and Primacy, sundry and diverse issues pertaining to the Christian's life and relationship to God are addressed; several distinct topics germane to the faith and practice of the community in its orientation to God are registered within the canon.[2] To this end, the polygeneric and transgeneric composition of the Bible plays a crucial role, drawing attention to the variety of its subject matter. Each genre, in its own particular manner and through its constituent pericopes, frames the world projected by the text, emphasizing one aspect or another of the plenary world projected by the canon as a whole. In other words, the canonical text projects a single world that comprises discrete segments featured by individual pericopes. A pericope therefore is essentially a self-intact sense unit bearing a relatively complete and integral idea that contributes to the whole, a defined portion of Scripture that reflects a unified span of thought and content.[3] In the periodic assemblies of the Church, the exposition of a particular pericope deals with the facet of life that is addressed by that pericopal sense unit. For the edification of believers, then, the employment of pericopal portions of the biblical text for preaching is of considerable significance.

Incontrovertible is the fact that no single sermon can capture and do justice to all the specific thrusts of all the pericopes in the canon, or even of all those smaller units within a single book. Instead, it is as individual pericopes that these portions of Scripture lend themselves to ecclesial use. The Rule of Substantiality, emphasizing the extraordinary content of the canon, prompts the interpreter, at any given gathering, to deal with the canonical text in small portions, densely packed as the whole corpus is with matters of moment and consequence. Considered one at a time, pericopes allow a more intensive exploration of the depth and force of the text, enabling the particularity and potency of each pericope to impact the congregation. Thus, sermon by sermon,

---

2. By the Rule of Singularity, the interpreter considers the canonical text as a single unit for application purposes; the Rule of Congruence bids readers assume broad coherence and consistency among the canonical witnesses; the Rule of Substantiality accords the content of Scripture the respect worthy of its priority and gravity; and the Rule of Primacy bases all biblical interpretation upon the person of Christ.

3. Often, the text itself demonstrates internal demarcations corresponding to its divisions into these discrete sense units. Textual clues that serve to locate the exposed seams between pericopes include: repeated terms or phrases (e.g., καὶ ἐγένετο ὅτε ἐτέλεσεν ὁ Ἰησοῦς in Mt. 7.28; 11.1; 13.53; 19.1; 26.1); significant discourse markers; rhetorical questions (e.g., וַאֲמַרְתֶּם, 'but you say…?' in Mal. 1.2, 6, 7, 12, 13; 2.14, 17; 3.7, 8, 13); changes in time, location, or setting, within narratives; thematic announcements (e.g., as with περὶ δὲ in 1 Cor. 7.1, 25; 8.1, [4]; 12.1; 16.1, 12); etc. See Walter C. Kaiser, Jr., *Toward an Exegetical Theology: Biblical Exegesis for Preaching and Teaching* (Grand Rapids: Baker, 1981), pp. 71–2.

pericope by pericope, the various aspects of Christian life, individual and corporate, are effectively brought into alignment with the will of God. The goal of a homiletical endeavour, after all, is not merely to explicate the content of the chosen pericope, but to expound it in such a way that its implications for current hearers are brought home with conviction, to transform lives for God's glory (the Rule of Applicability).[4] Life change is not a one-time phenomenon, and neither is it accomplished instantaneously; it involves a lifetime of progressive reorientation and realignment to the world in front of the text. Such an approach to the edification of God's people demands that a unit-sized pericopal block of Scripture, incorporating a single thrust or theme capable of being assimilated and applied, be the object of consideration in the weekly gatherings of the believers.

The liturgical use of Scripture

An example of the reading (and exposition) of a pericope is found in Luke's account of Jesus' activities in the synagogue at Nazareth (Lk. 4.16-30).[5] The narrator is careful to demonstrate not only the handling of a precisely demarcated text but also the preacher's taking into consideration the concerns and capacities of the audience. The unique situation of its auditors is reflected in this narrative: the hometown synagogue setting, the expectations of the congregation, the application to listeners' circumstances and the give-and-take in the reading and the reaction thereto. The event is set within the social context of a corporate gathering, and the evangelist describes in exquisite detail Jesus' standing to read, his being handed the book, the opening, reading and closing of the book before it is returned, and Jesus' resuming his seat at the conclusion of his exposition (4.16-20). It is a clear account of the homiletical utilization of a pericope in a very specific ecclesial environment and in a markedly liturgical format. This episode may validly be considered a paradigm of the sermonic undertaking in a defined setting of real life – the periodic assembly of the faithful.

The particulars of the process create a nearly perfect chiasm, emphasizing as its centrepiece the actual reading of Isa. 61.1-2 by Jesus.[6]

---

4. Tertullian stated: 'We assemble to read our sacred writings, ... with the sacred words we nourish our faith, we animate our hope, we make our confidence more steadfast; and no less by inculcations of God's precepts we confirm good habits' (*Apol.* 39). Such practices of reading for application were prevalent in the Jewish context as well. Philo observed that on the Sabbath people were taught lessons of virtues 'by which the whole of their lives may be improved' (*Spec. Laws* 2.15.62; also see *Creation* 128; and Josephus, *Ag. Ap.* 2.18).

5. This was probably not an isolated instance; Lk. 4.15, 16 and 31 indicate Jesus teaching in local synagogues with some frequency.

6. Jeffrey S. Siker, ' "First to the Gentiles": A Literary Analysis of Luke 4:16–30', *JBL* 111 (1992), pp. 73–90 (77).

4.16a	*A* Jesus enters the synagogue
4.16b	*B* He stands to read
4.17a	*C* He is handed the book of Isaiah
4.17b	*D* He opens the book
4.18-19	*E* He reads
4.20a	*D'* He closes the book
4.20b	*C'* He returns the book
4.20c	*B'* He sits down
4.20d	*A'* Those in the synagogue look at Jesus

The placement of the reading of the scroll of Isaiah in the crux of the chiasm emphasizes the importance of that event. The centrality of Scripture has always been integral to the corporate activities of the community of God. For instance, Timothy is enjoined in 1 Tim. 4.13 to give attention to the public reading of the Scriptures.[7] The corpus attended to there was, of course, the OT. With time, these communal transactions came to utilize every major portion of the Christian canon. That the Law and the Prophets were in use in the early Church is evident from Acts 13.15; Paul's sermon at Antioch is said to have commenced after the readings from these two sections of the OT. By the time of Justin Martyr (c. 150 CE), a weekly worship service in Rome also included readings of 'the memoirs [ἀπομνημονεύματα] of the apostles' along with the writings of the Prophets (*1 Apol.* 67).[8] Thus it appears that, by the mid-second century, at least some of the Gospels had also achieved authoritative liturgical status. In addition, even towards the close of the NT canon, the letters of Paul were beginning to be considered alongside the 'rest of the Scriptures' (2 Pet. 3.15-16).[9] Polycarp, late in the second century, asserts the pedagogical value of the Pauline Epistles, which 'if you carefully study, you will find to be the means of building you up in that faith which has been given you' (*Phil.* 3.2). In time, these missives also came to be included in the essential readings at corporate assemblies. Though of later origin (about the fourth century), the *Constitutions of the Holy Apostles* includes information about the lections of Scripture; the Clementine Liturgy therein (8.5) appears to call for several biblical readings in ecclesial gatherings – from the Law and the Prophets, the Epistles and the Gospels.[10] The historical evidence amply attests to the utilization of every major

7. This public undertaking is clearly distinguished from the private study of the sacred writings that Timothy was said to have been immersed in from his early days (2 Tim. 3.15).

8. In *1 Apol.* 66, Justin asserts that these memoirs were called 'gospels' (εὐαγγέλια).

9. Paul, himself, appears to have anticipated the authority of his writings; see 2 Thess. 2.15; 3.14.

10. *Constitutions of the Holy Apostles* has another description of the liturgy that prescribes

section of both Testaments for reading and exposition in the Church (as called for by the Rules of Completion, Singularity, Exclusivity and Applicability). The practice of reading from the various parts of the canon in the *same* gathering is the outworking of the Rules of Secondary Genre – those of Organization, Congruence, Intertextuality and Sequentiality.[11]

In the synagogue at Nazareth, Jesus proceeds to read Isa. 61.1-2, a defined pericope that Luke quotes in full, and upon which Jesus bases his homily. This reading of a pericope from the prophets functioned as the *haftarah* (הפתרה, the recitation of dismissal taken from the prophetic corpus including Joshua, Judges and Samuel-Kings) and followed the reading of the Pentateuch. The latter was ordered to be read consecutively in a three-yearly cycle, and so it is conceivable that the reading of the prophets, too, had been seriatim when Jesus opened the scroll of Isaiah.[12] While most of the evidence about the liturgical practice of the synagogue comes from the second century and later, it is clear that quite early on this pattern of communal utilization of Scripture in measured doses came to be directed by a lectionary. Appropriately divided sections of the text (pericopes) were read in continuous fashion (*lectio continua*), each subsequent reading taking up from where the previous reading had left off. This was the oldest approach to readings of the canonical text, and it was the standard practice on non-festival Sabbaths in Jewish synagogues.[13] In all likelihood, the protocol of continuous reading was bequeathed to the Church, and this mode of contact with Scripture appears to have been the norm for most of early Church history.[14]

readings from the OT, Acts, Epistles and Gospels, in that order (2.57). Also see F.E. Warren, *The Liturgy and Ritual of the Ante-Nicene Church* (2nd rev. edn; London: SPCK, 1912), pp. 257, 283.

11. The Rules of Completion and Exclusivity delimit the form and the books of the canon that may be productively employed for ecclesial purposes; the Rule of Singularity considers the canon a single integral unit and, with the Rule of Applicability, ensures that no part of the canon is neglected for application. The Rule of Congruence mandates a coherent and unified reading of Scripture. The Rules of Organization, Intertextuality and Sequentiality bid the interpreter respect the temporal and logical arrangements of the included texts and their contents, permitting dialogue between the components of this coherent canonical corpus, and thus justifying readings from different portions of the canon on the same occasion.

12. See Emil Schürer, *The History of the Jewish People in the Age of Jesus Christ (175 B.C– A.D. 135)* (eds Geza Vermes, Fergus Millar, and Matthew Black; Edinburgh: T. & T. Clark, 1979), vol. 2, pp. 450–4; and Asher Finkel, 'Jesus' Sermon at Nazareth (Luk. 4,16–30)', in *Abraham unser Vater: Juden und Christen im Gespräch über die Bibel* (eds Otto Betz, Martin Hengel and Peter Schmidt; Leiden: Brill, 1963), pp. 106–15 (107). The wear and tear on scrolls would probably have been considerable had readers been skipping discontinuously from text to text (Hughes Oliphant Old, *The Reading and Preaching of the Scriptures* [4 vols; Grand Rapids: Eerdmans, 1998], 1: 100 n. 109).

13. See the tractate *b. Meg.* 4; skipping passages of the Torah was looked upon with disfavour. Also see Harry Y. Gamble, *Books and Readers in the Early Church: A History of Early Christian Texts* (New Haven: Yale University Press, 1995), pp. 208–11, 217.

14. Among others, Origen, the Cappadocian Fathers, Cyril of Alexandria, John Chrysostom,

In weekly expositions of pericopes of Scripture for the community, especially with a hiatus of several days between these corporate encounters with the Bible, there is always the danger of dislodging a narrow sliver of text from its broader context. This threat is attenuated, no doubt, by the necessary explanatory glosses within the sermon that clarify and explain the textual locus and logical environs of the pericope. However, particularly effective for maintaining the continuity of the subject matter of the text from week to week, and for respecting its trajectory (its world projection) from reading to reading, is *lectio continua*. A tacit assumption operates under the practice of continuous reading: individual pericopes find their proper position in the context of the rest of the book and the canon, for there is an integrity to the whole that must not be fragmented – the 'Bible's own canonically organized patterns and internal relationships'. *Lectio continua* thus respects the Rules of Organization, Singularity and Congruence.[15] Preaching passages of Scripture that he suspected would be considered offensive to his listeners, Chrysostom pleaded, 'I have no wish to violate decency by discoursing upon such subjects, but I am compelled to it'; he was led perforce by providence to preach through all of the text.[16] Such an approach also reflects the Rule of Applicability that calls upon the interpreter to seek application in every portion of the canon.

By the time of the fifth century, however, the proliferation of feasts in the calendar and the allotment of specific biblical texts for each of those days rendered readings almost entirely *lectio selecta* ('reading selectively'), the textual assignment for an occasion being based upon the significance of a saint or that special feast. The complexity of the festal calendar required that texts allocated for particular occasions be listed formally, and lectionaries configured for this purpose came into existence.[17] Unlike for most of Church history, the Middle Ages, therefore, demonstrate a dearth of *lectio continua* sermons. It was not until the Reformers that this practice returned to popularity in churches. Martin

---

Ambrose of Milan, and Augustine abided by *lectio continua*, as evidenced in their methodical production of sermons from biblical books. See Old, *Reading and Preaching of the Scriptures*, 1: 344; 2: 36, 51–2, 83, 105–6, 173–4, 327, 345–68.

15. Christopher Seitz, 'The Lectionary as Theological Construction', in *Inhabiting Unity: Theological Perspectives in the Proposed Lutheran-Episcopal Concordat* (eds Ephraim Radner and R.R. Reno; Grand Rapids: Eerdmans, 1995), pp. 173–91 (179). Gerard S. Sloyan objects to a lectionary that is not continuous: 'Congregations are being protected from the insoluble mystery of God by a packaged providence, a packaged morality, even a packaged mystery of Christ' ('The Lectionary as a Context for Interpretation', *Int* 31 [1977], pp. 131–8 [138]). The Rule of Organization, in particular, affirms the need for the interpreter to pay heed to the arrangement of the Testaments and the individual books of the canon, as well as the ordering of time in Scripture.

16. John Chrysostom, *Hom. Col.* 8 (on Col. 3.5-7).

17. See Old, *Reading and Preaching of the Scripture*, 3: 85, 289; and John Reumann, 'A History of Lectionaries: From the Synagogue at Nazareth to Post-Vatican II', *Int* 31 (1977), pp. 116–30 (124).

Luther advised: 'one of the books should be selected and one or two chapters, or half a chapter, be read, until the book is finished. After that another book should be selected, and so on, until the entire Bible has been read through.' Huldrych Zwingli explained to the bishop of Constance in 1522 that he followed *lectio continua:* Matthew for a whole year, then Acts, then the letters to Timothy, the letters of Peter and Hebrews.[18] Martin Bucer, too, was an avid proponent of *lectio continua*, calling for such a practice among all pastors, a reversion to the custom of the ancient Church.[19] In sum, continuous reading and exposition emphasizes the relationship of the part to the whole: while the pericope is the smallest quantum of text attended to in a given gathering, the community affirms its indissoluble unity with its textual neighbourhood. Such an approach to Scripture also propagates the conviction that every part of the canon is worthy of exposition; the Rule of Applicability explicitly makes this assertion. As will be discussed later, a pericope frames a segment of the larger world projected by the canon, offering this segment for appropriation by the people of God. The sequential employment of contiguous pericopes thus enables the full breadth of the canonical world to be appropriated over time.

In Luke's report of the visit to the synagogue at Nazareth, Jesus commences his 'sermon' proper at 4.21 – the narrator notes that 'he began to say to them'. While the Lukan précis of the homily has Jesus only announcing the fulfilment of the Isaianic prophecy, it seems fair to assume there was more to the exposition than that brief comment; an extended discussion appears to be implied. Of particular interest to this work is Jesus' affirmation of the text's applicability in a day several centuries distant from the time of its original inscription – '*Today* this Scripture has been fulfilled'. The declaration marked the prophetic fulfilment of an ancient text; however, it is valid to see in this transhistorical use of Scripture an underlying affirmation of the implicit and potential contemporaneity of the text – its perennial significance that transcends the circumstances of its provenance.[20] What was written *then* is rendered effective *now*; properly

18. Martin Luther, 'Concerning the Order of Public Worship (1523)', in *Liturgy and Hymns* (vol. 53 of *Luther's Works*; trans. Paul Zeller Strodach; rev. Ulrich S. Leupold; Philadelphia: Fortress, 1965), pp. 7–14 (12); Gottfried Locher, *Zwingli's Thought: New Perspectives* (Leiden: Brill, 1981), p. 27.

19. Martin Bucer, *Martin Bucers Deutsches Schriften* (14 vols; ed. R. Stupperich; Gütersloh: Mohn, 1960–75), 7: 281. The Strasbourg Church Service (1525) promoted *lectio continua* rather than the preaching of 'chopped-up fragments' (*stuckwerk*) (Friedrich Hubert, *Die Strassburger Liturgische Ordnungen im Zeitalter der Reformation* [Göttingen: Vandenhoeck & Ruprecht, 1900], p. 79). Calvin, too, preached slowly and surely through most of the books of the Bible, meticulously abiding by *lectio continua*. See T.H.L. Parker, *Calvin's Preaching* (Edinburgh: T. & T. Clark, 1992), p. 80.

20. This perennial character of its writings, a property of the secondary genre of the canonical classic, is reinforced as Jesus urges the disciples of John, in Lk. 7.22, to report back to the latter (in prison, 3.20) that they had witnessed the blind receiving sight and the poor having the gospel

expounded, any text of Scripture is applicable in any particular 'present'. It comes as no surprise, therefore, that the Bible itself consistently asserts the relevance of its message for subsequent generations (the thrusts of the Rules of Substantiality and Applicability).[21]

Actualizations or realizations of Scripture in the 'here and now' – the application of the text to the circumstances and contexts of the current auditors of the word – is the ultimate end of all exposition of biblical pericopes in the ecclesial setting.[22] In achieving this goal of application, the formal utilization of a pericope in the context of the Church gathering plays a crucial theological role. Pericopes are not merely conveniently packaged textual units suitable for weekly uptake. Rather, their self-contained and defined nature, their potential use in *lectio continua* fashion, and their regular and periodic employment in Church assemblies for application, all render them agents of a unique and momentous phenomenon that serves to align the faithful with their God – the transaction of covenant renewal. This is the theological function of these units of Scripture in the life of the Christian community.

Theological function of pericopes

The theological role played by pericopes and their exposition in the worship of the Church has not been a matter that has attracted much academic interest. While attention has been lavished upon the theology of individual books and upon that of the canon as a whole, consideration of the theology of these liturgically and homiletically critical tracts of Scripture, the functional units of the canon that confront the people of God weekly in formal fashion, has languished. Such a neglect is all the more regrettable since it is by these regular encounters with demarcated entities of the biblical text that life change is addressed, so that individual and community may abide in the will of God. This work proposes that the central theological function of pericopes is the facilitation of covenant renewal, the restoration of God's people to a right relationship with him. Due respect for this instrumentality of pericopes is therefore essential for proper homiletical practice. Such an understanding of the role of pericopes is illustrated by the account of the prototypical transaction in Nehemiah 7–8.

---

preached to them; both events were actualizations of Isa. 61.1, the text that had been read in the synagogue at Nazareth (Lk. 4.18-19).

21. See Deut. 4.10; 6.6-25; 29.14-15; 2 Kgs 22–23; Neh. 7.73b–8.18; Mt. 28.19; Rom. 15.4; 1 Cor. 10.6, 11; 2 Tim. 3.16-17; etc. The Rule of Substantiality calls for the canonical text to be given the consideration due its materiality. Unaffected by the passage of time and the vagaries of culture, the canon sustains its substantiality across temporal spans and spatial boundaries.

22. The delivery of the sermon does not complete the event of the text-congregation encounter; integral to such an understanding is the element of actual praxis, of lives changed in response to the word preached, as God's people respond to him in worship, witness and service (Isa. 55.10-11).

Covenant renewal in Nehemiah 7.73b–8.12

The paradigmatic notion of God's people as 'purchased and delivered' by him reflects not only the primeval event of the exodus from Egypt but also all acts of deliverance that God performs for his people, especially the redemption wrought in Jesus Christ, the Passover Lamb.[23] The redeemed of God of all time thus become citizens of God's kingdom, for liberation by God involves a change of master – 'a passage from a distressing, foreign and arbitrary yoke to contentment and security under rightful authority'.[24] This extraordinary relationship between Creator and redeemed stipulates that the maintenance of such a filiation be given significant and constant attention in the corporate life of the people of God. The transaction of covenant renewal provides the perfect occasion for the community to focus jointly and formally upon its unique status under God. Reminding itself of the responsibilities of that privileged station, the community, in covenant renewal, commits itself to abiding by the will of its divine sovereign. Just as clauses of contemporaneous ancient Near Eastern treaties, repeatedly and publicly spelled out at recurrent intervals, helped preserve relationships between clients and overlords, regular and frequent readings of their foundational text played a critical role in the Israelites' covenant relationship with Yahweh, the one to whom they owed ultimate allegiance.[25] However, distinct from every other secular enterprise of this sort, Israel's covenant renewal was Torah centred, as she pledged loyalty and swore fealty to her Lord. In doing so, the nation placed itself under obligation to abide by the revealed will of God, implicitly acknowledging the Rules of Substantiality and Applicability that presume the gravity of Scripture and its potential for universal application. Historically, therefore, the reading of Scripture was always intertwined with this principle of covenant renewal; it is particularly exemplified in Ezra's proclamation of the law in c. 444 BCE.[26]

---

23. Moses' and Miriam's Song of the Sea (Exod. 15.1-21), that was considered in Chapter 2, clearly marked out the Israelites as having been bought and redeemed by Yahweh (Exod. 15.16). This theme is also reflected in the NT in 1 Cor. 6.20; 7.23; Tit. 2.14; 1 Pet. 1.18-19; 2.9; Rev. 5.9; etc.

24. David Daube, *The New Testament and Rabbinic Judaism* (London: Athlone, 1956), p. 273. For this concept of servanthood under God, see Lev. 25.55; Isa. 43.1; and, in the NT, Rom. 6.17-23; 1 Cor. 7.22; Col. 4.7; etc.

25. Ancient Near Eastern documents attest to the readings of treaties and the transactions of covenant renewal on a periodic basis to remind subjects of their responsibilities to their sovereign. It is conceivable that such practices as classically flourished in the environs of Israel influenced that nation's concept of her relationship with God and her dealings with him. See Robert H. Pfeiffer, *One Hundred New Selected Nuzi Texts* (trans. E.A. Speiser; New Haven: American Schools of Oriental Research, 1936), p. 103. Gary Beckman, *Hittite Diplomatic Texts* (Atlanta: Scholars, 1996), pp. 42, 47, 76 and 86, details treaties that mandated repeated reading. See also Moshe Weinfeld, *Deuteronomy and the Deuteronomic School* (Winona Lake, IN: Eisenbrauns, 1992), pp. 64–5.

26. Deuteronomy 31.10-13 reports on a similar transaction under Moses.

The reading of the law in Neh. 7.73b–8.12 is considered one of the oldest descriptions of a 'liturgy of the Word'.[27] This event was the watershed phenomenon in the life of the postexilic community of Israel: it forms the climax of the Ezra-Nehemiah joint corpus. The missions of the two protagonists, Ezra and Nehemiah, converge precisely within this enterprise, and for the first time they are mentioned together in this section (8.9). Within the larger body of the account (6.1–12.47), the renewal of covenant forms the centre of a chiasm.

6.1–7.4	*A* Completion of the city walls
7.5-73a	*B* List of ancestral inhabitants
7.73b–10.39	*C* Covenant renewal
11.1–12.26	*B'* Repopulation of Jerusalem
12.27–47	*A'* Dedication of the city walls

The location of the chiastic convergence is significant. The interpolation of covenant renewal within the broader undertaking that restored the Holy City signified the importance of this transaction as the singular event that definitively reconstituted the children of Israel. It provided both the pivot for the account of rebuilding and the prerequisite for the successful re-emergence and refounding of the nation after years of having been wrenched into exile. With this milestone, the identity of the nation was rediscovered, and its standing before God re-established.[28] In the accounting of this drama, the book of the law, rightly, occupied centre stage; indeed, covenant renewal is always Scripture centred and forms the basis of all realignment to God's will. Noteworthy in this regard is that of the twenty-one references to תּוֹרָה in Nehemiah, all but two are found in the section containing the covenant renewal account (7.73b–10.39). One might go so far as to assert that Scripture-centring always leads to covenant renewal, in that the priorities and purposes of God are established and realized in the life of the community. Bounded as it is between the detailed accounts of the rebuilding of the fortifications of Jerusalem, the act of covenant renewal under Nehemiah has wider theological ramifications for the community of God of all time. Covenant renewal, at the core of communal restructuring and reorientation to the will of God, may be considered the paradigm for the reading and exposition of Scripture undertaken in corporate contexts for the people of God.

The account in Neh. 7.73b–10.39 is itself tripartite, each portion involving an assembly for the reading of the Torah (7.73b–8.12; 8.13-18; and 9.1–10.39). Of particular interest is the first reading of the law, with its details of how the process was carried out. Nehemiah 7.73b–8.12 is bracketed by a gathering of

27. Old, *Reading and Preaching of the Scriptures*, 1: 95–6.

28. Michael W. Duggan, *The Covenant Renewal in Ezra-Nehemiah (Neh 7:72b–10:40): An Exegetical, Literary, and Theological Study* (Atlanta: SBL, 1996), p. 73.

'all the people' (כָּל־הָעָם, 8.1, 12). This assemblage of God's people, rather than Ezra, is the focus throughout the account, being mentioned sixteen times.[29] That Ezra was responding to the request of the people for the Torah to be read (8.1, 2) again indicates the leader's subordinate role as the 'minister' who merely mediated the book of the law to the community of God; it was for the benefit of the latter that the entire transaction was entered into.[30] The balanced cascade of five verbs each for leader and community (in 8.4-6) further emphasizes this occasion as having been for the whole body: Ezra stood, opened the book (× 2), was standing above and blessed God; 'all the people' had made the podium, they stood, answered, bowed low and worshipped. One led, the others responded. Flanked by thirteen 'lay' leaders (8.4), Ezra does not act unilaterally – this is a joint event of leaders and the led, affirming the importance and communal nature of this significant episode in the life of the people.[31]

What is actually read on the occasion fails to be mentioned. However, the liturgical responsibilities of the actants and the formality of the whole enterprise cannot be missed: the priest-scribe in solemn procession with the Torah scroll (8.2); his formalized, ritualized position at the forefront and above the assembly (8.4); the stationing of other leaders on either side of him (8.4); the unrolling of the scroll before the assembly (8.5); the people's rising to their feet in response (8.5); Ezra's invocation of a blessing (8.6); the people's responding in unison with 'Amen', while raising their hands and worshipping (8.6; Deut. 27.15-26 notes the covenantal connotations of this particular response); the presider's reading of the text to the assembly (Neh. 8.3); the Levites' interpreting the text to the people (8.7-8); and the leaders' instructing the people concerning the celebration of a subsequent festive meal (8.9-12). This was, indisputably, a liturgical gathering of the people of God before God. Notable, also, is that the reading was conducted in an easily accessible public place away from the temple precincts: none was barred from attending, hearing, understanding, or obeying. The parallels between this operation of covenant renewal and the

---

29. The community as a whole is indicated by 'sons of Israel' (7.73b); 'all the people' (8.1, 3, 5 [× 2], 6, 9, 11, 12); 'as one man' (8.1); 'the assembly' (8.2); 'men, women, and all who could listen with understanding' (8.2); 'men and women, those who could understand' (8.3); and 'the people' (8.7 [× 2], 9). When the covenant was renewed at Shechem, Joshua's address to the Israelites, likewise, designated the audience כָּל־הָעָם (Josh. 24.2, 27). Also see the renewal of the covenant in the time of Josiah (2 Kgs 23.1-3; 2 Chron. 34.30).

30. Neither was this an activity conducted impromptu, conjured up at the spur of the moment: Neh. 8.4 indicates planning in the construction of Ezra's podium, and 8.10 suggests that food preparation had also been going on in anticipation of the gathering.

31. Hittite treaties in the ancient Near East were also characterized by an evident 'democratization' of submission to the sovereign that devolved not only upon the vassal but also on the whole populace, a collective responsibility to maintain a right relationship with the suzerain. See John S. Holladay, Jr., 'Assyrian Statecraft and the Prophets of Israel', *HTR* 63 (1970), pp. 29–51 (38, 44, 49–50).

weekly worship of the Church with its formal encounter with Scripture are immediately noticeable.[32]

Especially pertinent to this work is the activity of the Levites in Neh. 8.7-8. Their task was to facilitate comprehension by the community of what God required of them. By the Rule of Substantiality, any reading of Scripture is to respect the immense significance of its content. It must therefore be ensured that such content is understood and its application apprehended by the auditors; this was the responsibility of the Levites (and continues to be that of theologian-homileticians today). The Levites' giving the sense of the reading involved an 'explanation' (מְפֹרָשׁ), the outcome of which was 'understanding'.[33] The root בין ('to understand') occurs six times in the account (8.2, 3, 7, 8, 9, 12), dramatizing the spiritual formation of the community through the comprehension of the Scriptures. Psalm 119.34 ('Give me understanding [בִין], that I may observe your law, and keep it with all my heart') indicates that the end-point of such understanding is obedience.[34] The exertions of the Levitical mediators of Scripture also bore fruit in the Israelites' subsequent response. Comprehension by the congregation included application of Scripture to their lives: an epistemological movement from worship, to hearing, to provisional understanding, to full cognition, to prompt and precise application – the celebration of the Feast of Tabernacles (Neh. 8.9-12, 16-18). The fundamental thrust of Nehemiah 8 is that Scripture reading with explanation leads to understanding, which in turn issues in joyful obedience (8.10-12, 17).[35] This is at the core of covenant renewal; the reading and exposition of the biblical text in a corporate, ecclesial context, an event mediated by the theologian-homiletician, culminates in application that readjusts the congregation to the covenant and restores them in it, thus reaffirming their status as those purchased and delivered by God.

Occurring as it does centuries removed from the giving of the law, covenant renewal in Nehemiah is an archetype of the hermeneutic of application and recontextualization espoused in this work. The Israelites in their restored post-exilic circumstances under Ezra and Nehemiah would no doubt have wondered how ancient Mosaic regulations pertaining to a theocratic state in which the will of God was law could have any commerce under the monarchical rule of the

---

32. See Duggan, *Covenant Renewal in Ezra-Nehemiah*, p. 110. In these transactions of the people of God, the Rule of Applicability is brought into prominence in that it accords the ancient writings universal validity for contemporary application. Such use of Scripture is to be conducted under the patronage of the community of believers (Rule of Ecclesiality).

33. The Aramaic term מפרש used in a document of c. 428 BCE denotes 'plainly, exactly, or separately set forth' (see A.E. Cowley, *Aramaic Papyri of the Fifth Century B.C.* [Oxford: Clarendon Press, 1923], pp. 51–2). The root of the word (פרש) in Lev. 24.12 and Num. 15.34 refers to legal judgements awaiting clarification.

34. The use of בין in the hiphil in Nehemiah 8 corresponds to its utilization in that stem in Prov. 28.7 – 'He who keeps the law is an understanding son': obedience is intrinsic to comprehension.

35. See H.G.M. Williamson, *Ezra, Nehemiah* (WBC; 16; Dallas: Word, 1985), pp. 286, 299.

Persian Empire of their time. It was the renewal of covenant that demonstrated how 'the principle of the Law could continue to be observed even when its letter was deadened by changed circumstances'.[36] The account in Nehemiah 7–8 was thus canonically intended to function as a prototype for all future communities that desire to orient themselves towards God and align themselves to his word. The ancient text is still capable of speaking to a modern audience with perennial significance for application; this is an intrinsic characteristic of the canonical classic. The Rule of Applicability renders the universal significance of the text a potential reality awaiting actualization. Such a conception of the role of pericopes of Scripture must necessarily result in a response to the demands of the text (application), without which, covenant renewal, the terminus of every biblical exposition, remains unrealized and inchoate.

Pericopes as literary instruments of covenant renewal
As the progenitor of the theological operation of pericopes regularly employed in an ecclesial setting, covenant renewal may be considered the conceptual model for all sermonic exposition of the Bible: it is a summons to God's people to return and renew a Scripture-centred relationship with the one who is truly their sovereign. The account of covenant renewal in Nehemiah 7–8 does duty as an outstanding exemplar of this endeavour. Set in a liturgical context, the entire event – the reading of Scripture, its subsequent exposition and the response of the congregation – serves as a helpful device for reflecting upon Scripture-centred transactions in the ecclesial context, activities that also comprise the same elements of reading, exposition and response. Pericopes of the biblical text, handled weekly in homiletical exercises, are therefore best construed as literary instruments of covenant renewal. A pericope performs its crucial function by featuring a segment of the canonical world projected by the text of Scripture. It is to this segment that individuals are bidden, in each homiletical event, to orient themselves. In so doing they align themselves to the particular aspects of the will of God prescribed by that pericope. Covenant renewal thus forms the permanent backdrop to all homiletical utilization of Scripture in the Church setting. It is an acknowledgement of the humanity of God's people and their tendency to drift away from the will of God; a periodic renewal of their standing with their Creator is therefore necessary. It is also a recognition of the distanciation of texts that necessitates its renewal for (reapplication to) a contemporary audience.

The goal of regular reading and exposition of pericopes of Scripture in the gathering of the Church, then, is application; at each such event a particular aspect of the life of the individual and community is addressed, as the pericope of that day dictates. Such an interpretive undertaking reflects the hermeneutic of covenant renewal and transformation, as readers respond to the text by 'inhabiting' the pericopal segment of the world projected in front of the canonical text.

---

36. Williamson, *Ezra, Nehemiah*, pp. xxxiv, 303–4.

In that each pericope considers only a specific facet of life lived in relationship with God, covenant renewal is the cumulative outcome of expositions of
pericopes conducted over time. The culmination of these ecclesial transactions
is the reorientation of the Church to the plenary world projected by the canon.
This canonical world depicts a mode of existence in which God's priorities are
supreme, where his principles operate and the practices of his Kingdom are
enacted. Such a world is a potential way of life open to those who, in obedience
to Scripture, choose to live in the will of God by aligning their lives to that
world. As biblical pericopes are applied in the lives of readers and hearers, the
projected world is appropriated by God's people, and covenant relationship is
renewed, week by week. Needless to say, the facilitation of covenant renewal
is the responsibility of the preacher, the one in the community of God entrusted
with the task of interpretation and application of the text, the chaperone of the
move from text to praxis. The mediation of covenant renewal between God and
his people, between sovereign and subjects, is a duty of immense gravity for the
theologian-homiletician, as emphasized in the mandate to Timothy: 'I solemnly
charge you in the presence of God and of Christ Jesus... preach the word'
(2 Tim. 4.1-2).[37]

The manner in which this preaching movement from Scripture to sermon
may be undertaken, in order to arrive at the destination of valid application
to accomplish covenant renewal, is at the heart of this work, and particularly
of this final chapter. It is in this transaction that world-projection achieves its
greatest utility. The world in front of the text, bearing a transhistorical intention,
and standing between ancient inscription and contemporary application, forms
the intermediary by which the reader is enabled to respond to the text. Distanciation and the ensuing decontextualization, a property of textuality, does not
quarantine the dated text from fruitful employment; rather, by world-projection,
conditions are created for recontextualization and application of the text to
proceed in the current circumstances of its readers. The *projection* of the world,
therefore, generates *projects* for action. In following this projected trajectory
of application, the dynamic course of the text is extended beyond itself and
covenant renewal is affected through the instrumentality of the pericope.[38]

What the regular utilization of pericopes is intended to achieve in a *general*
sense was the object of scrutiny in the last section – the concept of pericopes

37. Similarly, Ezra's reading and proclamation of the Law was an undertaking of great
moment, executed by one 'skilled in the law of Moses' (Ezra 7.6, 10), and one commissioned
by Artaxerxes to teach the 'law of your God' (7.25-6). See Duggan, *Covenant Renewal in Ezra-
Nehemiah*, p. 67.

38. Paul Ricoeur, *Hermeneutics and the Human Sciences: Essays on Language, Action and
Interpretation* (ed. and trans. John B. Thompson; Cambridge: Cambridge University Press, 1981),
p. 143; also see Charles E. Reagan and Paul Ricoeur, 'Interviews: Châtenay-Malabry, June 19,
1982', in Charles E. Reagan, *Paul Ricoeur: His Life and His Work* (Chicago: The University of
Chicago Press, 1996), pp. 100–9 (108).

as agents of covenant renewal in the setting of the Church assembly. The theologian-homiletician must also recognize how, in a more *specific* sense, each individual pericope contributes to covenant renewal. It is by the determination of the theology of that pericope and the derivation of valid application therefrom that covenant renewal is initiated. Pericopal theology and its application will therefore be the focus of the rest of this chapter.

Theology of pericopes

The biblical pericope is not only a literary object but also an instrument of action that projects a world that, when inhabited, renews God's people in a right relationship with their sovereign. As the *object* of a creative literary enterprise, the text must be investigated for what is 'behind' and 'within' the text (its rhetorical situation, linguistic particulars and specific content). Interpretation, however, must not cease with the elucidation of these essential entities, but, considering the text as an *instrument* of action, must proceed further to the discernment of the projected world 'in front of' the text in order to derive valid application of the text and accomplish covenant renewal.[39] This phenomenon of world-projection reflects the essential and crucial function of pericopes as 'concrete universals'.[40] As literary objects they depict what is concrete, specific, and particular; as literary instruments, the world they project gives pericopes their universal and transhistorical characteristic (perenniality). This section will explore the operation of pericopes as concrete universals. Furthermore, I shall argue that the portion of the world projected by the pericope (the universal) is the theology of that unit of text – *pericopal theology*, derived by a reading superintended by the Rules of Primary and Secondary Genre.

Concrete universals, projected world and theology

Given that a pericope is both an object and instrument of action, it has a twofold thrust: it is best considered a concrete universal – a 'plurisign' whereby it signifies a first-order referent that is 'close, immediate, and relatively obvious', as well as a second-order referent that possesses 'a universal and archetypal character' (the world in front of the text bearing a transhistorical intention; see Chapter 1). This is the mark of a classic text – its ability to function with this dual focus, concrete and universal. A concrete universal subsists in the particular and specific *qua* concrete, while it simultaneously yields a snapshot

---

39. Thomas G. Long stresses the need for homileticians to consider not only what the text says, but also what it does, for it is in the interplay between its saying and doing that 'the key to building the bridge between text and sermon' may be found (*The Witness of Preaching* [2nd edn; Louisville: Westminster/John Knox Press, 2005], p. 106).

40. Fred B. Craddock observed that 'it is in the particularity of a text that its universality lies' (*Preaching* [Nashville: Abingdon, 1985], p. 130).

of what is transcendent and general. In such texts, often, 'the universal is not announced explicitly, but stays implicit in, and yet is strongly affirmed by, the very individuality of the individual'.[41] It is this universal aspect of a text (its projected world) that generates a future-directed trajectory (its transhistorical intention). As a concrete universal, the classic text is thus rendered perennially significant: it now has potential for application across the temporal and spatial gulf created by distanciation. The Rule of Substantiality, in particular, affirming the gravity of the content of Scripture, directs a reading that recognizes, in the concrete particularities of the text, the canon's universally significant subject matter – God and his relationship to his creation. Moreover, in deference to the Rule of Ecclesiality, the people of God of *all* time have commissioned the reading and exposition of the Scriptures in the corporate setting, presuming upon the universal validity of its content. The legitimacy of such a hermeneutical enterprise that leads readers and hearers in every age from ancient text to contemporary praxis is therefore a given – an understanding further endorsed by the Rule of Applicability. These rules jointly accord Scripture the ability to speak its weighty matters to audiences and situations far removed from the circumstances of its provenance. It is as a concrete universal with world-projecting capabilities that a pericope overcomes the distanciation intrinsic to textuality.

The projected textual world (the universal) is the second-order pragmatic referent, unique to the text and derived from the particulars of its first-order referent. Such secondary referents of Scripture display to readers a world of divine values and demands, and offer to them the possibility of appropriating that world by subscription to those values and obedience to those demands. A new way of living – God's way – is depicted by the world projected by Scripture, and it is in the habitation of this world by the people of God that the text effects covenant renewal. The biblical canon as a whole projects a single world in front of itself, the canonical world. However, in the weekly homiletical transaction that moves the Church towards application, it is the pericope that remains the

---

41. Philip Wheelwright, *The Burning Fountain: A Study in the Language of Symbolism* (rev. edn; Bloomington, IN: Indiana University Press, 1968), p. 83. The concrete universality of Shakespearean writing, for instance, is widely acknowledged. The bard, Coleridge declared, could effect a 'union and interpenetration of the universal and the particular', characteristic of 'all works of decided genius and true science' ('The Friend: Section the Second, Essay IV', in *The Collected Works of Samuel Taylor Coleridge* [ed. Barbara E. Rooke; London: Routledge & Kegan Paul, 1969], pp. 448–57 [457]). Goethe asserted that the poet 'should seize the Particular and … thus represent the Universal' (J.W. Goethe, *Conversations with Eckermann (1823–1832)* [trans. John Oxenford; San Francisco: North Point, 1984], p. 95). A philosopher, Philip Sidney claimed, provides only the abstract and general precept; the historian, in contrast, gives only the concrete and particular. 'But both, not having both, do both halt', insufficient as they are to 'make men good'. Only 'doth the peerless poet perform both', supplying the general precept *and* the particular example – the concrete universal ('An Apology for Poetry', in *Criticism: The Major Statements* [2nd edn; ed. Charles Kaplan; New York: St. Martin's, 1986], pp. 108–48 [118–19]).

most basic textual component comprising the duality of concrete and universal elements. As the fundamental scriptural entity in ecclesial and homiletical use, and as the relatively irreducible textual element composing a single sense unit, each pericope projects a segment of that broader world projected by the canon. It is in, with and through an individual pericope (the concrete), that this specific segment of the canonical world (the universal) is revealed. The cumulative world-projections of all the individual pericopes of Scripture therefore constitute the plenary, singular world in front of the canonical text.[42] While the Rules of Primary Genre enable the identification of those pericopal sectors of the canonical world (see Chapter 2), the Rules of Secondary Genre beckon the interpreter to employ a reading that portrays the unity of the canonical world comprising the contributions of individual pericopes (see Chapter 3). It is the projected world that imbues a classic text with its prescriptive, perennial, and plural significance and it is to this world of Scripture that Christians are called to align their lives to accomplish covenant renewal.

The task of the theologian-homiletician, therefore, in interpreting a pericope for applicational purposes, is to move from the concrete biblical text via the intermediary of the universal (the world in front of the text) to arrive at another concrete element – relevant application in the modern day for specific listeners. Therein lies the genius of the projected world, for it is this entity, with its transhistorical, future-directed intention, that makes possible valid application in contexts far removed from those of the original utterance or discourse. Such a move from text to praxis involves the unfolding of a notion of transcendence, inherent in the world projected.[43] Moral judgements, especially, presuppose such a transcendence or implicit universality. By their very nature, these ethical principles point beyond the particularities of the concrete as they are 'generalized, abstracted and enlarged, and extended to an ideal communication community'.[44] What on the surface is concrete in its particularity turns out to

42. Countering Popper's argument against inferring universals from concrete statements or from singular ones – 'no matter how many instances of white swans we may have observed, this does not justify the conclusion that *all* swans are white' – Todorov replies that, though the hypothesis may be based on the observation of a limited number of the birds, it would still be 'perfectly legitimate' to so conclude, for cygnean whiteness is an organic and constitutional characteristic. Similarly, the universal is an intrinsic characteristic of the concrete text of the classic, and it can justly be derived therefrom. See Karl R. Popper, *The Logic of Scientific Discovery* (New York: Basic Books, 1959), p. 27; and Tzvetan Todorov, *The Fantastic: A Structural Approach to a Literary Genre* (trans. Richard Howard; Cleveland, OH: The Press of Case Western Reserve University, 1973), p. 4.

43. 'Essentially cognition is always oriented toward this essential aim, the articulation of the particular into a universal law and order' (Ernst Cassirer, *Language* [vol. 1 of *The Philosophy of Symbolic Forms*; trans. Ralph Mannheim; New Haven: Yale University Press, 1953], p. 77).

44. Jürgen Habermas, *Justification and Application: Remarks on Discourse Ethics* (trans. Ciaran Cronin; Cambridge: Polity, 1993), pp. 50, 52. For instance, the specific statement 'The car stopped because it ran out of petrol' implies the truth that 'All cars that run out of petrol will stop'.

be universal, subsuming large tracts of human life within itself. It is because of such inherent universality that a pericope, a literary instrument projecting a particular segment of the canonical world, can invite readers to consider this world and to organize their lives in accordance with it. Insofar as this move from text to praxis is accurately accomplished, and to the degree that the community, in obedient response, inhabits the world so projected, it participates in the ongoing and dynamic relationship between God and his creation – covenant renewal in operation.

What is proposed in this work is that the world projected in front of the text, the universal-in-the-concrete, is the theology of the text inasmuch as it portrays God and the covenantal relationship he intends to have with his people through the instrumentality of the text. It is a world wherein the economy of God is displayed, where kingdom priorities, principles and practices are portrayed. 'The proposed world that in biblical language is called a new creation, a new Covenant, the Kingdom of God, is the "issue" of the biblical text unfolded in front of this text.' Therefore it can rightly be called 'theology' – 'that skein of thought and language in which Christians understand themselves, the Bible, God, and their everyday world'.[45] Speaking as it does of God and his relationship with his creation, considering as it does the transcendentals of the universe – God (the divine attributes and Trinitarian nature; his purposes and plans), his creation (humanity; the community of God; and the *cosmos*, including sin and redemption) and the interaction of these actants between the two poles of eternity past and future – this projected world is the concern and focus of theology as a discipline. The theology projected by a pericope is a specific segment of the larger canonical world, and all such segments together compose a holistic understanding of God and his relationship to his people. This composite and integrated canonical world is the basis of biblical faith and the ground of cov-

---

Likewise, 'He should be punished for his theft' signifies that 'All who steal deserve punishment'. This, in the field of ethics, is called the principle of generalization, a process of justification or validation. '[A]n ethic without universals would be no ethic, a series of disconnected, arbitrary imperatives' (Oliver M.T. O'Donovan, 'The Possibility of a Biblical Ethic', *TSF Bull.* 67 [1973], pp. 15–23 [18]). Also see Marcus George Singer, *Generalization in Ethics* (London: Eyre & Spottiswoode, 1963), pp. 13–33, 34–46; and R.M. Hare, *Freedom and Reason* (Oxford: Clarendon Press, 1963), pp. 4–5, 10–13. 'The value of a generalization is that while it leaves out the specific features that are of the individual or of the moment, it expresses features that are general to a class' – the loss of specificity is a gain in applicability (Richard M. Weaver, *Language Is Sermonic: Richard M. Weaver on the Nature of Rhetoric* [eds Richard L. Johannesen, Rennard Strickland and Ralph T. Eubanks; Baton Rouge, LA: Louisiana State University Press, 1970], pp. 125–6). An example where Jesus himself sought to generalize a transhistorical intention from a narrative text is found in Mk 2.25-6 (employing 1 Sam. 21.1-7).

45. Paul L. Holmer, *The Grammar of Faith* (New York: Harper and Row, 1978), p. 9; Paul Ricoeur, 'Toward a Hermeneutic of the Idea of Revelation', in *Essays on Biblical Interpretation* (ed. Lewis S. Mudge; Philadelphia: Fortress, 1980), pp. 73–118 (103).

enant renewal.[46] Thus *pericopal theology* by definition is the theology specific to a particular pericope, that represents a segment of the plenary world in front of the canonical text, and that, bearing a transhistorical intention, functions as the crucial intermediary in the homiletical move from text to praxis that respects both the authority of the text and the circumstances of the hearer. It is such a world, projected by the pericope and unique to that text, that the congregation is invited to inhabit; by so doing, the ecclesial community renews its covenant relationship with God.

Pericopal theology as intermediary

The interpretation of a pericope at any gathering of the community of God, then, must discern the particular portion of the canonical world featured by that pericope; in other words, every homiletical undertaking must delineate the theology of the pericope. A reading of a pericope employing the Rules of Primary and Secondary Genres elucidates the segment of the canonical world framed by that given pericope; such a theological interpretation reflects what that specific text affirms about God and his relationship to mankind (an example is worked out below). What the pericope so affirms in its theology forms the basis of the subsequent homiletical move to derive application. As propounded herein, pericopal theology is a form of biblical theology and, as the theology of the specific pericope under consideration, it forms the station from which the interpreter may move on to the destination of application.[47] Pericopal theology is, therefore, neither the imposition of a systematic or confessional grid on textual data nor the result of an exclusively historical or sociological focus on the subject matter. Rather, it elucidates the textually mediated theological truth

46. Mudge likens the world in front of the text to a model in the natural sciences which functions as a heuristic device; in similar fashion, the projected world redescribes reality enabling readers to discover how that new world, a world according to God, may be actualized in their lives (Lewis S. Mudge, 'Paul Ricoeur on Biblical Interpretation', in Paul Ricoeur, *Essays on Biblical Interpretation* [ed. Lewis S. Mudge; Philadelphia: Fortress, 1980], pp. 1–37 [25]). Richard B. Hays suggests, likewise, that one mode of ethical discourse in the NT is the display of a symbolic world that creates perceptual categories for interpreting reality (Richard B. Hays, *The Moral Vison of the New Testament: Community, Cross, New Creation: A Contemporary Introduction to New Testament Ethics* [San Francisco: HarperSanFrancisco, 1996], pp. 208–9).

47. Biblical theology has been considered a thick description of the canon, an integrative accounting of the text as a divine, intentional act of communication. It is an interdisciplinary interpretive practice that emphasizes the unity of the canon, the 'work' of specific genres and the theological dimension of the hermeneutical undertaking. Such a 'redefined' biblical theology will gratefully mine the wisdom of the past, but will seek additional insights from contemporary hermeneutics as well, as this work attempts to do. See Francis B. Watson, *Text and Truth: Redefining Biblical Theology* (Grand Rapids: Eerdmans, 1997), pp. 8, 26; and Kevin J. Vanhoozer, 'Exegesis and Hermeneutics', in *New Dictionary of Biblical Theology* (eds T. Desmond Alexander and Brian S. Rosner; Downers Grove: InterVarsity, 2000), pp. 52–64 (53, 63).

of the pericope at hand, attending to the contribution of that particular quantum of text to the plenary canonical world that displays God and humanity rightly related to him. The cumulative integration of the theology of all the pericopes of Scripture thus constitutes the biblical theology of the canon – the plenary canonical world in front of the biblical text. In any gathering of the faithful, however, it is by the mediation of the theology of an individual pericope that the Scriptures may be brought to bear upon the situation of the hearers, thereby aligning the congregation to the world in front of the text. Week by week, and pericope by pericope, the community of God is progressively and increasingly reoriented to the will of God, gradually implementing covenant renewal.[48] The vector of such an interpretive transaction leads the theologian-homiletician from the text, via the posited world (pericopal theology) bearing a transhistorical intention, to arrive ultimately at application – the inhabitation of that projected world. Therefore in each expository undertaking geared for application, the theologian-homiletician sets the interpretive focus upon the theology of the particular text utilized. It is that one pericope chosen for the specific occasion in the gathered Christian community that must be applied via pericopal theology. As far as producing valid application is concerned, then, biblical interpretation that does not elucidate this crucial intermediary of pericopal theology is de facto incomplete.[49]

The theology of the pericope, generated by an interpretation supervised by the Rules of Primary and Secondary Genre, thus functions as the bridge between text and praxis, between the circumstances of the textual inscription and those of the reading community.[50] The utility of such a disposition of pericopal theol-

48. The Rule of Substantiality, asserting the density and wealth of material in all of the canon's constituent texts, promotes the handling of Scripture in smaller pericopal sizes for homiletical purposes. The Rules of Ecclesiality and Application also endorse this notion for implementing covenant renewal.

49. John Bright, *The Authority of the Old Testament* (Nashville: Abingdon, 1967), pp. 147–8, 173. David Buttrick agrees: 'The odd idea that preachers can move from text to sermon without recourse to theology by some exegetical magic or a leap of homiletic imagination is obvious nonsense' ('Interpretation and Preaching', *Int* 35 [1981], pp. 46–58 [57]).

50. Theology stands 'midway between the Bible and actual church preaching' (Heinrich Ott, *Theology and Preaching* [Philadelphia: Westminster, 1963], p. 17). Scobie, similarly, sees an intermediary role for biblical theology (Charles H.H. Scobie, 'The Challenge of Biblical Theology', *TynBul* 42.1 [1991], pp. 31–61 [49–51]; also see idem, *The Ways of Our God: An Approach to Biblical Theology* [Grand Rapids: Eerdmans, 2003], pp. 46–9). The concept of theology as a bridge between text and sermon has oft been proposed in the past, although how exactly it performs this role has not been explicated. See John Goldingay, *Approaches to Old Testament Interpretation* (Leicester, UK: InterVarsity, 1981), p. 43; John R.W. Stott, *Between Two Worlds: The Art of Preaching in the Twentieth Century* (Grand Rapids: Eerdmans, 1982), p. 137. For an insightful apprehension of the potential of this concept for preaching, see Timothy S. Warren, 'A Paradigm for Preaching', *BSac* 148 (1991), pp. 463–86; and idem, 'The Theological Process in Sermon Preparation', *BSac* 156 (1999), pp. 336–56.

ogy between text and praxis is in its facilitation of the interpretive move from canonical inscription to valid sermonic application.[51] What was there-and-then is thereby permitted to speak validly in the here-and-now. Divine discourse is thus forward looking, for the world in front of the text is the world that God is inviting his people to inhabit. This world is not necessarily the way the world actually *is*. Rather, it depicts God and his covenant relationship to his creation – a world that *should be* and *would be*, were God's people to align their lives to it: in a sense, an eschatological world. This eschatological world in front of the text guides believers to future action, to fresh appropriation of the pericope into their own particular contexts. Pericopal theology thus bears potential for the realization of God's kingdom; an eschatological concept, it is not yet completely fulfilled or operative until actualized in the future. It calls the Christian to a life lived in accord with the demands of God and to participate in the future endeavours of God, with God. The appropriation or application of the theology of the pericope is the remaking of the reader's world after the fashion of the world in front of the text, as 'the strange new eschatological world being created by the Spirit' is rendered real.[52] To this possibility, this potentiality, God's people are bidden to make their lives congruent, for application involves discovering the world projected in front of the text and aligning oneself to that world. Such an alignment restores the relationship between God and his community. A pericope, by way of its theology, thus contributes to the corporate mission of covenant renewal.

The explication of pericopal theology by the employment of the Rules of Primary and Secondary Genre enables the preacher to derive valid application. The resultant transformation of lives, as pericopal theology is applied and the projected world inhabited, reflects an alignment to the values of God's

---

51. J.P. Gabler also appears to have proposed such an intermediate position for biblical theology as early as the eighteenth century. Under biblical theology, he subsumed a 'pure' (*reine*) biblical theology that comprised an examination of texts for their 'universal ideas' that form 'the unchanging testament of Christian doctrine, and therefore pertain directly to us'. See his *Oratio de justo discrimine Theologiæ biblicæ et dogmaticæ regundisque recte utriusque finibus*, in John Sandys-Wunsch and Laurence Eldredge, 'J.P. Gabler and the Distinction between Biblical and Dogmatic Theology: Translation, Commentary, and Discussion of His Originality', *SJT* 33 (1980), pp. 133–58 (134–44; especially see 141–2, and 157 n. 1).

52. See Richard Briggs, *Reading the Bible Wisely* (London: SPCK, 2003), p. 111; and Kevin J. Vanhoozer, *The Drama of Doctrine: A Canonical-Linguistic Approach to Christian Theology* (Louisville: Westminster/John Knox Press, 2005), pp. 111, 318, 420. Ricoeur, too, acknowledges this eschatological nature of religious language. What is poetical in religion is, according to him, 'a capacity to create a new way of life and to open my eyes to new aspects of reality, new possibilities. You may call that eschatology in the sense that it's the horizon of another world, the promise of a new life' (Paul Ricoeur, 'Poetry and Possibility', in *A Ricoeur Reader: Reflection and Imagination* [ed. Mario J. Valdés; Hertfordshire: Harvester Wheatsheaf, 1991], pp. 448–62 [455]). This eschatological potential does not vitiate the veracity of textual assertions. Indeed, second-order referents, as was noted in Chapter 1, assume the validity of, and are built upon, such first-order referents without negating them.

kingdom. On a weekly basis in the ecclesial setting, as pericopes are sequentially preached from, the theology elucidated from each such textual unit contributes to the overall transaction of covenant renewal and the maintenance of a right relationship with the divine sovereign. This manner of 'doing' theology is integral to a proper homiletical approach to Scripture – one that seeks to move validly from text to praxis. Utilizing the Rules of Primary and Secondary Genres, the derivation of the theology of a specific pericope, 2 Sam. 11.1-27, will be demonstrated next.

Text to theology: 2 Samuel 11.1-27

Identifying the segment of the world projected by the pericope is an important goal of biblical interpretation, for it is via this critical intermediary that the theologian-homiletician can move from text to praxis, from inscription to application. An essential element of the sermonic undertaking in the ecclesial context is, therefore, the determination of pericopal theology. This section will attend to the theology of a particular pericope, 2 Sam. 11.1-27, a well-defined and self-contained quantum of the biblical text and potentially a prescribed lection in Church assemblies. The Rules of Genre (particularly those of the primary genre of narrative, Rules of Plot and Interaction) will be employed to unfold the theology inherent in the pericope.[53]

This accounting of the theology of 2 Sam. 11.1-27 will be conducted in the context of the theology of 1–2 Samuel as a whole.[54] While acknowledging the importance of the pericope as a fundamental textual unit of preaching and its singular role as the instrument of covenant renewal, the theologian-homiletician may not deny the unity of the wider text of which the pericope is part. Indeed, the theology of the pericope can be grasped only in light of the theology of the broader context; the segment of the world projected by the pericope is an integral element of the world projected by the larger body of text. The Rules of Singularity and Congruence explicitly assert the coherence of the biblical data, requiring the interpreter to reflect upon the relevance of the pericope in its wider literary and theological context.

In considering the entire corpus of 1–2 Samuel, the theme of faithfulness to Yahweh is found to be dominant. For instance, the two hymns that

---

53. The Rule of Plot enjoins a reading of the narrative that attends to the emplotted sequence of events revealing the moral framework of the story; by the Rule of Interaction, the interpreter examines the interpersonal transactions of the actants in the narrative to discern the projected world of the pericope.

54. In the choice of this canonical text for analysis, the following Rules of Secondary Genre are heeded: Rule of Completion (that respects the final form of the text); Rule of Exclusivity (that permits interpretation only of canonical texts); Rule of Applicability (that bids the interpreter heed all of Scripture and seek its application for all); and Rule of Substantiality (that recognizes the momentous nature of the content of Scripture).

bracket 1–2 Samuel (1 Sam. 2.1-10, Hannah's song; and 2 Sam. 22.1–23.7, the concluding hymn of David) emphasize this key principle of the world in front of the text: in both, Yahweh is exalted for his exploits and his excellence; the blissful lot of the faithful is extolled, while dire consequences are predicted for unfaithfulness. This characterization of God implicitly affirms that the one who rewards faithfulness with blessing must be trusted; the one who repays unfaithfulness with retribution must be feared (the operation of the two Rules of Hymnody).[55] As 2 Samuel 11 is exposited, these foundational assertions of who God is and what he expects from his people (faithfulness) will also undergird the sermon. Respecting the broader context of the pericope, the theologian-homiletician must attend to these larger themes as well, even though the sermonic undertaking focuses upon a narrower text.

Second Samuel 10–12 is structured by the framework of the Ammonite War that forms an *inclusio* for this section; it is within this plot enclosure that the shocking story of David is planted. The phrase וַיְהִי אַחֲרֵי־כֵן ('now it happened afterwards') begins both 2 Samuel 10 and the next section in 2 Samuel 13, isolating chapters 10–12 as a unit. The curtain falls on the narrative of 2 Samuel 10–12 with an obvious closure at 12.31 – 'then David and all the people returned to Jerusalem' – marking an end to the hostilities, as victor and army return in triumph to the capital. Though 2 Samuel 10–12 forms an integral narrative unit and part of a larger whole that spans chapters 9–20, for the purposes of this analysis the focus will be upon the specific pericope dealing with David's adultery and the murder of Uriah (11.1-27; the prophet Nathan's subsequent denunciation of David's unfaithfulness to God, in 2 Samuel 12, was considered separately in Chapter 2).

A striking feature of the opening episode of the narrative (2 Sam. 11.1-5) is the recurrence of the verb שׁלח ('to send'). Altogether in 2 Samuel 10–12, this term appears twenty-three times, while in the larger unit of 2 Samuel 9–20, it is utilized forty-four times; only thirteen instances occur in the rest of 2 Samuel. By the Rule of Congruence, the complementarity of the various parts of the canonical text points to the intentional inclusion of this conspicuous detail: the focused use of the term is clearly significant. For the most part, it is the king who does all the sending. This repeated element, then, appears to be a motif indicating regal power and authority, as David, supreme in his kingdom, sends people hither and thither; they all jump to do his bidding. The theologian-homiletician could therefore conceivably paint, in the sermon, the picture of a potentate abusing his power in the service of his immoral sensual desires. The

---

55. The Rule of Portrayal calls for an examination of how God is depicted in the hymnic text, and the Rule of Perspective urges the interpreter to seek the direction offered by the pericope on how the complexities and intricacies of daily life ought to be viewed, in the light of how God has been portrayed.

fateful sending, however, occurs when David decides to 'send' for Bathsheba (11.4), signalling the start of an uncontrolled downward spiral.[56]

The employment of the Rule of Plot reveals the thrust of the narrative and lays down an ethical framework upon which the narrative is constructed, a thrust that the sermon must not neglect. To appease his incontinent fleshly appetites, the king was abusing his power; indeed, this was power that was not inherently his, but that had been granted him in the first place. Yahweh, exercising his sovereignty, had chosen David from being a 'nobody', to replace a predecessor who had himself been warped by his own fantasies of omnipotence. David, exercising *his* 'sovereignty', had chosen to have his own way, not God's. The Rule of Interaction points to the conflict that is thereby generated between the two regents, divine and human. Such a conflict, developed further in the pericope, eventually forms a significant part of the theology of the text (and potentially of the sermon as well), portraying what readers and hearers should eschew at all costs. In the world projected by the pericope, a divine–human conflict has no place; instead faithful obedience and allegiance to God are the priorities to which believers are called to be aligned. The world in front of the text is gradually assuming shape as the Rules of Genre are employed; the interpreter is progressively discerning the various aspects of that world, the pericopal theology.

The Rules of Singularity and Congruence beckon the homiletician to attend to the similar theme of fidelity that is constantly in the background of the larger context of 1–2 Samuel: God's commission of his human agents entails, on their part, the responsibility to be faithful in their respective offices to the divine sovereign who appointed them. This principle was concretely (mis)represented in the lives of the two kings, Saul and David, whose individual dramas unfolded in 1 Samuel 13–2 Samuel 24. The first turned out to be unfaithful and, as a result, the Holy Spirit departed from him to come upon faithful David who then

---

56. John I. Lawlor, 'Theology and Art in the Narrative of the Ammonite War (2 Samuel 10–12)', *GTJ* 3 (1982), pp. 193–205 (195–6); Uriel Simon, 'The Poor Man's Ewe-Lamb: An Example of a Juridical Parable', *Bib* 48 (1967), pp. 207–42 (209). Bailey considers the ascription of the verb שלח to Bathsheba (2 Sam. 11.5) significant; apparently she wielded some authority as well. He notes that the only other women within Deuteronomic History who are subjects of this verb all exert influence of some sort (Rahab helps the Israelite spies escape, Josh 2.21; Deborah summons Barak to battle, Judg. 4.6; Delilah invites the Philistines to capture Samson, Judg. 16.18; and Jezebel plots against Elijah and Naboth, 1 Kgs 19.2; 21.8). The Rule of Singularity (seeing the canon as a single metanarrative) and the Rule of Intertextuality (respecting canonical citations and allusions) are thereby attended to in this reading. In addition, the threefold verb pattern of David's actions in 2 Sam. 11.2 and 11.3 is mirrored by a parallel array of three verbs with Bathsheba as subject in 11.5. Similarly, both David and Bathsheba are allotted two verbs each in 11.27. Some complicity on Bathsheba's part is perhaps being implied by the depiction of her actions in congruence with those of David (Randall C. Bailey, *David in Love and War: The Pursuit of Power in 2 Samuel 10–12* [Sheffield: JSOT, 1990], pp. 85–8, 99).

became Israel's anointed king (1 Sam. 16.13-14). The ark was subsequently returned to the nation, and blessing upon the land ensued (2 Samuel 6–8) – the projected world's principle of reward for faithfulness. But those halcyon days were not to last; Saul's flawed performance would not serve as a warning to David. Indeed, the catastrophic consequences of David's own subsequent transgressions would prove the principle of divine recompense for unfaithfulness. Whereas 1 Samuel 16–2 Samuel 8 lauds David's character and rule, 2 Samuel 9–20 laments its corruption and collapse – the regrettable, but not unexpected, consequence of the earthly king's infidelity towards the one who is truly king.[57] These principles of the projected world will doubtless make their appearance in the sermon, as the theologian-homiletician prepares to focus on the specifics of the pericope.

Though the presence of Yahweh is, undoubtedly, an established feature of biblical narrative by the Rule of Interaction (the Rule of Substantiality, attributing to Scripture a profundity of content, also recognizes the omnipresence of deity), the major interpersonal dealings in 2 Samuel 11 are between David and Uriah.[58] The Rule of Interaction is used to advantage here by the homiletician as further aspects of plot and conflict are unveiled. Uriah now becomes the subject of David's 'sending' (שלח, three times in 11.6; also see 11.12, 14), another victim of the king's power play, as David attempts to conceal his act of adultery.[59] Rather than taking Bathsheba for himself the moment she conceived, and immediately seeing to it that Uriah was disposed of, David concentrates, instead, on painting this elaborate façade of a paternity switch (it consumes a third of the chapter, 11.6-13). Clearly, his indulgence had been nothing more than a one-night stand to satisfy his own pleasures, a tryst that went awry. Engaged now in an ego-driven cover-up to defend his own name, he was more than willing to denigrate God's name in the process (12.9-14). The Rule of Interaction emphasizes David's selfish transactions with Uriah (and with Bathsheba who belonged to Uriah), callously undertaken and with an utter disregard for

---

57. The result of David's unfaithfulness was the dissipation of his authority, both over family and over nation, and attendant discord at home and disorder in the land. David's adultery and murder consumes significant textual space (2 Samuel 10–12), denoting its essential status as the *fons et origo* of the subsequent complications: incest, fratricide, rebellion and civil war (2 Samuel 13–20).

58. Bathsheba does not utter a word in the entire chapter; Joab and his messenger simply round out the story as David's agents. For God as a character, see below.

59. The leitmotif of שלח resurfaces in 2 Samuel 13 as well. It is David who *sends* Tamar to Amnon (13.7; she is the victim in an illicit sexual encounter); and it is he who *sends* Amnon with Absalom (13.27; Amnon is killed). In distinction to 2 Samuel 11, where David sends for the victims of his predatory actions, in 2 Samuel 13 he unwittingly sends his own children as victims, to have visited upon them the evils he perpetrated upon Bathsheba and Uriah (James S. Ackerman, 'Knowing Good and Evil: A Literary Analysis of the Court History in 2 Samuel 9–20 and 1 Kings 1–2', *JBL* 109 [1990], pp. 41–64 [48–9]).

consequences.[60] This is clearly not what God expects from his chosen; neither is the world in front of the text one that condones such odious behaviour – the shameless flaunting of power and the total contempt for the victims of abuse. This *negative* image of the projected world serves the homiletician well in the move towards praxis: already it is apparent what must be avoided by contemporary auditors who would be faithful toward God.

Markedly different are the reciprocal dealings of Uriah with David. Significant contrasts emerge between the Jewish king and the Hittite warrior as the narrative negotiates its nuanced turns. The Rule of Plot exposes the pungent irony. Uriah, at the battlefront with the army, was engaged in war; David, at home, was engaged in illicit pleasure, lying (שׁכב) with another man's wife (11.4). Uriah refused to succumb to the joys of rest and relaxation at home while his compatriots (and the ark) were encamping on open ground. This loyal soldier, instead, chose to lie (שׁכב) at the door of the king's house (11.9), rather than go home to lie (שׁכב) with his wife (11.11), as David was manipulating him to do. Later, even while inebriated, Uriah opted to 'lie' (שׁכב) with the servants of the king (11.13). Here, then, was the king of Israel, unfaithful and disloyal; deliberately and wilfully he had engaged in adultery with the spouse of one of his warriors, while those dedicated fighters, exemplified by the non-Israelite Uriah, were sacrificing themselves for their king and nation.[61] The Rule of Plot displays besotted Uriah emerging more faithful to Yahweh, liege and comrades, than does the sober and scheming David. Uriah is driven by loyalty, abstinence and self-sacrifice; David's actions, in contrast, are marked by disloyalty, indulgence and self-interest. Through the depiction of the contrast between the two, the faithful soldier is requisitioned as a foil for the unfaithful king. The overarching moral fabric of 1–2 Samuel – commending faithfulness and condemning unfaithfulness – is discernible in this particular portrayal of the protagonists of 2 Samuel 11. This framework, which helps construct the theology of the pericope, beckons the attention of the homiletician time and again in this narrative. The sermon cannot but be propelled along the trajectory that this theme sets up. What does it mean to be faithful to God, especially in the station of one whose resources, power and reputation are considerable?

In the narrative background of 1–2 Samuel, the Rule of Primacy points to a positive model in one greater than King David.[62] Integral to the broader account and the world it projects is a perceptible focus upon the eschatological reign of the anointed one of Yahweh; the Nathan Oracle and its promise of an everlasting kingdom and a glorious future were explored in Chapter 2. While the Davidic line would ultimately lose the throne with the fall of Jerusalem,

---

60. Meir Sternberg, *The Poetics of Biblical Narrative: Ideological Literature and the Drama of Reading* (Bloomington, IN: Indiana University Press, 1985), p. 210.

61. Lawlor, 'Theology and Art in the Narrative of the Ammonite War', p. 198.

62. The Rule of Primacy draws attention to the Christotelic orientation of biblical texts.

the fulfilment of an eternal kingdom would come to fruition with Jesus Christ, the king of the eschaton who would never be unfaithful (Heb. 3.5-6). This righteous king, whom the OT adumbrates in this very corpus (2 Sam. 7.12-16), and whom the NT calls in its very first verse 'the Son of David' (Mt. 1.1), would be a marked contrast to his eponymous ancestor, flawed and fallible. The Messiah alone would perfectly exemplify faithfulness to Yahweh.[63] Any sermon fashioned from this pericope must therefore proffer Christ as the paragon of fidelity. This grand theme of the faithfulness of the coming king forms the constant, albeit latent, background of the sorry story of 2 Samuel 11 (the application of the Rules of Singularity, Organization, Congruence, Sequentiality and Primacy). It must be remembered that, in the broad context of 1–2 Samuel, it was not only the nation's kings who were unfaithful. Even before the regents manifested their infidelity, the people, in calling for a monarchy, had themselves rejected Yahweh (1 Sam. 8.7). Therefore, for ruler and ruled – both unfaithful to the divine sovereign – the faithfulness of Christ serves as the model of fidelity to God.[64] Inhabitation of the world this pericope projects is clearly part of what it means to be Christlike.

The narrative plot thickens as Uriah refuses to succumb to David's stratagems. Evil is perpetrated upon evil, and David has Uriah killed in the frontlines of the ongoing war – another selfish 'interaction' with the soldier. David's fornication under cover of darkness ('evening', 2 Sam. 11.2) had now become cold-blooded murder in daylight ('morning', 11.14). Wanton sexual morals, rooted in base self-indulgence, had culminated in a tyrannical unconcern for the wounded 'third-party'. Uriah was heartlessly slaughtered, the culmination of an unbroken sequence of escalating malignity. Indeed, this last act succeeds in getting not just one man killed, but many, some of them the nation's best warriors ('valiant men', 11.16). By the Rule of Plot the irony of the narrative is again made palpable. The very loyalty of Uriah that had frustrated the king's machinations in the previous section was itself the instrument of this dedicated soldier's murder: Uriah faithfully bears the letter carrying his own death sentence, and his faithfulness

---

63. Significant is the fact that the elements associated with kingship as the monarchy was established in 1 Samuel – sovereign choice, divine anointing and Spirit gifting, and mighty deeds – reappear again together only in the ministry of Jesus Christ (all three are co-located in Mark 1). For Saul these regal elements are found in 1 Sam. 9.16; 10.1-13; and 11–15. For David, they occur in 16.1, 16.13; and 17.1-58. See William J. Dumbrell, 'The Content and Significance of the Books of Samuel: Their Place and Purpose within the Former Prophets', *JETS* 33 (1990), pp. 49–62 (54–5).

64. The Rule of Singularity sees the canon as an integral whole; the Rule of Organization respects the chronological arrangement of books within the canon; the Rule of Congruence recognizes the coherence of the discrete parts of the canon; the Rule of Sequentiality considers the temporal sequence of revelation in the canon. Together these rules integrate and interpret the canonical data as depicting Christ, who alone fulfilled all the demands of the Father in the power of the Spirit (the Rule of Primacy).

to his king, army and nation gets him killed on the battlefront.[65] Even after he is disposed of, the storyteller does not allow Uriah to vanish from the narrative: in 11.26, the awkward recurrence of that soldier's name in 'the wife of Uriah' and 'Uriah her husband', and the repeated assertion in the same verse of Bathsheba's marital status (אִישָׁהּ and בַּעְלָהּ, 'her husband') keep the focus unwaveringly upon the innocent victim of David's egregious actions.[66] The Rule of Plot helps the homiletician uncover the moral structure reinforcing this section of the story. He who ought to have been, as Yahweh's earthly representative, the guardian of the people's rights and the upholder of their justice, murders his loyal servant and causes the death of several other faithful soldiers. The condemnation of David's deeds is almost palpable; unfaithfulness to Yahweh could not be more starkly depicted, and the attendant theology of the pericope could hardly be more explicit. The extremes to which one will go to protect one's own name will surely be a grim reminder in the sermon of the dangers inherent in such an utterly self-focused and ego-serving abuse of God-given responsibilities. The Rules of Genre have thus furthered the homiletician's task by displaying cumulatively, facet by facet, the pericopal theology.

In light of the theology of 1–2 Samuel, one would expect this evil perpetrated by David to incur the wrath of Yahweh. However, quite strikingly, the narrative has thus far failed to make any mention of the divine sovereign. As the sin increases, so does the suspense – when will Yahweh intervene? That there is no explicit interaction between God and the human actants within the pericope, does not, of course, imply the absence of God as a character; unique to biblical narrative is an assumption of the constant presence of God permeating its every episode, whether such ubiquity of deity is expressed or not (the Rule of Interaction and the Rule of Substantiality).

At last, the final character in the dramatis personæ makes his appearance – Yahweh intervenes in 11.27b. Following right after David has just cavalierly remarked to Joab (through a messenger, 11.25), 'Do not let this thing be evil in your eyes' (בְּעֵינֶיךָ), the impact of Yahweh's riposte here could not be more striking. In the narrator's voice, divine disapprobation is registered in no uncertain terms (11.27b): 'But the thing that David had done was evil in the eyes of Yahweh' (בְּעֵינֵי יְהוָה). There appears to have been a major discrepancy between what David was 'seeing' and what Yahweh was 'seeing'. Already the larger plot had presented the symptoms of David's ophthalmic deficits: in contrast the Ammonites who saw firsthand the (mis)fortunes of war (10.6, 14, 15, 19),

---

65. J.P. Fokkelman, *King David (II Sam. 9–20 & I Kings 1–2)* (vol. 1 of *Narrative Art and Poetry in the Books of Samuel*; Assen, Netherlands: Van Gorcum, 1981), p. 60.

66. The child that is born to this illicit union is also referred to as 'the child that *Uriah's widow* bore' (2 Sam. 12.15). Uriah reappears at the conclusion of the book as well (in 23.39). The narrator does not intend that the reader forget this shocking episode and, to the very end, this brazen malfeasance blacklists David.

David had not seen; he had only heard, secondhand, the news from the front (10.5, 7, 17).[67] God and the king were not seeing eye to eye: what David considered 'not evil' was being expressly condemned as 'evil' by Yahweh. For the development of pericopal theology, this is an essential concept, a definite hint to the homiletician regarding the priorities of the projected world that must be displayed in the sermon: faithfulness to God involves recognizing evil for what it is, seeing sin as God does, and fleeing from such reprehensible behaviour – unfaithfulness. David, instead, had despised God's word and denigrated God's name (12.9, 14).

The conflict between David and God reaches its zenith at this juncture. Resolution is demanded by the Rule of Interaction: who would emerge victorious? If David imagined that God was nowhere present, he was deluding himself – God is one character that cannot be written out of the narrative script. Not only was Yahweh implicitly present as David went about his nefarious activities, but Yahweh had also seen! There is no deed so shrouded in darkness that it will be invisible to an all-seeing, omnipresent God. As if to rectify any misconception about the presence of deity on stage, from this point onwards, Yahweh, 'absent' in the previous scenes, becomes almost tangible: the Tetragrammaton occurs thirteen times in 2 Samuel 12, the section that details the judgement, sentence and punishment of the king. A reading of the text by the Rule of Substantiality (asserting that the matter of a biblical text is of moment and import – God himself) concurs with this observation of God's presence. He himself would now take action to bring justice and closure to this sinister episode; punishment was now inevitable. The final verse of the pericope, 11.27, turns out to be the focal point of the chiastic structure of 2 Samuel 10–12, emphasizing the crux of the narrative – what God considered 'evil in his eyes'.

10.1-19	*A* War – partial victory over the Ammonites
11.1-5	*B* Sin; Bathsheba conceives
11.6-13	*C* Concealment of David's sin
11.14-27a	*D* Murder of the innocent Uriah
11.27b	*E* Evil in the eyes of Yahweh
12.1-6	*D'* Murder of the lamb
12.7-15a	*C'* Exposure of David's sin
12.15b-25	*B'* Death; Bathsheba conceives
12.26-31	*A'* War – complete victory over the Ammonites

67. See Uriel Simon, *Reading Prophetic Narratives* (trans. Lenn J. Schramm; Bloomington, IN: Indiana University Press, 1997), p. 95. Such a coordinated reading, which sees a notable connection between these seemingly disparate details, respects the Rule of Congruence that asserts the complementarity of the various parts of the biblical texts to one another.

That the climax of the narrative has been reached in 11.27b is also indicated in the very next verse that has, for a change, Yahweh doing the sending (שׁלח), as Nathan is commissioned to play the prosecuting attorney (12.1). The tables had been turned! Resolution was forthcoming. The Rule of Interaction portrays a God who always sees; even when he is seemingly absent, this is a God whose presence is assured, whose eyesight never fails, whose judgement is sure. In the world in front of the text, the corollary to the priority of faithfulness to God is the principle that unfaithfulness will always get its just deserts. Therefore, in the movement from Scripture to sermon, this facet of the projected world must also be declared by the theologian-homiletician.

In summary, the Rules of Primary and Secondary Genre help frame the segment of the world projected by the pericope, a world that reflects – negatively, in this narrative of 11.1-27 – the same theological elements projected by 1–2 Samuel as a whole. Positively, a world is projected that endorses God's right to reign over his people through his chosen representatives, underscoring, in turn, the priority of subjects remaining faithful to their divine ruler. In its depiction of God as one who sees and labels evil for what it is, the pericope also virtually guarantees that punishment for unfaithfulness will follow. Specifically, the plot points to one sovereignly chosen by God, who developed a crack in the foundation of his character – unrestrained sexual desire that became a runaway disaster accumulating evil upon evil, and that resulted in his disparaging God's word and dishonouring God's name (as Nathan's accusation specified in 2 Sam. 12.9-14). God's reputation was no longer the pre-eminent priority; instead it was unbridled passion and abusive power that reigned supreme. The subsequent drive to protect self-honour without an iota of repentance demonstrated a descent to the depths of depravity, culminating in murder. Instead of demonstrating loyalty to God, subordinates and nation, here was a leader disloyal to all. The consequences would be severe; unfaithfulness would not remain unpunished; its ramifications would echo across generational divides: a period of blessing ends and an inexorable decline begins.[68] The pericope is thus a negative model of what the world in front of the text demands. However, implicit in the pericope, as the Rule of Substantiality and Primacy contend, is also a positive model. The theme of the righteous reign of Christ overarches 1–2 Samuel: this one alone would be absolutely faithful to his God, his comrades and his community; he was the one who kept God's word and glorified his name, and who would 'lay down his life for his friends' (Jn 8.55; 15.31; 17.4, 26); he is the only one able to inhabit perfectly the world in front of the text. In other words, to inhabit that world is to be Christlike.

Considering the narrative in its broader context, the theology of the pericope (the segment of the world in front of this text) may be summarized both

---

68. Forgiveness, though available, advanced by God and accepted by sinner, does not completely erase the consequences or the sentence of justice. Yet to the penitent and contrite, God offers restoration (as the events in 2 Samuel 12 prove).

negatively and positively: *Unfaithfulness to God, the true sovereign, negates blessing and promises punishment with tragic consequences for individual, family, community and society; such faithfulness as God demands – perfectly modelled by Christ, the Son of David, the righteous King – embraces an utmost regard for the word of God and the reputation of God, and is manifested in the restriction of sensual desires and in the reined exercise of power.* Borne by this world projected by the pericope is the implicit transhistorical intention that calls upon God's people everywhere to demonstrate faithfulness towards him in such matters as are dealt with in this text.

A key task of the homiletician in the move from text to praxis is the depiction, in the sermon, of this world in front of the text with its principles, priorities and practices – that is, pericopal theology. To be sure, the Rules of Genre need not be enunciated, nor do their actual operations need to be demonstrated, in the delivered sermon. However, the importance of elucidating the theology of the text cannot be underestimated: the Rules of Genre, as has been emphasized before, serve to focus the interpreter's attention upon the entity of pericopal theology. These rules are deployed for the analysis of the text with this particular end in view. Of note, in this analysis, almost all of the Rules of Genre were utilized in the derivation of the theology of 2 Sam. 11.1-27. It is only by discerning the pericopal theology that the theologian-homiletician can commence the final phase of the sermonic endeavour, the generation of valid application.[69]

As is evident in the analysis and summary of 2 Samuel 11, pericopal theology imparts to the textual particulars a significance that transcends their historical circumstances of origin. The semantic potency of a work of literary art, especially of one that is a classic and a concrete universal, causes it to go through a 'reversal', a movement from '*individual to universal* which constitutes the text's relevance' for its readers, rendering its significance perennial.[70] This is the function of the Rules of Primary and Secondary Genre operating upon the concrete universal of a pericope, enabling the discovery of a universal theme (pericopal theology) from concrete particulars, and thereby permitting the appropriation of the work's perennial meaning into the lives of readers (i.e., application, for which, see below). Ultimately, 2 Sam. 11.1-27 (and, indeed, the entire Davidic saga in 1–2 Samuel) is more than a narrative about a historical personage, 'but about the highest values in the narrated David (as shown or as violated by him) which are the same as those of our own human existence'. This work suggests that the proposed world in front of the text – the theology of the pericope – is the background in which these 'highest values', the priorities, principles and practices operating in the projected world, are propounded for appropriation by those readers who allow the transhistorical intention of the pericope to be

---

69. The next section deals with this aspect of interpretation. The derivation of application from this particular pericope (2 Samuel 11) will be considered there as well.

70. Fokkelman, *King David*, p. 421.

inscribed on their souls.[71] 'The David of the narrative is an artistic masterpiece of universal and transtemporal value and is a figure which through the reader's attention repeatedly rises up again in the Here and Now.' This was not merely history that was being written; the author was after 'psychagogy', adapting his material in such a way that the universal human value would be emphasized, allowing the past to flow over into the present.[72] It is, therefore, pericopal theology that mediates the ancient text's contemporary appropriation, and it is in such appropriation that that text becomes life in the one who reads.

Divine discourse projects a world in front of the text into which readers are called to enter. The same God who has thus discoursed yesterday is the same God of the Church today. It is in his presence, in the presence of one who is the same forever, that cultural dissonances and discrepancies between the times of the ancient text and those of the modern reader begin to fade in significance, and movement from text to praxis begins. Application can now be undertaken in the sermon: the people of God are urged to align their lives to the specificities of the world projected – the theology of the pericope – in order to accomplish covenant renewal. The final section of this chapter (and work) will therefore attend to application, the culmination of the homiletical endeavour.

Application

That theology involves praxis is undeniable. James 1.22-5 emphasizes the importance of application – 'prove yourselves doers of the word, and not merely hearers who delude themselves'; the one who applies the text is 'an effectual doer... blessed in what he does'. It is not enough to *know*; one must also *be*. Only in personal appropriation or application does the text accomplish its meaning; therefore, Gadamer could assert that application was an integral part of the hermeneutical process.[73] A response to the text from readers is thus essential, for

71. Borrowing from Socrates, Fokkelman notes that the goal of such a discourse written in the soul of the learner (γράφεται ἐν τῇ τοῦ μανθάνοντος ψυχῇ) is to provide guidance by means of words (ψυχαγωγία τις διὰ λόγων) (Plato, *Phaedr.* 261a, 276a, 278a). This goal is achieved insofar as the 'soul-inscription' is appropriated/applied by the learner. The particularly local significance subsides, but without being lost, as it makes room for its 'universal human significance'. See Fokkelman, *King David*, pp. 423–4.

72. Fokkelman believes that the writers of such texts were aware of the transtemporal values embedded in their work – the transhistorical intention of texts awaiting appropriation by the reader (Fokkelman, *King David*, pp. 424–5).

73. Hans-Georg Gadamer, *Truth and Method* (2nd rev. edn; trans. Joel Weinsheimer and Donald G. Marshall; London: Continuum, 2004), p. 307. 'Appropriation' was Ricoeur's translation of *Aneignung*. He notes that *aneignen* means to 'make one's own what was alien', the struggle to overcome distanciation. 'This goal is attained only insofar as interpretation actualizes the meaning of the text for the present reader' (*Hermeneutics and the Human Sciences*, pp. 85, 159). Also see Paul Ricoeur, 'Preface to Bultmann', in *The Conflict of Interpretations* (trans. Peter McCormick; ed. Don Ihde; Evanston: Northwestern University Press, 1974), pp. 384–401 (392).

the segment of the world projected by the pericope (and its future-directed intention) beckons and awaits an answer. Indeed, the text demands to be appropriated in this fashion, for Scripture is not content with its claim to be merely a historic reality; rather, its projected world is 'destined for autocracy', and, unlike other worlds spun to enchant or flatter, this world seeks the readers' subjection. Overcoming their reality, it calls individuals to fit their own lives in accordance with it, to align their days with the *chronos* of God's world projected before the text, thereby themselves becoming 'elements in its structure of universal history'.[74] A text thus projecting the possibility of praxis is more than informing; it is potentially transforming, for application of pericopal theology aligns lives with God's will, effecting covenant renewal within the community of saints. 'We may reject it. We may say, It is nothing; this is imagination, madness, this "God". But we may not deny nor prevent our being led by the Bible "history" far out beyond what is elsewhere called history – into a new world, into the world of God.'[75] It is as auditors accede to the demands of the text, inhabiting the world in front of the text, that covenant renewal becomes successful in the ecclesial setting.

Therefore, it is not enough to elucidate the theology of a text and the transhistorical intention therein; it is also incumbent upon the theologian-homiletician to approach, in each sermon, the intersection of that theology with the faith and practice of God's people – how exactly pericopal theology shapes and changes the lives of hearers. In the regular preaching of pericopes, the renewal of the covenant relationship between God and community is accomplished by a consistent, sequential projection of segments of the canonical world (pericopal theology) to which listeners are enjoined to orient themselves. The crucial nature of this transaction charges the preacher to generate, from theology, application that is valid, that is, exemplification, the specific response to be undertaken by hearers to the expounded pericope – what they must do to 'inhabit' its projected world. There is, thus, a twofold aspect to the overall homiletical undertaking: the exposition of the theology of the unit text, and the delineation of how the latter may be applied or appropriated in real life. The first move, from text to theology, draws meaning *from* the biblical text with authority; the second, from theology to praxis, directs meaning *to* the situations of listeners with relevance.[76] In so actualizing theol-

74. Erich Auerbach, *Mimesis: The Representation of Reality in Western Literature* (trans. Willard R. Trask; Princeton: Princeton University Press, 1953), pp. 14–15. Also see Amos N. Wilder, *Early Christian Rhetoric: The Language of the Gospel* (Cambridge, MA: Harvard University Press, 1971), p. 60.

75. Karl Barth, 'The Strange New World Within the Bible', in *The Word of God and the Word of Man* (trans. Douglas Horton; London: Hodder and Stoughton, 1928), pp. 28–50 (37). 'It is not out of order for theology to ask of preaching, What ultimate vision is held before us?' (Craddock, *Preaching*, p. 49).

76. 'The honest rhetorician therefore has two things in mind: a vision of how matters should go ideally and ethically and a consideration of the special circumstances of his auditors. Toward both of these he has a responsibility' (Weaver, *Language Is Sermonic*, p. 211).

ogy in the latter move into the discrete and specific circumstances of believers, the values of the cosmos are gradually subverted and undermined, and those of God's world are progressively established in the life of the community: covenant renewal is achieved. This is part of what it means to acknowledge, 'Thy kingdom come'.[77] The interpretive advance from pericopal theology to exemplification will be the focus of the remainder of Chapter 4. The discussion of this phase of the sermonic move from text to praxis will conclude the hermeneutics–homiletics dialogue.

Pericopal theology to exemplification

From the early days of the Church, Scripture was envisaged as a single, universal, but unfinished, story, the continuing relevance of which was to be explicated by the theologian-homiletician. A reading of Scripture by the Rule of Applicability countenances such an understanding of the contemporaneity of the ancient text. The language of the Bible enables a whole field of possible future meanings such that applications falling within that specific terrain of the theology of the pericope may be considered legitimate extensions of the meaning of that pericope, the continuation of the biblical story into the life of the current community of believers.[78] It is this layered sense of Scriptural meaning – original textual sense, theology of the pericope bearing a transhistorical intention and exemplifications (the tripartite scheme of meaning introduced in Chapter 1) – that enables the canon to be applied in later circumstances by its readers, giving it prescriptivity, perenniality and plurality of meaning. The concern of interpreters, both ancient and modern, has never simply been the reconstruction of the *Sitz im Leben* of the text but also the elucidation of its *Sitz in unserem Leben*, its situation in *our* life, in the situation of current readers of the text and hearers of the sermon. This is the process of generating valid application, a recontextualization of pericopal theology into the faith and practice of the community of God. Theology, Vanhoozer notes perceptively, 'is less a matter of *in*doctrination than it is of *ex*doctrination: the living out of Christian teaching'.[79]

---

77. The world projected in front of the text comprises strategies for believers to be Christlike in their own contemporary situations. The life of Christ alone perfectly fits the world projected in front of the text and perfectly conforms to the theology of the pericope. The world in front of the text may, therefore, be considered a theologically thick description of Jesus Christ, the one who fulfilled the Father's will and the demands of the projected world. Thus, if the canon is faith's *norm*, then Christ is faith's *form*. Appropriating the theology of scriptural pericopes and indwelling the projected world is to participate in the drama of God's economy by which the Holy Spirit conforms readers to the image of Christ. See Vanhoozer, *Drama of Doctrine*, p. 229.

78. The Rule of Substantiality also affirms the critical importance of this ongoing narrative for every generation of the Church.

79. Vanhoozer, *The Drama of Doctrine*, p. 400. Also see N.T. Wright, 'How Can the Bible Be Authoritative?' *Vox Evangelica* 21 (1991), pp. 7–32 (27–8); David C. Steinmetz, 'The Superiority of Pre-Critical Exegesis', *ThTo* 37 (1980), pp. 27–38 (32); and Brian E. Daley, 'Is Patristic

The second half of the interpretive move – from theology to praxis, from the universal back to the concreteness of auditors' lives – is rendered faithful to the text insofar as the particular exemplification generated is within the boundaries of the theology of the pericope (and the transhistorical intention it bears), the essential intermediary between inscription and application. Application, while beholden to the text, however, is not an attempt to repeat what is in the text or to reiterate the historical event that stands behind it. 'Rather, creativity must be involved as we seek to mediate, translate, interpret its meaning – the meaning in front of the text – into our own horizon.'[80] This is a call for application that is relevant to the contemporary community of hearers. *Fidelity* to what has gone on before is essential, for the Church remains under the authority of the text of Scripture and seeks to be faithful to it in its application. This is the restraint imposed by pericopal theology that is grounded firmly upon the text and derived therefrom. In contrast, *novelty* is also called for in the fresh context of current auditors, as the Church recontextualizes an ancient text to its own modern setting. This is the release afforded, in that there is liberty to render pericopal theology and its transhistorical intention into application that is relevant to the particularities of the hearers' circumstances. Fidelity and novelty are, thus, at the heart of exemplification, endowing it with both authority and relevance.

Verbatim and unimaginative imitation of what transpired in the previous acts of the drama is inadequate and inappropriate in the new context of the present troupe of performers.[81] Instead, a novel reading of the unchanged (and unchangeable) text has to occur in a changed context in order to maintain fidelity to the normative text – 'a kind of relativism, to be sure, but one that *establishes* rather than undermines biblical authority'. For instance, to disregard the change in the context of the text '2/12/1991' written in the UK, but read in the USA, would thoroughly mislead the reader: that sequence of digits, depending on one's location, could either stand for 2 December 1991 or 12 February 1991. In America, the British text '2/12/1991' must be read as '12/2/1991' in order for the reading

---

Exegesis Still Usable? Some Reflections on Early Christian Interpretation of the Psalms', in *The Art of Reading Scripture* (eds Ellen F. Davis and Richard B. Hays; Grand Rapids: Eerdmans, 2003), pp. 69–88 (77–8).

80. David Tracy, 'Creativity in the Interpretation of Religion: The Question of Radical Pluralism', *NLH* 15 (1984), pp. 289–309 (298); also see Michael J. Quicke, *360-Degree Preaching: Hearing, Speaking, and Living the Word* (Grand Rapids: Baker, 2003), p. 159, who advocates preachers exhibit creativity that is constrained by rigorous exegesis.

81. Vanhoozer, *Drama of Doctrine*, pp. 260–1. In Vanhoozer's concept of the theo-dramatic rendition of the script (Scripture), the Father is the playwright and producer of the play, the Son the principal actor and the Holy Spirit the director. Pastors and homileticians, and elders and Church leaders are assistant directors, with the theologian taking the role of the dramaturge, a technical adviser to the dramatic company that is the Church, the troupe of actors (106, 244, 247).

to remain faithful to the originary transhistorical intention ('the second day of the twelfth month of the year 1991 CE'). Obviously, classic and normative texts cannot themselves be altered, but readings can and should be changed, to maintain fidelity to the thrust of the original utterance. Such a reading is not an option; it is necessary *in order that* the interpretation may remain faithful to the original in a new reading context.[82]

As the end of the Gospels and the beginning of Acts make clear (Mt. 28.18-20; Acts 1.8), God desires to involve his people in the ongoing drama of creation and redemption. Believers are to undertake their own 'improvisations' that demonstrate faithfulness to the past and newness towards the future – not the aping of deeds once done, nor the repetition of words once uttered, but a rearticulation and representation of the ongoing saga with fidelity and novelty. The entire operation, from text to theology and from theology to praxis, is the task of the Church in every age, and pericopal theology is the authoritative guide for this faithful-yet-new performance of the text in unprecedented situations. It is this theology that ensures the bidirectional congruity in this move towards exemplification: congruity to the word of Scripture that maintains the authority of the text (fidelity), and congruity to the world of the hearer that manifests the relevance of the text (novelty).

Fidelity in this transaction involves sustaining the identity of exemplifications with the original textual sense. As was noted in Chapter 1, it is the preservation of *ipse*-identity between text and exemplifications that credits the latter with fidelity. While maintenance of *idem*-identity calls only for slavish imitation, *ipse*-identity calls for skilful improvisation. One is passive, the other demands training and a developed sensibility for what is fitting in a given situation, a transaction best directed, in biblical exposition, by those who 'by practice have their senses trained to discern good and evil' (Heb. 5.14). It requires of the theologian-homiletician attentiveness to new contexts of interpretation, sensitivity to the unfolding continuities of the work, and responsibility for, and accountability to, the particular community of co-performers, fellow-improvisers, and auditors.[83] However, the creativity of the expositor in generating such exemplifications must be exercised with due respect for the original work, lest '[t]he license to create-to-preserve quickly becomes indistinguishable from the license simply to create'.[84] Exemplification is not an act of creation *ex nihilo*,

82. See Lawrence Lessig, 'The Limits of Lieber', *Cardozo L. Rev.* 16 (1995), pp. 2249–72 (2258, 2260, 2262); idem, 'Fidelity in Translation', *Texas L. Rev.* 71 (1992–93), pp. 1165–1268 (1170); and idem, 'Fidelity and Constraint', *Fordham L. Rev.* 65 (1996–97), pp. 1365–1434 (1370).

83. Titus 2.1 appropriately urges that a Church leader is to 'speak what is fitting for sound doctrine'. In the same vein, Thucydides lauded Themistocles: '[He] was of all men the best able to extemporize the right thing to be done' (αὐτοσχεδιάζειν τὰ δέοντα) – improvisation upon principle (*History* 1.138.3).

84. Lessig, 'Fidelity in Translation', p. 1206. Utilizing the same Ricoeurian concept of *ipse-*

but rather a *re*creation, an application of the text to the fresh context of current hearers. Scripture is the plenary source, the authoritative playbook of action, with each pericope contributing specific instructions for the 'performance' of the segment of the canonical world it projects. Valid exemplification is generated from the text by a reading characterized by fidelity and novelty. For the maintenance of fidelity and novelty, pericopal theology is critical; it is this intermediary that enables the sermon to be both authoritative and relevant, as the preacher moves from text to praxis.

In sum, the task of the theologian-homiletician is to improvise, delving into the past and suggesting in the present how the past may be creatively exemplified in the future. Keith Johnstone's analogy is apt: 'The improviser has to be like a man walking backwards.'[85] This is one who, with eyes on the past, must be guided by it – the canonical Scriptures. Yet the improviser, it must be remembered, is also headed 'forwards', away from the past of the text, transposing it into the future of hearers. Thus the situation of the auditors must also be an important parameter that governs the activities of the interpreter. When the same text is 'performed' in different contexts to produce discrete improvisations on the same theme, the same pericopal theology is brought to bear upon those different reading situations in order to generate faithful applications, exemplifications that are relevant to each individual context. Such exemplifications, though administered by the same theology, may – and, indeed, should – look different, for each reader, hearer, congregation and context is different. However, insofar as these varied applications fall within the bounds of the same pericopal theology, they are but instances of a single type, exemplifications of a single transhistorical intention, and therefore all such improvisations remain faithful to the text.[86]

identity, Vanhoozer characterizes these improvisations as 'creative fidelity' or 'ruled spontaneity' (*Drama of Doctrine*, pp. 128–9). Also see Martha C. Nussbaum, *Love's Knowledge: Essays on Philosophy and Literature* (New York: Oxford University Press, 1990), pp. 155–6.

85. Keith Johnstone, *Impro: Improvisation and the Theatre* (London: Methuen, 1981), p. 116.

86. For an insightful analysis of improvisation in jazz, with clear parallels for the present discussion, see James O. Young and Carl Matheson, 'The Metaphysics of Jazz', *J Aes Art Crit* 58 (2000), pp. 125–33. Musicians performing this genre recognize 'jazz standards' as providing instructions for improvising. Such operations are not *totally* spontaneous for, to be an instance of a jazz standard, the performance has to be in accord with a given set of guidelines embodied by the standard. Young and Matheson discuss what they call the 'canonical model' of such tacit rules that constitute a standard: introduction, head (statement of the melody), improvisations, recapitulation of the head and ending. According to the model, two jazz performances are instances of the same standard if their heads utilize the same melody and their improvisations are grounded on the chord patterns of the head ('theology'? the 'transhistorical intention' it bears?), while yet being obviously very different from each other. Indeed, many of these performances are based on *The Real Book*, a set of unauthorized, but ubiquitous, volumes (there are recent legal versions as well [3 vols; Milwaukee, WI: Hal Leonard, 2006]), scoring the melody and chord changes of an exhaustive listing of jazz standards. All paginated identically (chapter and verse?) and coming in

To arrive at praxis that is faithful to text and relevant to auditors is the goal of the homiletical undertaking. The burden of the theologian-homiletician is, therefore, to move validly from Scripture to sermon, enabling the community of God to align itself to the world in front of the text and thus enact covenant renewal.

Generating exemplifications

This notion of exemplification pertains not only to religious literature but to legal literature as well, ancient texts that homiletician and jurist seek to apply to their contemporary eras. There is much that may be learned by comparing theological and legal hermeneutics, for the tasks of practitioners in both fields are conceptually parallel. Therefore, before illustrating the derivation of exemplifications from the theology of specific pericopes, exemplification in judicial interpretation will be briefly surveyed.

Exemplification in legal hermeneutics

It has been observed that interpretation of legal texts, such as the *US Constitution*, is 'bringing into the present a text of the past', a straddling of two worlds simultaneously.[87] The continuing life of a binding legal or religious classic depends on ongoing recontextualization in new circumstances. Like the Scriptures, a constitution, too, is 'intended to endure for ages to come, and, consequently, to be adapted to the various *crises* of human affairs'.[88] The similarity between the hermeneutics of law and Scripture are considerable: both judge and preacher are hermeneuts handling classic texts; both mediate those texts for their hearers and readers; and the literature of both fields exists to be actualized in specific situations in subsequent time, one to serve the execution of justice through pronouncing verdicts, the other to serve the exercise of faith through preaching sermons. Generating exemplifications is the task of the judge who moves from the text of law to judicial philosophy and thence to the adjudication of the case currently at the bar; the homiletician, this work proposes,

editions to suit B♭, E♭ and C instruments (multiple translations/versions?), these tomes, in a sense, form the 'canon' of jazz.

87. James Boyd White, 'Judicial Criticism', in *Interpreting Law and Literature: A Hermeneutic Reader* (eds Sanford Levinson and Steven Mailloux; Evanston: Northwestern University Press, 1988), pp. 393–410 (403).

88. US Supreme Court Chief Justice John Marshall, *McCulloch v. The State of Maryland*, US Reports 17 (4 Wheaton) (1819): 316–437 (415). 'They are not ephemeral enactments, designed to meet passing occasions. They are, to use the words of Chief Justice Marshall, "designed to approach immortality as nearly as human institutions can approach it"… In the application of a constitution, therefore, our contemplation cannot be only of what has been but of what may be' (US Supreme Court Justice Joseph McKenna, *Weems v. United States*, US Reports 217 [1910]: 349–413 (373); the citation of Chief Justice Marshall is from *Cohens v. Virginia*, US Reports 19 [1821]: 264–448 [387]).

generates exemplifications similarly by moving from the pericope of Scripture to theology before arriving at application for the congregation currently in the pews.[89] 'This implies that the text, whether law or gospel, if it is to be understood properly – i.e., according to the claim it makes – must be understood at every moment, in every concrete situation, in a new and different way', the novelty of interpretation that, at the same time, maintains fidelity to the text.[90] Of particular interest, then, is this congruence between exemplifications in legal and scriptural interpretation.

Legal literature is replete with examples of such a movement from original textual sense through transhistorical intention to future exemplification. The passage of time introduces new conditions and contingencies and, therefore, legal classics are constructed (and construed) to be perennially relevant. Textual distanciation renders necessary the movement to generate future exemplifications with validity in situations and circumstances distant from, and unforeseen at, the event of the original inscription. For instance, the *US Constitution* empowers Congress '[t]o raise and support armies', '[t]o provide and maintain a navy' and '[t]o make rules for the government and regulation of the land and naval forces' (Article I, ¶8, clauses 12 and 13). As written, this edict is silent about any support for an air force. However, despite the absence of any explicit reference in the *US Constitution* to this branch of the armed forces, the US government continues to raise and support, provide and maintain, govern and regulate an air force. Presumably, the concrete terms 'army' and 'navy' in that late eighteenth-century document were comprehensive universals signifying the broad categories they attempted to particularize, namely, all manner of national defence undertakings. The transhistorical and pragmatic intention of the declaration was, clearly, to designate any conceivable military force as worthy of establishment and maintenance by Congress; such an intention would necessarily include an air force and, potentially, even a space force as future exemplifications.[91] An interpretation that moves in this fashion from

---

89. Upon the jurist falls 'the task of translating the majestic generalities of the Bill of Rights [a component of the *US Constitution*], conceived as part of the pattern of liberal government in the eighteenth century, into concrete restraints on officials dealing with the problems of the twentieth century' (US Supreme Court Justice Robert H. Jackson, *West Virginia State Board of Education et al.* v. *Barnette et al.*, US Reports 319 [1942]: 624–71 [639]). Likewise, upon the theologian-homiletician is the onus of deriving application from the ancient text of Scripture for contemporary auditors of the sermon who have to struggle with real-life issues of their current day.

90. Gadamer, *Truth and Method*, pp. 307–8, 325–6, 328. Also see Frederick Schauer, 'An Essay on Constitutional Language', in *Interpreting Law and Literature: A Hermeneutic Reader* (eds Sanford Levinson and Steven Mailloux; Evanston: Northwestern University Press, 1988), pp. 133–53 (137–8, 141–3).

91. See Lessig, 'Fidelity and Constraint', pp. 1376–77. Within such a transhistorical intention, perhaps even a robotic force could be imagined as a valid application (exemplification)!

original textual sense to exemplification via transhistorical intention is essential for the interpretation of a distanciated text, especially one that falls into the category of the classic. No canonical corpus can be expected to bear the burden of explicitly expressing *all* possible future exemplifications: 'A constitution, to contain an accurate detail of all the subdivisions of which its great powers will admit, and of all the means by which they may be carried into execution, would partake of the prolixity of a legal code, and could scarcely be embraced by the human mind'.[92] In the Christian canon, it is the theology of the pericope (and the transhistorical intention it carries) that implicitly encompasses every legitimate option of exemplification and thus oversees what may be considered faithful to the particular portion of Scripture exposited in the ecclesial setting. The original words of such texts as the *US Constitution* or the Bible establish the direction of meaning of what is written therein, and this trajectory functions as the standard by which the validity of all subsequent interpretive endeavours must be gauged.[93] For biblical hermeneutics the trajectory of the pericope is captured in its theology which thereby becomes the arbiter of the legitimacy of the praxis proclaimed and preached by the theologian-homiletician.

Exemplification in theological hermeneutics
The final homiletical move, from theology to praxis, is the culmination of the preacher's undertaking that began as an encounter with a pericope of Scripture in an ecclesial context. Whereas the first interpretive movement (*theological*: text to pericopal theology) takes the hermeneut from the concrete to the universal, the second movement (*homiletical*: pericopal theology to praxis) brings the interpreter back to the concrete. In this latter stage, the particular cares of the day are to be diligently considered by the theologian-homiletician, as the universal is now couched in the concrete, the transhistorical in the timely context of the hearers. Such a move is, in effect, a return to the lingua franca, '[f]or what else is good preaching but vernacular theology?' This is the re-expression of an ancient text in the language and circumstances of contemporary time, without which the antiquarian interest is simply a futile endeavour 'to massage the dead'.[94] The theologian-homiletician must grap-

---

92. Marshall, *McCulloch* v. *Maryland*, p. 407.

93. The interpreter's goal is 'never ... to copy what is said, but to place himself in the direction of what is said (i.e., in its meaning) in order to carry over what is to be said into the direction of his own saying' (Hans-Georg Gadamer, *Philosophical Hermeneutics* [trans. and ed. David E. Linge; Berkeley, CA: University of California Press, 1976], p. 68).

94. Holmer, *Grammar of Faith*, pp. 14, 16. Only historical ignorance or cultural chauvinism, notes Hays, would lead one to presume that no such hermeneutical operation – 'metaphor-making' – is required for the meaning of the ancient text of Scripture to be carried into the contemporary context of the Church (Richard B. Hays, *The Moral Vision of the New Testament: Community, Cross, New Creation: A Contemporary Introduction to New Testament Ethics* [New York: HarperCollins, 1996], p. 6).

ple, therefore, with both the canon of God and the concerns of mankind, and employ pericopal theology (with its transhistorical intention) as a mediator between the two, maintaining the dialectic of improvisation between fidelity and novelty, sameness and change. Not only must the sermon expound theology but also it must express exemplifications that are specific and concrete, tailored to the congregation to whom the message is delivered.[95] '[T]o make a general principle worth anything, you must give it a body; you must show in what way and how far it would be applied actually in an actual system'.[96] The 'embodiment' of pericopal theology in exemplification is the ultimate goal of the homiletical undertaking.

The terminus of exemplification renders possible the transaction of covenant renewal between God and his people, as lives are transformed according to the will of God. It is therefore critical that this move be performed in a manner that guarantees the validity of application. In that exemplifications are instances subsumed by the theology and transhistorical intention of the text, *ipse*-identity between original textual sense and the different exemplifications is preserved, rendering these applications faithful to the text, and therefore authoritative. In that exemplifications are appropriate for the specific circumstances of the community being preached to, these applications are relevant. Applications that are both authoritative and relevant are, by definition, valid.

In all such transactions, however, it must be borne in mind that it is the scriptural text that ultimately remains normative for the community of God's people. Therefore the authority behind exemplifications depends upon the cogency of the interpretive process by which they have been generated – primarily upon the careful and correct employment of the Rules of Primary and Secondary Genre to derive pericopal theology. To the degree that these hermeneutical operations upon the text have been performed with due diligence, the triadic components of textual meaning (original textual sense, theology/transhistorical

---

95. Exemplifications may operate with different trajectories. Classical rhetoric knows of three directions of audience responses sought by a rhetor: a *judicial* assessment of past events (for instance, the goal of Paul's apologetic for his early ministry in Corinth, in 2 Corinthians), a *deliberative* resolve with regard to future actions of the audience (e.g., parabolic teachings that call for explicit responses), or an *epideictic* appreciation of particular beliefs or values in the present (as put forward by Jesus in his farewell discourse in John 14–16). See Quintilian, *Inst.* 3.7-9; Anaximenes, *Rhet. Alex.* 1421b; also see C. Clifton Black, 'Rhetorical Criticism', in *Hearing the New Testament: Strategies for Interpretation* (ed. Joel B. Green; Grand Rapids: Eerdmans, 1995), pp. 256–77 (261). Application, in parallel to this threefold shape of rhetorical purpose, may also be considered broadly as responses culminating in a change of mind (a response of cognition), a change of action (a response of volition) or a change of feeling (a response of emotion).

96. Oliver Wendell Holmes, 'The Use of Law Schools', in *Speeches by Oliver Wendell Holmes* (Boston: Little, Brown, and Company, 1934), pp. 28–40 (34–5); this oration is dated 5 November 1886.

intention and exemplifications) bear the vigour of the text itself in its prescriptivity, perenniality and plurality.[97]

The analysis of two pericopes, Eph. 5.15-20 and 2 Sam. 11.1-27, for the derivation of their exemplifications will conclude this final phase of the dialogue
between hermeneutics and homiletics.

Ephesians 5.15-20. Ephesians 5.18 is an integral part of a discrete pericope,
5.15-20, itself embedded in the larger context of the letter to Ephesus.[98] While
a pericope must be considered on its own merit to discover its unique theology and to generate specific exemplification, its membership in the larger body
of the surrounding text must never be overlooked. The Rules of Singularity
and Congruence, in particular, but all the other Rules of Secondary Genre as
well, sponsor the reading of the canon as an integral whole; therein is a unity
of thought that is not dissolved in the individuality of pericopal content. For
the purposes of ongoing covenant renewal, such unity and continuity of matter
is a given, especially when pericopes are handled sequentially in regular and
frequent assemblies.

In considering the imperative, 'be not drunk with wine' (Eph. 5.18), one
might ask what transhistorical intention is conveyed by 'wine' and what
exemplifications are possible therefrom. Are all alcoholic concoctions subsumed by that intention, or would it be acceptable to be drunk with an alcoholic
beverage other than wine? Distanciation of the text and the resultant change in
context call for that imperative to be recontextualized in order to generate valid
application, a transaction engaged in by the theologian-homiletician, employing
the Rules of Genre. Though the particular rules of epistolary literature might be
operative in this instance, considering that Eph. 5.18 is an imperative, the rules
employed here are those of the primary genre of law – the Rules of Directive
and Rationale.[99]

---

97. It may be noted here that the concept of inspiration implies that the entirety of the canonical speech act – including all the components of meaning – is attributed to divine authorship and
is therefore authoritative (see Gregg R. Allison, 'Speech Act Theory and Its Implications for the
Doctrine of the Inerrancy/Infallibility of Scripture', *Phil. Christi* 8 [1995], pp. 1–23). Poythress
also agrees that authority attaches to valid applications generated from the text (Vern Sheridan
Poythress, 'Divine Meaning of Scripture', *WTJ* 48 [1986], pp. 241–79 [251]). Yet, the hermeneut
must grasp all these interpretive results with a degree of humility, for they are derivations from
the normative text and no interpreter is infallible. 'Our metaphorical readings must be tested
prayerfully within the community of faith by others who seek God's will along with us through
close reading of the text' (Hays, *Moral Vision of the New Testament*, p. 304). This is also the
demand of the Rule of Ecclesiality.

98. Hymnic material has just closed out the preceding paraenetic section, and this pericope,
Eph. 5.15-20, transitions seamlessly into a relatively newer topic – submission – in a new pericope
bookended by 'fear' (5.21-33). Thus, 5.15-20 is itself a well-demarcated pericope. See Andrew
T. Lincoln, *Ephesians* (WBC, 42; Dallas: Word, 1990), p. 338.

99. The Rule of Directive urges the interpreter to attend to both the content of the law and

Community governance is in view in the latter half of Ephesians, with guide-lines for living embedded in a cascade of contrasts between the dynamics of the 'new self' and the 'old self' (4.17–5.14).[100] The pericope of 5.15-20 itself contains three contrasts (μὴ...ἀλλὰ): between those who are wise and those who are not (5.15-16), between being foolish and understanding the will of the Lord (5.17) and between being drunk with wine and being filled by the Holy Spirit (5.18-20). Drunkenness is thus paralleled with walking unwisely and being foolish, and is explicitly labelled ἀσωτία ('dissipation'), used elsewhere in the NT only in Tit. 1.6 (1.7 mentions addiction to wine) and 1 Pet. 4.4 (4.3 has drunkenness).[101] Wine, while its use is not condemned in the NT (see 1 Tim. 5.23), is clearly not to be abused (1 Tim. 3.3, 8; Tit. 1.7; 2.3). The Rule of Directive thus marks inebriation as folly and as a characteristic of those who operate in the lifestyle of the old self. Filling by the Spirit, in contrast, is a characteristic of the wise, those displaying the lifestyle of the new self.[102] The consequences of such a filling and such a walk – speech, singing and thanksgiving appropriate to 'spiritual' worship (Eph. 5.19-20) – are explicitly delineated by the Rule of Directive.

Instead of being drunk, therefore, the Ephesians are enjoined to be 'filled by the Spirit' (ἐν πνεύματι). The injunction is clarified in the instrumental use of the preposition that indicates that the Holy Spirit is the means by which this presence is mediated, just as the instrumentality of wine mediates the state of inebriation.[103] Spiritual filling, therefore, refers to the presence and control of God in Christ mediated by the Spirit with, in and among his people (also see Eph. 1.23; 3.19; 4.13). With the thrust of the passage upon the conduct of the

its literary context; the Rule of Rationale calls attention to the motive or justification operating behind the imperative.

100. Timothy G. Gombis, 'Being the Fullness of God in Christ by the Spirit: Ephesians 5:18 in Its Epistolary Setting', *TynBul* 53 (2002), pp. 259–71 (265); Peter T. O'Brien, *The Letter to the Ephesians* (Grand Rapids: Eerdmans, 1999), pp. 379–81.

101. Rogers considers the possibility that the drunken fertility practices of Dionysian worship, widespread over the Roman Empire and established in every stratum of society, may have formed the cultural background for Eph. 5.18. There appears to have been a cult of that god extant at Ephesus: Plutarch describes Mark Antony's entrance into Ephesus in 41 BCE celebrated by Dionysian cultic ceremonies (*Ant.* 24.3). The inebriation, frenzied dancing and uncontrolled ravings that accompanied these bacchanalia were intended to lead Dionysius to 'possess' the worship-per with the 'enthusiasm' of the god. See Cleon L. Rogers, Jr., 'The Dionysian Background of Ephesians 5:18', *BSac* 136 (1979), pp. 249–57 (250–2, 254); Stanley E. Porter, 'Ephesians 5.18–19 and Its Dionysian Background', in *Testimony and Interpretation: Early Christology in Its Judeo-Hellenistic Milieu* (eds Jiří Mrázek and Jan Roskovec; London: T. & T. Clark, 2004), pp. 69–80 (72–9); and Peter W. Gosnell, 'Ephesians 5:18–20 and Mealtime Propriety', *TynBul* 44 (1992), pp. 363–71 (366).

102. Interestingly enough, in the book of Acts, the ministry of the Spirit was mistaken for drunkenness (2.4, 13, 15).

103. Also see Eph. 2.22 and 4.30 for similar instrumental uses of ἐν. The emphasis on the Holy Spirit percolates throughout this letter: 1.3, 13, 14, 17; 2.18, 22; 3.16; 4.30; 5.18; 6.17-18.

community that distinguishes it from the world around them, this focus upon God's indwelling through the Spirit enables the Rule of Rationale to discover the motive behind the proscription of wine-induced drunkenness. In exhorting the Ephesians to be filled by the Spirit rather than be drunk with wine, Paul is essentially commanding them to become, corporately, the unique temple of God, the dwelling place of God in Christ, by the Spirit, and to exhibit the Spirit's control. Corresponding to the πλήρωμα language of the OT that depicted the glory of God in the temple, in Ephesians, the Church is the new temple of God serving his presence, where the fullness of Christ dwells (1.23) – the new body comprising both Jews and Gentiles, 'a holy temple in the Lord', 'a dwelling of God in the Spirit' (2.19-22; also 3.16-19).[104] Remaining filled in this fashion, the Christian community is to engage in spiritual worship.

The theology of the pericope, derived by the Rules of Directive and Rationale; might be summarized thus: Rather than remaining under the control of alcohol – unwise and foolish – members of the Christian community live wisely, understanding God's will and in a manner befitting the temple of God, controlled instead by the presence of God in Christ mediated by the Spirit, the consequence of which is spiritual worship. In this projected world, in particular relation to Eph. 5.18 and wine, an embedded transhistorical intention may be discerned: where the original textual sense considers *wine* (concrete), the transhistorical intention accounts for *all alcoholic beverages capable of rendering one intoxicated* (universal).[105] Wine, then, is a 'concrete universal' – concrete in its label of a particular drink of certain alcoholic content, and universal in its tagging of any alcoholic potion capable of rendering one drunken when it is abused. The consequences for application are evident: drunkenness is proscribed, whether it be with vodka, whiskey or any conceivable ethanol-containing concoction.[106]

---

104. Isa. 6.1-4; Ezek. 10.4; 43.5; 44.4; Hag. 2.7; etc. See Gombis, 'Being the Fullness of God', p. 268; and Lincoln, *Ephesians*, p. 348.

105. One could hypothetically broaden this transhistorical intention to 'all *drugs* capable of rendering one intoxicated', thereby encompassing other ingested, inhaled or injected substances as its exemplifications. However, in the light of the considerable focus on 'filling' (a fluid-related phenomenon), and on the contrast between the results of Spirit-filling and the manifestations of wine-filling – manifestations that are generally more common with the abuse of alcohol than that of other chemicals – it seems prudent to restrict the transhistorical intention to 'alcohol'. There is clearly a degree of interpretive freedom here.

106. It is worth considering, in the case of Eph. 5.18, what might constitute 'significance' – application that is *not* bounded by the transhistorical intention and therefore *not* part of the 'meaning' of the text (see Chapter 1). If one were addressing, for instance, recovering alcoholics, one might suggest that those prone to the addiction should not even enter an establishment that sells liquor, lest temptation overwhelm them. Such an application is obviously not subsumed by the transhistorical intention of 5.18, which simply proscribes drunkenness with alcohol. Disbarment from entry into liquor stores would therefore be a significance, clearly outside the broad concept of the meaning of the text. However, that is not to deny that such sermonic application may be sensible or appropriate, for, as in this case, the 'invalid' application (significance) of

The transhistorical intention embedded in the pericopal theology thus forms the basis for the derivation of these exemplifications.

Second Samuel 11.1-27. The elucidation of theology from the particulars of the pericope was demonstrated earlier in this Chapter with 2 Sam. 11.1-27: Unfaithfulness to God, the true sovereign, negates blessing and promises punishment with tragic consequences for individual, family, community and society; such faithfulness as God demands – perfectly modelled by Christ, the Son of David, the righteous King – embraces an utmost regard for the word of God and the reputation of God, and is manifested in the restriction of sensual desires and in the reined exercise of power. The theology of this quantum of text warns against unfaithfulness to God manifesting in uncontrolled desire and sexual incontinence, combined with an outrageous abuse of power. Unchecked, such a disregard for God's reputation and the demands of his word only leads one deeper into a maelstrom of misdeeds. Even human life becomes of dubious value in the eyes of one who is more interested in preserving his or her own reputation, rather than God's. Faithfulness to God clearly involves a vigilant, tenacious and unyielding commitment to the values of God for the sake of his reputation. Implicit in the narrative of 1–2 Samuel is the perfect model of faithfulness to God – the Son of David, Jesus Christ. In contrast to the unfaithful human king, the divine regent is the exemplar of absolute faithfulness, fulfilling God's word and glorifying God's name. Therefore, part of what it means to be Christlike is to be faithful to God in this fashion.

The specific exemplification of this theology in the lives of hearers will, of course, be determined to a great extent upon characteristics of the congregation. The case study of King David is a dramatic example of how discontent and concupiscence, abetted by power run amok, when unrestrained by a respect for God's word or name, can plunge one deeper into the abyss of transgression (the brunt of Nathan's accusation, 2 Sam. 12.9, 14). This drama of David (and its dire consequences) serves, in its theology, as an unmistakable deterrent for the one tempted to slide in that downward direction of unfaithfulness to God. Considering the position of the king as one wielding considerable authority, the thrust of this narrative may also be brought home effectively to those who are in positions of leadership and authority. If one would live faithfully under the hand of God in such situations, one must be resolute about exercising power with utmost responsibility, with great care and concern for one's subordinates, especially when tempted by lusts of the flesh to fall into dissolution and debauchery. Obviously not all in a congregation are heads of state or those who administer the kind of power that was wantonly abused by David. Nevertheless, whether in the workplace or at home, among classmates or coworkers, in the field or in the marketplace, most individuals exercise some degree of authority by virtue

keeping away from businesses purveying alcohol may indeed be a means of actualizing the *valid* application (exemplification) of remaining sober.

of official capacity, social standing or organizational membership. Even for one who might not be part of any such hierarchy, the lesson of turpitude degenerating into further baseness, when uncurbed by the moral demands of God to honour his name and his word, is one to be taken to heart, for many a Christian has fallen – and, sadly, many continue to fall – prey to such licentiousness. No doubt, 2 Sam. 11.1-27 bears potential for general application to all readers, the specificities of exemplification being governed by the situation of address and the station of the addressees.[107]

A controlled exercise of passion and power as demanded by the theology of this pericope necessitates accountability to God (and to his agents) as the one with authority strives to 'see' things the way God does, to live humbly and contentedly under him who alone holds supreme power, and to recognize immoral behaviour as evil in the eyes of God. The theologian-homiletician might therefore consider proposing, as significance (application outside the realm of meaning; see Chapter 1), the setting up of an accountability group of godly, responsible people that, corporately personifying the prophet Nathan's office, would be granted the freedom and authority by individual Christians to proffer them counsel, as well as to provide correction, when necessary. Such a significance, when put into practice, is a means of realizing the valid application of living faithfully unto God, under God.

In sum, the move from original textual sense to exemplification is made possible by the transhistorical intention borne by pericopal theology; thereby improvisation is undertaken with fidelity and novelty. Exemplifications subsumed by pericopal theology demonstrate fidelity to the text of Scripture under consideration; the novelty of improvisation is reflected in the relevant adaptation of application to the specificities of auditors' contexts. The theologian-homiletician thus serves as the conscience of application for the community of God, with the dual responsibility to understand what God has said (text), and to generate valid application (praxis) in order that God's people may be aligned to the world projected in front of the text. Covenant renewal is thus accomplished in the Church. The task of the theologian-homiletician is therefore one of great moment and consequence for the community of God's people. John R.W. Stott charged preachers with this solemn duty:[108]

---

107. While 1–2 Samuel appears to deal primarily with the iniquities of two Israelite kings, the lessons therein for the people of the nation (and for subsequent readers and hearers of the text) must not be neglected. In opting for monarchy, the people had themselves rejected God (1 Sam. 8.7). The misdoings of their rulers reflected the people's own unfaithfulness to God; this endows the text with potential for universal applicability – for both crown and commoner.

108. John R.W. Stott, *Between Two Worlds: The Art of Preaching in the Twentieth Century* (Grand Rapids: Eerdmans, 1982), p. 145. '[T]ruth and timeliness together make the full preacher' – fidelity to the text and novelty towards audience (Phillips Brooks, *Lectures on Preaching, Delivered before the Divinity School of Yale College in January and February, 1877* [New York: E.P. Dutton, 1877], pp. 220–1).

> Our bridges ... must be firmly anchored on both sides of the chasm, by refusing either
> to compromise the divine content of the message or to ignore the human context in
> which it has to be spoken. We have to plunge fearlessly into both worlds, ancient and
> modern, biblical and contemporary, and to listen attentively to both. For only then
> shall we understand what each is saying, and so discern the Spirit's message to the
> present generation.

Thus the theologian-homiletician (whose role conflates the crucial responsibilities of both theologian and homiletician) is a mediator between the text
and Church, script and actors. It is this one's task to interpret the text for the
community and to propose how it may be applied in valid praxis. Combin-
ing canonical script analysis and contextual situation analysis – the dialogue
between hermeneutics and homiletics – the sermon bridges text and praxis
via theology, in an operation governed by the Rules of Primary and Secondary Genre. It is the resulting *ipse*-identity of text and praxis made possible by
pericopal theology that renders application both authoritative and relevant. By
such valid application, the Church renews its covenant with its God. The pericope has, thus, performed its role as an instrument of covenant renewal in the
ecclesial context, and the theologian-homiletician has fulfilled the mandate to
mediate this crucial undertaking to the people of God.

Summary: pericopal theology and application

The final chapter of this work has concluded the engagement of hermeneutics
with homiletics, focusing upon the move made by the theologian-homiletician
from text to praxis – the passage from pericope through theology to application.
The function of pericopes in ecclesial settings was established as promoting
covenant renewal, the restoration of a right relationship between God and his
people. In the weekly employment of pericopes in the life of the Church, these
assimilable portions of the canon function as concrete universals, projecting,
in and through their concrete particulars, segments of the universal canonical
world projected by Scripture. Each such segment constitutes the theology of that
particular pericope. It is pericopal theology that serves as the intermediary in
the movement from text to praxis, bidding readers inhabit the world so framed.
Such an understanding of the role of pericopal theology calls upon the theologian-homiletician to expound that entity in every sermonic proclamation.

That theology has been long considered a key intermediary in this undertaking is acknowledged; this work has sought to further that understanding and
to enable that concept to be utilized more precisely by a narrower definition
of the theological entity as pericopal theology, by hermeneutically following
its derivation *via* the Rules of Genre, and by delineating the potential for the
employment of pericopal theology in discovering application. Interpretation,
to be sure, is not complete with the discovery of pericopal theology, the move
from text to theology. The theologian-homiletician must also consummate the

hermeneutical and homiletical undertaking by proceeding further, from theology to praxis. The former undertaking (text to theology) sustains the authority of the text in the sermon; the latter (theology to praxis) endows the sermon with relevance. Under the auspices of pericopal theology, authority and relevance are thus maintained in balance, as valid application is generated. The people of God are now enabled to obey Scripture, implementing covenant renewal and aligning individual and community to the will of God for the glory of God.

This work has described a means to move validly from text to praxis by engaging hermeneutics and homiletics in dialogue. Chapter 4 has taken the final step towards that end, proposing the critical intermediary, pericopal theology, as the guardian of the sermonic move from ancient inscription to contemporary application. Derived from the pericope in question, pericopal theology grounds the entire hermeneutical and homiletical operation in the particulars of the text – the restraint. At the same time, by means of the transhistorical intention it bears, pericopal theology grants release by allowing the theologian-homiletician to tailor application to the specific circumstances of hearers. Insofar as the sermon affirms the theology portrayed by the pericope, and insofar as the applications proposed lie within the boundaries of its transhistorical intention and are appropriate for the particular audience, the passage from Scripture to sermon has been validly conducted; the journey from text to praxis has been successfully undertaken. The dialogue between hermeneutics and homiletics has borne fruit.

CONCLUSION: SUMMARY AND PROSPECTS

The burden of this work has been to determine how the move from Scripture to sermon may be conducted with validity. Such legitimacy in the homiletical transaction is not merely a documentation of the sermon's authority – its grounding upon Scripture. The interpretive operation that culminates in application must also take into consideration the circumstances of the congregation to which that portion of Scripture is exposited. In other words, the sermon must not only have *authority*, it must also have *relevance*. In maintaining its focus on the text, a sermon obtains its authority; by attending to praxis that is specific for its auditors, the sermon becomes relevant. These two poles in the homiletical endeavour, text and praxis, this work proposed, are linked by the mediating agency of pericopal theology. It is acknowledged that the concept of theology as the mediating entity between Scripture and sermon has been proposed in the past by others. This work furthers that notion, defining the theological entity more sharply as *pericopal theology*, showing how it might be discerned by the judicious use of the Rules of Genre and demonstrating how pericopal theology serves as the fountainhead for deriving application. This intermediary, a projection of the text, endows the sermon with authority and, orienting application within the boundaries of its transhistorical intention, pericopal theology enables the sermon to have relevance for the listening community as well. In the sermonic proclamation of Scripture with authority and relevance, God's people are called to renew their covenant relationship with the divine sovereign. The consequence of covenant renewal is the realization of covenantal blessings in their lives, upon their families and within their societies. Therefore, the generation of authoritative and relevant praxis from a biblical text is not a trivial matter for one who would preach the word of God faithfully. To the task of aiding the preacher in this solemn undertaking, this work addressed itself.

Summary

Engaging hermeneutics and homiletics in dialogue enabled the theologian-homiletician to move from text to praxis in valid fashion, with both authority and relevance, constrained by the text of Scripture and conformed to the circumstances of the community. Broadly, Chapters 1, 2 and 3 bore the hermeneutical burden of this interlocution. Chapter 4, primarily homiletical in focus, undertook the integration of the concepts derived in earlier chapters with the liturgical and ecclesial event of preaching.

Chapter 1 provided much of the theoretical bases for this work, surveying the operating principles and literary entities within the domain of general hermeneutics: language-games, textuality and genres. Establishing that texts play Wittgensteinian language-games, it was shown that these activities operate by rules – rules that do not command but rather guide writers' and readers' transactions of these linguistic exercises. Textuality and its tumultuous consequences for discourse were considered, especially the ramifications of distanciation for medium, speaker, hearer, code and referent. Of significant moment to this work was the referential function of written discourse, the projection of what Ricoeur labelled the *world in front of the text* – the second-order referent of texts and an element of the pragmatics of discourse. The two species of biblical language-games, primary and secondary genre, facilitate such world projections. Primary genre permits the perception of these worlds by framing them in particular ways, each genre in its own fashion projecting a segment of the larger canonical world. Secondary genre, that of the classic, creates for Scripture a unique set of properties: this language-game grants the biblical text prescriptive, perennial and plural significance. By virtue of these singular characteristics, the future-directedness of the Bible becomes manifest in the transhistorical intentions borne by the projected world. The actualization of these intentions in the futurity of readers and hearers constitutes exemplifications (valid applications). This work asserted that 'meaning', therefore, comprises the integrally linked triad of original textual sense, transhistorical intention and future exemplifications. In such a scheme, the distanciation effected by textuality is neutralized, for the projected world with its transhistorical intention enables application even in circumstances far removed in time and space from the originary utterance. Indeed, textuality may be seen as the property of a discourse that confers upon it the capacity of overcoming the temporo-spatial restrictions imposed by orality. This emancipation of communication renders movement from ancient text to future praxis viable.

Chapters 2 and 3 proposed rules for the two language-games played by the biblical text. These rules enable the recognition of the segment of the world projected by individual genres and texts, and the plenary world projected by the canon. Chapter 2 enumerated the Rules of Primary Genre. A fundamental hurdle to be overcome in the analysis of primary genres is that of classification, a complexity that was underscored by the examination of two NT genres, epistle and gospel. The arduousness of this task, however, is not necessarily disabling for interpretation. Indeed, this very complication emphasizes the attribute of genres as 'works', instruments requisitioned and specifically refigured by authors to achieve their purposes and to evoke particular responses from readers. Despite the difficulty of categorization, sufficient family resemblances obtain within broad generic classes to render discrimination between genres possible. Four prominent text-types were utilized to display the Rules of Primary Genre and their role in world projection: narrative (Rules of Plot and Interaction), prophecy (Rules of Anticipation and Correction), law (Rules of Directive and Rationale) and hymnody (Rules of Portrayal and Perspective).

Chapter 3 proceeded to list the Rules of Secondary Genre. These rules were grouped by the part they play in presiding over the structure, function and content of the canon. The Rules of Structure (Rules of Completion, Singularity and Organization) form and shape the source material for the world projected by the text. The Rules of Function (Rules of Exclusivity, Applicability, Congruence and Ecclesiality) demarcate those texts that may contribute to the canon's world-projection, and govern the manner of their reading. The Rules of Content (Rules of Substantiality, Intertextuality, Sequentiality and Primacy) help elucidate the critical core and content of the world in front of the text. Together, the Rules of Primary and Secondary Genre enable the theologian-homiletician to discern the world in front of the text – the segment of the world projected by each text in its primary genre and the composite of these segments that constitutes the world projected by the canon.

Chapter 4 completed the hermeneutical-homiletical dialogue as the focus of investigation narrowed from language-games and texts (Chapter 1), through genres (Chapters 2 and 3), to converge, finally, upon specific texts of Scripture, pericopes, utilized for sermons in liturgical settings. This work contended that these fundamental units of text function as literary instruments of covenant renewal between God and his people. The exposition of pericopes of Scripture in the weekly gatherings of the Church serves as the formal event for motivating and moulding the submission of the community to its Creator. Such a corporate transaction, that helps sustain a right relationship between God and his people, involves application, the response of readers and hearers to the world in front of the text. Application, therefore, was envisaged as the inhabitation of that projected world and the alignment of auditors' lives to the priorities, principles and practices of this world.

In this homiletical operation, the pericope is, in effect, a concrete universal subsisting in the specific and particular, while simultaneously portraying what is general and transcendent. By means of its textual particulars (the concrete), each pericope projects a facet of the canonical world (the universal).[1] This

---

1. The cumulative world-depictions by pericopes constitute the plenary world projected by the canon. There are, in principle, an indefinite number of worlds (theories) that could conceivably fit the matter of the written discourse adequately; this is the potential problem of underdetermination of theory by data. In practice, however, the quantum of data available, when ample, restricts the number of such theories that may be propounded; a certain convergence occurs when adequate evidence is included in the calculus. Therefore, not *all* theories or projected worlds are equally underdetermined; most are excluded by the specificity of textual content, simplicity of explanation, correspondence with empirical data, plausibility of the world portrayed and intrasystematic coherence between segments thereof. The sizeable volume of data and context provided

work proposed that the world so portrayed is *pericopal theology* – theology specific to a particular pericope, which represents a segment of the plenary world in front of the canonical text and which, bearing a transhistorical intention, functions as the crucial intermediary in the homiletical move from text to praxis that respects both the authority of the text and the circumstances of the hearer. In other words, while demonstrating *fidelity* to the thrust of the text, the exemplified praxis is also to display *novelty* in its adaptation to the situations of listeners. This balance, the dialectic between fidelity and novelty mediated by pericopal theology, is a form of improvisation – faithfulness to the text and freshness toward the context of hearers. To the extent that the sermon proclaims this 'constancy in change', the homiletical undertaking may be said to have been performed with validity; the move from text to praxis has been made with authority and relevance. Hermeneutics has thus made a successful rendezvous with homiletics.

Prospects

A theological hermeneutic for preaching was propounded in this work to answer the question of how the homiletician may move validly from text to praxis. Pericopal theology was identified as the key intermediary between text and sermon that lends validity to the entire transaction. This work has therefore facilitated the preacher becoming a *theologian*-homiletician, one who employs pericopal theology to bridge the much-bemoaned lacuna between inscription and interpretation. It is this proposed manœuvre from text through theology to praxis that alone will enable the production of a sermon that is both authoritative and relevant; only such a product will mediate covenant renewal between God and his people. It is hoped, therefore, that this work will alleviate, at least to some extent, the angst in the pastor's study that accompanies the weekly agonies of fashioning a sermon that is faithful to Scripture and fitting for parishioners.

Further work, no doubt, remains to be undertaken to broaden the scope of what has been essayed herein. The list of the Rules of Primary Genre could be expanded to include guidelines for other genres (and, perhaps, sub-genres) as well – Wisdom literature, NT Epistles, apocalyptic writings, parables, etc. Fruitful terrain for further exploration will also include the use of the Old Testament in the New. Could it be discerned that in their employment of the OT, the NT writers comprehended the theology of those OT passages, subsequently applying that theology to their own post-resurrection contexts? With the paradigm put forth in this work that posits meaning as comprising original textual sense,

by the biblical text maintains this convergence upon a limited number of possibilities. See Mary Hesse, *Revolutions and Reconstructions in the Philosophy of Science* (Bloomington, IN: Indiana University Press, 1980), pp. vii–viii; and David K. Clark, *To Know and Love God* (Wheaton, IL: Crossway, 2003), p. 140.

transhistorical intention and exemplifications, it may well be that the postulation of *sensus plenior* ('fuller sense' – the deeper meaning intended by God, but not clearly intended by the human author of the biblical text) is unnecessary to demonstrate the logic of Old Testament citations in the New. The exemplifications of a text *can* go beyond its original sense and exceed anything the human author could have consciously intended, so long as those exemplifications remain within the bounds of the pericopal theology (and its transhistorical intention). All instances of interpretation of biblical texts that resort to *sensus plenior* could conceivably be explained more simply by employing this triad of meaning. A substantiation of this assertion with a text-by-text analysis of NT writers' use of antecedent Scripture is an undertaking that holds much promise.

A sermon is not merely the product of a strategic employment of rules; homiletics, to be sure, cannot be reduced to following recipes. While facility in hermeneutics (the domain of this work) and skill in rhetoric are essential for the making of an effective preacher, neither is sufficient. The role of the Holy Spirit and the spiritual formation of the theologian-homiletician can be ignored only with great loss to the preacher, to the preaching endeavour and to those at the receiving end of this enterprise. It would be a miscarriage of the theme of covenant renewal were the theologian-homiletician to undertake this august task with nary a thought for the divine operation of the Spirit that makes such renewal possible and such relationship with God successful. These aspects of spirituality in homiletics remain to be examined. Perhaps the hermeneutical foundations laid by this work will stimulate investigation in these arenas.

Prospective inquiries notwithstanding, it is anticipated that the concepts propounded herein will have an impact not only upon homiletics and homiletical pedagogy but also upon the faith and practice of the Church, as the people of God are directed to apply the precepts of Scripture to their own lives validly, enabling covenant renewal, facilitating covenant blessing and furthering the kingdom of this God who deigns, in love, to have a relationship with his redeemed.

BIBLIOGRAPHY

Ancient texts

'Abot de Rabbi Nathan (The Fathers according to Rabbi Nathan) (trans. Judah Goldin; New Haven: Yale University Press, 1955).

Amphilochius, 'The Canon of Amphilochius of Iconium', in Bruce M. Metzger, *The Canon of the New Testament: Its Origin, Development, and Significance* (Oxford: Clarendon Press, 1987), pp. 313–14.

Anaximenes, *Rhetorica ad Alexandrum* (trans. H. Rackham; LCL, 317; Cambridge, MA: Harvard University Press, 1970).

Aquinas, Thomas, *Summa theologica* (trans. the Fathers of the English Dominican Province; ed. Daniel J. Sullivan; London: Encyclopædia Britannica, 1952).

Aristotle, *Poetics* (trans. W. Hamilton Fyfe; LCL, 199; Cambridge, MA: Harvard University Press, 1982).

Athanasius, *De decretis*, NPNF Series II, vol. 4, pp. 149–72.

—*Epistula ad Serapionem de more Arii*, NPNF Series II, vol. 4, pp. 564–6.

—*Epistulæ festales*, NPNF Series II, vol. 4, pp. 506–53.

Augustine, *De doctrina christiana* (trans. R.P.H. Green; Oxford: Oxford University Press, 1997).

Bucer, Martin, *Martin Bucers Deutsches Schriften* (14 vols; ed. R. Stupperich; Gütersloh: Mohn, 1960–75).

Chrysostom, John, *Homiliæ in Genesim*, PG 53.

—*Homiliæ in epistulam ad Colossenses*, NPNF Series I, pp. 257–314.

Cicero, *Brutus* (trans. G.L. Hendrickson; LCL, 342; Cambridge, MA: Harvard University Press, 1962).

—*De oratore* (trans. E.W. Sutton and H. Rackham; LCL, 348; Cambridge, MA: Harvard University Press, 1948).

—*Orator ad M. Brutum* (trans. H.M. Hubbell; LCL, 342; Cambridge, MA: Harvard University Press, 1962).

Clement of Alexandria, *Stromata*, ANF, vol. 2, pp. 299–568.

Clement of Rome, *1 Clement*, ANF, vol. 1, pp. 1–21.

Constitutions of the Holy Apostles, ANF, vol. 7, pp. 385–508.

Council of Laodicea, *Canons*, NPNF Series II, vol. 14, pp. 123–60.

Cyril of Alexandria, *Commentary on Isaiah*, PG, vol. 70, sections 557–858.

Dead Sea Scrolls, 4Q174 (Florilegium), in Geza Vermes, *The Complete Dead Sea Scrolls in English* (London: Allen Lane, 1997), pp. 493–4.

Demetrius, *De elocutione*, in *Poetics, On the Sublime, On Style* (trans. W. Rhys Roberts; LCL, 199; Cambridge, MA: Harvard University Press, 1982), pp. 255–487.

Ephrem the Syrian, *Saint Ephrem's Commentary on Tatian's Diatessaron* (trans. C. McCarthy; Oxford: Oxford University Press, 1993).

Epiphanius, *Panarion: Book II and III (Sections 47–80)* (trans. Frank Williams; Leiden: E.J. Brill, 1993).

Eusebius, *Historia ecclesiastica* (trans. Kirsopp Lake and J.E.L. Oulton; 2 vols; LCL, 153, 265; Cambridge, MA: Harvard University Press, 1926, 1932).

—*Quaestiones ad Marinum*, in James A. Kelhoffer, 'The Witness of Eusebius' *ad Marinum* and Other Christian Writings to Text-Critical Debates concerning the Original Conclusion to Mark's Gospel', *ZNW* 92 (2001), pp. 78–112 (83–9).

Gabler, J.P., *Oratio de justo discrimine Theologiæ biblicæ et dogmaticæ regundisque recte utriusque finibus*, in John Sandys-Wunsch and Laurence Eldredge, 'J.P. Gabler and the Distinction between Biblical and Dogmatic Theology: Translation, Commentary, and Discussion of His Originality', *SJT* 33 (1980), pp. 133–58 (134–44).

Gregory the Great, *Epistula ad Theodorum medicum*, PL, vol. 77, section 706.

Irenaeus, *Adversus haereses*, ANF, vol. 1, pp. 309–567.

Isocrates, *Evagoras* (trans. La Rue Van Hook; LCL, 373; Cambridge, MA: Harvard University Press, 1945).

Jerome, *Epistula ad Dardanum*, in *Sancti Hieronymi Epistulae* (Paris: Société d'Edition 'Les Belles Lettres', 1961), pp. 160–1.

—*Epistula ad Hedybiam*, NPNF, Series II, vol. 6, p. 224.

—*Epistula ad Paula*, NPNF, Series II, vol. 6, p. 45.

—*Prefaces to the Books of the Vulgate: Samuel and Kings*, NPNF, Series II, vol. 6, pp. 489–90.

Josephus, *Against Apion* (trans. H.St.J. Thackeray; LCL, 186; Cambridge, MA: Harvard University Press, 1926).

—*Jewish War* (trans. H.St.J. Thackeray; LCL, 203; Cambridge, MA: Harvard University Press, 1927).

Justin Martyr, *Dialogue with Trypho*, ANF, vol. 1, pp. 194–270.

—*First Apology*, ANF, vol. 1, pp. 159–87.

Lucian, *Demonax* (trans. A.M. Harmon; LCL, 14; Cambridge, MA: Harvard University Press, 1913).

Luther, Martin, 'Concerning the Order of Public Worship (1523)', in *Liturgy and Hymns* (vol. 53 of *Luther's Works*; trans. Paul Zeller Strodach; rev. Ulrich S. Leupold; Philadelphia: Fortress, 1965), pp. 7–14.

Macarius Magnes, *Apocriticus* (trans. T.W. Craffer; London: SPCK, 1919).

Muratorian Canon, in Bruce M. Metzger, *The Canon of the New Testament: Its Origin, Development, and Significance* (Oxford: Clarendon Press, 1987), pp. 305–7.

Origen, *Commentarii in evangelium Joannis*, ANF, vol. 9, pp. 297–345.

—*De principiis*, ANF, vol. 4, pp. 239–384.

Philo, *Hypothetica* (trans. F.H. Colson; LCL, 363; Cambridge, MA: Harvard University Press, 1941).

—*On the Creation of the World*, in Philo (trans. F.H. Colson; LCL, 226; Cambridge, MA: Harvard University Press, 1929), vol. 1, pp. 1–140.

—*On the Embassy to Gaius* (trans. F.H. Colson; LCL, 379; Cambridge, MA: Harvard University Press, 1962).

—*On the Life of Moses* (trans. F.H. Colson; LCL, 289; Cambridge, MA: Harvard University Press, 1935).

—*On the Special Laws* (trans. F.H. Colson; LCL, 320; Cambridge, MA: Harvard University Press, 1937).

Plato, *Phaedrus* (trans. R. Hackforth; Cambridge: Cambridge University Press, 1972).

Plutarch, *Antonius*, *Parallel Lives* (trans. Bernadotte Perrin; LCL, 101: Cambridge, MA: Harvard University Press, 1920), vol. 9, pp. 139–333.

—*Cato Minor* (ed. J. Murrell; London: Association of Classical Teachers, 1984).

Polycarp, *Epistle to the Philippians*, ANF, vol. 1, pp. 33–6.

Pseudo Demetrius, Τύποι 'Επιστολικοι, in Abraham J. Malherbe, 'Ancient Epistolary Theorists', *Ohio Journal of Religious Studies* 5 (1977), pp. 3–77 (30–41).

Pseudo Libanius, Ἐπιστολιμαῖοι Χαρακτῆρες, in Abraham J. Malherbe, 'Ancient Epistolary Theorists', *Ohio Journal of Religious Studies* 5 (1977), pp. 3–77 (66–81).

Quintilian, *Institutio oratoria* (trans. Donald A. Russell; 5 vols; LCL, 124–7, 494; Cambridge, MA: Harvard University Press, 2001).

Satyrus, *Life of Euripides*, in *The Oxyrhynchus Papyri IX* (ed. Arthur S. Hunt; London: Egypt Exploration Fund Graeco-Roman Branch, 1912), P. Oxy. No. 1176, pp. 124–82.

Tacitus, *Agricola* (trans. M. Hutton; LCL, 35; Cambridge, MA: Harvard University Press, 1914).

Talmud, Babylonian tractate *Megillah*, Vol. 8, *Mo'ed Qaṭan* (ed. I. Epstein; London: Soncino, 1938).

Talmud, Babylonian tractate *Soṭah*, Vol. 6, *Našim* (ed. I. Epstein; London: Soncino, 1936).

Talmud, Mishnah tractate *Pesaḥim*, Vol. 4, *Mo'ed Qaṭan* (ed. H. Freedman; London: Soncino, 1938).

Talmud, Tosefta tractate *Sanhedrin*, in *The Tosefta* (trans. Jacob Neusner; Peabody, MA: Hendrickson, 2002), vol. 2, pp. 1143–197.

Tertullian, *Adversus Marcionem*, ANF, vol. 3, pp. 269–475.

—*Apology*, ANF, vol. 3, pp. 1–60.

—*De praescriptione haereticorum*, ANF, vol. 3, pp. 243–67.

Thucydides, *History of the Peloponnesian War* (trans. C.F. Smith; 4 vols; LCL, 108–10, 169; Cambridge, MA: Harvard University Press, 1919–23).

US Constitution, in *Documents of American Constitutional and Legal History* (2nd edn; eds Melvin I. Urofsky and Paul Finkelman; New York: Oxford University Press, 2001), vol. 1, pp. 85–102.

Wilkins, John, *Ecclesiastes, or A discourse concerning the Gift of Preaching As it fals under the Rules of Art: Shewing The most proper Rules and Directions, for Method, Invention, Books, Expressions, whereby a Minister may be furnished with such abilities as may make him a Workman that needs not to be ashamed* (3rd edn; London: Samuel Gellibrand, 1651).

Xenophon, *Agesilaus* (trans. E.C. Marchant; LCL, 183; Cambridge, MA: Harvard University Press, 1925).

General bibliography

Ackerman, James S., 'Knowing Good and Evil: A Literary Analysis of the Court History in 2 Samuel 9–20 and 1 Kings 1–2', *JBL* 109 (1990), pp. 41–64.

Aichele, George, *The Control of Biblical Meaning: Canon as Semiotic Mechanism* (Harrisburg, PN: Trinity, 2001).

Allison, Gregg R., 'Speech Act Theory and Its Implications for the Doctrine of the Inerrancy/Infallibility of Scripture', *Phil. Chris.* 8 (1995), pp. 1–23.

Alter, Robert, *The Art of Biblical Narrative* (New York: Basic Books, 1981).

Altieri, Charles 'The Poem as Act: A Way to Reconcile Presentational and Mimetic Theories', *Iowa Rev.* 6.3-4 (1975), pp. 103–24.

Auerbach, Erich, *Mimesis: The Representation of Reality in Western Literature* (trans. Willard R. Trask; Princeton: Princeton University Press, 1953).

Austin, J.L., *How to Do Things with Words* (2nd edn; eds J.O. Urmson and Marina Sbisà; Cambridge, MA: Harvard University Press, 1975).

Avioz, Michael, *Nathan's Oracle (2 Samuel 7) and Its Interpreters* (Bern, Switzerland: Peter Lang, 2005).

Bach, Kent, and Robert M. Harnish, *Linguistic Communication and Speech Acts* (Cambridge, MA: MIT Press, 1979).

Bailey, Randall C., *David in Love and War: The Pursuit of Power in 2 Samuel 10–12* (Sheffield: JSOT, 1990).

Bakhtin, Mikhail, *The Dialogical Imagination: Four Essays* (trans. Caryl Emerson and Michael Holquist; ed. Michael Holquist; Austin, TX: University of Texas Press, 1981).

—'The Problem of Speech Genres', in *Modern Genre Theory* (ed. David Duff; Essex, UK: Pearson, 2000), pp. 82–97.

Barr, James, 'A New Look at *Kethibh-Qere*', in *Remembering All the Way ...* (OTS, 21; ed. B. Albrektson; Leiden: E.J. Brill, 1981), pp. 19–37.

Barker, William S., and W. Robert Godfrey (eds), *Theonomy: A Reformed Critique* (Grand Rapids: Zondervan, 1990).

Barth, Karl, *Church Dogmatics* Vol. 1, part 2 (trans. G.T. Thomson and Harold Knight; eds G.W. Bromiley and T.F. Torrance; Edinburgh: T. & T. Clark, 1956).

—'The Strange New World within the Bible', in *The Word of God and the Word of Man* (trans. Douglas Horton; London: Hodder and Stoughton, 1928), pp. 28–50.

Barton, John, *Holy Writings, Sacred Text: The Canon in Early Christianity* (Louisville: Westminster/John Knox Press, 1997).

—*The Spirit and the Letter: Studies in the Biblical Canon* (London: SPCK, 1997).

Bauckham, Richard, 'Reading Scripture as a Coherent Story', in *The Art of Reading Scripture* (eds Ellen F. Davis and Richard B. Hays; Grand Rapids: Eerdmans, 2003), pp. 38–53.

Bawarshi, Anis, 'The Genre Function', *College English* 62 (2000), pp. 335–60.

Beckman, Gary, *Hittite Diplomatic Texts* (Atlanta: Scholars, 1996).

Beckwith, Roger, *The Old Testament Canon of the New Testament Church* (London: SPCK, 1985).

Bertman, Stephen, 'Tasseled Garments in the Ancient East Mediterranean', *Biblical Archaeologist* 24 (1961), pp. 119–28.

Bitzer, Lloyd F., 'The Rhetorical Situation', *P&R* 1 (1968), pp. 1–14.

Black, C. Clifton, 'Rhetorical Criticism', in *Hearing the New Testament: Strategies for Interpretation* (ed. Joel B. Green; Grand Rapids: Eerdmans, 1995), pp. 256–77.

Bloomfield, Morton W., 'Allegory as Interpretation', *NLH* 3 (1972), pp. 301–17.

Bock, Darrell L., 'Why I Am a Dispensationalist with a Small "d" ', *JETS* 41 (1998), pp. 383–96.

Bodner, Keith, 'Nathan: Prophet, Politician and Novelist?', *JSOT* 95 (2001), pp. 43–54.

Booth, Wayne C., *The Company We Keep: An Ethics of Fiction* (Berkeley, CA: University of California Press, 1988).

Brennan, Joseph P., 'Psalms 1–8: Some Hidden Harmonies', *BTB* 10 (1980), pp. 25–9.

Brenner, Martin L., *The Song of the Sea: Ex 15:1–21* (BZAW, 195; Berlin: de Gruyter, 1991).

Briggs, Richard, *Reading the Bible Wisely* (London: SPCK, 2003).

Bright, John, *The Authority of the Old Testament* (Nashville: Abingdon, 1967).

Brooks, Phillips, *Lectures on Preaching, Delivered before the Divinity School of Yale College in January and February, 1877* (New York: E.P. Dutton, 1877).

Bruce, F.F., *The Canon of Scripture* (Downers Grove: InterVarsity, 1988).

Burridge, Richard A, *Four Gospels, One Jesus? A Symbolic Reading* (London: SPCK, 1994).

—'The Gospels and Acts', in *Handbook of Classical Rhetoric in the Hellenistic Period 330 B.C.–A.D. 400* (ed. Stanley E. Porter; Leiden: E.J. Brill, 2001), pp. 507–32.

—*What Are the Gospels? A Comparison with Graeco-Roman Biography* (2nd edn; Grand Rapids: Zondervan, 2004).

Buttrick, David. A., *Captive Voice: The Liberation of Preaching* (Louisville: Westminster/John Knox Press, 1994).

—'Interpretation and Preaching', *Int* 35 (1981), pp. 46–58.

Campbell, Barth L., *Honor, Shame, and the Rhetoric of 1 Peter* (Atlanta: Scholars, 1998).

Carmichael, Calum, *The Spirit of Biblical Law* (Athens, GA: University of Georgia Press, 1996).

Cassirer, Ernst, *Language*, Vol. 1 of *The Philosophy of Symbolic Forms* (trans. Ralph Mannheim; New Haven: Yale University Press, 1953).

The Catechism of the Catholic Church (2nd edn; New York: Doubleday, 2003).

Chatman, Seymour, *Reading Narrative Fiction* (New York: Macmillan, 1993).

—*Story and Discourse: Narrative Structure in Fiction and Film* (Ithaca, NY: Cornell University Press, 1978).

Childs, Brevard S., *Biblical Theology in Crisis* (Philadelphia: Westminster, 1970).

—*Biblical Theology of the Old and New Testaments: Theological Reflection on the Christian Bible* (London: SCM Press, 1992).

—*Exodus: A Commentary* (London: SCM Press, 1974).

—*Introduction to the Old Testament as Scripture* (London: SCM Press, 1979).

Clark, David K., *To Know and Love God* (Wheaton, IL: Crossway, 2003).

Clements, Ronald. E., *The Conscience of the Nation: A Study of Early Israelite Prophecy* (London: Oxford University Press, 1967).

—*Old Testament Prophecy: From Oracles to Canon* (Louisville: Westminster/John Knox Press, 1996).

Cohen, Ralph, 'History and Genre', *NLH* 17 (1986), pp. 203–18.

Coleridge, Samuel Taylor, 'The Friend: Section the Second, Essay IV', in *The Collected Works of Samuel Taylor Coleridge* (ed. Barbara E. Rooke; London: Routledge & Kegan Paul, 1969), pp. 448–57.

Comstock, Gary, 'Truth or Meaning: Ricoeur versus Frei on Biblical Narrative', *JR* 66 (1986), pp. 117–40.

Cosgrove, Charles H., 'Toward a Postmodern Hermeneutica Sacra: Guiding Considerations in Choosing between Competing Plausible Interpretations of Scripture', in *The Meanings We Choose: Hermeneutical Ethics, Indeterminacy and the Conflict of Interpretations* (ed. Charles H. Cosgrove; London: T. & T. Clark, 2004), pp. 39–61.

Cowley, A. E., *Aramaic Papyri of the Fifth Century B.C.* (Oxford: Clarendon Press, 1923).

Craddock, Fred B., *As One without Authority* (Nashville: Abingdon, 1981).

—*Preaching* (Nashville: Abingdon, 1985).

Craig, Kenneth M., Jr., 'The Character(ization) of God in 2 Samuel 7:1–17', *Semeia* 63 (1993), pp. 159–76.

Craigie, Peter C., *The Problem of War in the Old Testament* (Grand Rapids: Eerdmans, 1978).

—*Ugarit and the Old Testament* (Grand Rapids: Eerdmans, 1983).

Crouzel, Henri, *Origen* (trans. A.S. Worrall; Edinburgh: T. & T. Clark, 1989).

Culler, Jonathan, *Structuralist Poetics: Structuralism, Linguistics, and the Study of Literature* (London: Routledge & Kegan Paul, 1975).

Cullman, Oscar, *The Early Church* (London: SCM Press, 1956).

Daley, Brian E., 'Is Patristic Exegesis Still Usable? Some Reflections on Early Christian Interpretation of the Psalms', in *The Art of Reading Scripture* (eds Ellen F. Davis and Richard B. Hays; Grand Rapids: Eerdmans, 2003), pp. 69–88.

Daube, David, *The New Testament and Rabbinic Judaism* (London: Athlone, 1956).

Derrida, Jacques, 'The Law of Genre', trans. Avital Ronell, *Critical Inquiry* 7 (1980), pp. 55–81.

Devitt, Amy J., 'Generalizing about Genre: New Conceptions of an Old Concept', *CCC* 44 (1993), pp. 573–86.

Dorsey, David A., 'The Law of Moses and the Christian: A Compromise', *JETS* 34 (1991), pp. 322–34.

—'The Use of the OT Law in Christian Life: A Theocentric Approach', *EvJ* 17 (1998), pp. 1–18.

Douglas, Mary, *Implicit Meanings: Selected Essays in Anthropology* (2nd edn; London: Routledge, 1999).

Dubrow, Heather, *Genre* (London: Methuen, 1982).

Duggan, Michael W., *The Covenant Renewal in Ezra-Nehemiah (Neh 7:72b–10:40): An Exegetical, Literary, and Theological Study* (Atlanta: SBL, 1996).

Dumbrell, William J., 'The Content and Significance of the Books of Samuel: Their Place and Purpose within the Former Prophets', *JETS* 33 (1990), pp. 49–62.

—'Genesis 2:1–17: A Foreshadowing of the New Creation', in *Biblical Theology: Retrospect and Prospect* (ed. Scott J. Hafemann; Downers Grove: InterVarsity, 2002), pp. 53–65.

Dyck, Elmer, 'Jonah among the Prophets: A Study in Canonical Context', *JETS* 33 (1990), pp. 63–73.

Eco, Umberto, *The Limits of Interpretation* (Bloomington, IN: Indiana University Press, 1990).

Ellis, E. Earle, 'Biblical Interpretation in the New Testament Church', in *Mikra: Text, Translation, Reading and Interpretation of the Hebrew Bible in Ancient Judaism and Early Christianity* (ed. Martin Jan Mulder; Philadelphia: Fortress, 1988), pp. 691–725.

Enns, Peter, 'Apostolic Hermeneutics and an Evangelical Doctrine of Scripture: Moving beyond a Modernist Impasse', *WTJ* 65 (2003), pp. 263–87.

Erickson, Millard J., *Evangelical Interpretation: Perspectives on Hermeneutical Issues* (Grand Rapids: Baker, 1993).

Finkel, Asher, 'Jesus' Sermon at Nazareth (Luk. 4,16–30)', in *Abraham unser Vater: Juden und Christen im Gespräch über die Bibel* (eds Otto Betz, Martin Hengel and Peter Schmidt; Leiden: E.J. Brill, 1963), pp. 106–15.

Flusser, D., 'Two Notes on the Midrash on 2 Sam. vii', *IEJ* (1959), pp. 99–109.

Fodor, James, *Christian Hermeneutics: Paul Ricoeur and the Refiguring of Theology* (Oxford: Clarendon Press, 1995).

Fokkelman, J.P., *King David (II Sam. 9–20 & I Kings 1–2)*, Vol. 1 of *Narrative Art and Poetry in the Books of Samuel* (Assen, Netherlands: Van Gorcum, 1981).

—*Reading Biblical Narrative: An Introductory Guide* (trans. Ineke Smit; Louisville: Westminster/John Knox Press, 1999).

—*Throne and City (II Sam. 2–8 & 21–24)*, Vol. 3 of *Narrative Art and Poetry in the Books of Samuel* (Assen, Netherlands: Van Gorcum, 1990).

Fowl, Stephen, 'The Canonical Approach of Brevard Childs', *ExpTim* 96 (1985), pp. 173–76.

—*Engaging Scripture: A Model for Theological Interpretation* (Malden, MA: Blackwell, 1998).

Frege, Gottlob, 'On *Sinn* and *Bedeutung*', in *The Frege Reader* (ed. Michael Beaney; Malden, MA: Blackwell, 1997), pp. 150–80.

Frei, Hans W., *The Eclipse of Biblical Narrative: A Study in Eighteenth and Nineteenth Century Hermeneutics* (New Haven: Yale University Press, 1974).

—*The Identity of Jesus Christ: The Hermeneutical Bases of Dogmatic Theology* (Philadelphia: Fortress, 1975).

—'The "Literal Reading" of the Biblical Narrative in the Christian Tradition: Does It Stretch or Will It Break?', in *The Bible and the Narrative Tradition* (ed. Frank McConnell; New York: Oxford University Press, 1986), pp. 36–77.

—'Response to "Narrative Theology: An Evangelical Appraisal"', *TrinJ* 8 (1987), pp. 21–4.

—*Types of Christian Theology* (ed. George Hunsinger and William C. Placher; New Haven: Yale University Press, 1992).

Frye, Northrop, *Anatomy of Criticism: Four Essays* (Princeton: Princeton University Press, 1957).

—*The Educated Imagination* (Bloomington, IN: Indiana University Press, 1964).

—*The Great Code: The Bible and Literature* (New York: Harcourt Brace, 1982).

Gadamer, Hans-Georg, *Philosophical Hermeneutics* (trans. and ed. David E. Linge; Berkeley, CA: University of California Press, 1976).

—*Truth and Method* (2nd rev. edn; trans Joel Weinsheimer and Donald G. Marshall; London: Continuum, 2004).

Gamble, Harry Y., *Books and Readers in the Early Church: A History of Early Christian Texts* (New Haven: Yale University Press, 1995).

—*The New Testament Canon: Its Making and Meaning* (Philadelphia: Fortress, 1985).

Geertz, Clifford, *The Interpretation of Cultures* (London: Fontana, 1993).

Gemser, B., 'The Importance of the Motive Clause in Old Testament Law', in *Congress Volume: Copenhagen* (VTSup, 1; Leiden: E.J. Brill, 1953), pp. 50–66.

Gibbs, Raymond W., Jr., *Intentions in the Experience of Meaning* (Cambridge: Cambridge University Press, 1999).

—'Nonliteral Speech Acts in Text and Discourse', in *The Handbook of Discourse Processes* (eds Arthur C. Graesser, Morton Ann Gernsbacher and Susan R. Goldman; Mahwah, NJ: Erlbaum, 2003), pp. 357–93.

Goethe, J.W., *Conversations with Eckermann (1823–1832)* (trans. John Oxenford; San Francisco: North Point, 1984), pp. 357–93.

Goldingay, John, *Approaches to Old Testament Interpretation* (Leicester, UK: InterVarsity, 1981).

—*Models for Interpretation of Scripture* (Grand Rapids: Eerdmans, 1995).

Goldsmith, Dale, 'Acts 13:33–37: A Pesher on II Samuel 7', *JBL* 87 (1968), pp. 321–4.

Goldsworthy, Graeme, *Gospel-Centred Hermeneutics: Biblical-Theological Foundations and Principles* (Nottingham, UK: Apollos, 2006).

Gombis, Timothy G., 'Being the Fullness of God in Christ by the Spirit: Ephesians 5:18 in Its Epistolary Setting', *TynBul* 53 (2002), pp. 259–71.

Gosnell, Peter W., 'Ephesians 5:18–20 and Mealtime Propriety', *TynBul* 44 (1992), pp. 363–71.

Green, Joel B., 'Reading the Gospels and Acts as Narrative', in *Narrative Reading, Narrative Preaching: Reuniting New Testament Interpretation and Proclamation* (eds Joel B. Green and Michael Pasquarello III; Grand Rapids: Baker, 2003), pp. 37–66.

Guest, Stephen, *Ronald Dworkin* (Stanford, CA: Stanford University Press, 1991).

Gunn, David M., and Danna Nolan Fewell, *Narrative in the Hebrew Bible* (Oxford: Oxford University Press, 1993).

Habermas, Jürgen, *Justification and Application: Remarks on Discourse Ethics* (trans. Ciaran Cronin; Cambridge: Polity, 1993).

Hare, R.M., *Freedom and Reason* (Oxford: Clarendon Press, 1963).

Harnack, Adolf von, *Marcion: The Gospel of the Alien God* (trans. John E. Steely and Lyle D. Bierma; Durham, NC: Labyrinth, 1990).

Hays, Richard B., *Echoes of Scripture in the Letters of Paul* (New Haven: Yale University Press, 1989).

—*The Moral Vision of the New Testament: Community, Cross, New Creation: A Contemporary Introduction to New Testament Ethics* (San Francisco: HarperSanFrancisco, 1996).

Hesse, Mary, *Revolutions and Reconstructions in the Philosophy of Science* (Bloomington, IN: Indiana University Press, 1980).

High, Dallas M., *Language, Persons, and Belief: Studies in Wittgenstein's* Philosophical Investigations *and Religious Use of Language* (New York: Oxford University Press, 1967).

Hirsch, E.D., Jr., *The Aims of Interpretation* (Chicago: The University of Chicago Press, 1976).

—'Counterfactuals in Interpretation', in *Interpreting Law and Literature: A Hermeneutic Reader* (eds Sanford Levinson and Steven Mailloux; Evanston: Northwestern University Press, 1988), pp. 55–68.

—'Criticism and Countertheses: On Justifying Interpretive Norms', *J Aes Art Crit* 43 (1984), pp. 89–91.

—'Meaning and Significance Reinterpreted', *CI* 11 (1984), pp. 202–25.

—'Past Intentions and Present Meanings', *Ess. Crit.* 33 (1983), pp. 79–98.

—'The Politics of Theories of Interpretation', in *The Politics of Interpretation* (ed. W.J.T. Mitchell; Chicago: The University of Chicago Press, 1983), pp. 321–33.

—'Transhistorical Intentions and the Persistence of Allegory', *NLH* 25 (1994), pp. 549–67.

—*Validity in Interpretation* (New Haven: Yale University Press, 1967).

Holbert, John C., ' "Deliverance Belongs to Yahweh!": Satire in the Book of Jonah', *JSOT* 21 (1981), pp. 59–81.

Holladay, John S., Jr., 'Assyrian Statecraft and the Prophets of Israel', *HTR* 63 (1970), pp. 29–51.

Holmer, Paul L., *The Grammar of Faith* (New York: Harper and Row, 1978).

Holmes, Oliver Wendell, 'The Use of Law Schools', in *Speeches by Oliver Wendell Holmes* (Boston: Little, Brown, and Company, 1934), pp. 28–40.

Hubert, Friedrich, *Die Strassburger Liturgische Ordnungen im Zeitalter der Reformation* (Göttingen: Vandenhoeck & Ruprecht, 1900).

Iser, Wolfgang, *The Act of Reading* (Baltimore: Johns Hopkins University Press, 1978).

Jackson, US Supreme Court Justice Robert H., *West Virginia State Board of Education et al.* v. *Barnette et al.*, US Reports 319 (1942), pp. 624–71.

Janzen, J. Gerald, 'Song of Moses, Song of Miriam: Who Is Seconding Whom?', *CBQ* 54 (1992), pp. 211–20.

Jauss, Hans Robert, *Toward an Aesthetic of Reception* (trans. Timothy Bahti; Brighton, UK: Harvester, 1982).

Jeanrond, Werner G., *Text and Interpretation as Categories of Theological Thinking* (trans. Thomas J. Wilson; New York: Crossroad, 1988).

Johnstone, Keith, *Impro: Improvisation and the Theatre* (London: Methuen, 1981).

Jones, Gwilym H., *The Nathan Narratives* (Sheffield: Sheffield Academic Press, 1990).

Juhl, P.D., *Interpretation: An Essay in the Philosophy of Literary Criticism* (Princeton: Princeton University Press, 1980).

Kaiser, Walter C., Jr., *Toward an Exegetical Theology: Biblical Exegesis for Preaching and Teaching* (Grand Rapids: Baker, 1981).

Kelhoffer, James A., 'The Witness of Eusebius' *ad Marinum* and Other Christian Writings to Text-Critical Debates concerning the Original Conclusion to Mark's Gospel', *ZNW* 92 (2001), pp. 78–112.

Kelly, J.N.D., *Golden Mouth: The Story of John Chrysostom – Ascetic, Preacher, Bishop* (London: Duckworth, 1995).

Kelsey, David H., 'The Bible and Christian Theology', *JAAR* 48 (1980), pp. 385–402.

—*The Uses of Scripture in Recent Theology* (Philadelphia: Fortress, 1975).

Kermode, Frank, *The Classic* (London: Faber & Faber, 1975).

—'A Modern Way with the Classic', *NLH* (1974), pp. 415–34.

Kerr, Fergus, *Theology after Wittgenstein* (London: SPCK, 1997).

Kierkegaard, Søren, *For Self-Examination, Judge for Yourself!* Vol. 21 of *Kierkegaard's Writ-*

ings (ed. and trans. Howard V. Hong and Edna H. Hong; Princeton: Princeton University Press, 1990).

Knapp, Steven, and Walter Benn Michaels, 'Against Theory', *CI* 8 (1982), pp. 723–42.

—'Against Theory 2: Hermeneutics and Deconstruction', *CI* 14 (1987), pp. 49–68.

Kugel, James L., and Rowan A. Greer, *Early Biblical Interpretation* (Philadelphia: Westminster, 1986).

Lawlor, John I., 'Theology and Art in the Narrative of the Ammonite War (2 Samuel 10–12)', *GTJ* 3 (1982), pp. 193–205.

Lessig, Lawrence, 'Fidelity and Constraint', *Fordham L. Rev.* 65 (1996–97), pp. 1365–1434.

—'Fidelity in Translation', *Texas L. Rev.* 71 (1992–3), pp. 1165–268.

—'The Limits of Lieber', *Cardozo L. Rev.* 16 (1995), pp. 2249–72.

Levenson, Jon D. 'The Theologies of Commandment in Biblical Israel', *HTR* 73 (1980), pp. 17–33.

Levin, Michael, 'What Makes a Classic in Political Theory?', *Pol. Sci. Q.* 88 (1973), pp. 462–76.

Levinson, Stephen C., *Pragmatics* (Cambridge: Cambridge University Press, 1983).

—*Presumptive Meanings: The Theory of Generalized Conversational Implicature* (Cambridge, MA: The MIT Press, 2000).

Lewis, C.S., *A Preface to Paradise Lost* (rev. edn; London: Oxford University Press, 1960).

Lincoln, Andrew T., *Ephesians* (WBC, 42; Dallas: Word, 1990).

Locher, Gottfried, *Zwingli's Thought: New Perspectives* (Leiden: E.J. Brill, 1981).

Long, Thomas G., *The Witness of Preaching* (2nd edn; Louisville: Westminster/John Knox Press, 2005).

Longenecker, Richard N., *Biblical Exegesis in the Apostolic Period* (2nd edn; Grand Rapids: Eerdmans, 1999).

Longman, Tremper, III, 'Form Criticism, Recent Developments in Genre Theory, and the Evangelical', *WTJ* 47 (1985), pp. 47–68.

Lubeck, R.J., 'Prophetic Sabotage: A Look at Jonah 3:2–4', *TrinJ* 9 (1988), pp. 37–46.

McCarthy, Dennis J., 'II Samuel 7 and the Structure of the Detueronomic History', *JBL* 84 (1965), pp. 131–8.

McGinn, Marie, *Wittgenstein and the* Philosophical Investigations (London: Routledge, 1997).

McKenna, US Supreme Court Justice Joseph, *Weems* v. *United States*, US Reports 217 (1910), pp. 349–413.

Magowan, Robin, 'A Note on Genre', *Coll. Eng.* 30 (1969), pp. 534–38.

Mailloux, Stephen, 'Rhetorical Hermeneutics', *CI* 11 (1985), pp. 620–41.

Marshall, US Supreme Court Chief Justice John, *Cohens* v. *Virginia*, US Reports 19 (1821), pp. 264–448.

—*McCulloch* v. *The State of Maryland et al.*, US Reports 17 (4 Wheaton) (1819), pp. 316–437.

Mayer, Wendy, and Pauline Allen, *John Chrysostom* (London: Routledge, 2000).

Metzger, Bruce M., *The Canon of the New Testament: Its Origin, Development, and Significance* (Oxford: Clarendon Press, 1987).

Michaels, J. Ramsey, *1 Peter* (WBC, 49; Dallas, TX: Word, 1988).

Milgrom, Jacob, 'Of Hems and Tassels', *BAR* 9 (1983), pp. 61–5.

Miller, Carolyn R., 'Genre as Social Action', *QJS* 79 (1984), pp. 151–67.

Miller, John W., *The Origins of the Bible: Rethinking Canon History* (Mahwah, NJ: Paulist, 1994).

Morgan, Robert, 'The Hermeneutical Significance of the Four Gospels', *Int* 33 (1979), pp. 376–88.

Morson, Gary Saul, *The Boundaries of Genre: Dostoevsky's* Diary of a Writer *and the Tradition of Literary Utopia* (Austin, TX: University of Texas Press, 1981).

Morson, Gary Saul, and Caryl Emerson, *Mikhail Bakhtin: Creation of Prosaics* (Stanford, CA: Stanford University Press, 1990).

Mudge, Lewis S., 'Paul Ricoeur on Biblical Interpretation', in Paul Ricoeur, *Essays on Biblical Interpretation* (ed. Lewis S. Mudge; Philadelphia: Fortress, 1980), pp. 1–37.

Murphy, James J., and Richard A. Katula, *A Synoptic History of Classical Rhetoric* (2nd edn; Davis, CA: Hermagoras, 1994).

Noble, Paul R., *A Canonical Approach: A Critical Reconstruction of the Hermeneutics of Brevard S. Childs* (Leiden: E.J. Brill, 1995).

Nussbaum, Martha C., *Love's Knowledge: Essays on Philosophy and Literature* (New York: Oxford University Press, 1990).

—*Poetic Justice: The Literary Imagination and Public Life* (Boston: Beacon, 1995).

Nystrand, Martin, 'An Analysis of Errors in Written Communication', in *What Writers Know* (ed. Martin Nystrand; New York: Academic, 1982), pp. 57–74.

O'Brien, Peter T., *The Letter to the Ephesians* (Grand Rapids: Eerdmans, 1999).

O'Donovan, Oliver M.T., 'The Possibility of a Biblical Ethic', *TSF Bull.* 67 (1973), pp. 15–23.

Old, Hughes Oliphant, *The Reading and Preaching of the Scriptures* (4 vols; Grand Rapids: Eerdmans, 1998).

Ong, Walter J., *Orality and Literacy: The Technologizing of the Word* (London: Routledge, 1982).

Osborne, Grant R., *The Hermeneutical Spiral: A Comprehensive Introduction to Biblical Interpretation* (Downers Grove: InterVarsity, 1991).

Ott, Heinrich, *Theology and Preaching* (Philadelphia: Westminster, 1963).

Parker, T.H.L., *Calvin's Preaching* (Edinburgh: T. & T. Clark, 1992).

Patrick, Dale, and Allen Scult, *Rhetoric and Biblical Interpretation* (Sheffield: Almond, 1990).

Patterson, Richard D., 'Victory at Sea: Prose and Poetry in Exodus 14–15', *BSac* 161 (2004), pp. 42–54.

Pavel, Thomas, 'Literary Genres as Norms and Good Habits', *NLH* 34 (2003), pp. 201–10.

Pellauer, David, 'The Significance of the Text in Paul Ricoeur's Hermeneutical Theory', in *Studies in the Philosophy of Paul Ricoeur* (ed. Charles E. Reagan; Athens, OH: Ohio University Press, 1979), pp. 98–114.

Petrey, Sandy, *Speech Acts and Literary Theory* (New York: Routledge, 1990).

Pfeiffer, Robert H., *One Hundred New Selected Nuzi Texts* (trans. E.A. Speiser; New Haven: American Schools of Oriental Research, 1936).

Polzin, Robert, *David and the Deuteronomist* (part 3 of *A Literary Study of Deuteronomic History (2 Samuel)*; Bloomington, IN: Indiana University Press, 1993).

Popper, Karl R., *The Logic of Scientific Discovery* (New York: Basic Books, 1959).

Porter, Stanley E., 'Ephesians 5.18–19 and Its Dionysian Background', in *Testimony and Interpretation: Early Christology in Its Judeo-Hellenistic Milieu* (eds Jiří Mrázek and Jan Roskovec; London: T. & T. Clark, 2004), pp. 69–80.

Poythress, Vern Sheridan, 'Divine Meaning of Scripture', *WTJ* 48 (1986), pp. 241–79.

Pratt, Mary Louise, *Toward a Speech Act Theory of Literary Discourse* (Bloomington, IN: Indiana University Press, 1977).

Puskas, Charles B., Jr., *The Letters of Paul: An Introduction* (Collegeville, MN: The Liturgical Press, 1993).

Putnam, Hilary, *Mind, Language and Reality* (vol. 2 of *Philosophical Papers*; Cambridge: Cambridge University Press, 1975).

Quicke, Michael J., *360-Degree Preaching: Hearing, Speaking, and Living the Word* (Grand Rapids: Baker, 2003).

Ratner, Sidney, 'Presupposition and Objectivity in History', *Phil. Sci.* 7 (1940), pp. 499–505.

Reagan, Charles E., and Paul Ricoeur, 'Interviews: Châtenay-Malabry, June 19, 1982', in Charles E. Reagan, *Paul Ricoeur: His Life and His Work* (Chicago: The University of Chicago Press, 1996), pp. 100–9.

The Real Book (3 vols; Milwaukee, WI: Hal Leonard, 2006).

Recanati, François, *Meaning and Force: The Pragmatics of Performative Utterances* (Cambridge: Cambridge University Press, 1987).

Reed, Jeffrey T., 'Using Ancient Rhetorical Categories to Interpret Paul's Letters: A Question of Genre', in *Rhetoric and the New Testament: Essays from the 1992 Heidelberg Conference* (eds Stanley E. Porter and Thomas H. Olbricht; Sheffield: JSOT, 1993), pp. 292–324.

Reumann, John, 'A History of Lectionaries: From the Synagogue at Nazareth to Post-Vatican II', *Int* 31 (1977), pp. 116–30.

Richard, Ramesh P., 'Selected Issues in Theoretical Hermeneutics', *BSac* 143 (1986), pp. 14–25.

Richards, E. Randolph, *The Secretary in the Letters of Paul* (Tübingen: J.C.B. Mohr, 1991).

Ricoeur, Paul, 'The Bible and the Imagination', in *The Bible as a Document of the University* (ed. Hans Dieter Betz; Chico, CA: Scholars, 1981), pp. 49–75.

—'Biblical Hermeneutics', *Semeia* 4 (1975), pp. 27–148.

—'Biblical Time', in Paul Ricoeur, *Figuring the Sacred: Religion, Narrative, and Imagination* (trans. David Pellauer; ed. Mark I. Wallace; Minneapolis: Fortress, 1995), pp. 167–80.

—*The Course of Recognition* (trans. David Pellauer; Cambridge, MA: Harvard University Press, 2005).

—'Dialogues with Paul Ricoeur', in *Dialogues with Contemporary Continental Thinkers: The Phenomenological Heritage* (ed. Richard Kearney; Manchester, UK: Manchester University Press, 1984), pp. 15–46.

—*Du texte à l'action: Essais d'herméneutique, II* (Paris: Seuil, 1986).

—'Existence and Hermeneutics', in *The Conflict of Interpretations* (trans. Kathleen McLaughlin; ed. Don Ihde; Evanston: Northwestern University Press, 1974, repr. 2004), pp. 3–24.

—*From Text to Action: Essays in Hermeneutics, II* (trans. Kathleen Blamey and John B. Thompson; Evanston: Northwestern University Press, 1991).

—*Hermeneutics and the Human Sciences: Essays on Language, Action and Interpretation* (ed. and trans. John B. Thompson; Cambridge: Cambridge University Press, 1981).

—'The Hermeneutics of Symbols and Philosophical Reflection: I', in *The Conflict of Interpretations* (trans. Denis Savage; ed. Don Ihde; Evanston: Northwestern University Press, 1974, repr. 2004), pp. 278–314.

—*Interpretation Theory: Discourse and the Surplus of Meaning* (Fort Worth, TX: Texas Christian University Press, 1976).

—'Naming God', *USQR* 34 (1979), pp. 215–27.

—'The Narrative Function', *Semeia* 13 (1978), pp. 177–202.

—'On Narrative', *CI* 7 (1980), pp. 169–90.

—*Oneself as Another* (trans. Kathleen Blamey; Chicago: The University of Chicago Press, 1992).

—'Philosophical Hermeneutics and Theological Hermeneutics: Ideology, Utopia, and Faith', in *Protocol of the Seventeenth Colloquy, 4 November 1975* (ed. W. Wuellner; Berkeley: The Center for Hermeneutical Studies in Hellenistic and Modern Culture, 1976), pp. 1–28.

—'Philosophy and Religious Language', *JR* 54 (1974), pp. 71–85.

—'Poetry and Possibility', in *A Ricoeur Reader: Reflection and Imagination* (ed. Mario J. Valdés; Hertfordshire: Harvester Wheatsheaf, 1991), pp. 448–62.

—'Preface to Bultmann', *The Conflict of Interpretations* (trans. Peter McCormick; ed. Don Ihde; Evanston: Northwestern University Press, 1974, repr. 2004), pp. 384–401.

—'The Problem of Double Meaning as Hermeneutic Problem and as Semantic Problem', *The Conflict of Interpretations* (trans. Kathleen McLaughlin; ed. Don Ihde; Evanston: Northwestern University Press, 1974, repr. 2004), pp. 63–78.

—'Reply to Lewis S. Mudge', *Essays on Biblical Interpretation* (ed. Lewis S. Mudge; Philadelphia: Fortress, 1980), pp. 41–5.

—*The Rule of Metaphor: Multi-disciplinary Studies on the Creation of Meaning in Language* (trans. Robert Czerny, with Kathleen McLaughlin and John Costello; London: Routledge & Kegan Paul, 1978).

—'Sentinel of Imminence', in *Thinking Biblically: Exegetical and Hermeneutical Studies*, by André LaCocque and Paul Ricoeur (trans. David Pellauer; Chicago: The University of Chicago Press, 1998), pp. 165–83.

—'Structure and Hermeneutics', *The Conflict of Interpretations* (trans. Kathleen McLaughlin; ed. Don Ihde; Evanston: Northwestern University Press, 1974, repr. 2004), pp. 27–61.

—'Structure, Word, Event', *The Conflict of Interpretations* (trans. Robert Sweeney; ed. Don Ihde; Evanston: Northwestern University Press, 1974), pp. 79–96.

—*The Symbolism of Evil* (trans. Emerson Buchanan; Boston: Beacon, 1967).

—'The Text as Dynamic Identity', in *Identity of the Literary Text* (eds Mario J. Valdés and Owen Miller; Toronto: University of Toronto Press, 1985), pp. 175–86.

—*Time and Narrative* (trans. Kathleen McLaughlin and David Pellauer; 3 vols; Chicago: The University of Chicago Press, 1984–8).

—'Toward a Hermeneutic of the Idea of Revelation', *Essays on Biblical Interpretation* (ed. Lewis S. Mudge; Philadelphia: Fortress, 1980), pp. 73–118.

—'Word, Polysemy, Metaphor: Creativity in Language', *A Ricoeur Reader: Reflection and Imagination* (ed. Mario J. Valdés; Hertfordshire: Harvester Wheatsheaf, 1991), pp. 65–85.

—'Writing as a Problem for Literary Criticism and Philosophical Hermeneutics', in *A Ricoeur Reader: Reflection and Imagination* (ed. Mario J. Valdés; Hertfordshire: Harvester Wheatsheaf, 1991), pp. 320–37.

Robbins, Vernon K., 'Writing as a Rhetorical Act in Plutarch and the Gospels', in *Persuasive Artistry: Studies in New Testament Rhetoric in Honor of George A. Kennedy* (ed. Duane F. Watson; Sheffield: JSOT, 1991), pp. 142–68.

Roberts, Robert C., 'Narrative Ethics', in *A Companion to Philosophy of Religion* (eds Philip L. Quinn and Charles Taliaferro; Cambridge, MA: Blackwell, 1997), pp. 473–80.

Roetzel, Calvin J., *The Letters of Paul: Conversations in Context* (4th edn; Louisville: Westminster/John Knox Press, 1998).

Rogers, Cleon L., Jr., 'The Dionysian Background of Ephesians 5:18', *BSac* 136 (1979), pp. 249–57.

Ryle, Gilbert, *Collected Essays* (vol. 2 of *Collected Papers*; New York: Barnes and Noble, 1971).

Sailhamer, John H., *The Pentateuch as Narrative: A Biblical-Theological Commentary* (Grand Rapids: Zondervan, 1992).

Sanders, James A., *Canon and Community: A Guide to Canonical Criticism* (Philadelphia: Fortress, 1984).

Sandys-Wunsch, John, and Laurence Eldredge, 'J.P. Gabler and the Distinction between Biblical and Dogmatic Theology: Translation, Commentary, and Discussion of His Originality', *SJT* 33 (1980), pp. 133–58.

Schauer, Frederick, 'An Essay on Constitutional Language', in *Interpreting Law and Litera-*

ture: A Hermeneutic Reader (eds Sanford Levinson and Steven Mailloux; Evanston: Northwestern University Press, 1988), pp. 133–53.

—*Playing by the Rules: A Philosophical Examination of Rule-Based Decision-Making in Law and Life* (Oxford: Clarendon Press, 1991).

Schleiermacher, Friedrich, *The Christian Faith* (eds H.R. Mackintosh and J.S. Stewart; Edinburgh: T. & T. Clark, 1928).

—'Hermeneutics and Criticism', in *Hermeneutics and Criticism and Other Writings* (ed. Andrew Bowie; Cambridge: Cambridge University Press, 1998), pp. 1–224.

Schneiders, Sandra M., 'The Paschal Imagination: Objectivity and Subjectivity in New Testament Interpretation', *TS* 46 (1982), pp. 52–68.

Schnittjer, Gary Edward, 'The Narrative Multiverse within the Universe of the Bible: The Question of "Borderlines" and "Intertextuality"', *WTJ* 2 (2002), pp. 231–52.

Schürer, Emil, *The History of the Jewish People in the Age of Jesus Christ (175 B.C–A.D. 135)* (vol. 2; eds Geza Vermes, Fergus Millar and Matthew Black; Edinburgh: T. & T. Clark, 1979).

Scobie, Charles H.H., 'The Challenge of Biblical Theology', *TynBul* 42.1 (1991), pp. 31–61.

—*The Ways of our God: An Approach to Biblical Theology* (Grand Rapids: Eerdmans, 2003).

Searle, John R., *Expression and Meaning: Studies in the Theory of Speech Acts* (Cambridge: Cambridge University Press, 1979).

—*Speech Acts: An Essay in the Philosophy of Language* (Cambridge: Cambridge University Press, 1969).

Seitel, Peter, 'Theorizing Genres – Interpreting Works', *NLH* 34 (2003), pp. 275–97.

Seitz, Christopher, 'The Lectionary as Theological Construction', in *Inhabiting Unity: Theological Perspectives in the Proposed Lutheran-Episcopal Concordat* (eds Ephraim Radner and R.R. Reno; Grand Rapids: Eerdmans, 1995), pp. 173–91.

Sherry, Patrick, *Religion, Truth and Language-Games* (London: Macmillan, 1977).

Sidney, Philip, 'An Apology for Poetry', in *Criticism: The Major Statements* (2nd edn; ed. Charles Kaplan; New York: St. Martin's, 1986), pp. 108–48.

Siker, Jeffrey S., '"First to the Gentiles": A Literary Analysis of Luke 4:16–30', *JBL* 111 (1992), pp. 73–90.

Simon, Uriel, 'The Poor Man's Ewe-Lamb: An Example of a Juridical Parable', *Bib* 48 (1967), pp. 207–42.

—*Reading Prophetic Narratives* (trans. Lenn J. Schramm; Bloomington, IN: Indiana University Press, 1997).

Singer, Marcus George, *Generalization in Ethics* (London: Eyre & Spottiswoode, 1963).

Skeat, T. C., 'The Origins of the Christian Codex', *ZPE* 102 (1994), pp. 263–8.

Skinner, Quentin, 'Motives, Intentions and the Interpretation of Texts', *NLH* 3 (1972), pp. 393–408.

Sloyan, Gerard S., 'The Lectionary as a Context for Interpretation', *Int* 31 (1977), pp. 131–8.

Smart, James D., *The Strange Silence of the Bible in the Church: A Study in Hermeneutics* (London: SCM Press, 1970).

Sonsino, Rifat, *Motive Clauses in Hebrew Law: Biblical Forms and Near Eastern Parallels* (Chico, CA: Scholars, 1980).

Stanton, Graham N., 'The Fourfold Gospel', *NTS* 43 (1997), pp. 317–46.

Steiner, George, *After Babel: Aspects of Language and Translation* (London: Oxford University Press, 1975).

—'"Critic"/"Reader"', *NLH* 10 (1979), pp. 423–52.

—*Real Presences* (Chicago: The University of Chicago Press, 1989).

Steinmetz, David C., 'The Superiority of Pre-Critical Exegesis', *ThTo* 37 (1980), pp. 27–38.

Stendahl, Krister, 'The Bible as a Classic and the Bible as Holy Scripture', *JBL* 103 (1984), pp. 3–10.

Sternberg, Meir, *The Poetics of Biblical Narrative: Ideological Literature and the Drama of Reading* (Bloomington, IN: Indiana University Press, 1985).

Stirewalt, M. Luther, Jr., *Studies in Ancient Greek Epistolography* (Atlanta: Scholars Press, 1993).

Stiver, Dan R., *Theology after Ricoeur: New Directions in Hermeneutical Theology* (Louisville: Westminster/John Knox Press, 2001).

Stott, John R.W., *Between Two Worlds: The Art of Preaching in the Twentieth Century* (Grand Rapids: Eerdmans, 1982).

Stowers, Stanley K., *Letter Writing in Graeco-Roman Antiquity* (Philadelphia: Westminster, 1986).

Thomas, W.H. Griffith, *The Principles of Theology: An Introduction to the Thirty-Nine Articles* (London: Longmans, 1930).

Thompson, John B., 'Editor's Introduction', in Pierre Bourdieu, *Language and Symbolic Power* (trans. Gino Raymond and Matthew Adamson; ed. John B. Thompson; Cambridge: Polity, 1991), pp. 1–31.

Todorov, Tzvetan, *The Fantastic: A Structural Approach to a Literary Genre* (trans. Richard Howard; Cleveland, OH: The Press of Case Western Reserve University, 1973).

—*Symbolism and Interpretation* (trans. Catherine Porter; Ithaca, NY: Cornell University Press, 1982).

Tracy, David, *The Analogical Imagination: Christian Theology and the Culture of Pluralism* (New York: Crossroad, 1981).

—'Creativity in the Interpretation of Religion: The Question of Radical Pluralism', *NLH* 15 (1984), pp. 289–309.

—*Plurality and Ambiguity: Hermeneutics, Religion, Hope* (San Francisco: Harper and Row, 1987).

Traugott, Elizabeth Closs, and Mary Louise Pratt, *Linguistics for Students of Literature* (New York: Harcourt Brace Jovanovich, 1980).

Vanderveken, Daniel, 'Non-Literal Speech Acts and Conversational Maxims', in *John Searle and His Critics* (eds Ernest Lepore and Robert Van Gulick; Cambridge, MA: Basil Blackwell, 1991), pp. 371–84.

Vanhoozer, Kevin J., *Biblical Narrative in the Philosophy of Paul Ricoeur: A Study in Hermeneutics and Theology* (Cambridge: Cambridge University Press, 1990).

—*The Drama of Doctrine: A Canonical-Linguistic Approach to Christian Theology* (Louisville: Westminster/John Knox Press, 2005).

—'Exegesis and Hermeneutics', in *New Dictionary of Biblical Theology* (eds T. Desmond Alexander and Brian S. Rosner; Downers Grove: InterVarsity, 2000), pp. 52–64.

—*First Theology: God, Scripture and Hermeneutics* (Downers Grove: InterVarsity, 2002).

—'From Canon to Concept: "Same" and "Other" in the Relation between Biblical and Systematic Theology', *SBET* 12 (1994), pp. 96–124.

—'From Speech Acts to Scripture Acts: The Covenant of Discourse and the Discourse of the Covenant', in *After Pentecost: Language and Biblical Interpretation* (eds Craig Bartholomew, Colin Greene and Karl Möller; Grand Rapids: Zondervan, 2001), pp. 1–49.

—'God's Mighty Speech-Acts: The Doctrine of Scripture Today', in *A Pathway into the Holy Scripture* (eds P.E. Satterthwaite and D.F. Wright; Grand Rapids: Eerdmans, 1994), pp. 143–81.

—*Is There a Meaning in This Text? The Bible, the Reader, and the Morality of Literary Knowledge* (Grand Rapids: Zondervan, 1998).

—'Language, Literature, Hermeneutics, and Biblical Theology: What's Theological about a

Theological Dictionary?', in Vol. 1 of *New International Dictionary of Old Testament Theology and Exegesis* (ed. William VanGemeren; Grand Rapids: Zondervan, 1997), pp. 15–50.

—'The Spirit of Understanding: Special Revelation and General Hermeneutics', in *Disciplining Hermeneutics: Interpretation in Christian Perspective* (ed. Roger Lundin; Grand Rapids: Eerdmans, 1997), pp. 131–65.

Wall, Robert W., 'Reading the New Testament in Canonical Context', in *Hearing the New Testament: Strategies for Interpretation* (ed. Joel B. Green; Grand Rapids: Eerdmans, 1995), pp. 370–93.

Wallace, Mark I., 'Ricoeur, Rorty, and the Question of Revelation', in *Meanings in Texts and Action: Questioning Paul Ricoeur* (eds David E. Klemm and William Schweiker; Charlottesville, VA: University Press of Virginia, 1993), pp. 234–54.

—*The Second Naiveté: Barth, Ricoeur, and the New Yale Theology* (2nd edn; Macon, GA: Mercer University Press, 1995).

Warren, F.E., *The Liturgy and Ritual of the Ante-Nicene Church* (2nd rev. edn; London: SPCK, 1912).

Warren, Timothy S., 'A Paradigm for Preaching', *BSac* 148 (1991), pp. 463–86.

—'The Theological Process in Sermon Preparation', *BSac* 156 (1999), pp. 336–56.

Watson, Francis B., *Text and Truth: Redefining Biblical Theology* (Grand Rapids: Eerdmans, 1997).

—*Text, Church and World: Biblical Interpretation in Theological Perspective* (Grand Rapids: Eerdmans, 1994).

Watts, James W., *Psalm and Story: Inset Hymns in Hebrew Narrative* (Sheffield: JSOT, 1992).

—*Reading Law: The Rhetorical Shaping of the Pentateuch* (Sheffield: Sheffield Academic Press, 1999).

—'Song and the Ancient Reader', *PRSt* 22 (1995), pp. 135–47.

Weaver, Richard M., *Language Is Sermonic: Richard M. Weaver on the Nature of Rhetoric* (eds Richard L. Johannesen, Rennard Strickland and Ralph T. Eubanks; Baton Rouge, LA: Louisiana State University Press, 1970).

Webster, John, *Word and Church: Essays in Christian Dogmatics* (Edinburgh: T. & T. Clark, 2001).

Weinfeld, Moshe, *Deuteronomy and the Deuteronomic School* (Winona Lake, IN: Eisenbrauns, 1992).

Wellek, René, and Austin Warren, *Theory of Literature* (3rd edn; New York: Harcourt Brace Jovanovich, 1977).

Wendland, Ernst R., 'Text Analysis and the Genre of Jonah (Part 1)', *JETS* 39 (1996), pp. 191–206.

Wenham, Gordon, *Story as Torah: Reading Old Testament Narrative Ethically* (Grand Rapids: Baker, 2000).

Wheelwright, Philip, *The Burning Fountain: A Study in the Language of Symbolism* (rev. edn; Bloomington, IN: Indiana University Press, 1968).

White, Hayden, 'The Narrativization of Real Events', in *On Narrative* (ed. W.J.T. Mitchell; Chicago: The University of Chicago Press, 1981), pp. 249–54.

—'The Value of Narrativity in the Representation of Reality', in *On Narrative* (ed. W.J.T. Mitchell; Chicago: The University of Chicago Press, 1981), pp. 1–23.

White, James Boyd, 'Judicial Criticism', in *Interpreting Law and Literature: A Hermeneutic Reader* (eds Sanford Levinson and Steven Mailloux; Evanston: Northwestern University Press, 1988), pp. 393–410.

White, John L., *Light from Ancient Letters* (Philadelphia: Fortress, 1986).

Wilder, Amos N., *Early Christian Rhetoric: The Language of the Gospel* (Cambridge, MA: Harvard University Press, 1971).

Williamson, H.G.M., *Ezra, Nehemiah* (WBC, 16; Dallas: Word, 1985).

Williamson, W. Paul, and Howard R. Pollio, 'The Phenomenology of Religious Serpent Handling: A Rationale and Thematic Study of Extemporaneous Sermons', *JSSR* 38 (1999), pp. 203–18.

Wittgenstein, Ludwig, *The Blue and Brown Books: Preliminary Studies for the 'Philosophical Investigations'* (2nd edn; ed. R. Rhees; New York: Harper and Row, 1960).

—*Lectures and Conversations on Aesthetics, Psychology and Religious Belief* (ed. Cyril Barrett; Oxford: Blackwell, 1966).

— 'Notes for Lectures on "Private Experience" and "Sense Data"', ed. R. Rhees, *Phil. Rev.* 77 (1968), pp. 275–320.

—*On Certainty* (eds G.E.M. Anscombe and G.H. von Wright; trans. Denis Paul and G.E.M. Anscombe; San Francisco: Harper and Row, 1969).

—*Philosophical Investigations* (2nd edn; trans. G.E.M. Anscombe; London: Basil Blackwell, 1958).

—*Remarks on the Foundations of Mathematics* (ed. G.H. von Wright; Oxford: Basil Blackwell, 1956).

Wolff, Hans Walter, 'The Understanding of History in the Old Testament Prophets', in *Essays on Old Testament Interpretation* (trans. Keith R. Crim; ed. Claus Westermann; London: SCM Press, 1963), pp. 336–65.

Wolterstorff, Nicholas, *Art in Action: Toward a Christian Aesthetic* (Grand Rapids: Eerdmans, 1980).

—*Divine Discourse: Philosophical Reflections on the Claim that God Speaks* (Cambridge: Cambridge University Press, 1995).

—'The Importance of Hermeneutics for a Christian Worldview', in *Disciplining Hermeneutics: Interpretation in Christian Perspective* (ed. Roger Lundin; Grand Rapids: Eerdmans, 1997), pp. 25–47.

—*Works and Worlds of Art* (Oxford: Clarendon Press, 1980).

Wood, Charles M., *The Formation of Christian Understanding* (Philadelphia: Westminster, 1981).

Wright, N.T., 'How Can the Bible Be Authoritative?', *Vox Evangelica* 21 (1991), pp. 7–32.

Yadin, Y., 'A Midrash on 2 Sam. vii and Ps. i–ii (4QFlorilegium)', *IEJ* 9 (1959), pp. 95–8.

Young, Frances, 'Allegory and the Ethics of Reading', in *The Open Text: New Directions for Biblical Studies?* (ed. Francis B. Watson; London: SCM Press, 1993), pp. 103–20.

—'The "Mind" of Scripture: Theological Readings of the Bible in the Fathers', *IJST* 7 (2005), pp. 126–41.

Young, James O., and Carl Matheson, 'The Metaphysics of Jazz', *J Aes Art Crit* 58 (2000), pp. 125–33.

Index of Biblical Citations

Old Testament

INDEX OF OTHER CITATIONS

Index of Authors